REFLECTING ON MY LIFE IN HIGH SCHOOL

BY HACHIMAN HIKIGAYA CLASS 2-F

YOUTH IS LIES; YOUTH IS EVIL.

YOUTH IS LIES; YOUTH IS EVIL.

THOSE WHO INCESSANTLY CELEBRATE THEIR TEENAGED YEARS ARE LYING BOTH TO THEMSELVES AND TO THOSE AROUND THEM. THEIR PRINCIPLES ARE ENTIRELY BASED ON THEIR OWN CONVENIENCE.

THUS, THEIR PRINCIPLES ARE DECEIT. LIES, DECEIT, SECRETS, AND FRAUD ARE ALL REPREHENSIBLE THINGS.

THESE PEOPLE ARE EVIL.

THESE PEOPLE ARE EVIL.

AND THAT MEANS, PARADOXICALLY, THAT THOSE WHO DO NOT CELEBRATE THE TEEN YEARS ARE CORRECT AND RIGHTEOUS.

S0-BMZ-592

IN CONCLUSION,

CHAPTER ··· **ANYWAY, HACHIMAN HIKIGAYA IS ROTTEN.**

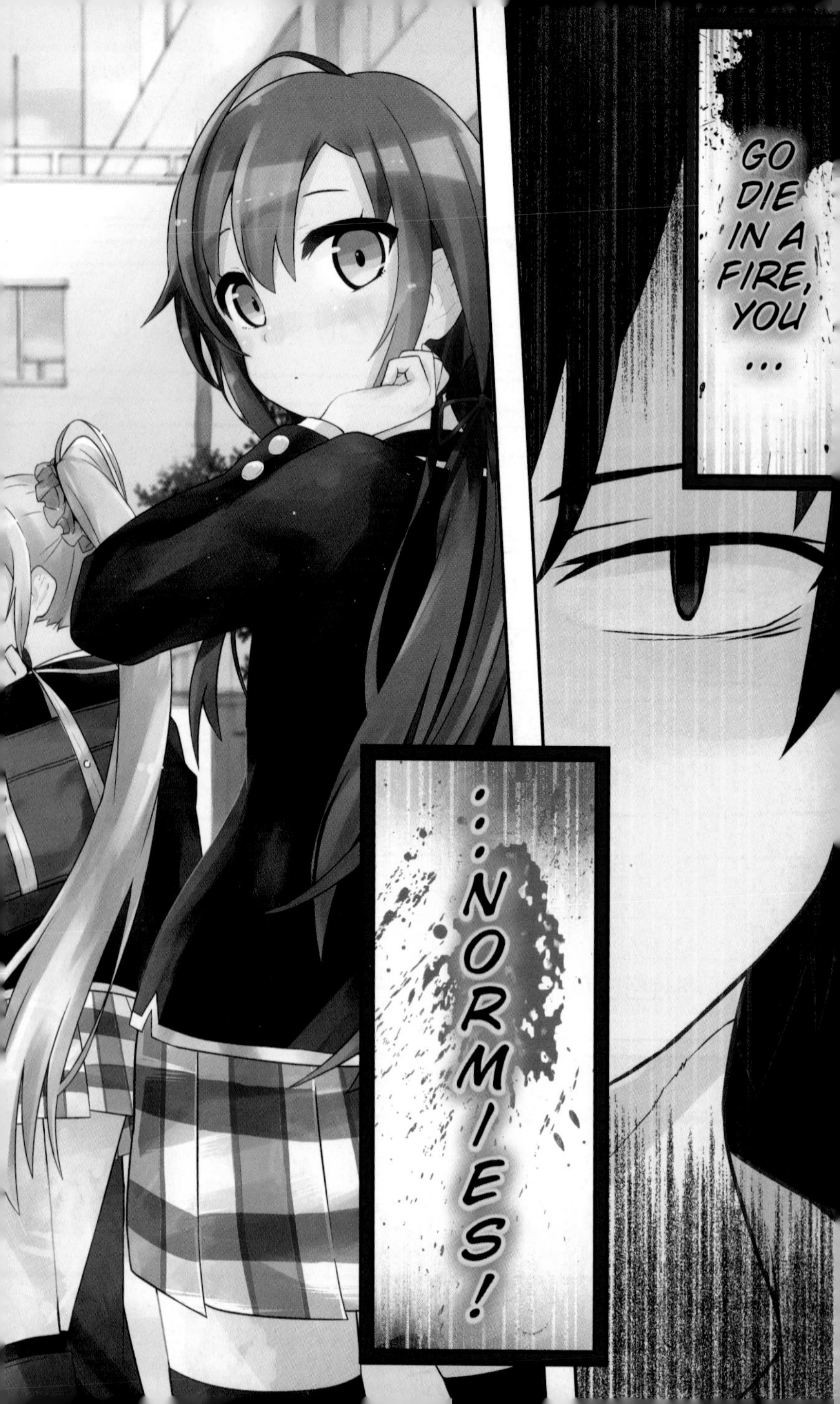
GO DIE IN A FIRE, YOU ...
...NORMIES!

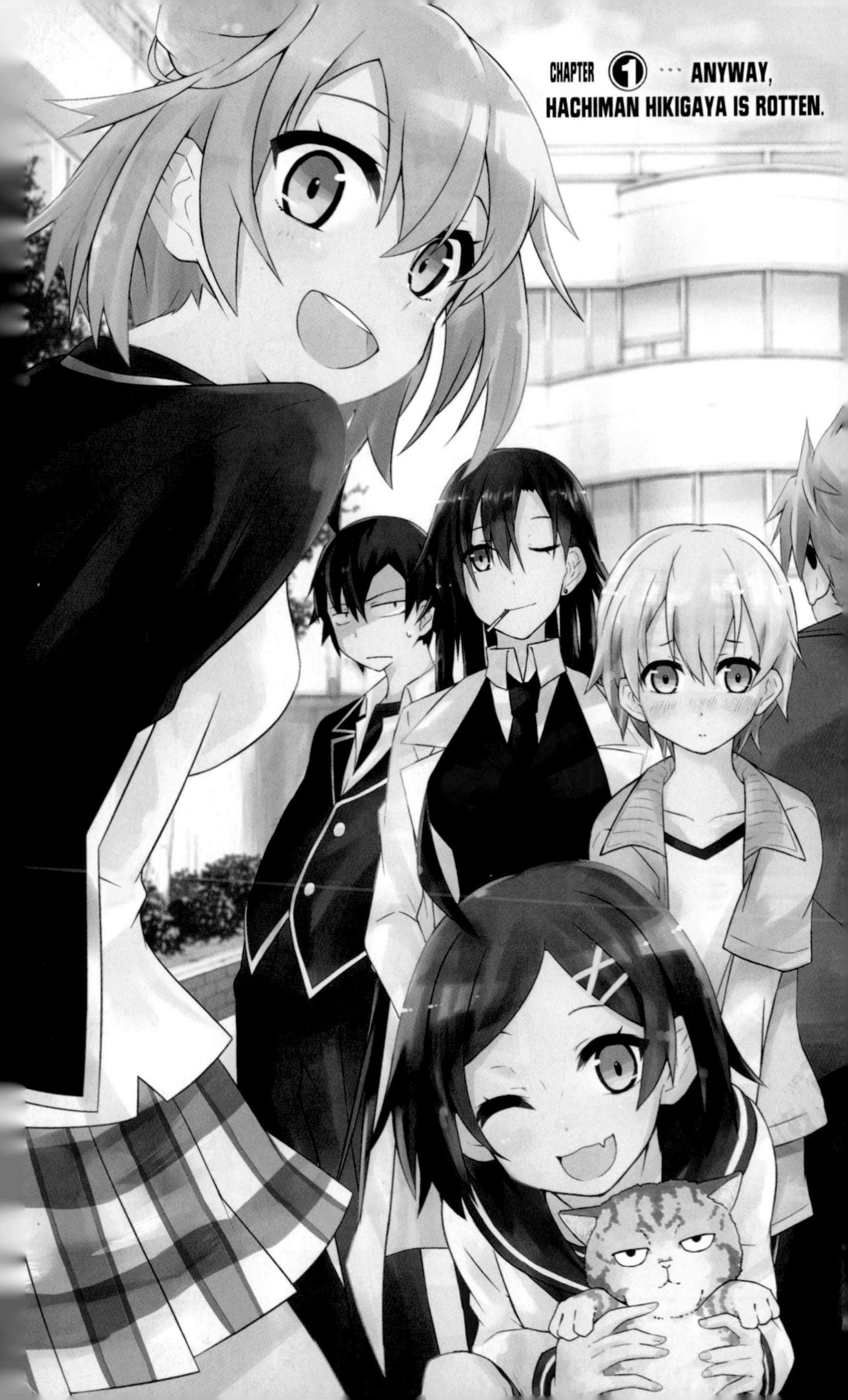
CHAPTER 1 … ANYWAY, HACHIMAN HIKIGAYA IS ROTTEN.

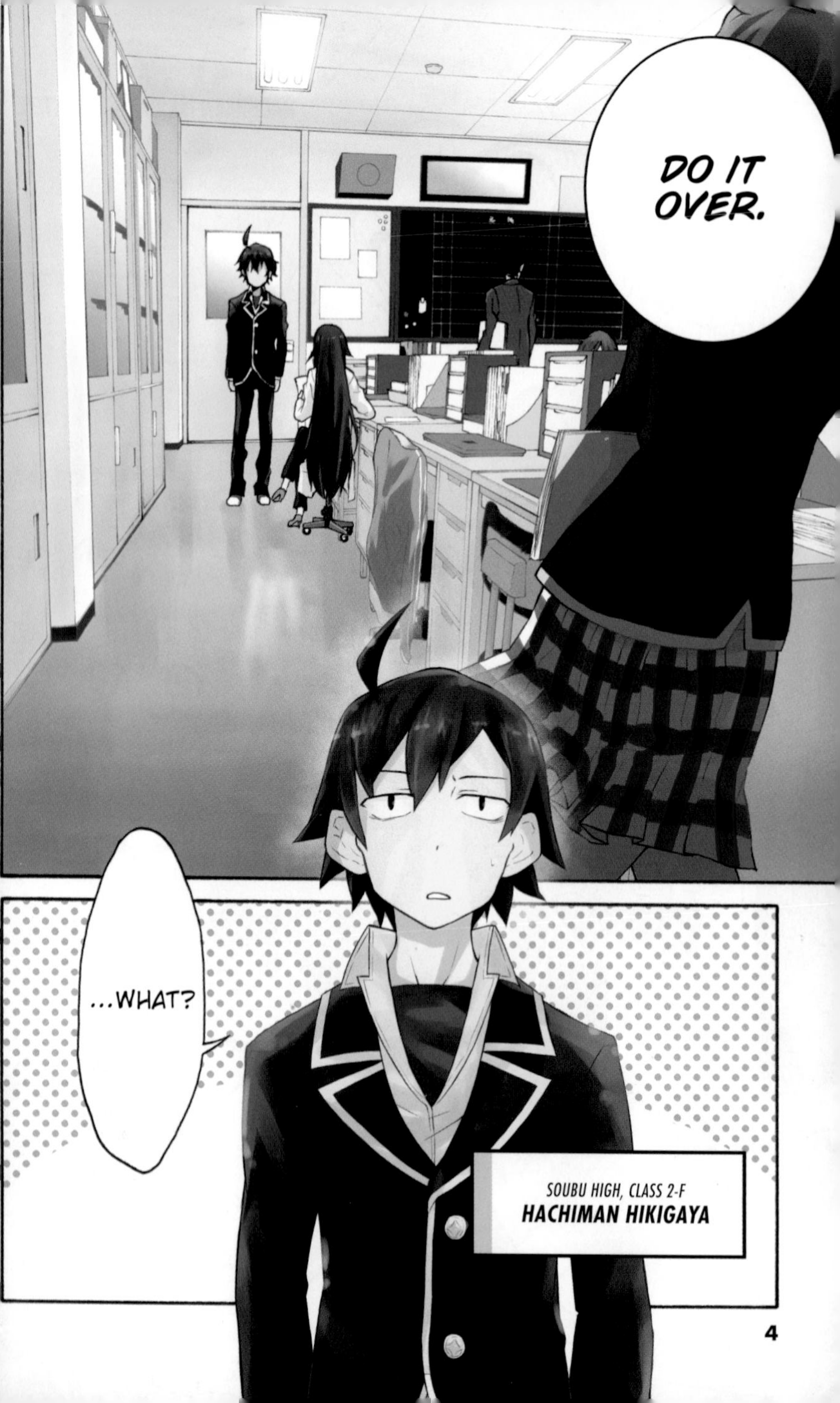
DO IT OVER.
...WHAT?
SOUBU HIGH, CLASS 2-F
HACHIMAN HIKIGAYA

MY YOUTH R♥MANTIC COMEDY is WRØNG, AS I EXPECTED @comic 01

Original Story
Wataru Watari

Art
Naomichi Io

Character Design
Ponkan⑧

— CONTENTS —

MADE IN COOPERATION WITH THE CHIBA CITY LOCATION SERVICE

DON'T GIVE ME THAT.

HAA (SIGH)

HIKIGAYA, THIS WAS SUPPOSED TO BE THE HOMEWORK I ASSIGNED TO YOU, AN ESSAY REFLECTING ON YOUR LIFE AT SCHOOL.

PARA (RUSTLE)

REPORT WORKSHEET

REFLECTING ON MY LIFE IN HIGH SCHOOL.

YOUTH IS LIES; YOUTH IS E
THOSE WHO INCESSANT'
LYING BOTH TO THEM;
PRINCIPLES ARE ENT'
THUS, THEIR PRINC'
'RAUD ARE '

THIS READS LIKE THE PRELUDE TO A SCHOOL MASSACRE.

BORI (SCRATCH)

YOU'RE RIGHT. I GUESS IT COMES OFF AS NOTHING MORE THAN A KID'S WILD IDEAS...

JAPANESE LANGUAGE TEACHER AND GUIDANCE COUNSELOR
SHIZUKA HIRATSUKA

...TO A WOMAN OF YOUR AGE.

GO (WHAM)

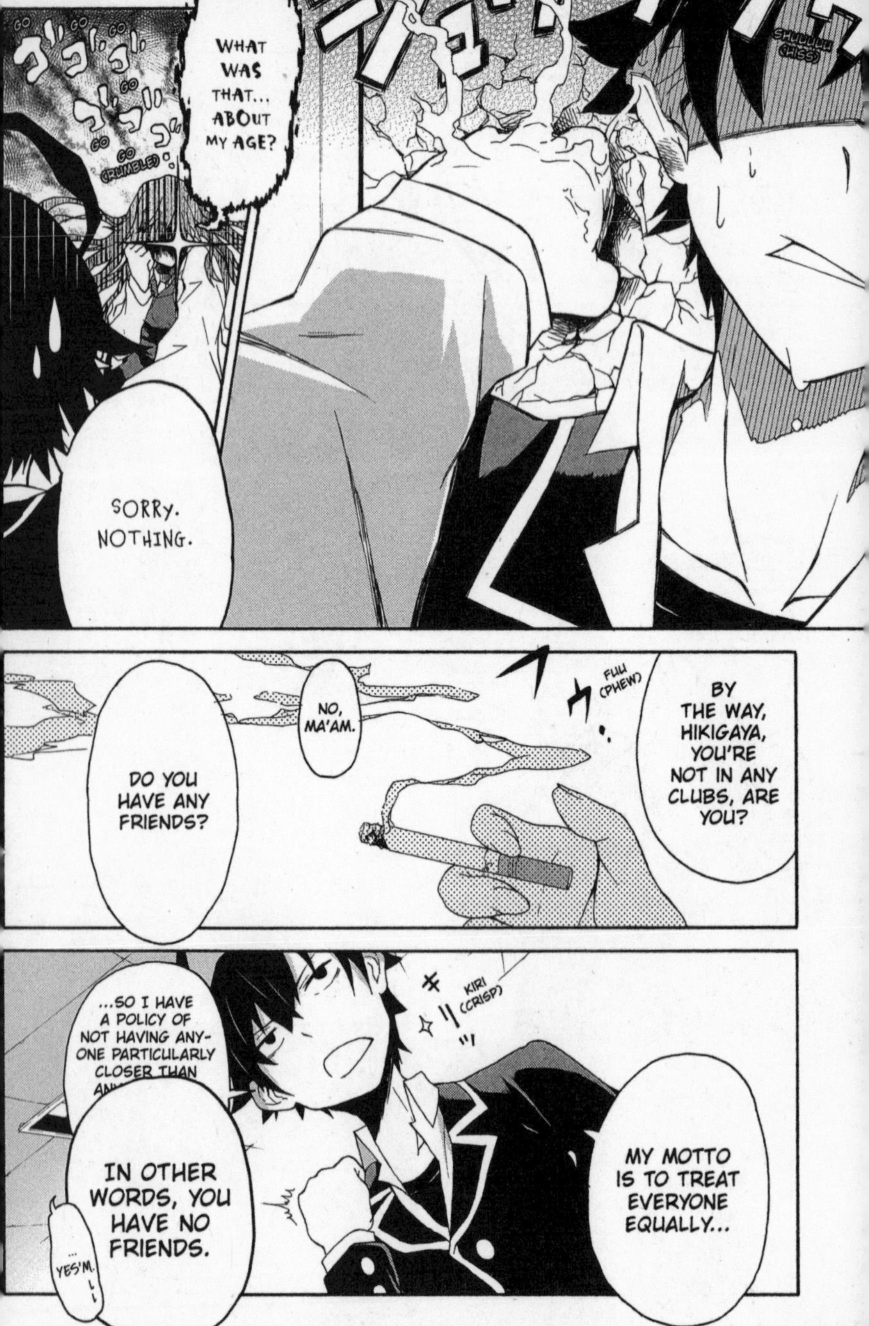
SHUUUUU (HISS)
WHAT WAS THAT... ABOUT MY AGE?
GO GO GO GO GO GO (RUMBLE)
SORRY. NOTHING.
BY THE WAY, HIKIGAYA, YOU'RE NOT IN ANY CLUBS, ARE YOU?
FUU (PHEW)
NO, MA'AM.
DO YOU HAVE ANY FRIENDS?
KIRI (CRISP)
MY MOTTO IS TO TREAT EVERYONE EQUALLY...
...SO I HAVE A POLICY OF NOT HAVING ANY-ONE PARTICULARLY CLOSER THAN
IN OTHER WORDS, YOU HAVE NO FRIENDS.
... YES'M.

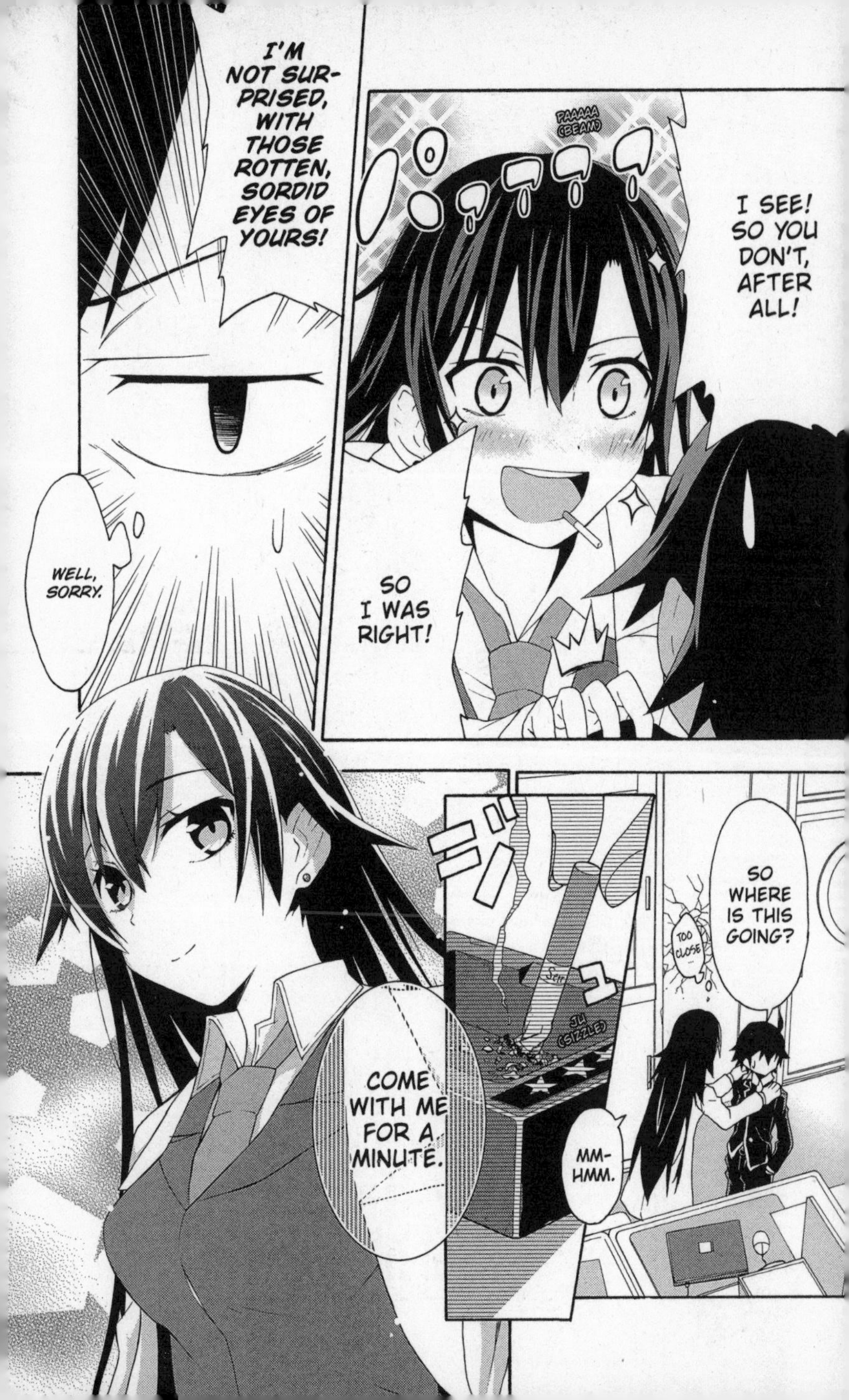
PAAAAA (BEAM)
I SEE! SO YOU DON'T, AFTER ALL!
SO I WAS RIGHT!
I'M NOT SURPRISED, WITH THOSE ROTTEN, SORDID EYES OF YOURS!
WELL, SORRY.
SO WHERE IS THIS GOING?
TOO CLOSE...
JU (SIZZLE)
MM-HMM.
COME WITH ME FOR A MINUTE.

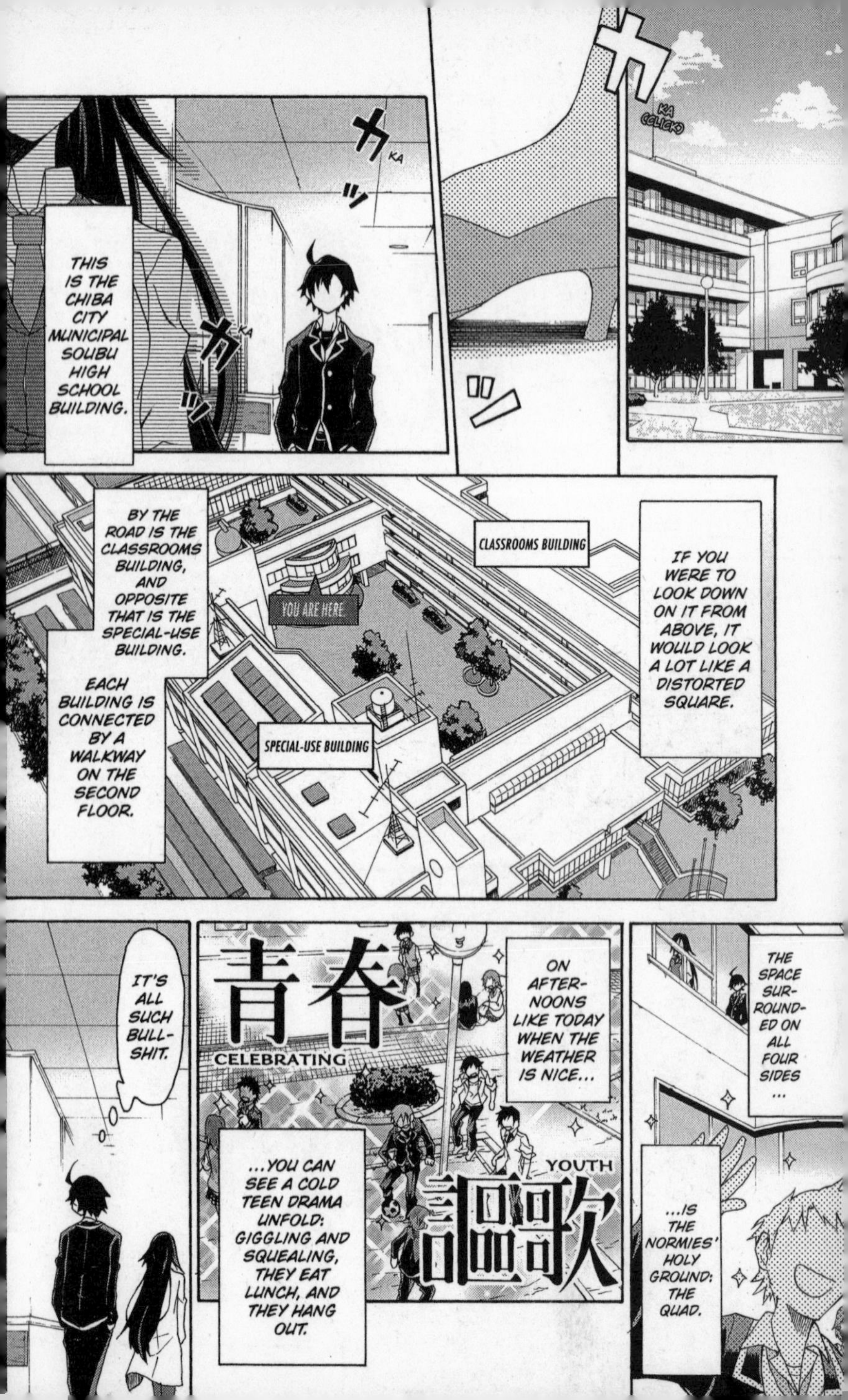
KA (CLICK)
KA
KA
THIS IS THE CHIBA CITY MUNICIPAL SOUBU HIGH SCHOOL BUILDING.
IF YOU WERE TO LOOK DOWN ON IT FROM ABOVE, IT WOULD LOOK A LOT LIKE A DISTORTED SQUARE.
CLASSROOMS BUILDING
YOU ARE HERE.
BY THE ROAD IS THE CLASSROOMS BUILDING, AND OPPOSITE THAT IS THE SPECIAL-USE BUILDING.
EACH BUILDING IS CONNECTED BY A WALKWAY ON THE SECOND FLOOR.
SPECIAL-USE BUILDING
THE SPACE SURROUNDED ON ALL FOUR SIDES...
...IS THE NORMIES' HOLY GROUND: THE QUAD.
ON AFTERNOONS LIKE TODAY WHEN THE WEATHER IS NICE...
青春
CELEBRATING
YOUTH
謳歌
...YOU CAN SEE A COLD TEEN DRAMA UNFOLD: GIGGLING AND SQUEALING, THEY EAT LUNCH, AND THEY HANG OUT.
IT'S ALL SUCH BULLSHIT.

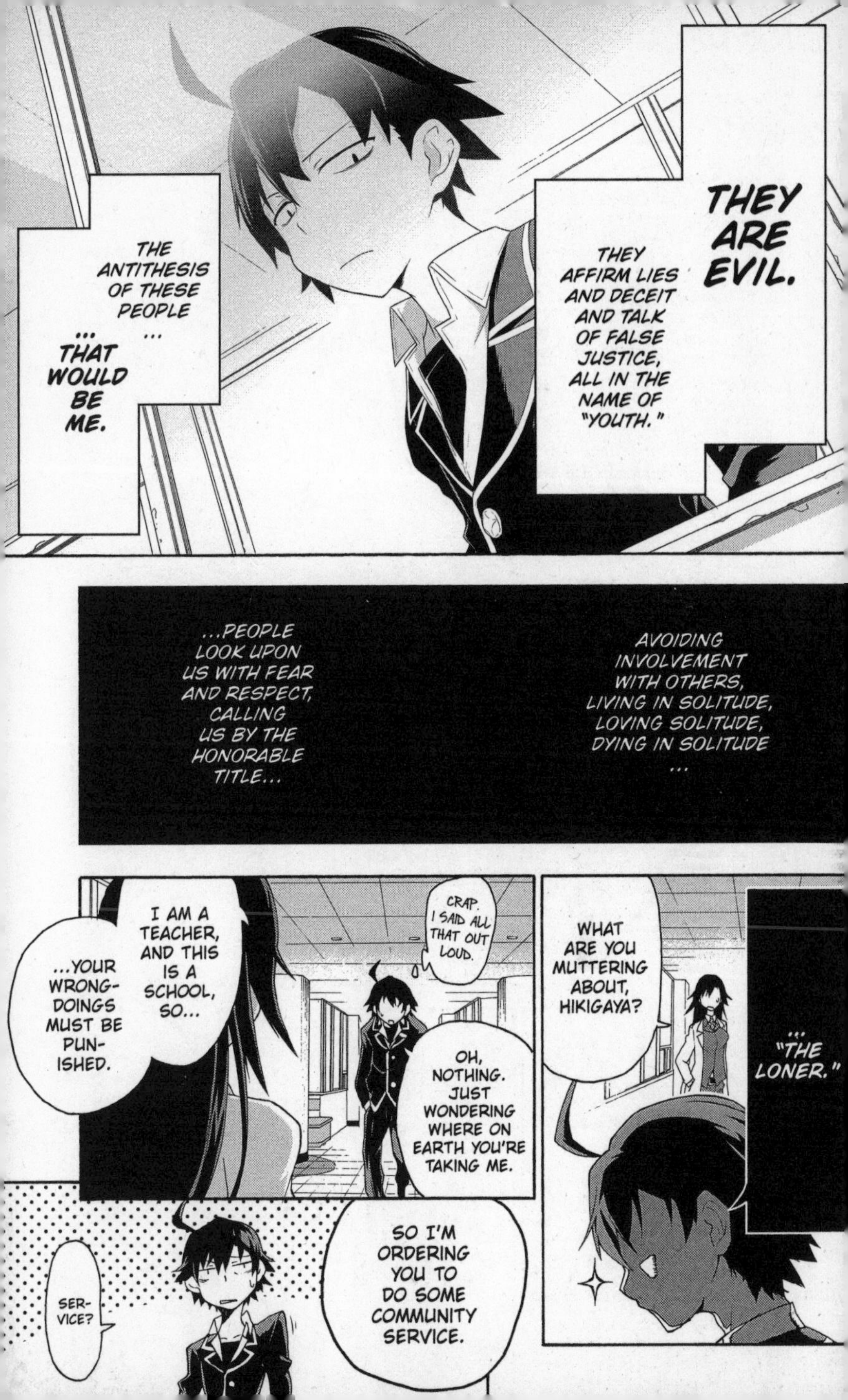
THEY AFFIRM LIES AND DECEIT AND TALK OF FALSE JUSTICE, ALL IN THE NAME OF "YOUTH."
THEY ARE EVIL.
THE ANTITHESIS OF THESE PEOPLE ... ... THAT WOULD BE ME.
AVOIDING INVOLVEMENT WITH OTHERS, LIVING IN SOLITUDE, LOVING SOLITUDE, DYING IN SOLITUDE ...
...PEOPLE LOOK UPON US WITH FEAR AND RESPECT, CALLING US BY THE HONORABLE TITLE...
... "THE LONER."
WHAT ARE YOU MUTTERING ABOUT, HIKIGAYA?
CRAP. I SAID ALL THAT OUT LOUD.
OH, NOTHING. JUST WONDERING WHERE ON EARTH YOU'RE TAKING ME.
I AM A TEACHER, AND THIS IS A SCHOOL, SO...
...YOUR WRONG-DOINGS MUST BE PUN-ISHED.
SO I'M ORDERING YOU TO DO SOME COMMUNITY SERVICE.
SER-VICE?

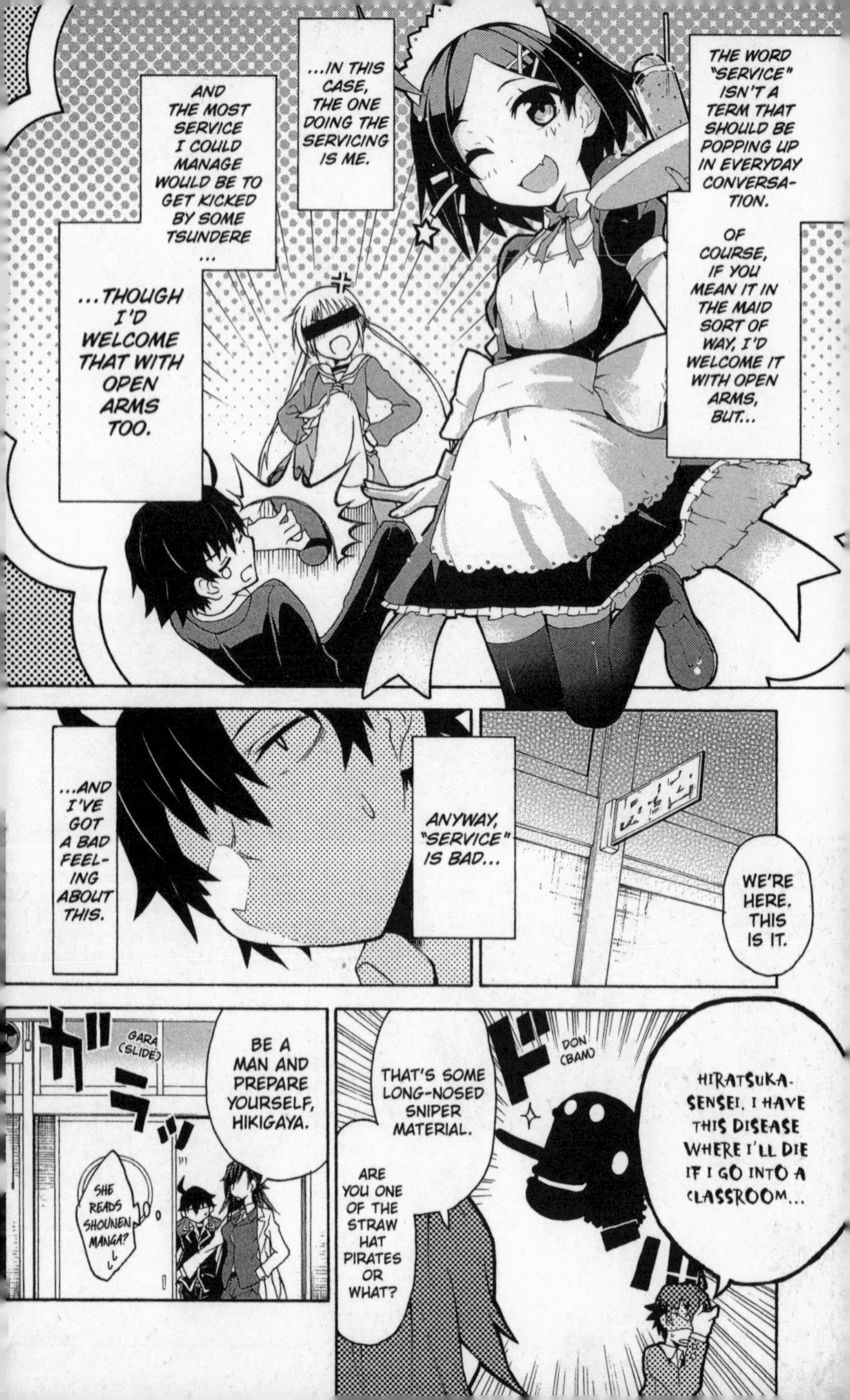

THE WORD "SERVICE" ISN'T A TERM THAT SHOULD BE POPPING UP IN EVERYDAY CONVERSA-TION.
OF COURSE, IF YOU MEAN IT IN THE MAID SORT OF WAY, I'D WELCOME IT WITH OPEN ARMS, BUT...
...IN THIS CASE, THE ONE DOING THE SERVICING IS ME.
AND THE MOST SERVICE I COULD MANAGE WOULD BE TO GET KICKED BY SOME TSUNDERE ...
...THOUGH I'D WELCOME THAT WITH OPEN ARMS TOO.
WE'RE HERE. THIS IS IT.
ANYWAY, "SERVICE" IS BAD...
...AND I'VE GOT A BAD FEEL-ING ABOUT THIS.
HIRATSUKA-SENSEI, I HAVE THIS DISEASE WHERE I'LL DIE IF I GO INTO A CLASSROOM...
DON (BAM)
THAT'S SOME LONG-NOSED SNIPER MATERIAL.
ARE YOU ONE OF THE STRAW HAT PIRATES OR WHAT?
BE A MAN AND PREPARE YOURSELF, HIKIGAYA.
GARA (SLIDE)
SHE READS SHOUNEN MANGA?

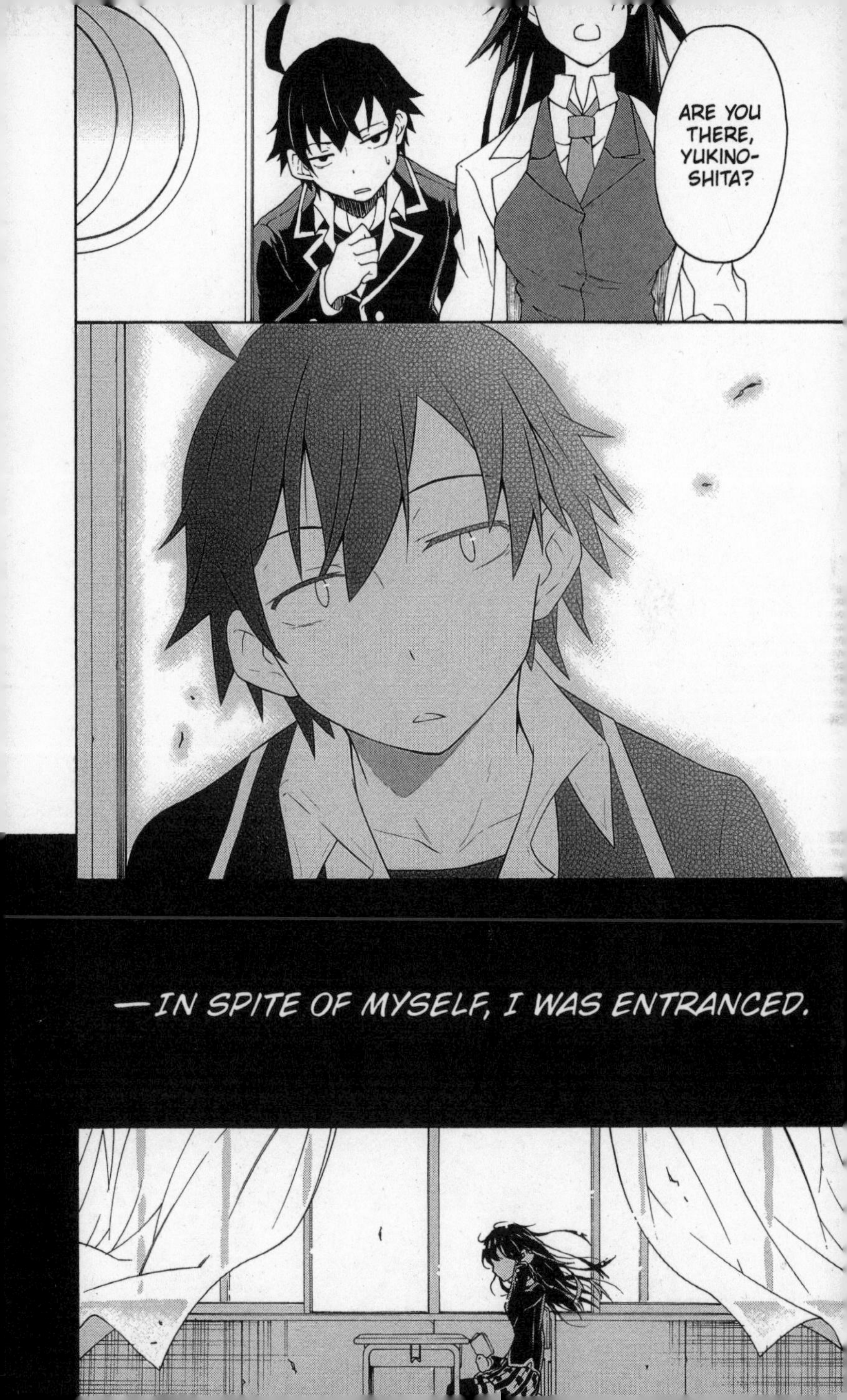
ARE YOU THERE, YUKINO-SHITA?
—IN SPITE OF MYSELF, I WAS ENTRANCED.

FLWA
(FWOO)

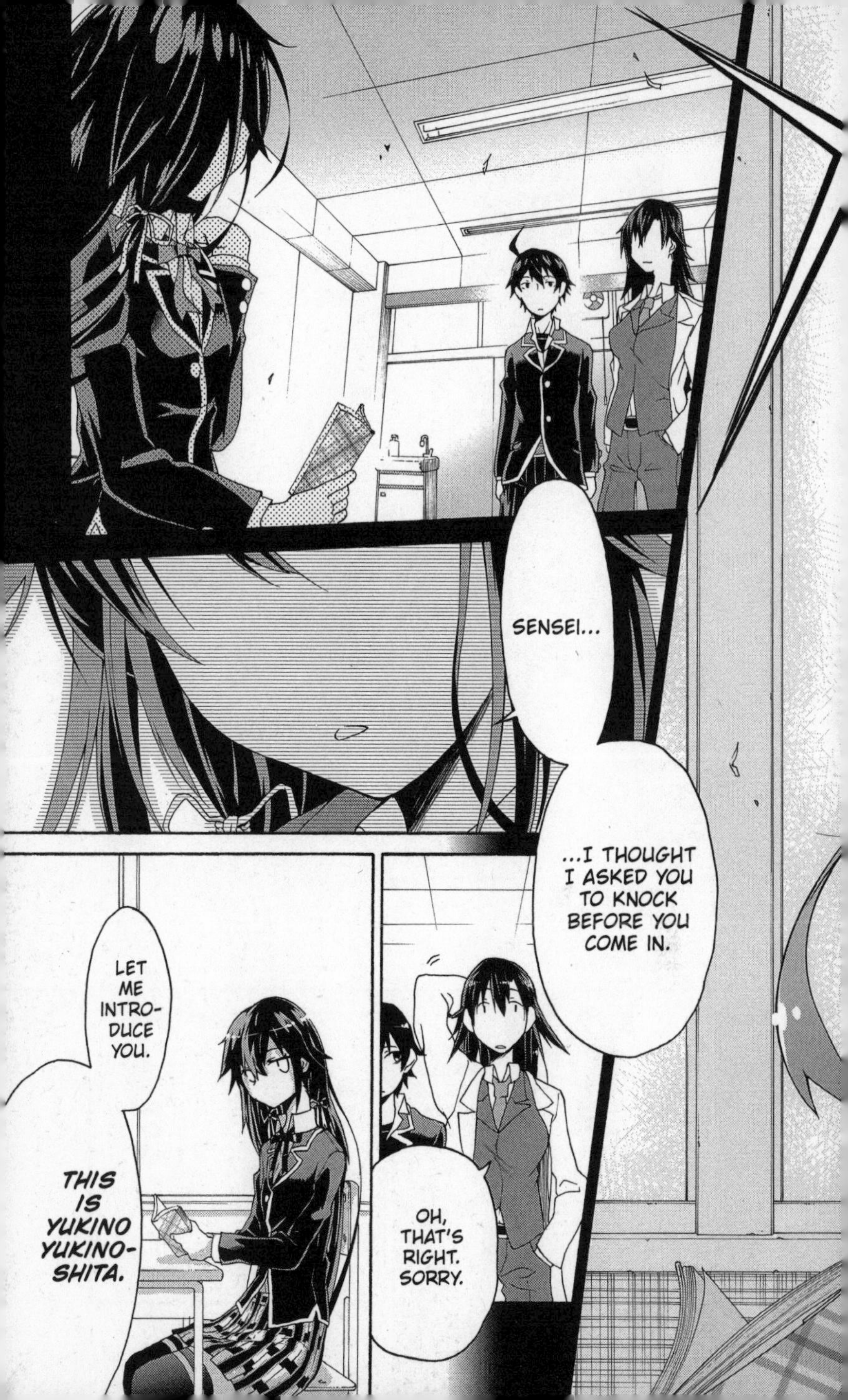
SENSEI...
...I THOUGHT I ASKED YOU TO KNOCK BEFORE YOU COME IN.
OH, THAT'S RIGHT. SORRY.
LET ME INTRO-DUCE YOU.
THIS IS YUKINO YUKINO-SHITA.

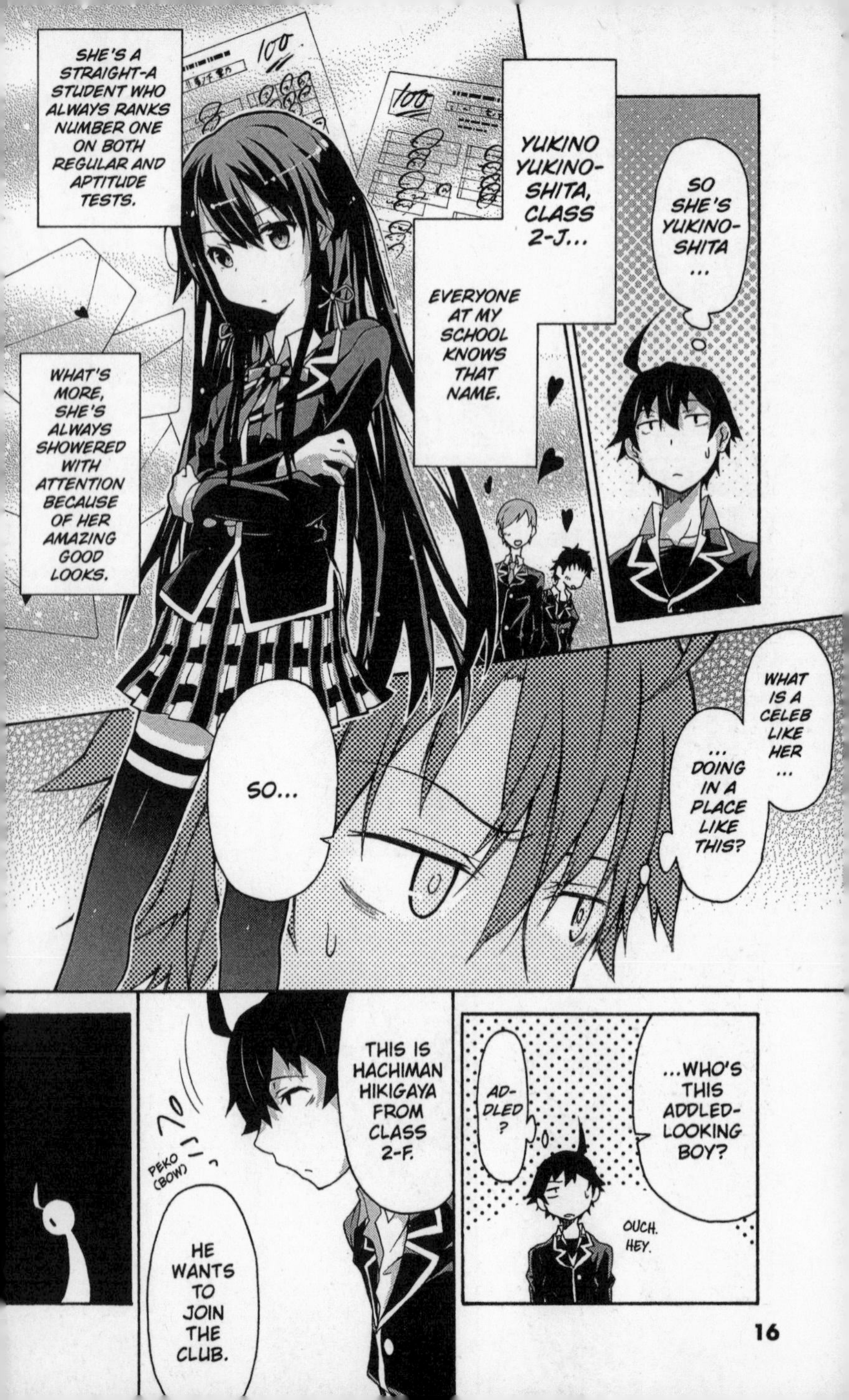
SO SHE'S YUKINOSHITA ...
YUKINO YUKINOSHITA, CLASS 2-J...
EVERYONE AT MY SCHOOL KNOWS THAT NAME.
SHE'S A STRAIGHT-A STUDENT WHO ALWAYS RANKS NUMBER ONE ON BOTH REGULAR AND APTITUDE TESTS.
WHAT'S MORE, SHE'S ALWAYS SHOWERED WITH ATTENTION BECAUSE OF HER AMAZING GOOD LOOKS.
WHAT IS A CELEB LIKE HER ... ... DOING IN A PLACE LIKE THIS?
SO...
...WHO'S THIS ADDLED-LOOKING BOY?
AD-DLED?
OUCH. HEY.
THIS IS HACHIMAN HIKIGAYA FROM CLASS 2-F.
PEKO (BOW)
HE WANTS TO JOIN THE CLUB.

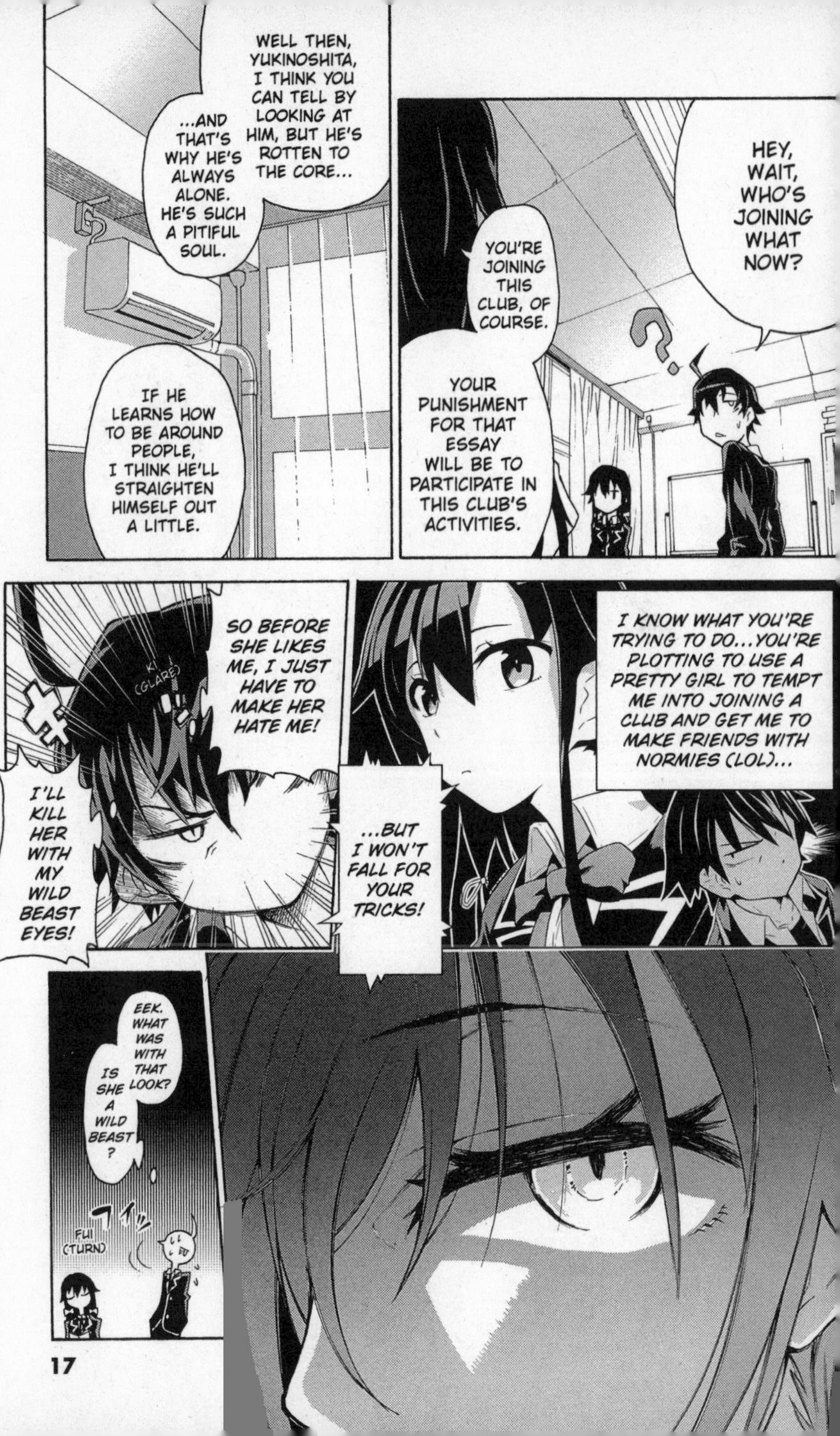

HEY, WAIT, WHO'S JOINING WHAT NOW?
YOU'RE JOINING THIS CLUB, OF COURSE.
YOUR PUNISHMENT FOR THAT ESSAY WILL BE TO PARTICIPATE IN THIS CLUB'S ACTIVITIES.
WELL THEN, YUKINOSHITA, I THINK YOU CAN TELL BY LOOKING AT HIM, BUT HE'S ROTTEN TO THE CORE...
...AND THAT'S WHY HE'S ALWAYS ALONE. HE'S SUCH A PITIFUL SOUL.
IF HE LEARNS HOW TO BE AROUND PEOPLE, I THINK HE'LL STRAIGHTEN HIMSELF OUT A LITTLE.
I KNOW WHAT YOU'RE TRYING TO DO...YOU'RE PLOTTING TO USE A PRETTY GIRL TO TEMPT ME INTO JOINING A CLUB AND GET ME TO MAKE FRIENDS WITH NORMIES (LOL)...
...BUT I WON'T FALL FOR YOUR TRICKS!
SO BEFORE SHE LIKES ME, I JUST HAVE TO MAKE HER HATE ME!
KI (GLARE)
I'LL KILL HER WITH MY WILD BEAST EYES!
EEK. WHAT WAS WITH THAT LOOK?
IS SHE A WILD BEAST?
FUI (TURN)

SEEING THOSE LEWD EYES OF HIS BRIMMING WITH ULTERIOR MOTIVES, I FEEL THERE IS A THREAT TO MY PERSON.

I REFUSE.

LOW-LEVEL CREEP... I SEE.

HEY, LOW-LEVEL CREEP?

HE'S JUST A MILD, LOW-LEVEL CREEP. HE'D NEVER DO ANYTHING THAT WOULD GET HIM ARRESTED.

RELAX, YUKINO-SHITA.

SHE'S ACCEPTING THAT!?

KYU (SQUEEZE)

NOBODY'S LOOKING AT YOUR MEAGER CHEST!

NO REALLY, IT'S TRUE. SERIOUSLY.

WELL, IF IT'S A REQUEST FROM YOU, I CAN'T JUST REFUSE...

I WILL COMPLY.

MM-HMM.

NOT ONLY IS THAT HARD TO UNDERSTAND, THOSE REFERENCES ARE GIVING AWAY YOUR AGE.

YOU WILL WORK TO TRANSFORM YOURSELF HERE AS WELL.

HIKIGAYA, THE GOAL OF THIS CLUB IS TO STIMULATE PERSONAL TRANS-FORMATION AND RESOLVE PROBLEMS.

OW, OW, OW!!!

THINK OF IT AS THE HYPERBOLIC TIME CHAMBER...

...OR WOULD IT BE EASIER TO UNDERSTAND IF I JUST CALLED IT *REVOLUTIONARY GIRL UTENA*?

YANK

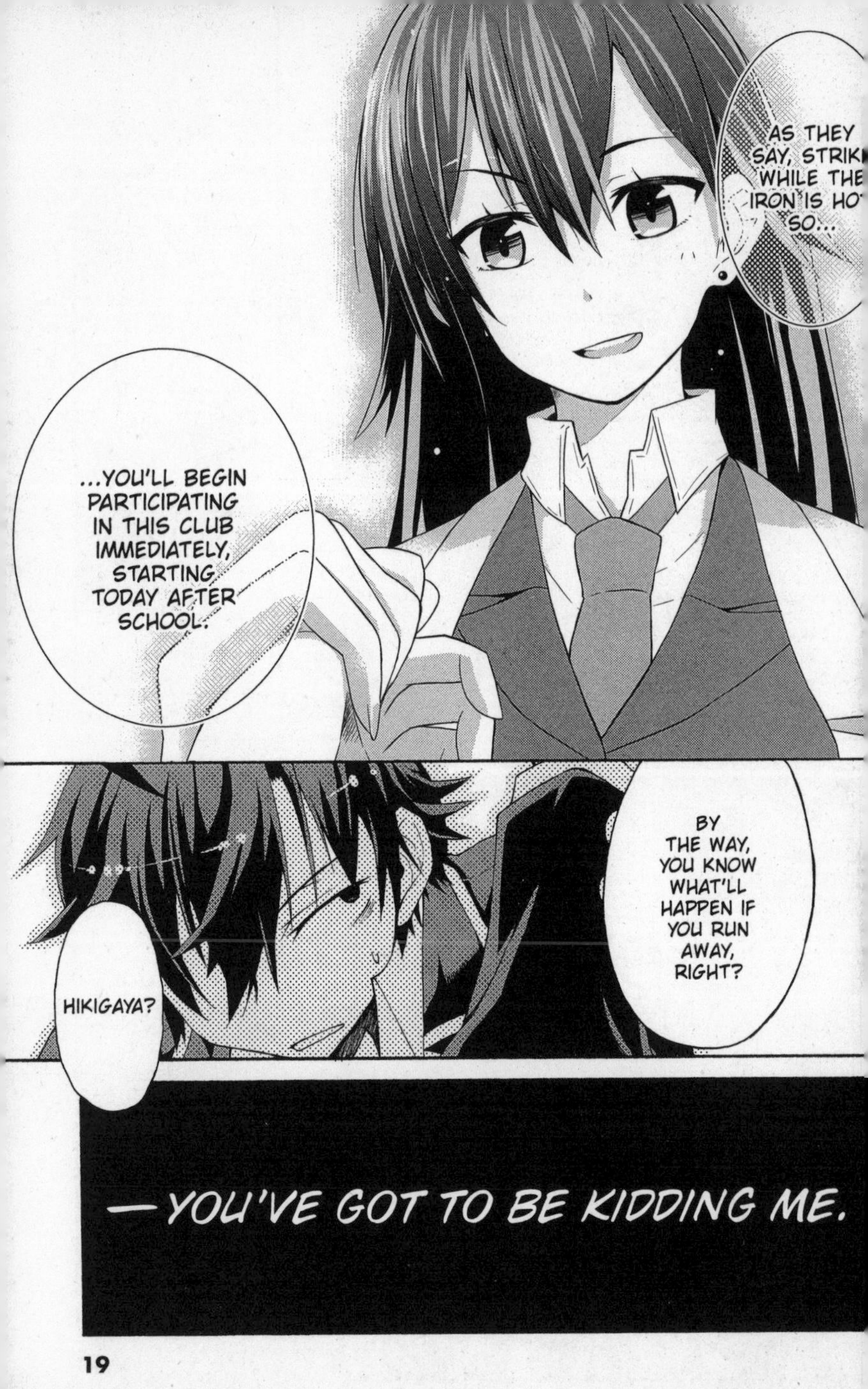
AS THEY SAY, STRIKE WHILE THE IRON IS HOT SO...
...YOU'LL BEGIN PARTICIPATING IN THIS CLUB IMMEDIATELY, STARTING TODAY AFTER SCHOOL.
BY THE WAY, YOU KNOW WHAT'LL HAPPEN IF YOU RUN AWAY, RIGHT?
HIKIGAYA?
—YOU'VE GOT TO BE KIDDING ME.

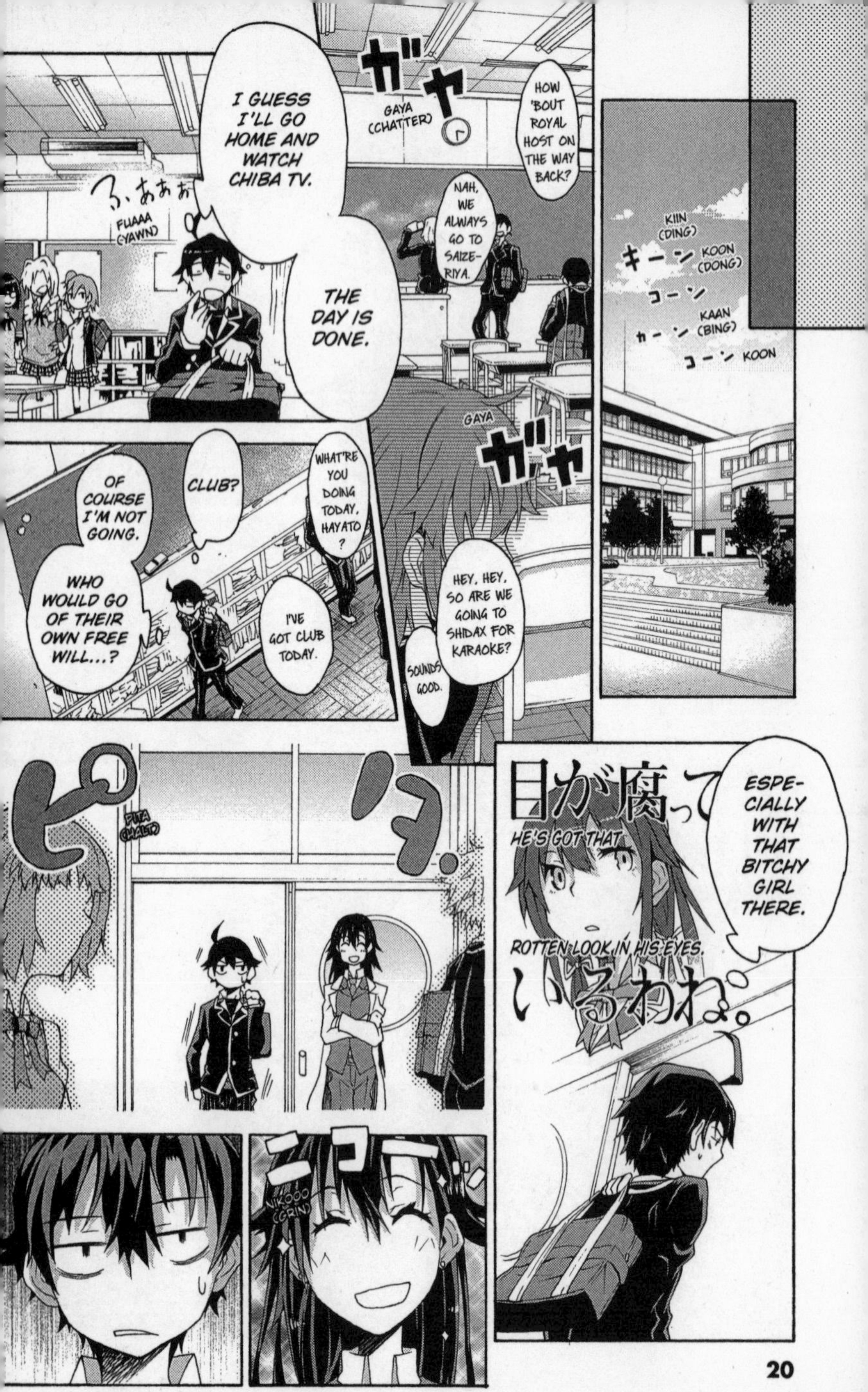

キーン
KIIN (DING)
コーン
KOON (DONG)
カーン
KAAN (BING)
コーン
KOON
ガヤ
GAYA (CHATTER)
HOW 'BOUT ROYAL HOST ON THE WAY BACK?
NAH, WE ALWAYS GO TO SAIZE-RIYA.
ふぁあぁ
FUAAA (YAWN)
I GUESS I'LL GO HOME AND WATCH CHIBA TV.
THE DAY IS DONE.
ガヤ
GAYA
HEY, HEY, SO ARE WE GOING TO SHIDAX FOR KARAOKE?
SOUNDS GOOD.
WHAT'RE YOU DOING TODAY, HAYATO?
I'VE GOT CLUB TODAY.
CLUB?
OF COURSE I'M NOT GOING.
WHO WOULD GO OF THEIR OWN FREE WILL...?
目が腐っているわね。
HE'S GOT THAT ROTTEN LOOK IN HIS EYES.
ESPE-CIALLY WITH THAT BITCHY GIRL THERE.
ピタッ
PITA (HALT)
ニコー
NIKOOO (GRIN)

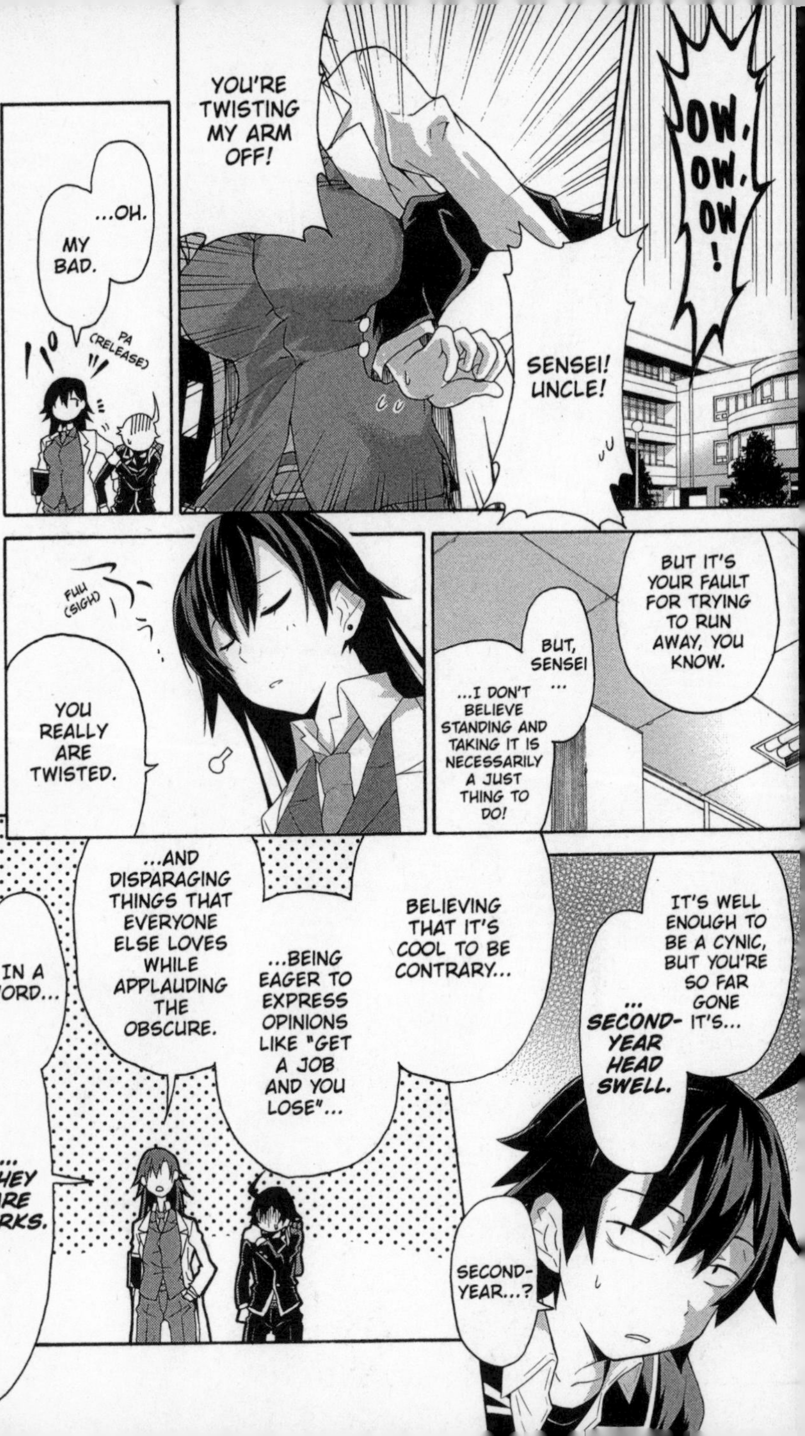
OW, OW, OW!
YOU'RE TWISTING MY ARM OFF!
SENSEI! UNCLE!
...OH. MY BAD.
PA (RELEASE)
BUT IT'S YOUR FAULT FOR TRYING TO RUN AWAY, YOU KNOW.
BUT, SENSEI...
...I DON'T BELIEVE STANDING AND TAKING IT IS NECESSARILY A JUST THING TO DO!
FUU (SIGH)
YOU REALLY ARE TWISTED.
IT'S WELL ENOUGH TO BE A CYNIC, BUT YOU'RE SO FAR GONE IT'S...
...SECOND-YEAR HEAD SWELL.
SECOND-YEAR...?
BELIEVING THAT IT'S COOL TO BE CONTRARY...
...BEING EAGER TO EXPRESS OPINIONS LIKE "GET A JOB AND YOU LOSE"...
...AND DISPARAGING THINGS THAT EVERYONE ELSE LOVES WHILE APPLAUDING THE OBSCURE.
IN A WORD...
...THEY ARE JERKS.

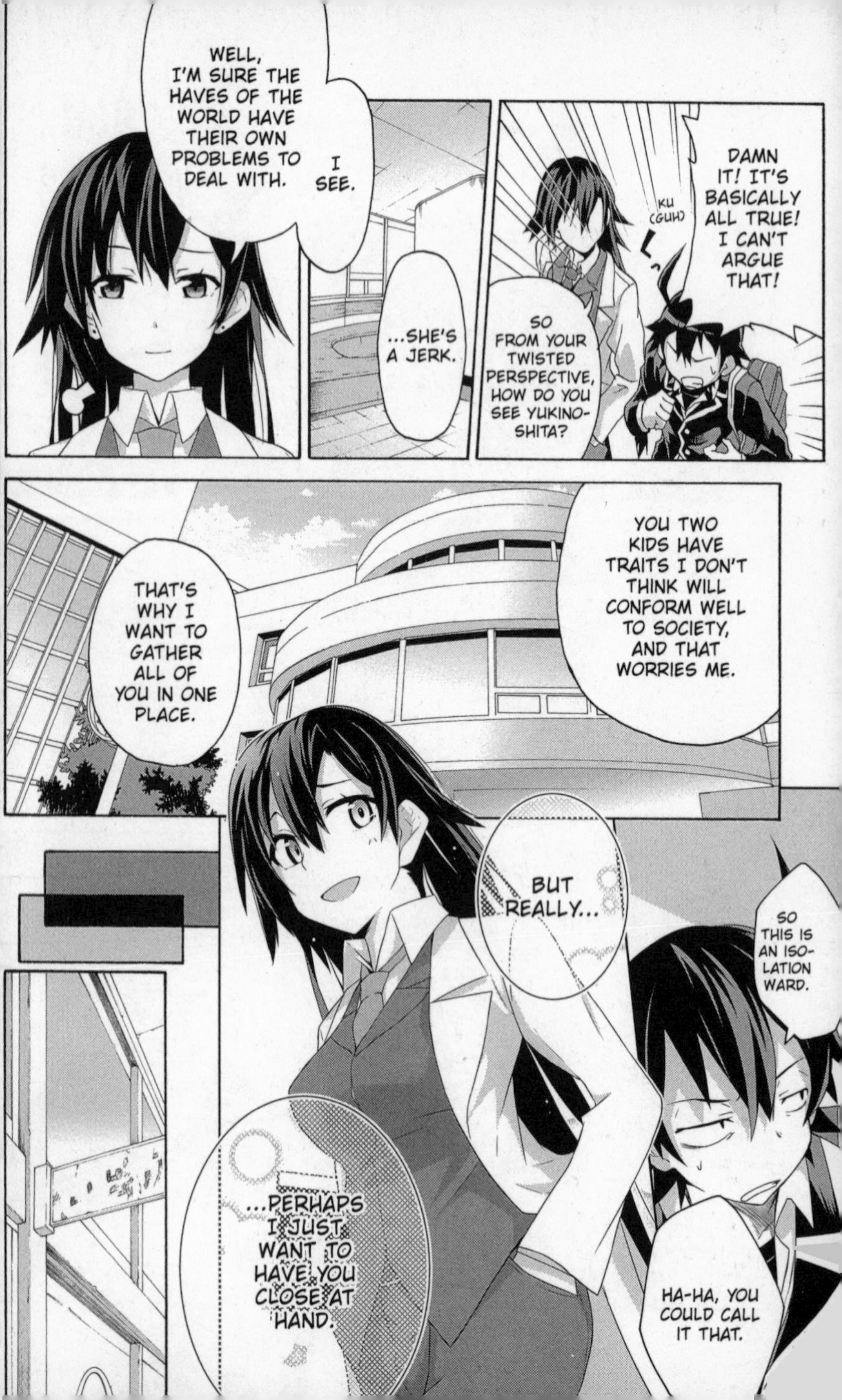
DAMN IT! IT'S BASICALLY ALL TRUE! I CAN'T ARGUE THAT!
KU (GUH)
SO FROM YOUR TWISTED PERSPECTIVE, HOW DO YOU SEE YUKINO-SHITA?
...SHE'S A JERK.
I SEE.
WELL, I'M SURE THE HAVES OF THE WORLD HAVE THEIR OWN PROBLEMS TO DEAL WITH.
YOU TWO KIDS HAVE TRAITS I DON'T THINK WILL CONFORM WELL TO SOCIETY, AND THAT WORRIES ME.
THAT'S WHY I WANT TO GATHER ALL OF YOU IN ONE PLACE.
SO THIS IS AN ISO-LATION WARD.
HA-HA, YOU COULD CALL IT THAT.
BUT REALLY...
...PERHAPS I JUST WANT TO HAVE YOU CLOSE AT HAND.

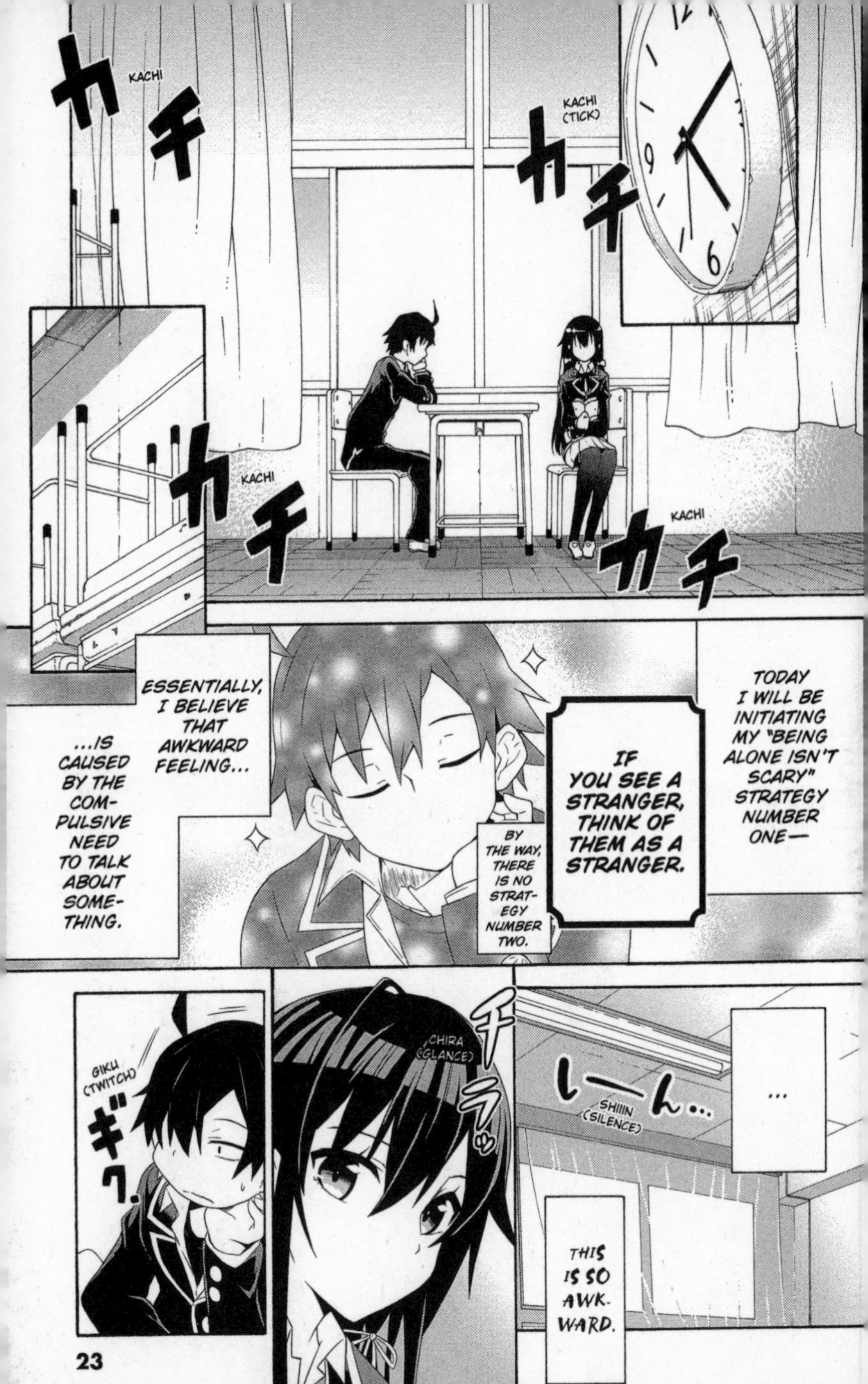
カチ
KACHI (TICK)
カチ
KACHI
カチ
KACHI
カチ
KACHI
TODAY I WILL BE INITIATING MY "BEING ALONE ISN'T SCARY" STRATEGY NUMBER ONE—
IF YOU SEE A STRANGER, THINK OF THEM AS A STRANGER.
BY THE WAY, THERE IS NO STRATEGY NUMBER TWO.
ESSENTIALLY, I BELIEVE THAT AWKWARD FEELING...
...IS CAUSED BY THE COMPULSIVE NEED TO TALK ABOUT SOMETHING.
...
しーん...
SHIIIN (SILENCE)
THIS IS SO AWKWARD.
チラ
CHIRA (GLANCE)
ギク
GIKU (TWITCH)

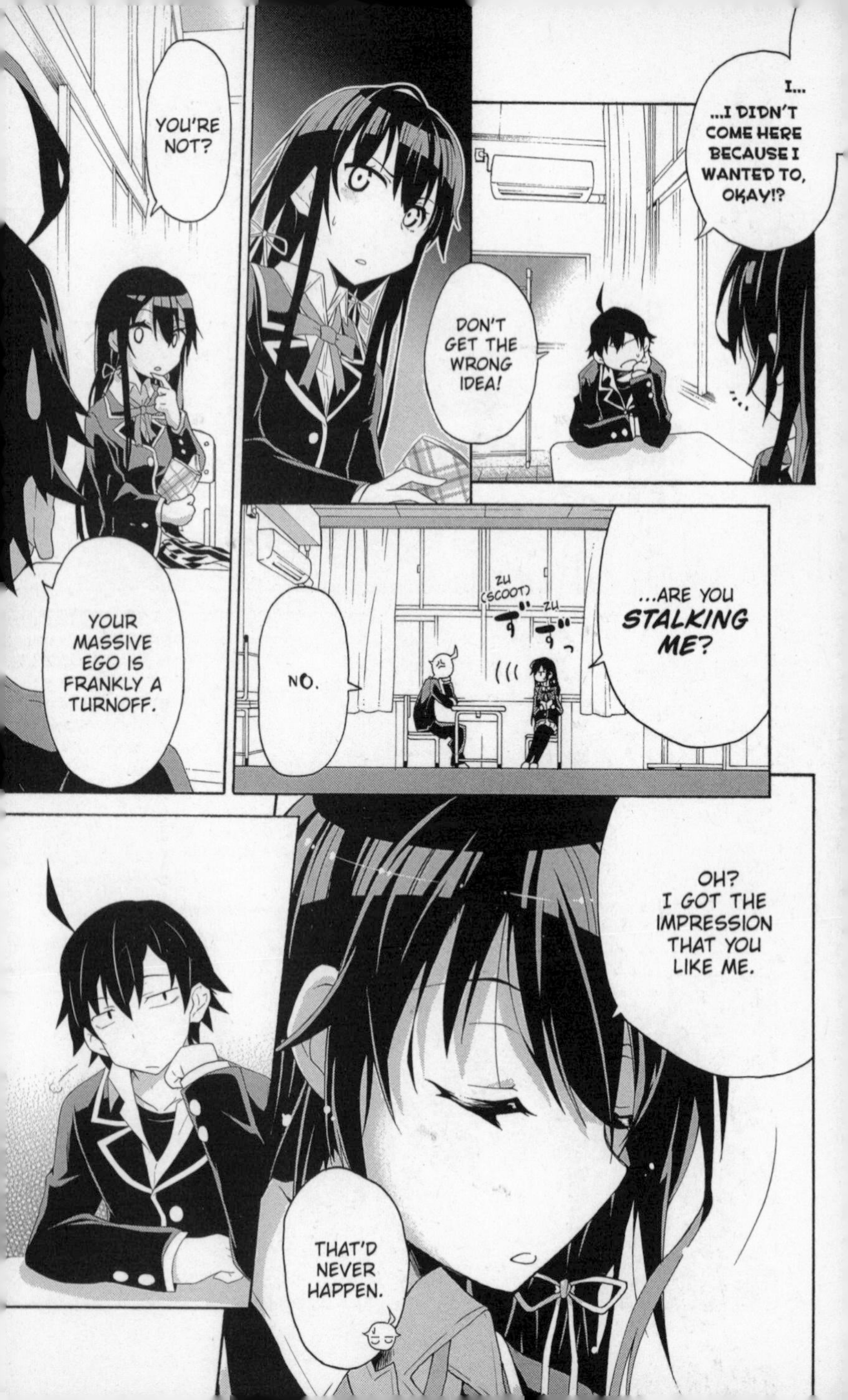
I...
...I DIDN'T COME HERE BECAUSE I WANTED TO, OKAY!?
DON'T GET THE WRONG IDEA!
YOU'RE NOT?
...ARE YOU STALKING ME?
ZU (SCOOT)
ZU
NO.
YOUR MASSIVE EGO IS FRANKLY A TURNOFF.
OH? I GOT THE IMPRESSION THAT YOU LIKE ME.
THAT'D NEVER HAPPEN.

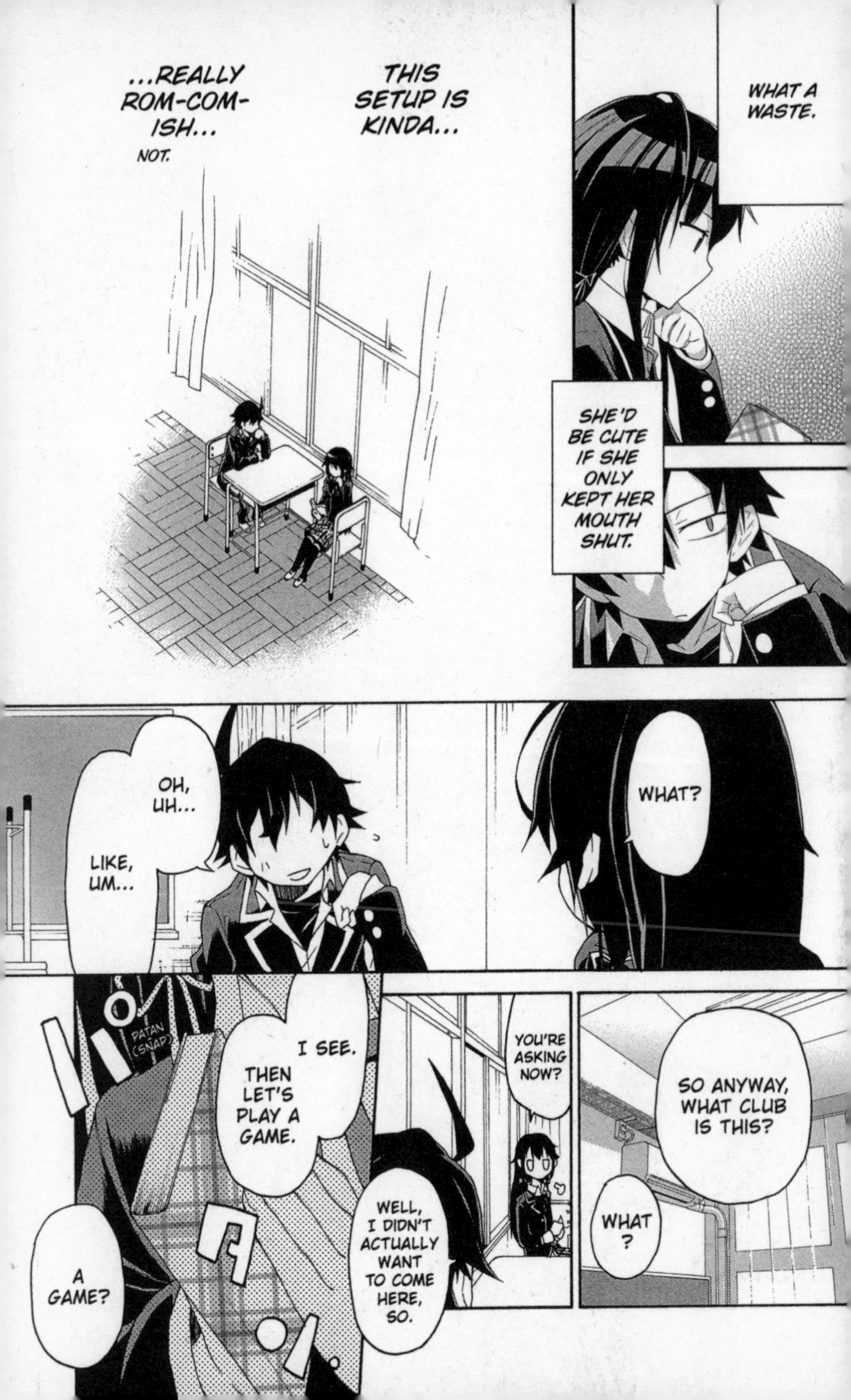
WHAT A WASTE.
SHE'D BE CUTE IF SHE ONLY KEPT HER MOUTH SHUT.
THIS SETUP IS KINDA...
...REALLY ROM-COM-ISH...
NOT.
WHAT?
OH, UH...
LIKE, UM...
SO ANYWAY, WHAT CLUB IS THIS?
WHAT?
YOU'RE ASKING NOW?
WELL, I DIDN'T ACTUALLY WANT TO COME HERE, SO.
PATAN (SNAP)
I SEE.
THEN LET'S PLAY A GAME.
A GAME?

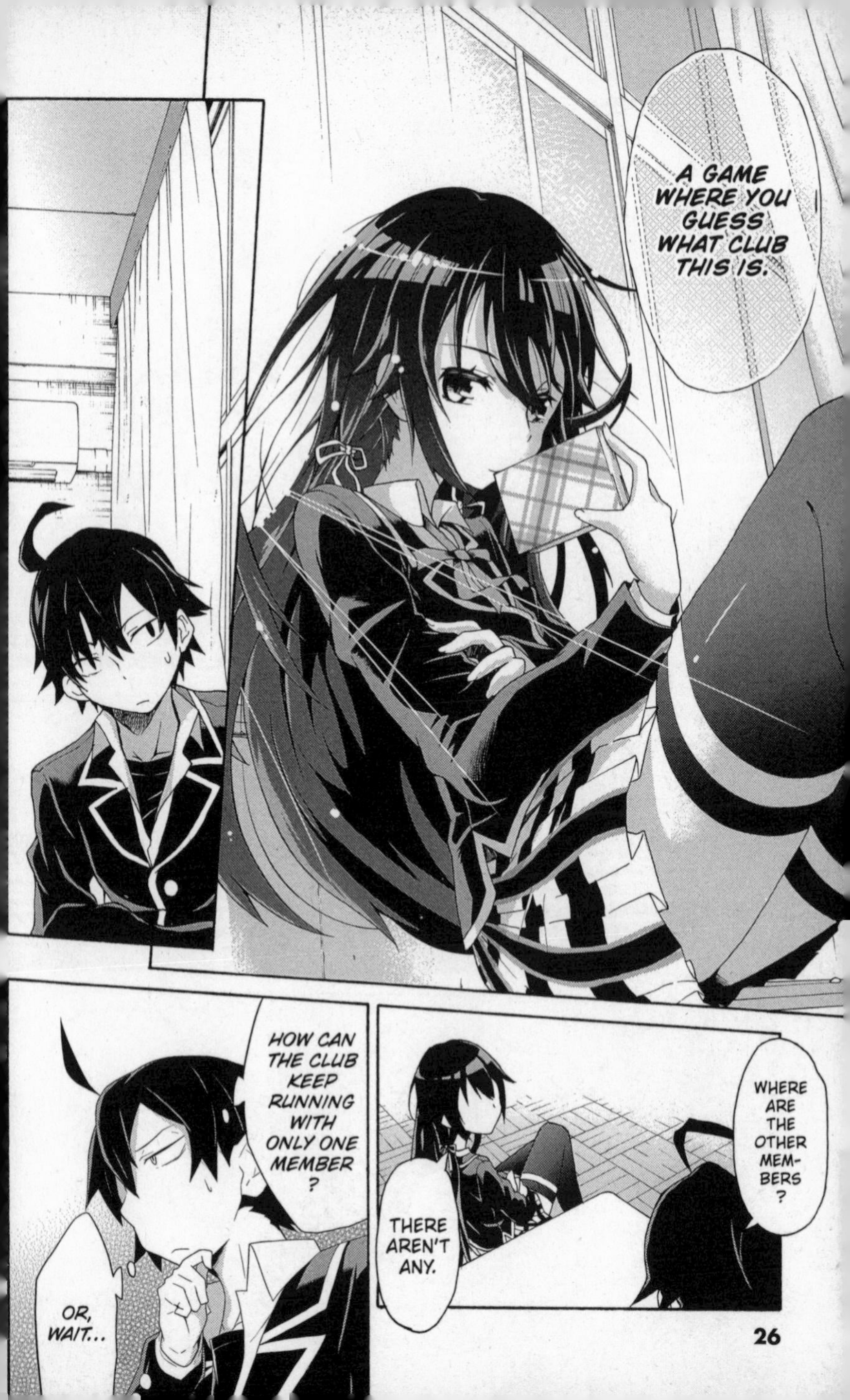
A GAME WHERE YOU GUESS WHAT CLUB THIS IS.
WHERE ARE THE OTHER MEM-BERS?
THERE AREN'T ANY.
HOW CAN THE CLUB KEEP RUNNING WITH ONLY ONE MEMBER?
OR, WAIT...

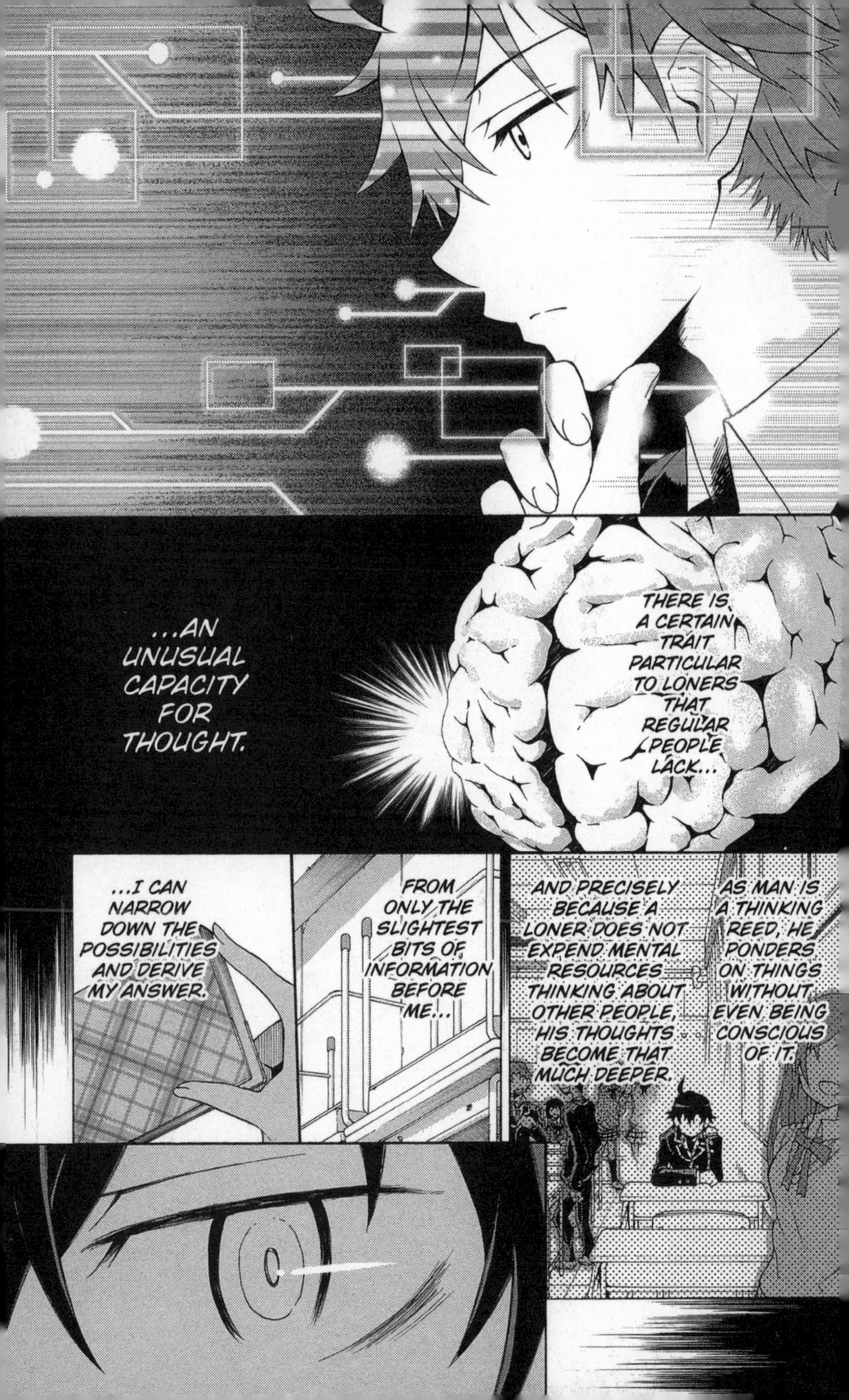
THERE IS A CERTAIN TRAIT PARTICULAR TO LONERS THAT REGULAR PEOPLE LACK...
...AN UNUSUAL CAPACITY FOR THOUGHT.
AS MAN IS A THINKING REED, HE PONDERS ON THINGS WITHOUT EVEN BEING CONSCIOUS OF IT.
AND PRECISELY BECAUSE A LONER DOES NOT EXPEND MENTAL RESOURCES THINKING ABOUT OTHER PEOPLE, HIS THOUGHTS BECOME THAT MUCH DEEPER.
FROM ONLY THE SLIGHTEST BITS OF INFORMATION BEFORE ME...
...I CAN NARROW DOWN THE POSSIBILITIES AND DERIVE MY ANSWER.

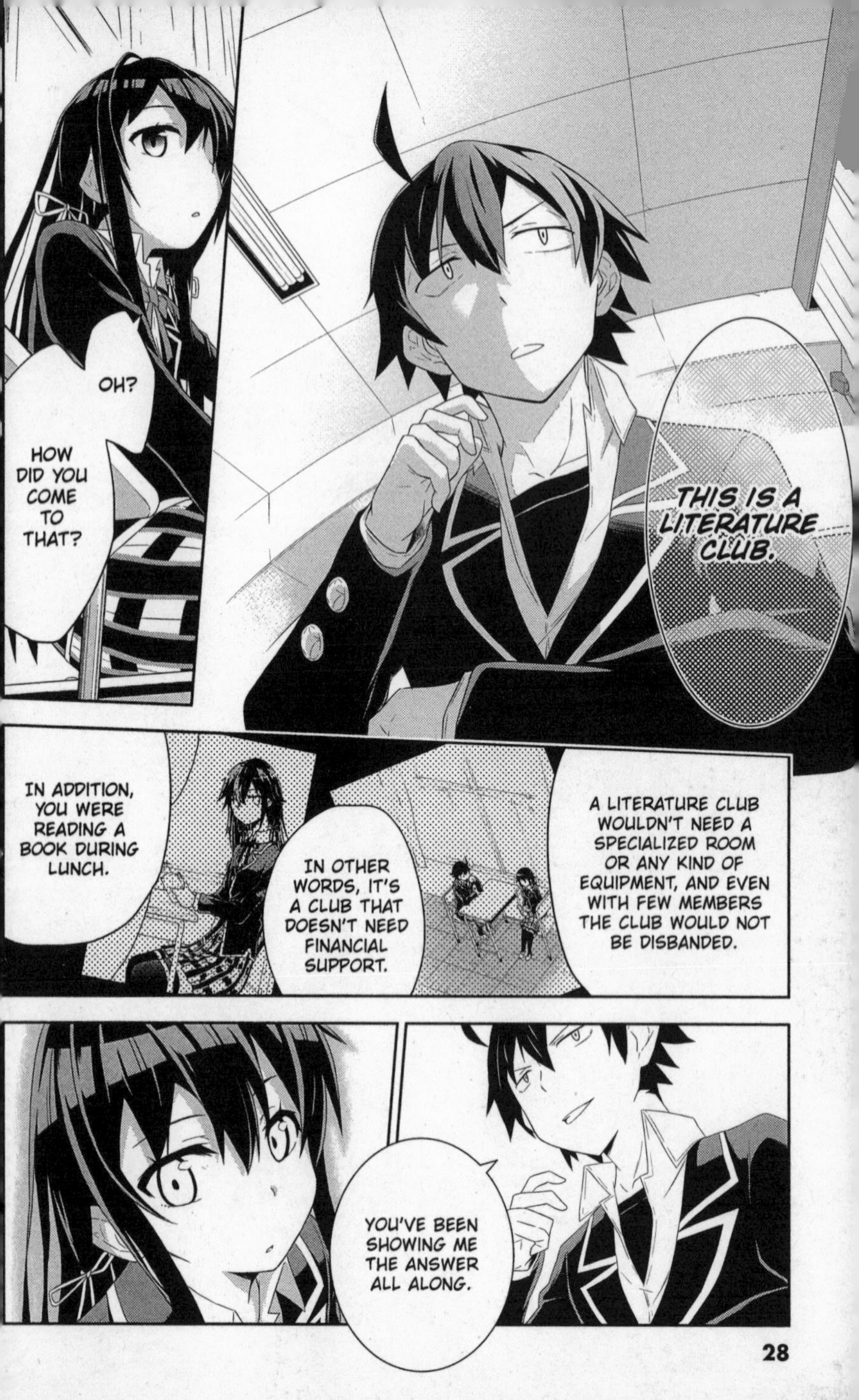
THIS IS A LITERATURE CLUB.
OH?
HOW DID YOU COME TO THAT?
A LITERATURE CLUB WOULDN'T NEED A SPECIALIZED ROOM OR ANY KIND OF EQUIPMENT, AND EVEN WITH FEW MEMBERS THE CLUB WOULD NOT BE DISBANDED.
IN OTHER WORDS, IT'S A CLUB THAT DOESN'T NEED FINANCIAL SUPPORT.
IN ADDITION, YOU WERE READING A BOOK DURING LUNCH.
YOU'VE BEEN SHOWING ME THE ANSWER ALL ALONG.

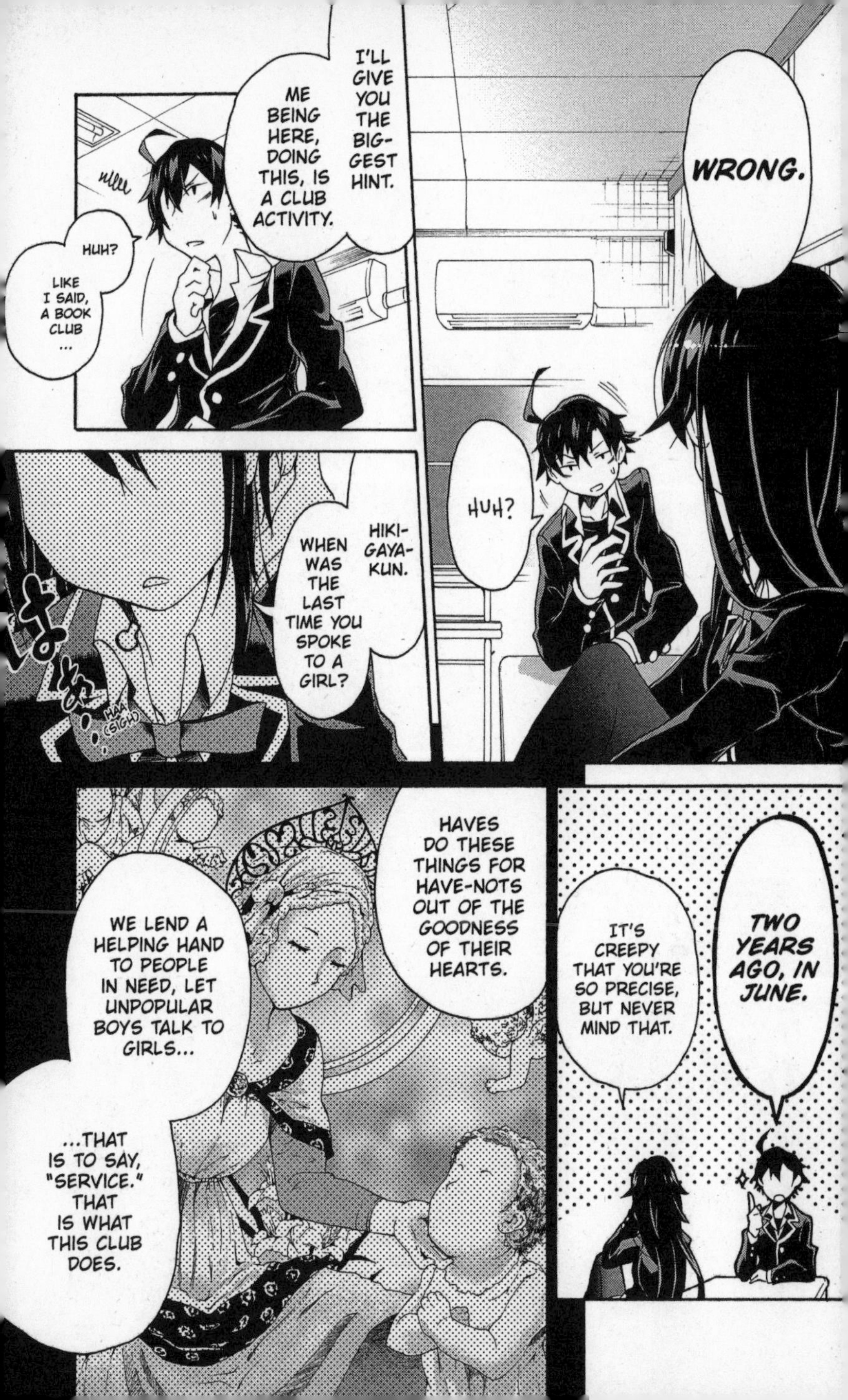
WRONG.
HUH?
I'LL GIVE YOU THE BIG-GEST HINT.
ME BEING HERE, DOING THIS, IS A CLUB ACTIVITY.
HUH?
LIKE I SAID, A BOOK CLUB ...
HIKI-GAYA-KUN.
WHEN WAS THE LAST TIME YOU SPOKE TO A GIRL?
HAA (SIGH)
TWO YEARS AGO, IN JUNE.
IT'S CREEPY THAT YOU'RE SO PRECISE, BUT NEVER MIND THAT.
HAVES DO THESE THINGS FOR HAVE-NOTS OUT OF THE GOODNESS OF THEIR HEARTS.
WE LEND A HELPING HAND TO PEOPLE IN NEED, LET UNPOPULAR BOYS TALK TO GIRLS...
...THAT IS TO SAY, "SERVICE." THAT IS WHAT THIS CLUB DOES.

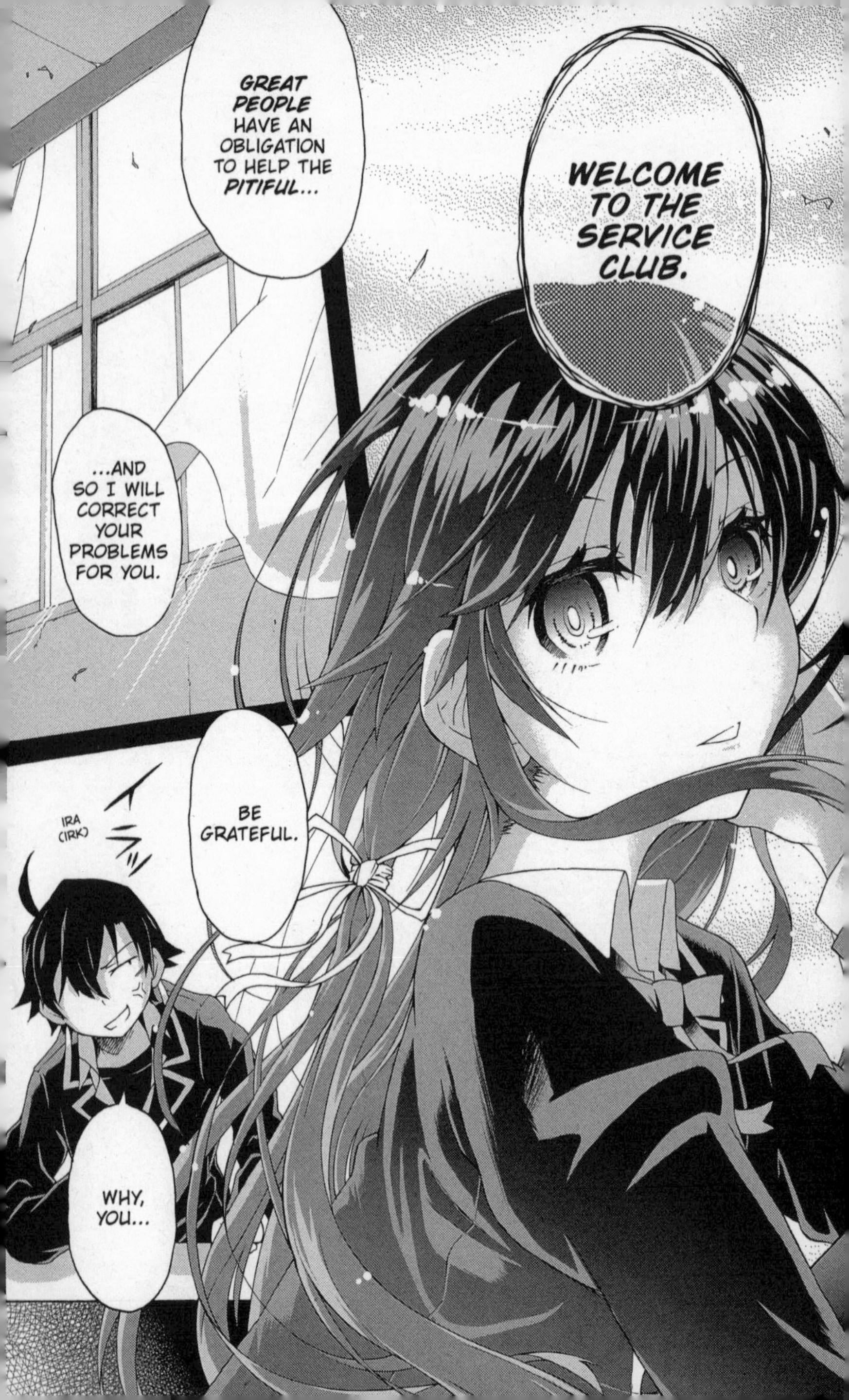
WELCOME TO THE SERVICE CLUB.
GREAT PEOPLE HAVE AN OBLIGATION TO HELP THE PITIFUL...
...AND SO I WILL CORRECT YOUR PROBLEMS FOR YOU.
BE GRATEFUL.
IRA (IRK)
WHY, YOU...

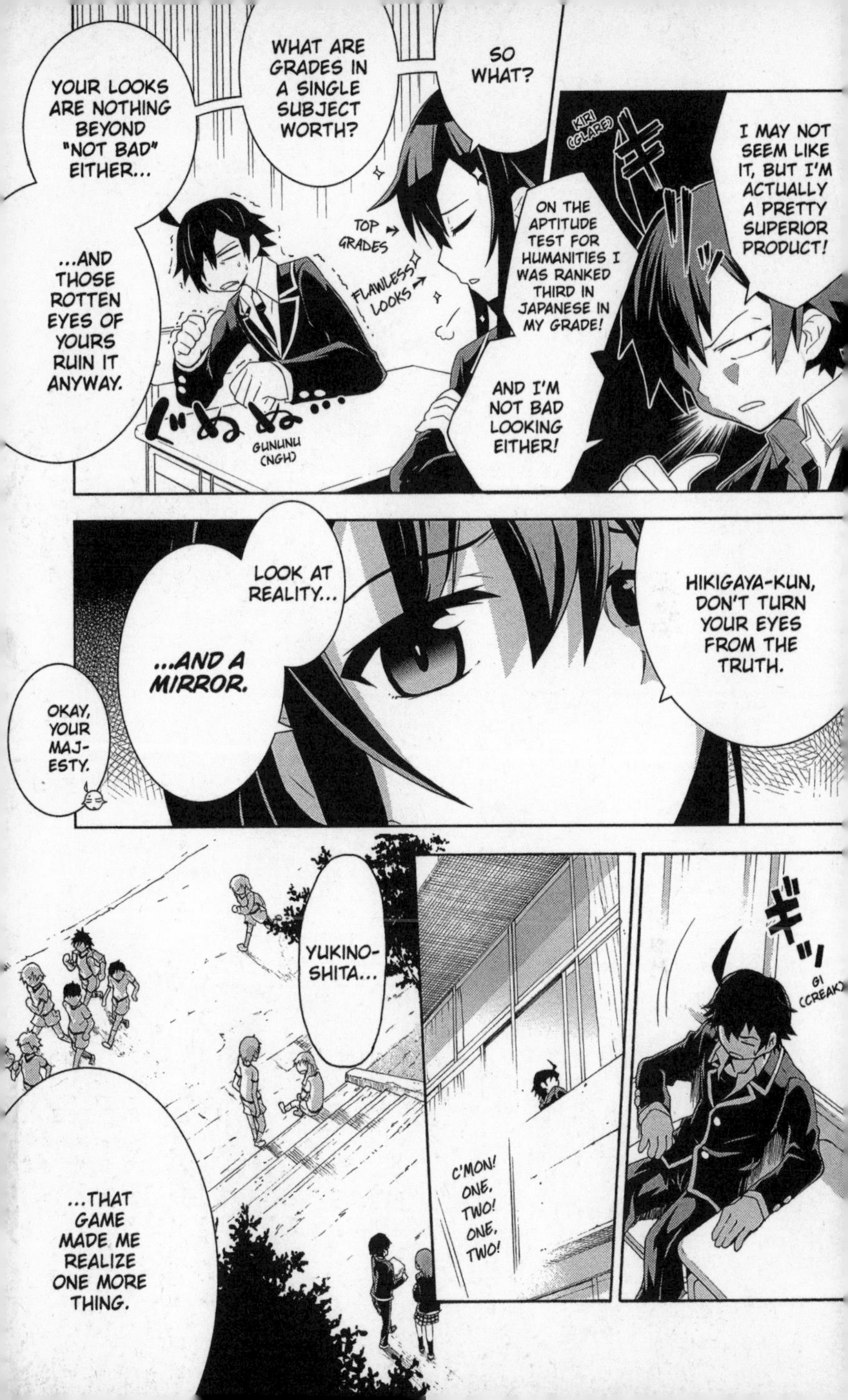
I MAY NOT SEEM LIKE IT, BUT I'M ACTUALLY A PRETTY SUPERIOR PRODUCT!
KIRI (GLARE)
ON THE APTITUDE TEST FOR HUMANITIES I WAS RANKED THIRD IN JAPANESE IN MY GRADE!
AND I'M NOT BAD LOOKING EITHER!
SO WHAT?
WHAT ARE GRADES IN A SINGLE SUBJECT WORTH?
TOP GRADES
FLAWLESS LOOKS
YOUR LOOKS ARE NOTHING BEYOND "NOT BAD" EITHER...
...AND THOSE ROTTEN EYES OF YOURS RUIN IT ANYWAY.
ぐぬぬ…
GUNUNU (NGH)
HIKIGAYA-KUN, DON'T TURN YOUR EYES FROM THE TRUTH.
LOOK AT REALITY...
...AND A MIRROR.
OKAY, YOUR MAJESTY.
ギッ
GI (CREAK)
C'MON! ONE, TWO! ONE, TWO!
YUKINO-SHITA...
...THAT GAME MADE ME REALIZE ONE MORE THING.

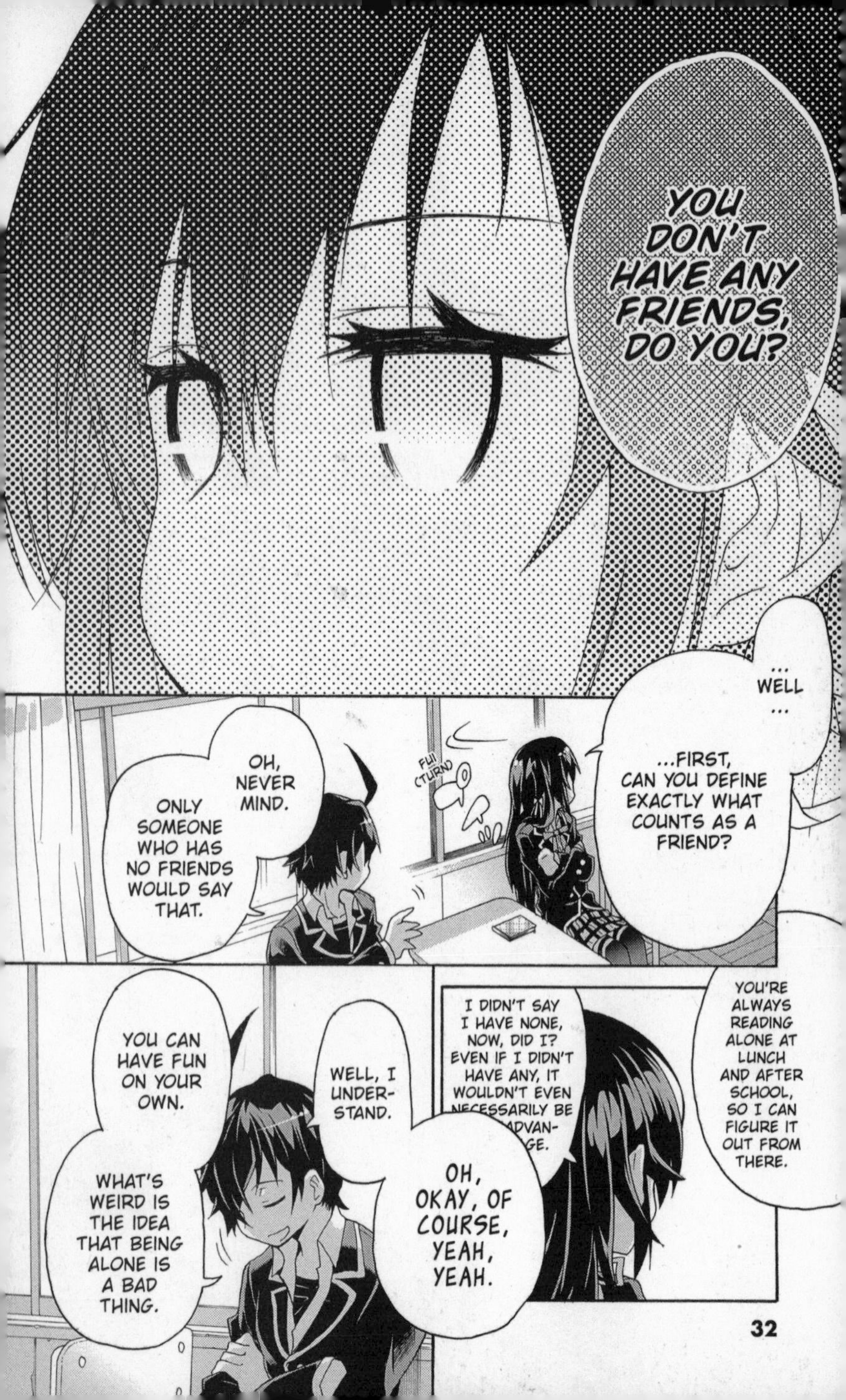
YOU DON'T HAVE ANY FRIENDS, DO YOU?
... WELL ...
...FIRST, CAN YOU DEFINE EXACTLY WHAT COUNTS AS A FRIEND?
FUI (TURN)
OH, NEVER MIND.
ONLY SOMEONE WHO HAS NO FRIENDS WOULD SAY THAT.
YOU'RE ALWAYS READING ALONE AT LUNCH AND AFTER SCHOOL, SO I CAN FIGURE IT OUT FROM THERE.
I DIDN'T SAY I HAVE NONE, NOW, DID I? EVEN IF I DIDN'T HAVE ANY, IT WOULDN'T EVEN NECESSARILY BE ADVAN- GE.
OH, OKAY, OF COURSE, YEAH, YEAH.
WELL, I UNDER-STAND.
YOU CAN HAVE FUN ON YOUR OWN.
WHAT'S WEIRD IS THE IDEA THAT BEING ALONE IS A BAD THING.

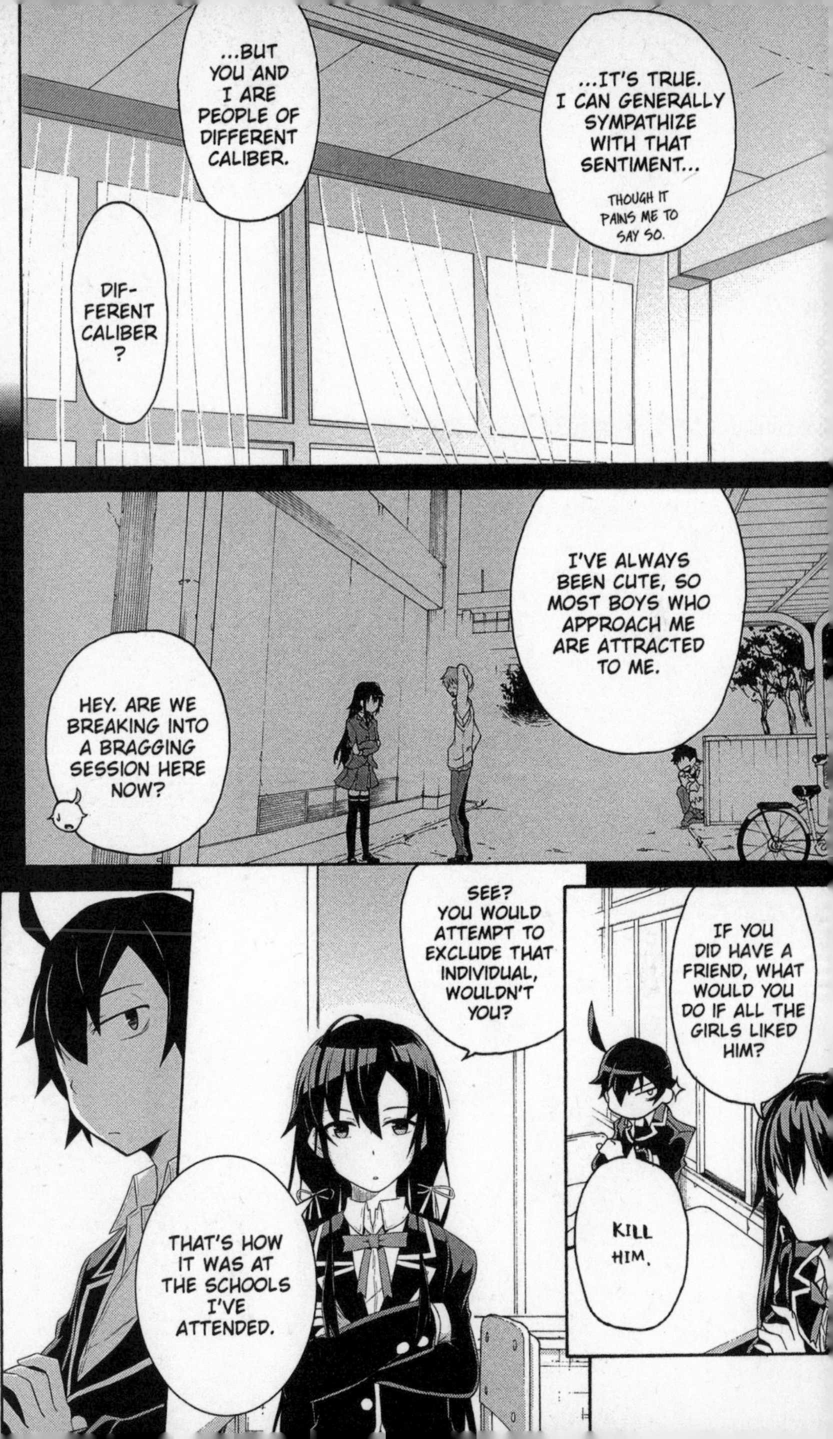
...IT'S TRUE. I CAN GENERALLY SYMPATHIZE WITH THAT SENTIMENT...
THOUGH IT PAINS ME TO SAY SO.
...BUT YOU AND I ARE PEOPLE OF DIFFERENT CALIBER.
DIF-FERENT CALIBER?
I'VE ALWAYS BEEN CUTE, SO MOST BOYS WHO APPROACH ME ARE ATTRACTED TO ME.
HEY. ARE WE BREAKING INTO A BRAGGING SESSION HERE NOW?
IF YOU DID HAVE A FRIEND, WHAT WOULD YOU DO IF ALL THE GIRLS LIKED HIM?
KILL HIM.
SEE? YOU WOULD ATTEMPT TO EXCLUDE THAT INDIVIDUAL, WOULDN'T YOU?
THAT'S HOW IT WAS AT THE SCHOOLS I'VE ATTENDED.

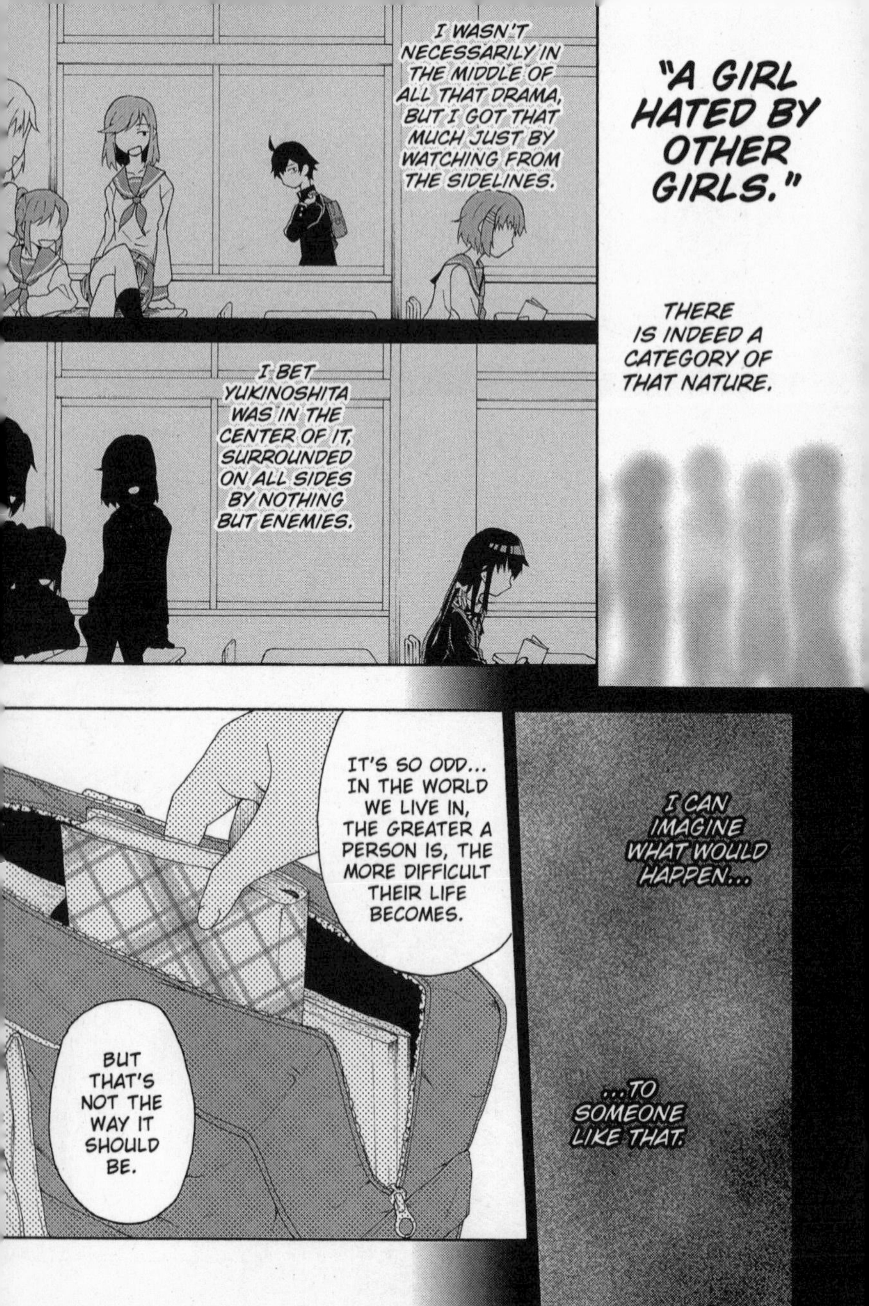
"A GIRL HATED BY OTHER GIRLS."
THERE IS INDEED A CATEGORY OF THAT NATURE.
I WASN'T NECESSARILY IN THE MIDDLE OF ALL THAT DRAMA, BUT I GOT THAT MUCH JUST BY WATCHING FROM THE SIDELINES.
I BET YUKINOSHITA WAS IN THE CENTER OF IT, SURROUNDED ON ALL SIDES BY NOTHING BUT ENEMIES.
I CAN IMAGINE WHAT WOULD HAPPEN...
...TO SOMEONE LIKE THAT.
IT'S SO ODD... IN THE WORLD WE LIVE IN, THE GREATER A PERSON IS, THE MORE DIFFICULT THEIR LIFE BECOMES.
BUT THAT'S NOT THE WAY IT SHOULD BE.

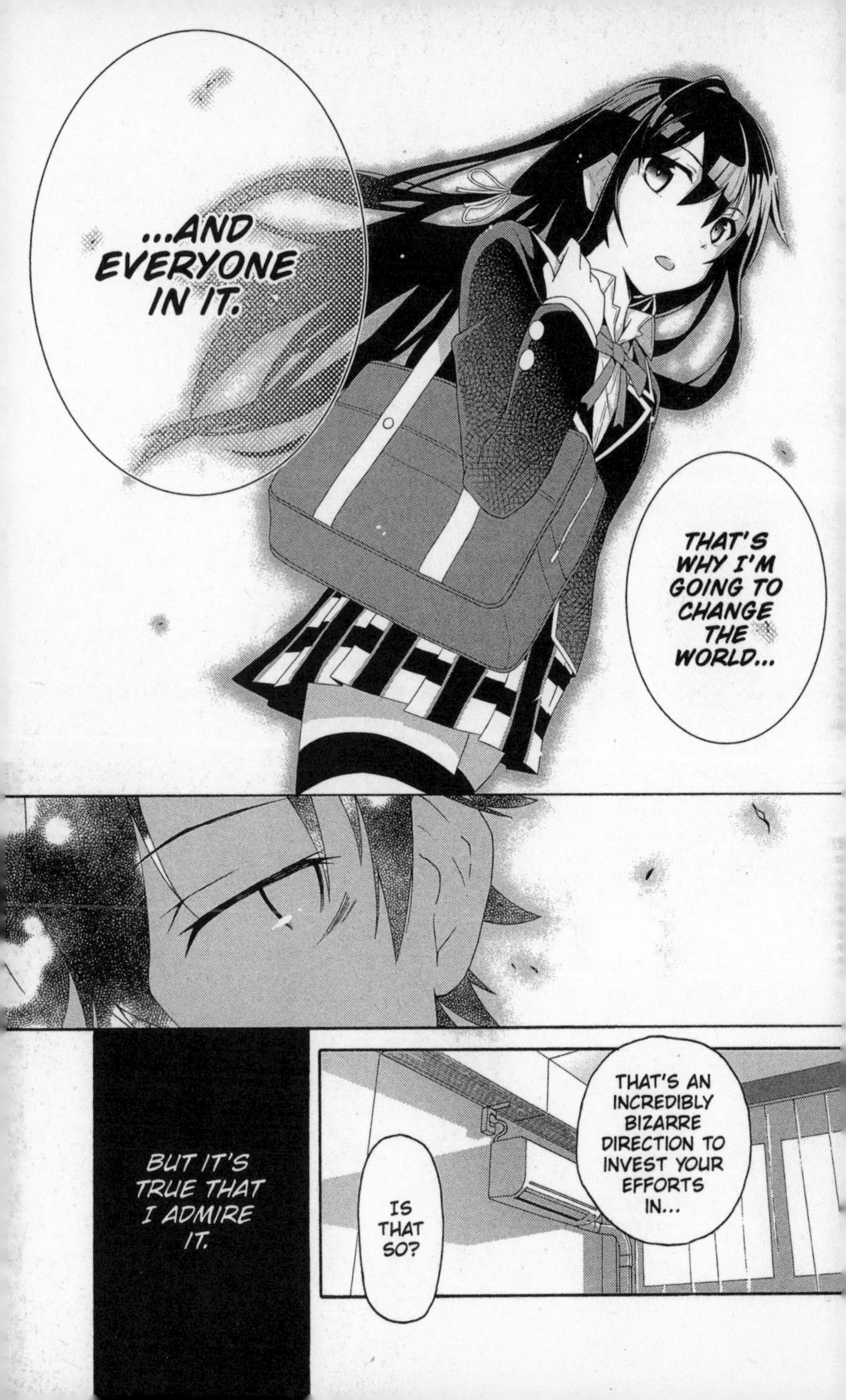
THAT'S WHY I'M GOING TO CHANGE THE WORLD...
...AND EVERYONE IN IT.
THAT'S AN INCREDIBLY BIZARRE DIRECTION TO INVEST YOUR EFFORTS IN...
IS THAT SO?
BUT IT'S TRUE THAT I ADMIRE IT.

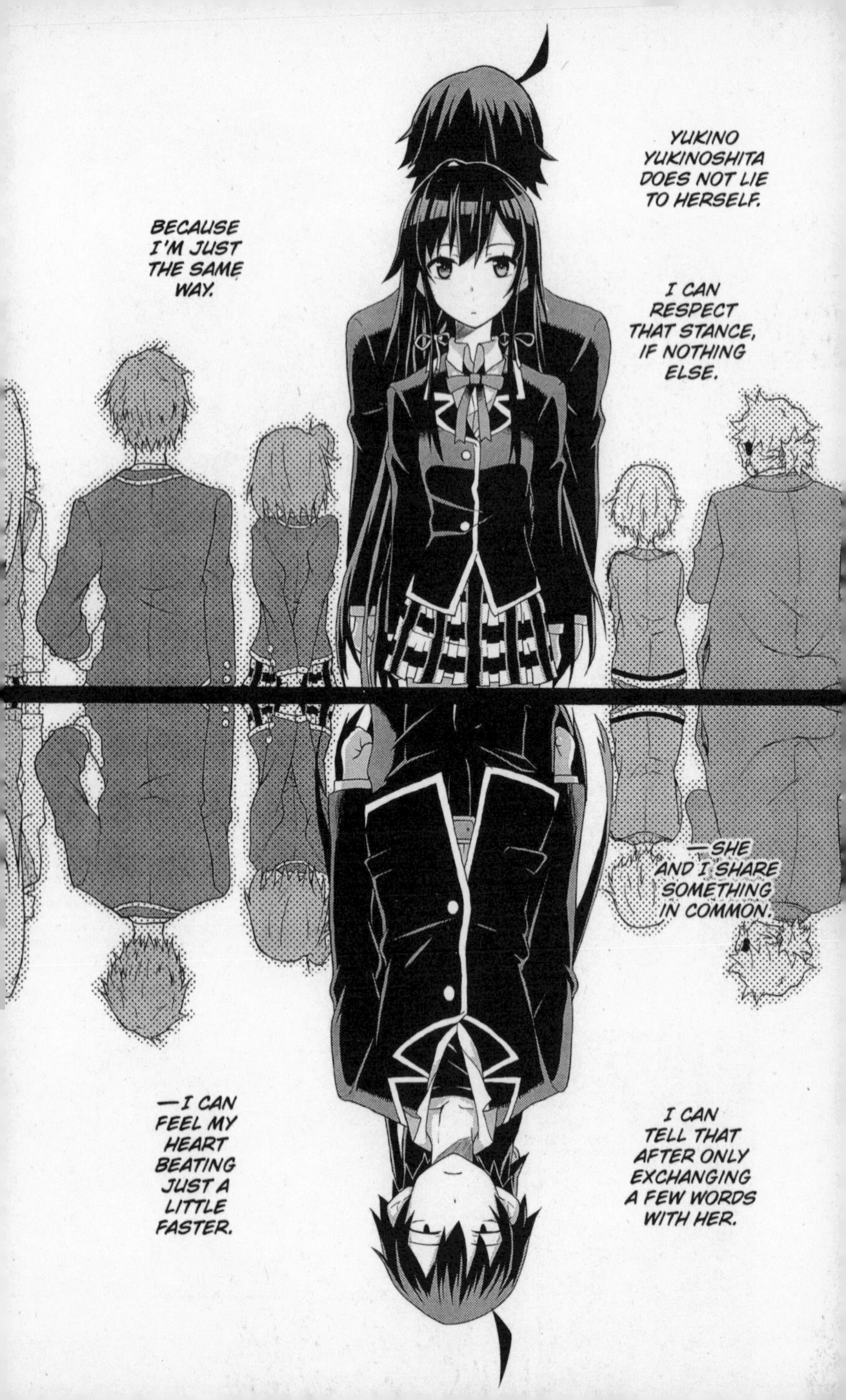
YUKINO YUKINOSHITA DOES NOT LIE TO HERSELF.
I CAN RESPECT THAT STANCE, IF NOTHING ELSE.
BECAUSE I'M JUST THE SAME WAY.
—SHE AND I SHARE SOMETHING IN COMMON.
I CAN TELL THAT AFTER ONLY EXCHANGING A FEW WORDS WITH HER.
—I CAN FEEL MY HEART BEATING JUST A LITTLE FASTER.

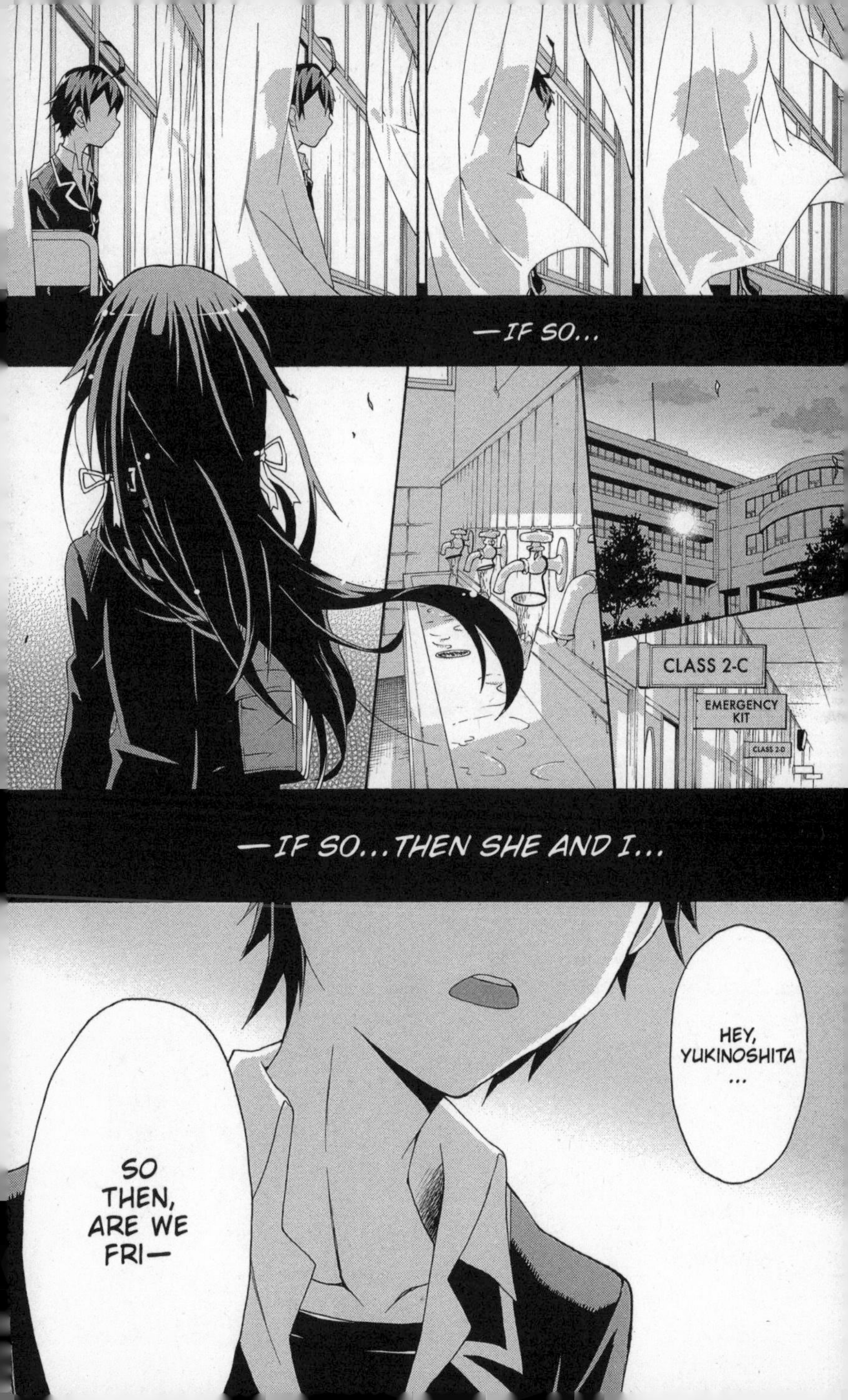
—IF SO...
CLASS 2-C
EMERGENCY KIT
CLASS 2-D
—IF SO...THEN SHE AND I...
HEY, YUKINOSHITA ...
SO THEN, ARE WE FRI—

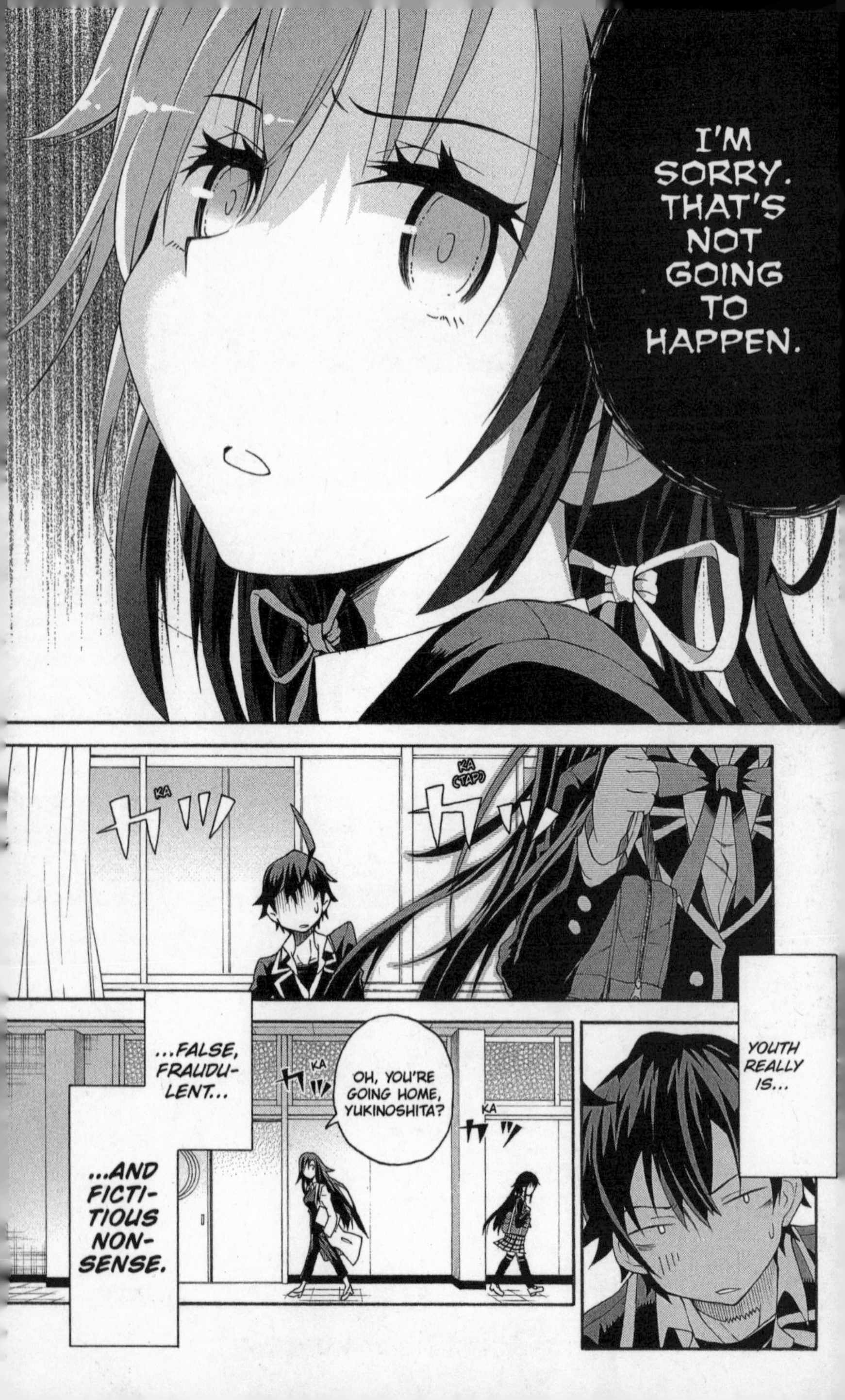
I'M SORRY. THAT'S NOT GOING TO HAPPEN.
KA (TAP)
KA
YOUTH REALLY IS...
KA
OH, YOU'RE GOING HOME, YUKINOSHITA?
KA
...FALSE, FRAUDU-LENT...
...AND FICTI-TIOUS NON-SENSE.

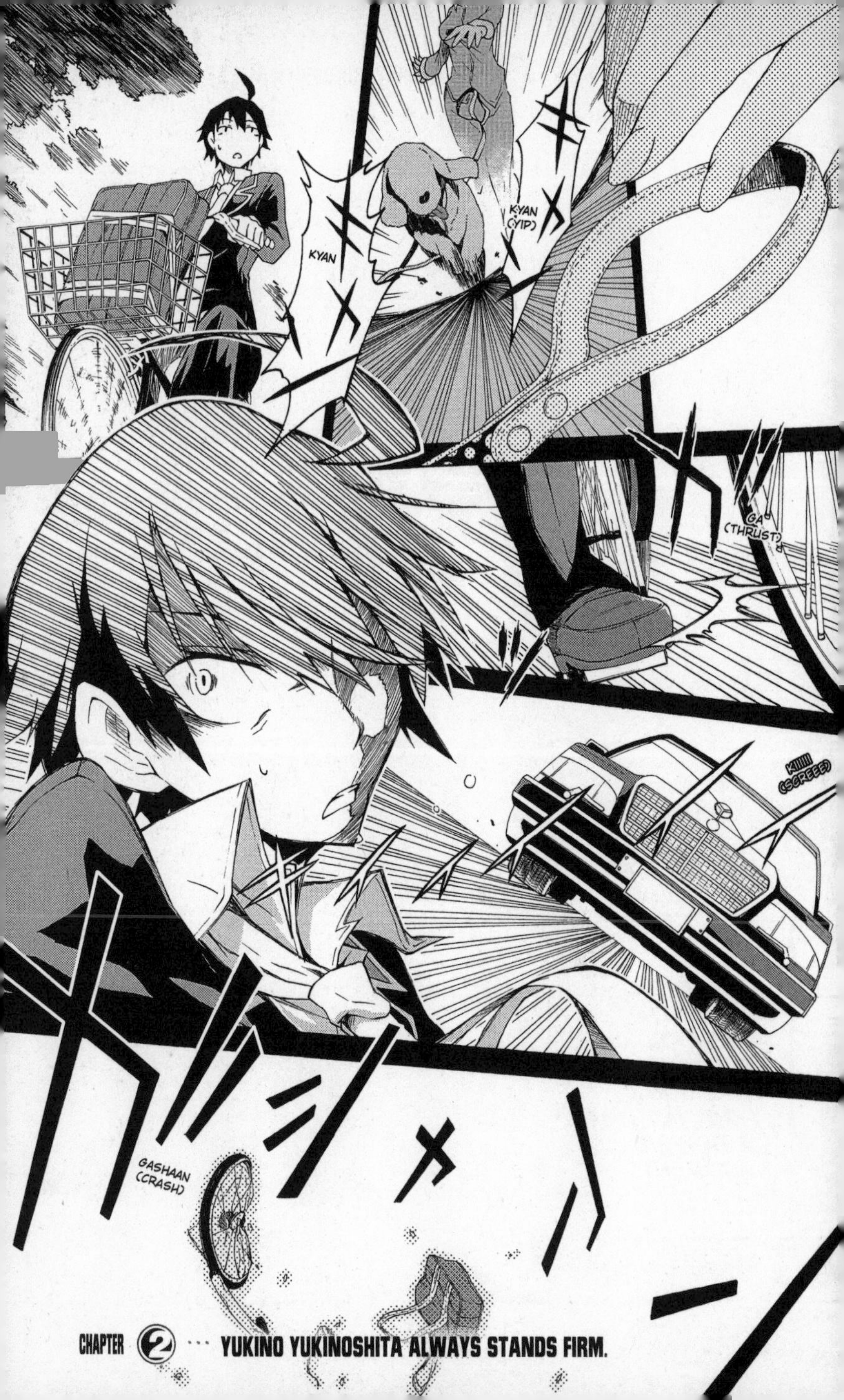
KYAN (YIP)
KYAN
GA (THRUST)
KIIIII (SCREEE)
GASHAAN (CRASH)

CHAPTER 2 ... YUKINO YUKINOSHITA ALWAYS STANDS FIRM.

CHAPTER 2 … YUKINO YUKINOSHITA ALWAYS STANDS FIRM.

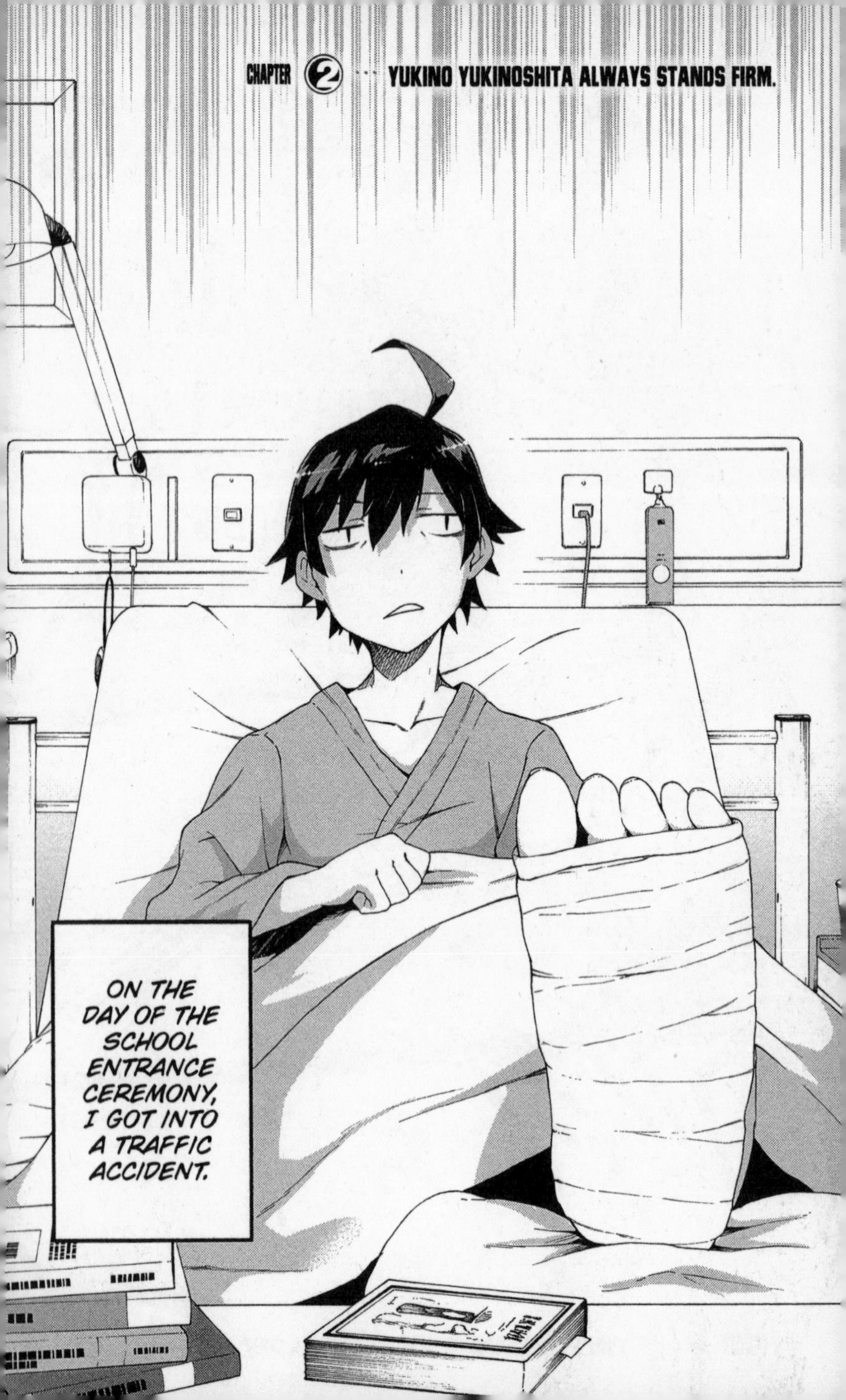
ON THE DAY OF THE SCHOOL ENTRANCE CEREMONY, I GOT INTO A TRAFFIC ACCIDENT.

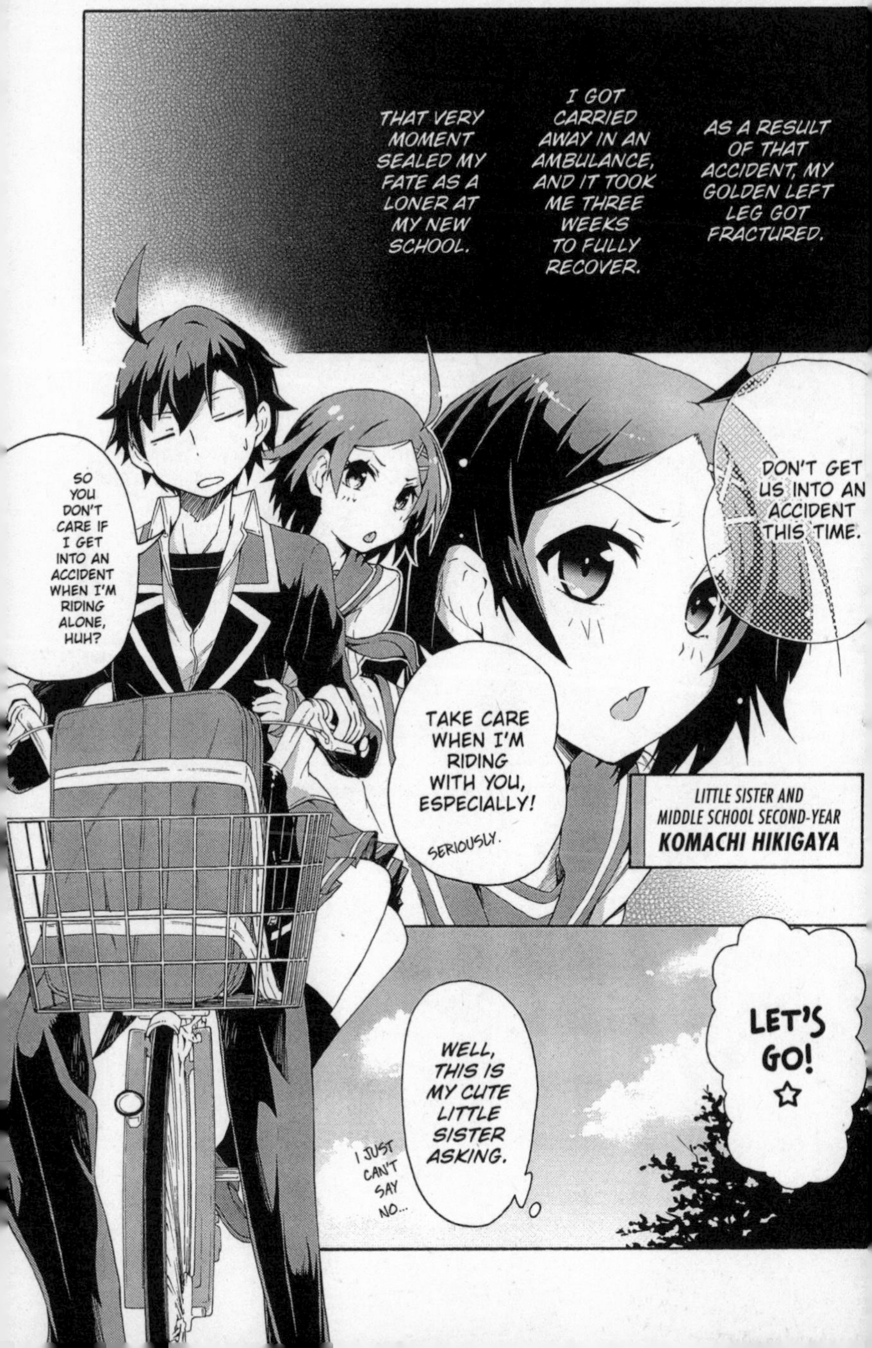
AS A RESULT OF THAT ACCIDENT, MY GOLDEN LEFT LEG GOT FRACTURED.
I GOT CARRIED AWAY IN AN AMBULANCE, AND IT TOOK ME THREE WEEKS TO FULLY RECOVER.
THAT VERY MOMENT SEALED MY FATE AS A LONER AT MY NEW SCHOOL.
DON'T GET US INTO AN ACCIDENT THIS TIME.
LITTLE SISTER AND MIDDLE SCHOOL SECOND-YEAR KOMACHI HIKIGAYA
TAKE CARE WHEN I'M RIDING WITH YOU, ESPECIALLY!
SERIOUSLY.
SO YOU DON'T CARE IF I GET INTO AN ACCIDENT WHEN I'M RIDING ALONE, HUH?
LET'S GO! ☆
WELL, THIS IS MY CUTE LITTLE SISTER ASKING.
I JUST CAN'T SAY NO...

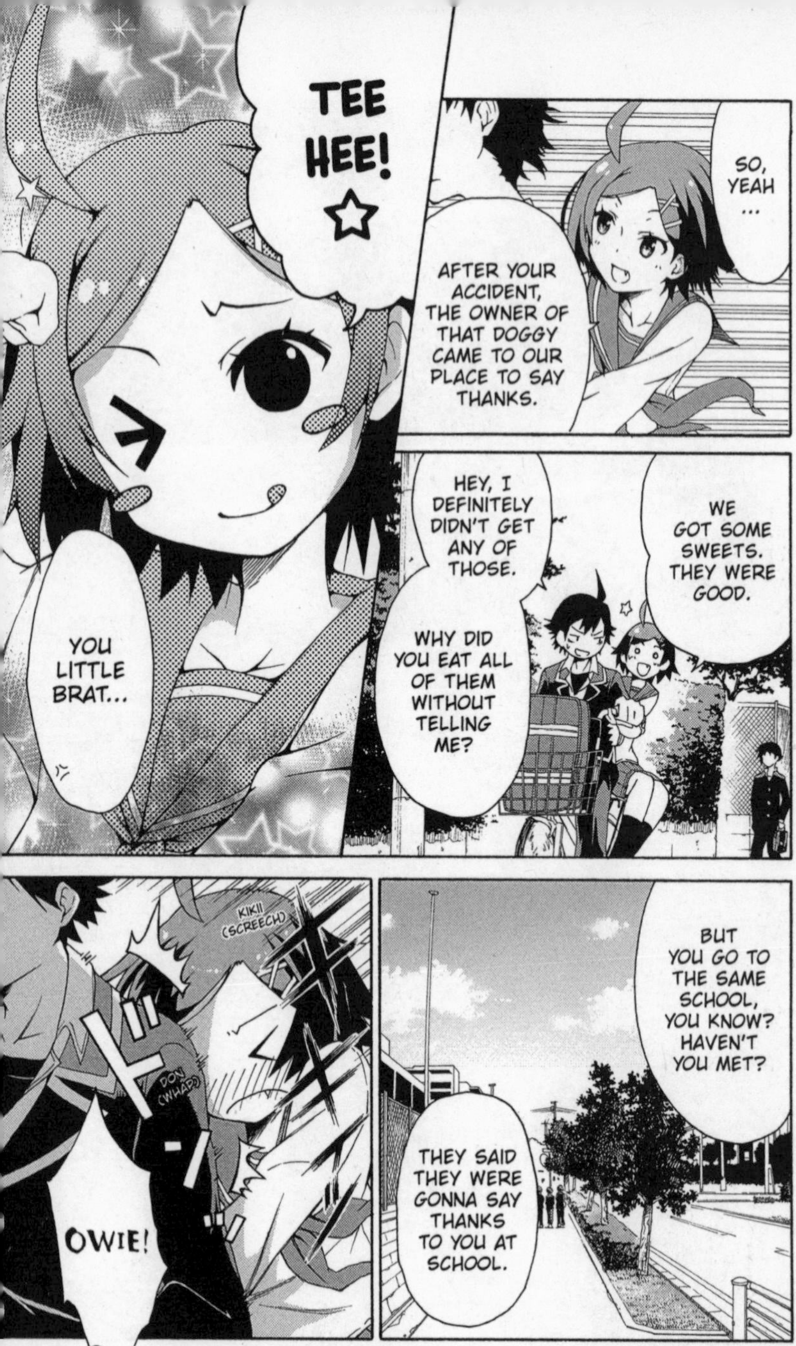
SO, YEAH ...
AFTER YOUR ACCIDENT, THE OWNER OF THAT DOGGY CAME TO OUR PLACE TO SAY THANKS.
WE GOT SOME SWEETS. THEY WERE GOOD.
HEY, I DEFINITELY DIDN'T GET ANY OF THOSE.
WHY DID YOU EAT ALL OF THEM WITHOUT TELLING ME?
TEE HEE! ☆
YOU LITTLE BRAT...
BUT YOU GO TO THE SAME SCHOOL, YOU KNOW? HAVEN'T YOU MET?
THEY SAID THEY WERE GONNA SAY THANKS TO YOU AT SCHOOL.
KIKII (SCREECH)
DON (WHAP)
OWIE!

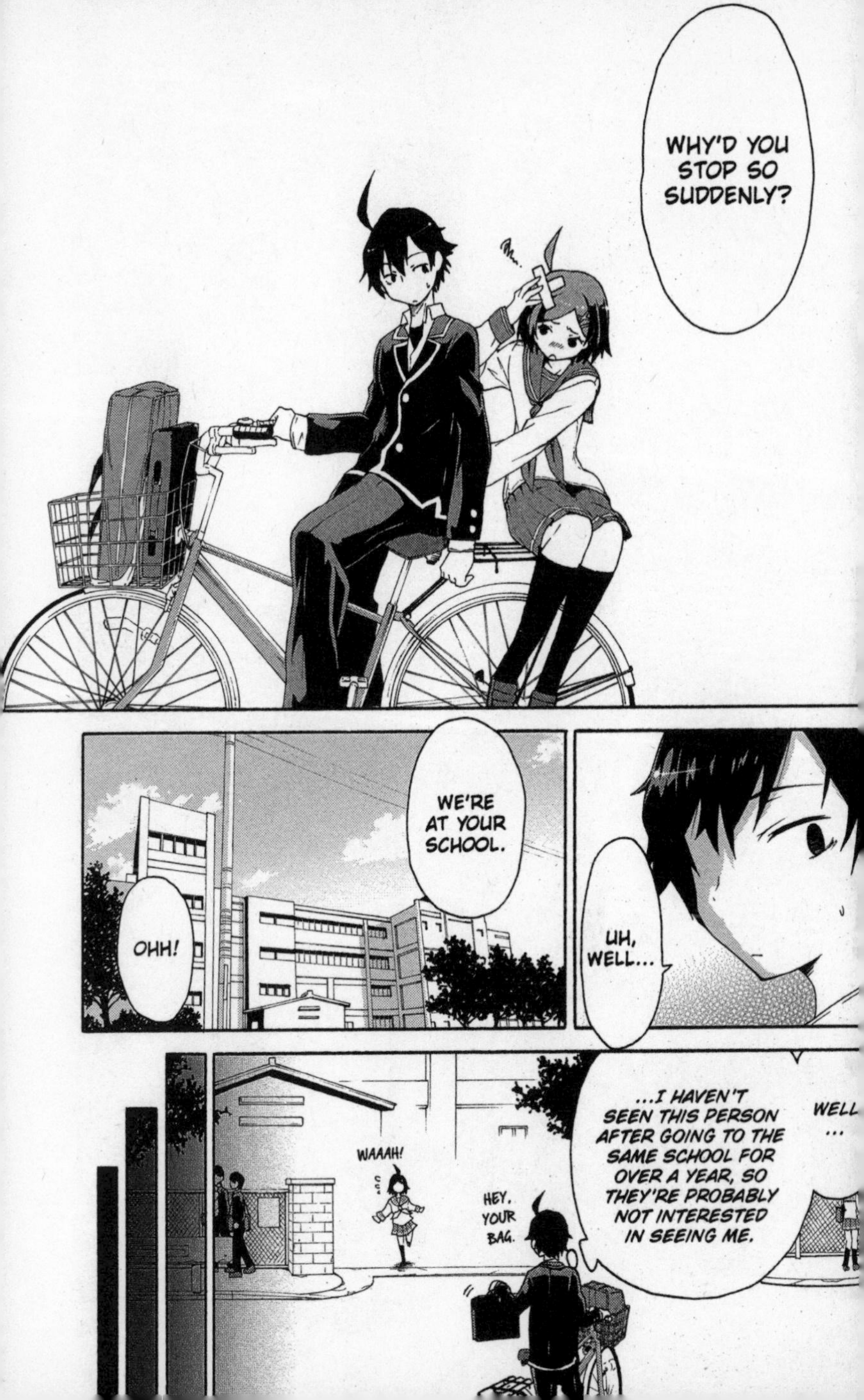
WHY'D YOU STOP SO SUDDENLY?
UH, WELL...
WE'RE AT YOUR SCHOOL.
OHH!
WELL ...
...I HAVEN'T SEEN THIS PERSON AFTER GOING TO THE SAME SCHOOL FOR OVER A YEAR, SO THEY'RE PROBABLY NOT INTERESTED IN SEEING ME.
HEY. YOUR BAG.
WAAAH!

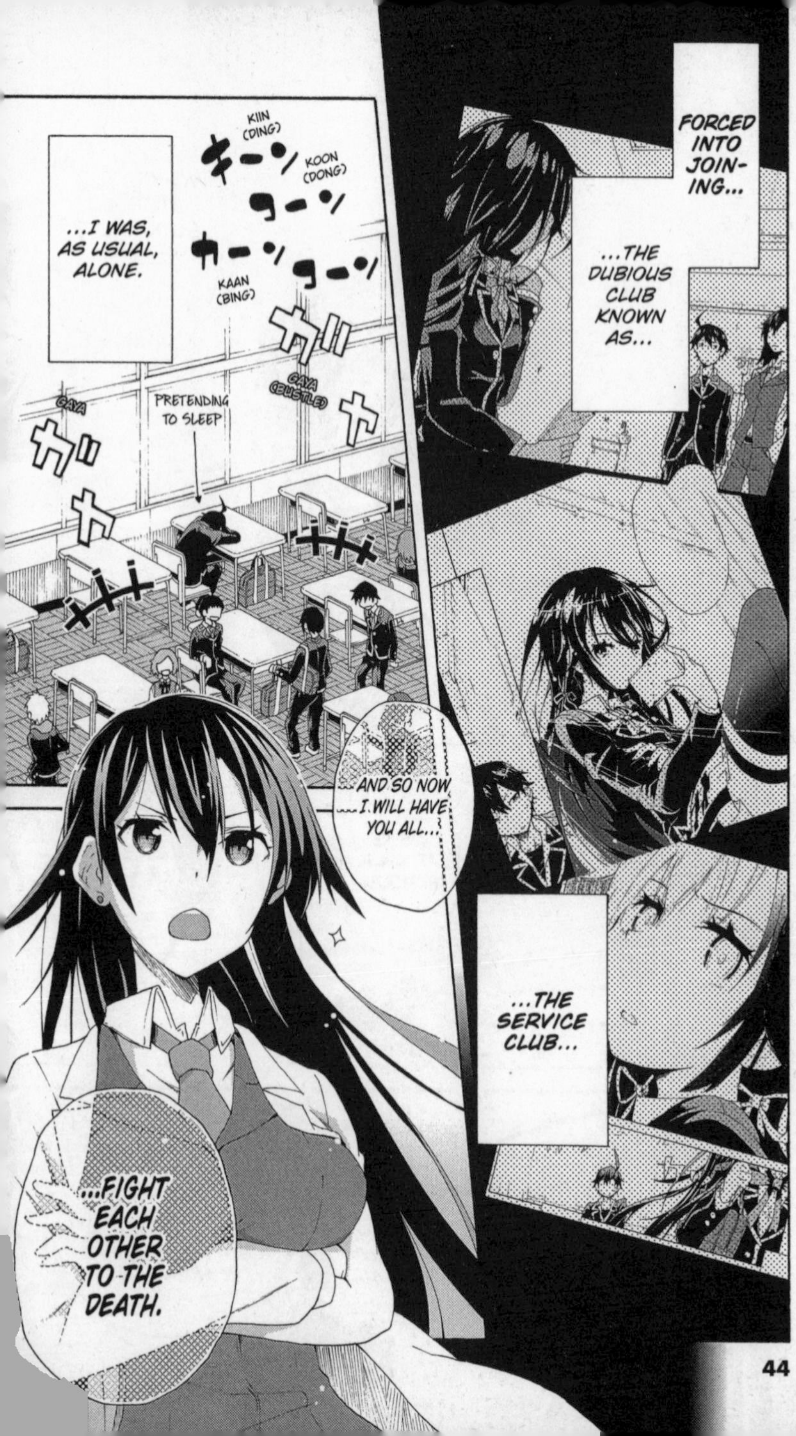
FORCED INTO JOIN-ING...
...THE DUBIOUS CLUB KNOWN AS...
...THE SERVICE CLUB...
...I WAS, AS USUAL, ALONE.
KIIN (DING)
KOON (DONG)
KAAN (BING)
GAYA (BUSTLE)
GAYA
PRETENDING TO SLEEP
AND SO NOW I WILL HAVE YOU ALL...
...FIGHT EACH OTHER TO THE DEATH.

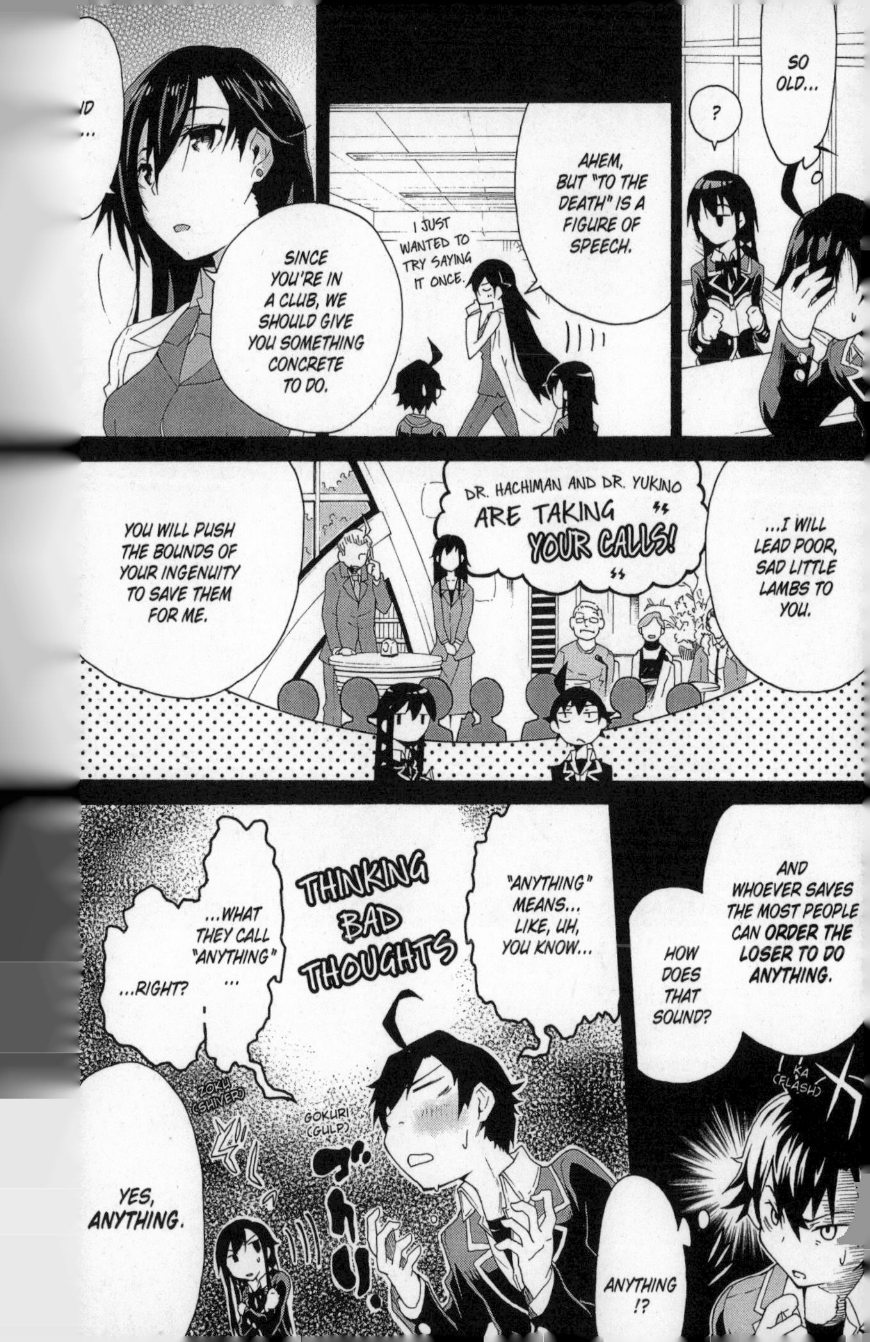
SO OLD...
?
AHEM, BUT "TO THE DEATH" IS A FIGURE OF SPEECH.
I JUST WANTED TO TRY SAYING IT ONCE.
SINCE YOU'RE IN A CLUB, WE SHOULD GIVE YOU SOMETHING CONCRETE TO DO.
...I WILL LEAD POOR, SAD LITTLE LAMBS TO YOU.
DR. HACHIMAN AND DR. YUKINO ARE TAKING YOUR CALLS!
YOU WILL PUSH THE BOUNDS OF YOUR INGENUITY TO SAVE THEM FOR ME.
AND WHOEVER SAVES THE MOST PEOPLE CAN ORDER THE LOSER TO DO ANYTHING.
HOW DOES THAT SOUND?
KA (FLASH)
ANYTHING !?
"ANYTHING" MEANS... LIKE, UH, YOU KNOW...
THINKING BAD THOUGHTS
...WHAT THEY CALL "ANYTHING" ...
...RIGHT?
GOKURI (GULP)
ZOKU (SHIVER)
YES, ANYTHING.

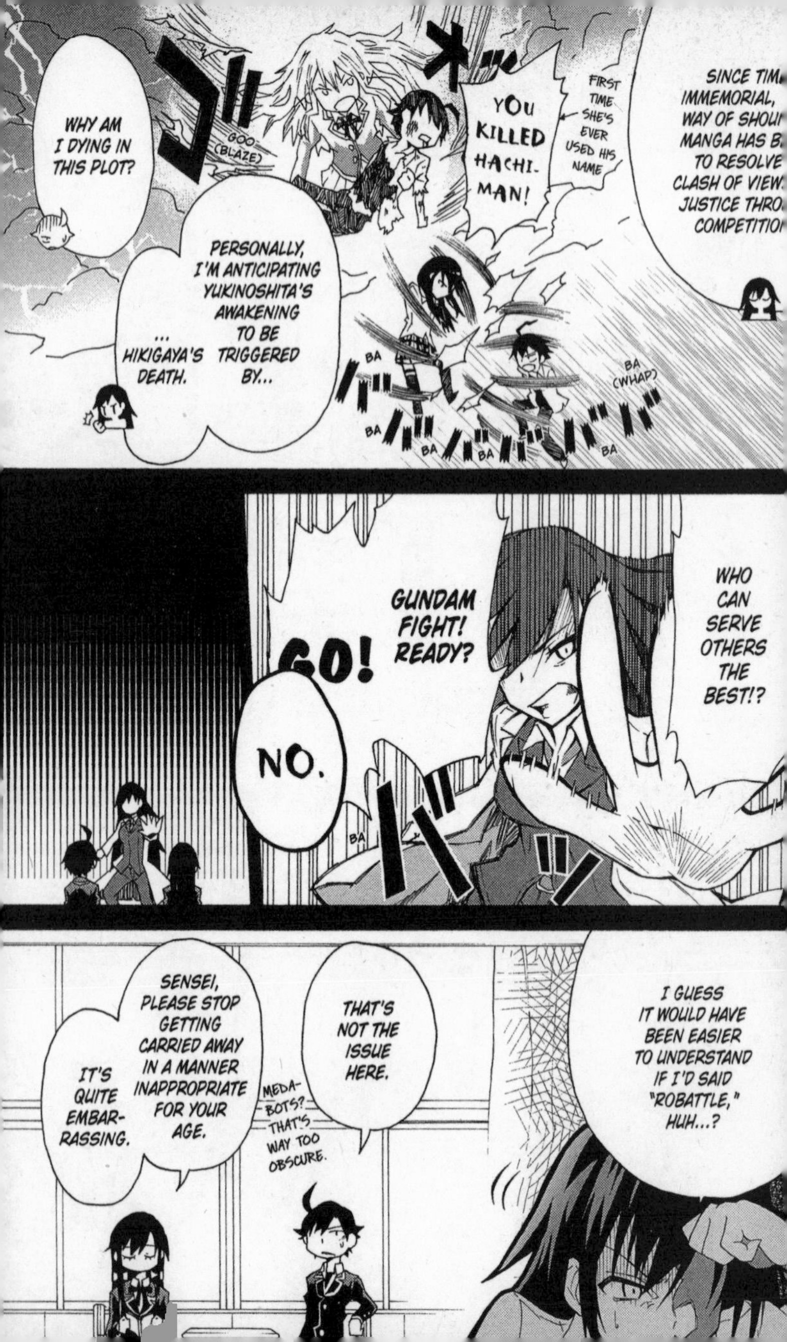
SINCE TIM
IMMEMORIAL,
WAY OF SHOU
MANGA HAS B
TO RESOLVE
CLASH OF VIEW
JUSTICE THRO
COMPETITIO
FIRST TIME SHE'S EVER USED HIS NAME
YOU KILLED HACHI-MAN!
GOO (BLAZE)
WHY AM I DYING IN THIS PLOT?
PERSONALLY, I'M ANTICIPATING YUKINOSHITA'S AWAKENING TO BE TRIGGERED BY...
...HIKIGAYA'S DEATH.
BA (WHAP)
BA
BA
BA
BA
BA
WHO CAN SERVE OTHERS THE BEST!?
GUNDAM FIGHT! READY?
GO!
NO.
BA
I GUESS IT WOULD HAVE BEEN EASIER TO UNDERSTAND IF I'D SAID "ROBATTLE," HUH...?
THAT'S NOT THE ISSUE HERE.
MEDA-BOTS? THAT'S WAY TOO OBSCURE.
SENSEI, PLEASE STOP GETTING CARRIED AWAY IN A MANNER INAPPROPRIATE FOR YOUR AGE.
IT'S QUITE EMBAR-RASSING.

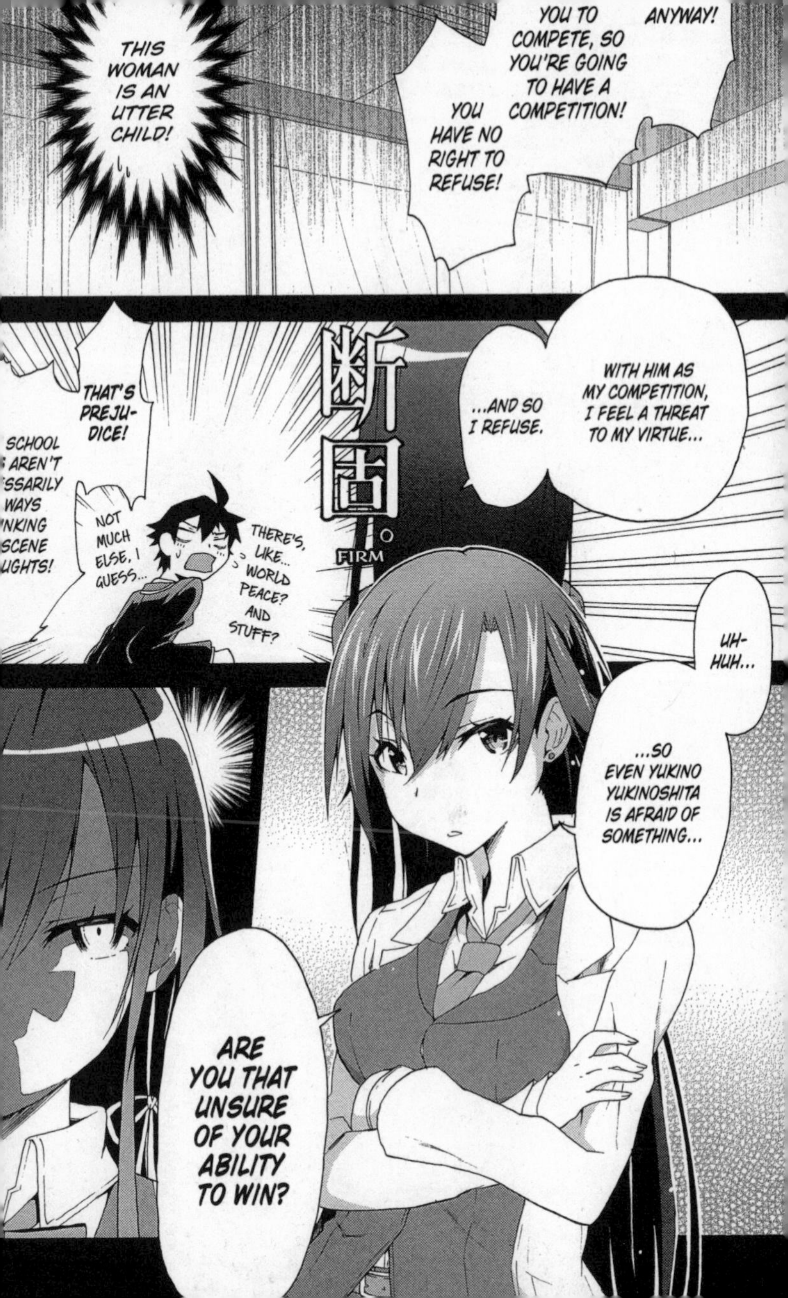
ANYWAY!
YOU TO COMPETE, SO YOU'RE GOING TO HAVE A COMPETITION!
YOU HAVE NO RIGHT TO REFUSE!
THIS WOMAN IS AN UTTER CHILD!
WITH HIM AS MY COMPETITION, I FEEL A THREAT TO MY VIRTUE...
...AND SO I REFUSE.
断固。
FIRM
THERE'S, LIKE... WORLD PEACE? AND STUFF?
NOT MUCH ELSE, I GUESS...
THAT'S PREJU-DICE!
SCHOOL AREN'T
UH-HUH...
...SO EVEN YUKINO YUKINOSHITA IS AFRAID OF SOMETHING...
ARE YOU THAT UNSURE OF YOUR ABILITY TO WIN?

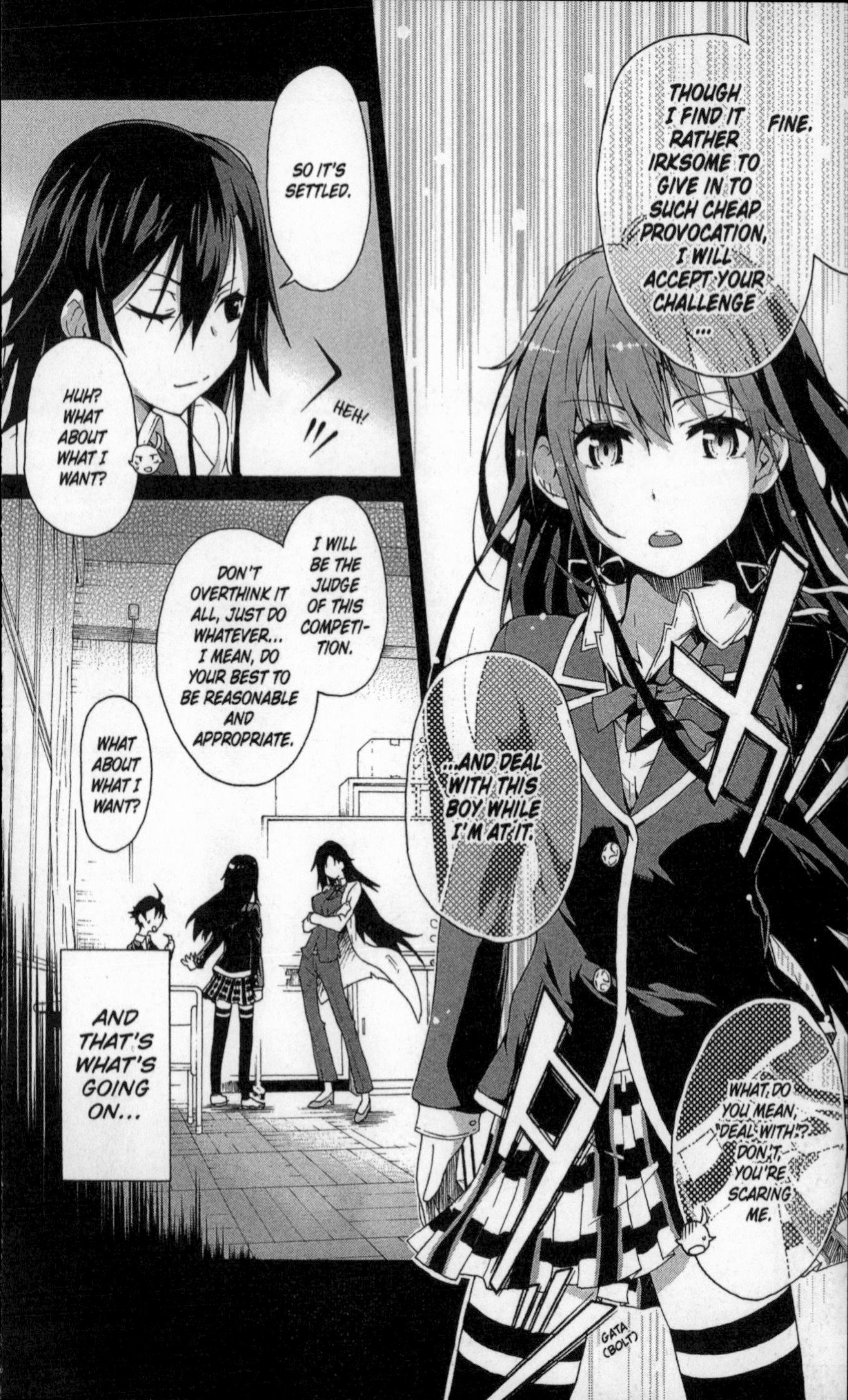
FINE.
THOUGH I FIND IT RATHER IRKSOME TO GIVE IN TO SUCH CHEAP PROVOCATION, I WILL ACCEPT YOUR CHALLENGE ...
...AND DEAL WITH THIS BOY WHILE I'M AT IT.
WHAT DO YOU MEAN, "DEAL WITH"? DON'T, YOU'RE SCARING ME.
GATA (BOLT)
SO IT'S SETTLED.
HEH!
HUH? WHAT ABOUT WHAT I WANT?
I WILL BE THE JUDGE OF THIS COMPETITION.
DON'T OVERTHINK IT ALL, JUST DO WHATEVER... I MEAN, DO YOUR BEST TO BE REASONABLE AND APPROPRIATE.
WHAT ABOUT WHAT I WANT?
AND THAT'S WHAT'S GOING ON...

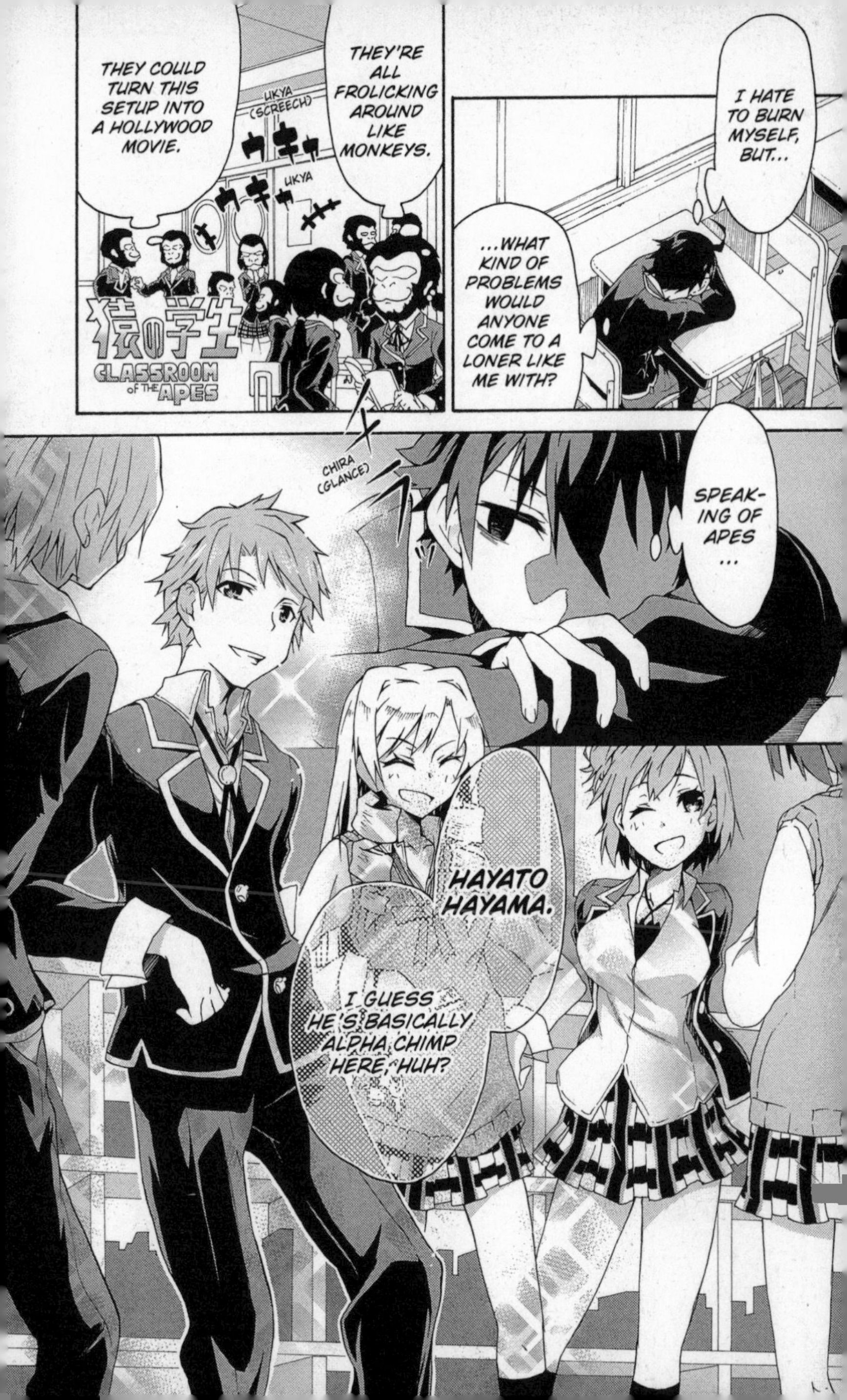
I HATE TO BURN MYSELF, BUT...
...WHAT KIND OF PROBLEMS WOULD ANYONE COME TO A LONER LIKE ME WITH?
THEY'RE ALL FROLICKING AROUND LIKE MONKEYS.
THEY COULD TURN THIS SETUP INTO A HOLLYWOOD MOVIE.
UKYA (SCREECH)
ウキャ
UKYA
ウキャ
猿の学生
CLASSROOM of THE APES
CHIRA (GLANCE)
SPEAK-ING OF APES...
HAYATO HAYAMA.
I GUESS HE'S BASICALLY ALPHA CHIMP HERE, HUH?

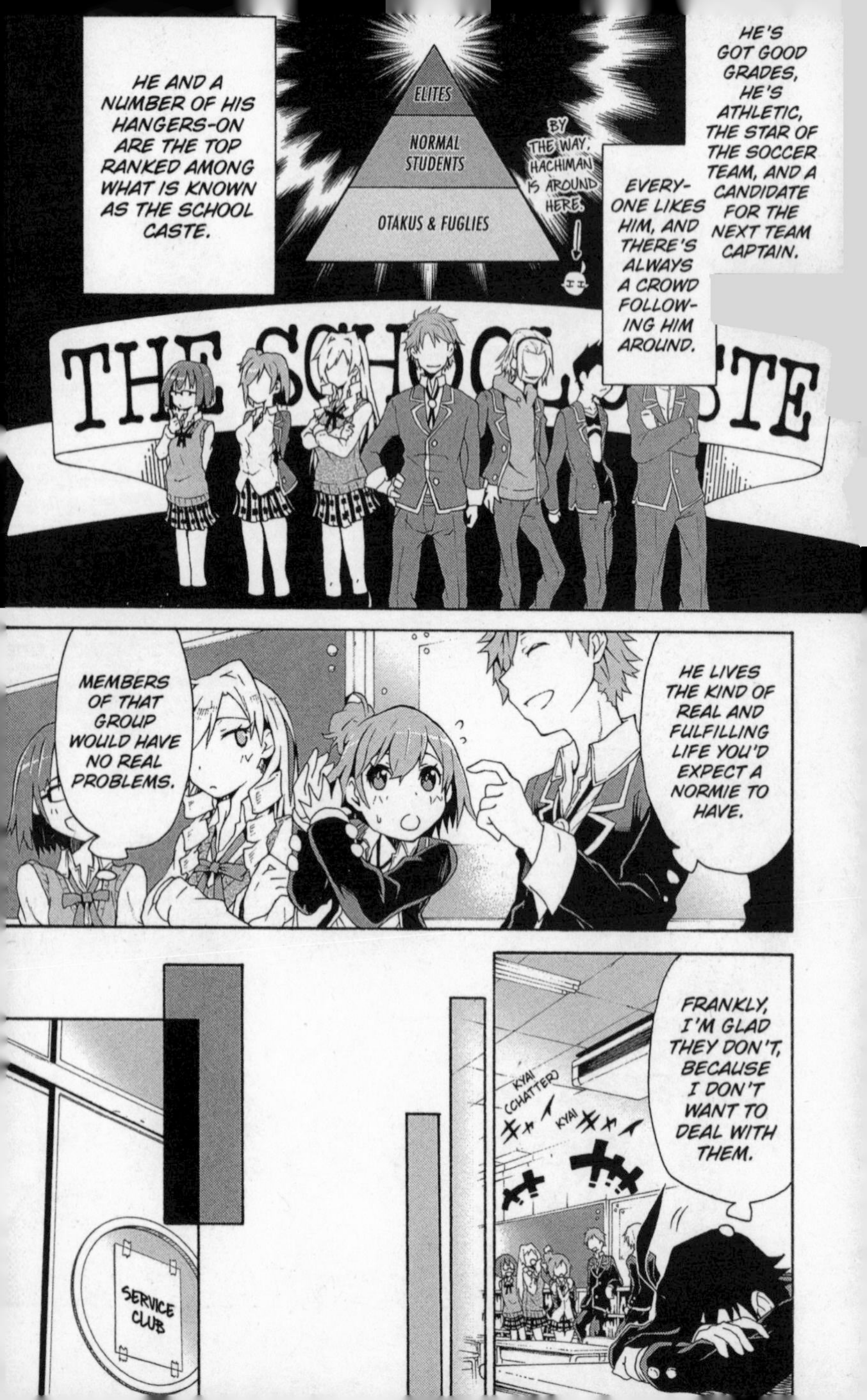
HE'S GOT GOOD GRADES, HE'S ATHLETIC, THE STAR OF THE SOCCER TEAM, AND A CANDIDATE FOR THE NEXT TEAM CAPTAIN.
EVERYONE LIKES HIM, AND THERE'S ALWAYS A CROWD FOLLOWING HIM AROUND.
BY THE WAY, HACHIMAN IS AROUND HERE.
ELITES
NORMAL STUDENTS
OTAKUS & FUGLIES
HE AND A NUMBER OF HIS HANGERS-ON ARE THE TOP RANKED AMONG WHAT IS KNOWN AS THE SCHOOL CASTE.
HE LIVES THE KIND OF REAL AND FULFILLING LIFE YOU'D EXPECT A NORMIE TO HAVE.
MEMBERS OF THAT GROUP WOULD HAVE NO REAL PROBLEMS.
FRANKLY, I'M GLAD THEY DON'T, BECAUSE I DON'T WANT TO DEAL WITH THEM.
KYAI (CHATTER)
KYAI
SERVICE CLUB

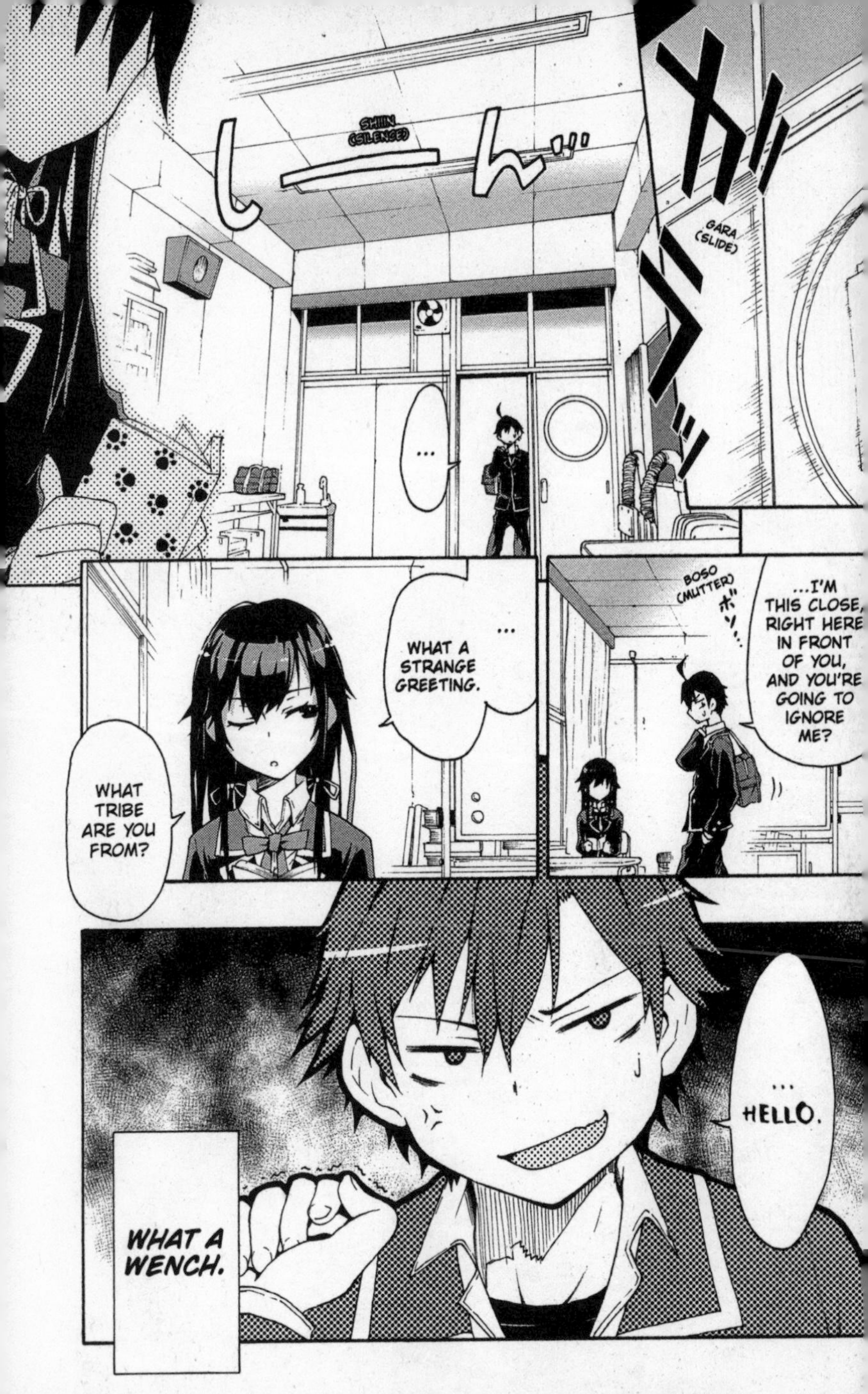
GARA (SLIDE)
SHIIN (SILENCE)
...
...I'M THIS CLOSE, RIGHT HERE IN FRONT OF YOU, AND YOU'RE GOING TO IGNORE ME?
BOSO (MUTTER)
... WHAT A STRANGE GREETING.
WHAT TRIBE ARE YOU FROM?
... HELLO.
WHAT A WENCH.

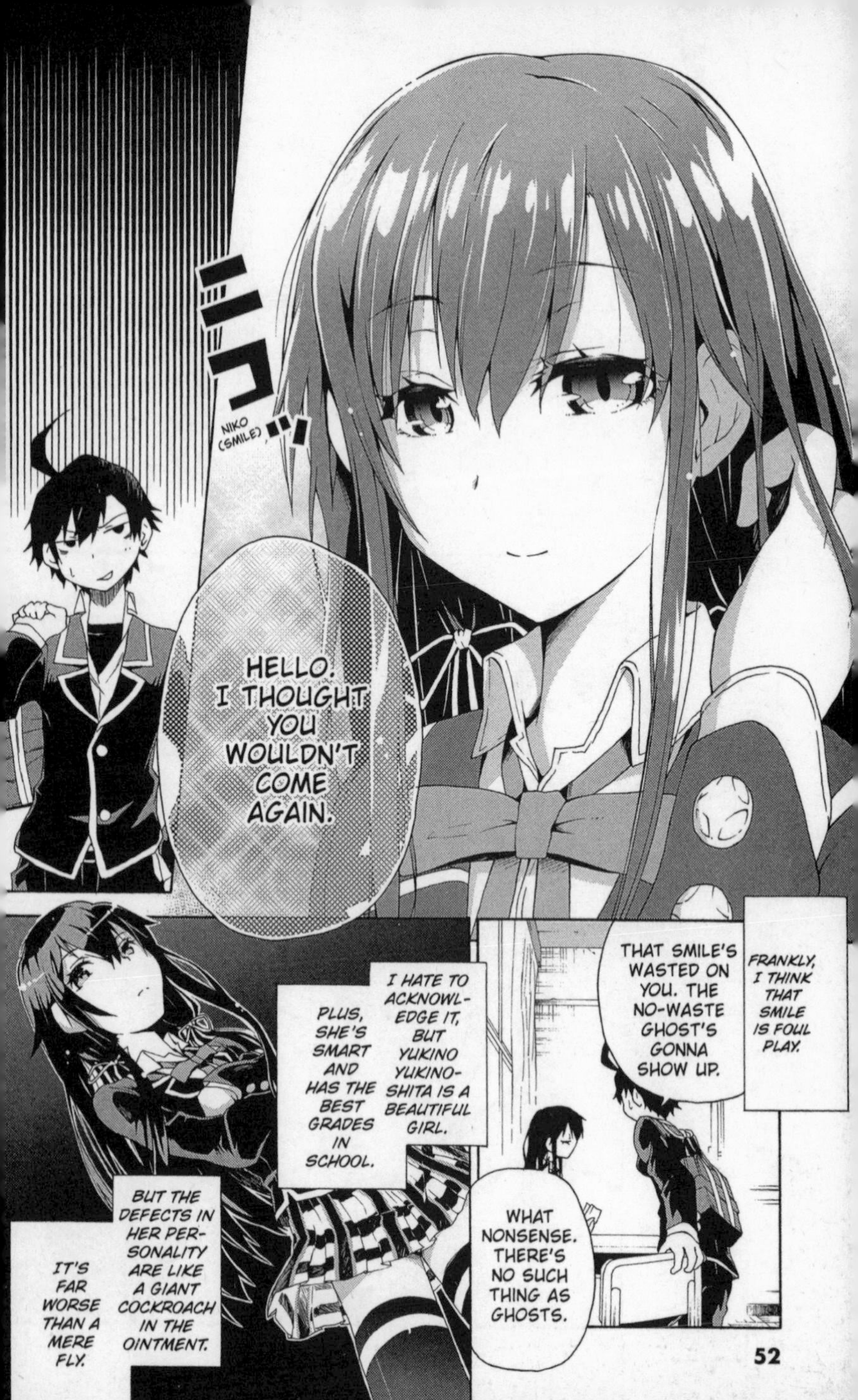

NIKO (SMILE)
HELLO. I THOUGHT YOU WOULDN'T COME AGAIN.
FRANKLY, I THINK THAT SMILE IS FOUL PLAY.
THAT SMILE'S WASTED ON YOU. THE NO-WASTE GHOST'S GONNA SHOW UP.
WHAT NONSENSE. THERE'S NO SUCH THING AS GHOSTS.
I HATE TO ACKNOWL-EDGE IT, BUT YUKINO YUKINO-SHITA IS A BEAUTIFUL GIRL.
PLUS, SHE'S SMART AND HAS THE BEST GRADES IN SCHOOL.
BUT THE DEFECTS IN HER PER-SONALITY ARE LIKE A GIANT COCKROACH IN THE OINTMENT.
IT'S FAR WORSE THAN A MERE FLY.

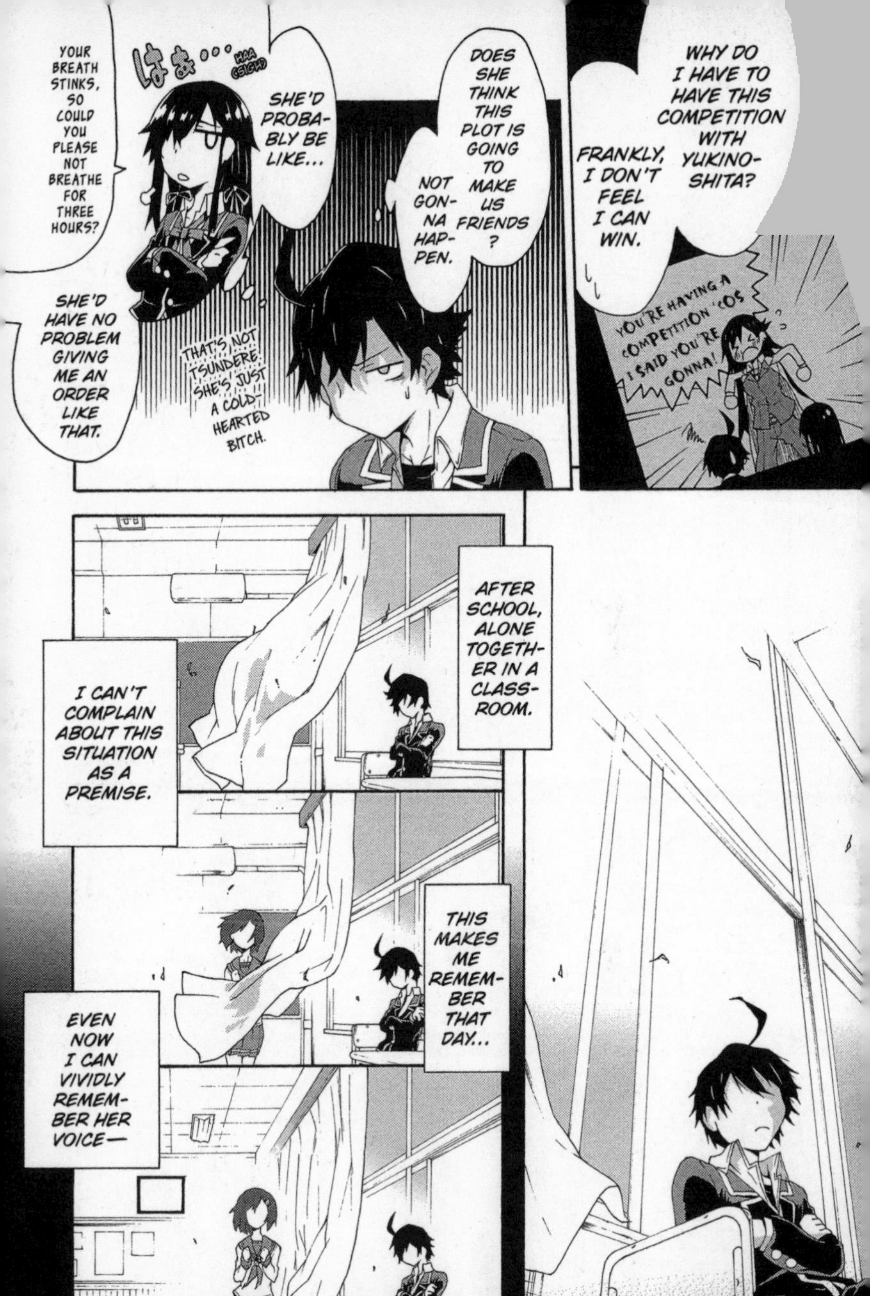
WHY DO I HAVE TO HAVE THIS COMPETITION WITH YUKINO-SHITA?
FRANKLY, I DON'T FEEL I CAN WIN.
YOU'RE HAVING A COMPETITION 'COS I SAID YOU'RE GONNA!
DOES SHE THINK THIS PLOT IS GOING TO MAKE US FRIENDS?
NOT GON-NA HAP-PEN.
SHE'D PROBA-BLY BE LIKE...
はぁ・・・ HAA (SIGH)
YOUR BREATH STINKS, SO COULD YOU PLEASE NOT BREATHE FOR THREE HOURS?
SHE'D HAVE NO PROBLEM GIVING ME AN ORDER LIKE THAT.
THAT'S NOT TSUNDERE. SHE'S JUST A COLD-HEARTED BITCH.
AFTER SCHOOL, ALONE TOGETH-ER IN A CLASS-ROOM.
I CAN'T COMPLAIN ABOUT THIS SITUATION AS A PREMISE.
THIS MAKES ME REMEM-BER THAT DAY...
EVEN NOW I CAN VIVIDLY REMEM-BER HER VOICE—

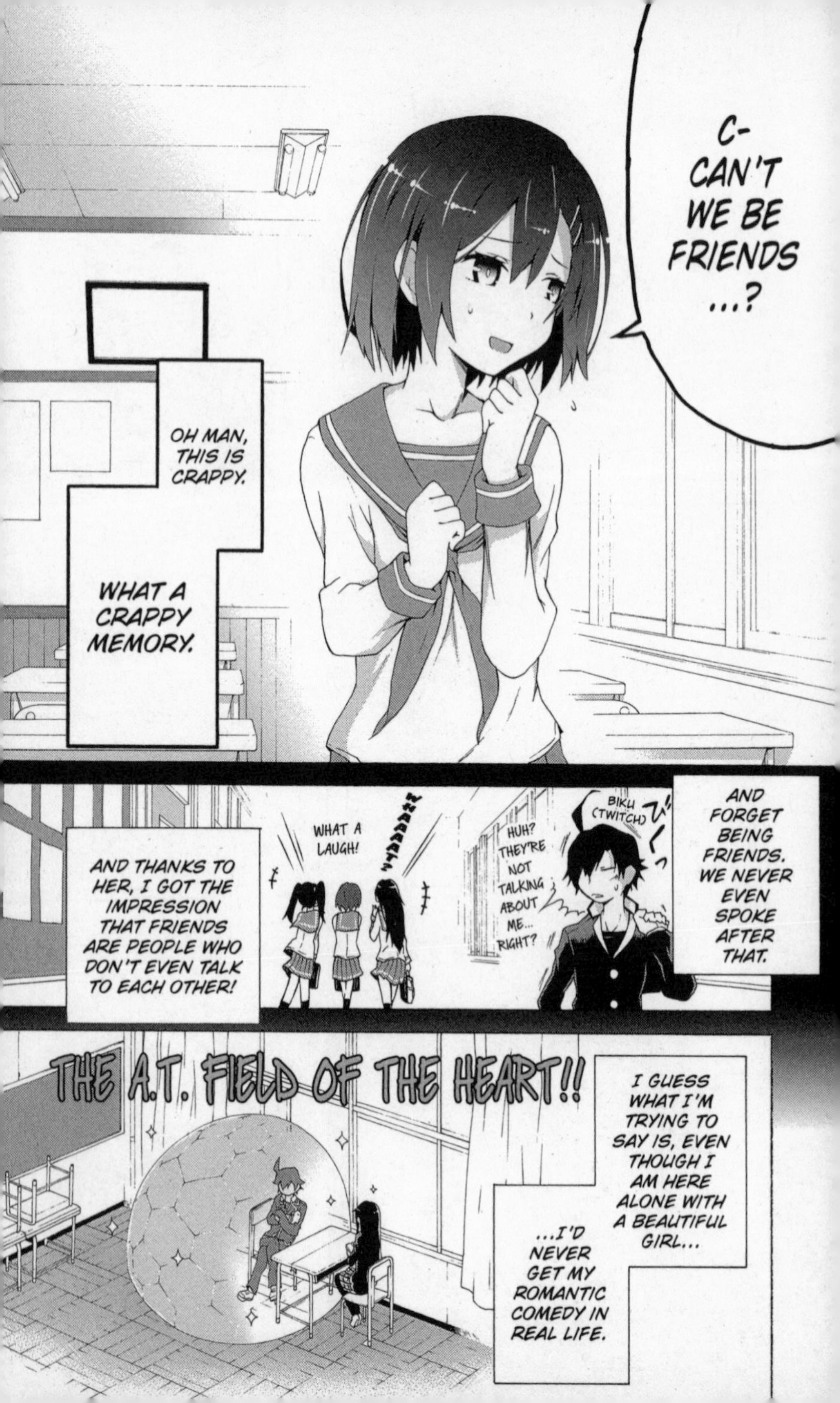
C-CAN'T WE BE FRIENDS ...?
OH MAN, THIS IS CRAPPY.
WHAT A CRAPPY MEMORY.
AND FORGET BEING FRIENDS. WE NEVER EVEN SPOKE AFTER THAT.
BIKU (TWITCH)
HUH? THEY'RE NOT TALKING ABOUT ME... RIGHT?
WHAAAAAT?
WHAT A LAUGH!
AND THANKS TO HER, I GOT THE IMPRESSION THAT FRIENDS ARE PEOPLE WHO DON'T EVEN TALK TO EACH OTHER!
I GUESS WHAT I'M TRYING TO SAY IS, EVEN THOUGH I AM HERE ALONE WITH A BEAUTIFUL GIRL...
...I'D NEVER GET MY ROMANTIC COMEDY IN REAL LIFE.
THE A.T. FIELD OF THE HEART!!

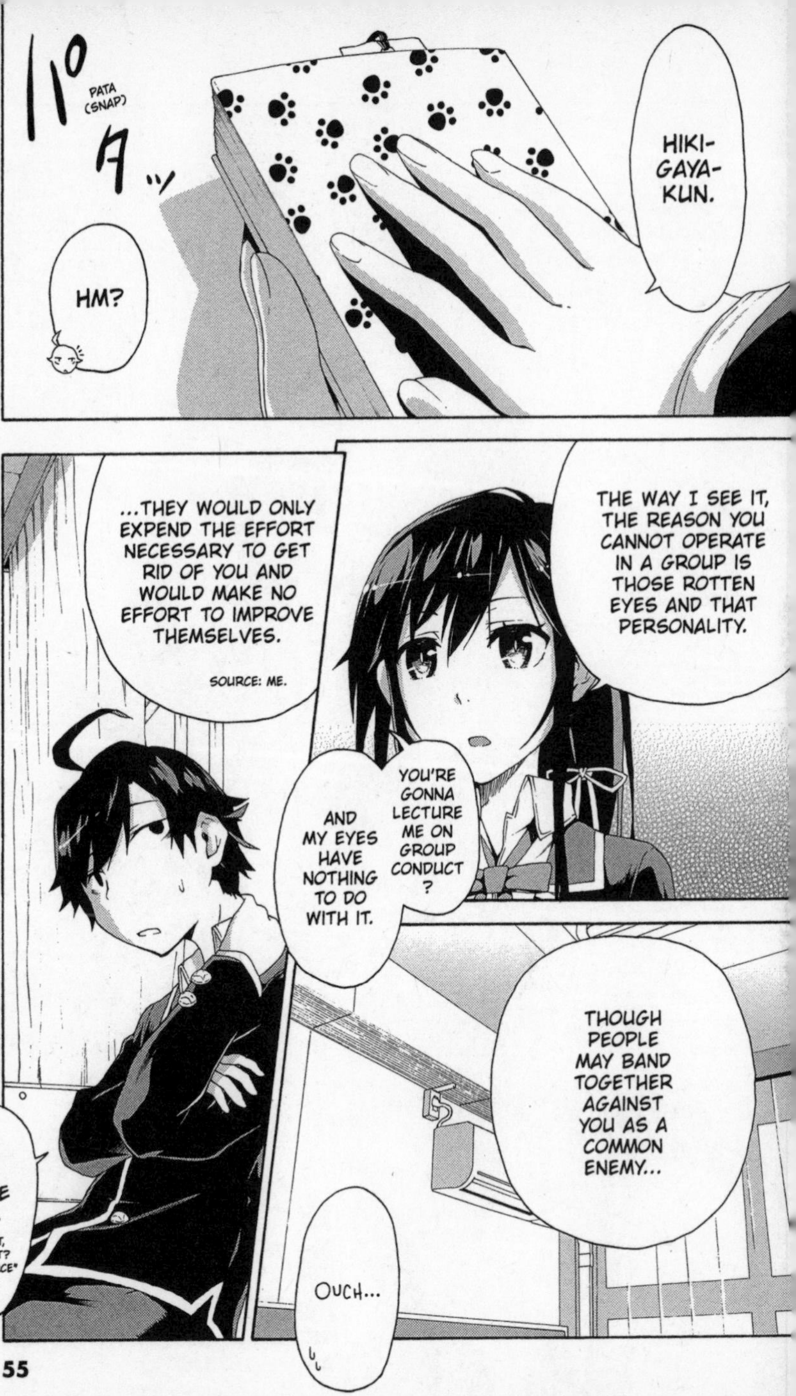
HIKI-GAYA-KUN.
PATA (SNAP)
HM?
THE WAY I SEE IT, THE REASON YOU CANNOT OPERATE IN A GROUP IS THOSE ROTTEN EYES AND THAT PERSONALITY.
YOU'RE GONNA LECTURE ME ON GROUP CONDUCT?
THOUGH PEOPLE MAY BAND TOGETHER AGAINST YOU AS A COMMON ENEMY...
OUCH...
...THEY WOULD ONLY EXPEND THE EFFORT NECESSARY TO GET RID OF YOU AND WOULD MAKE NO EFFORT TO IMPROVE THEMSELVES.
SOURCE: ME.
AND MY EYES HAVE NOTHING TO DO WITH IT.
I SEE...
WAIT, WHAT? "SOURCE"?

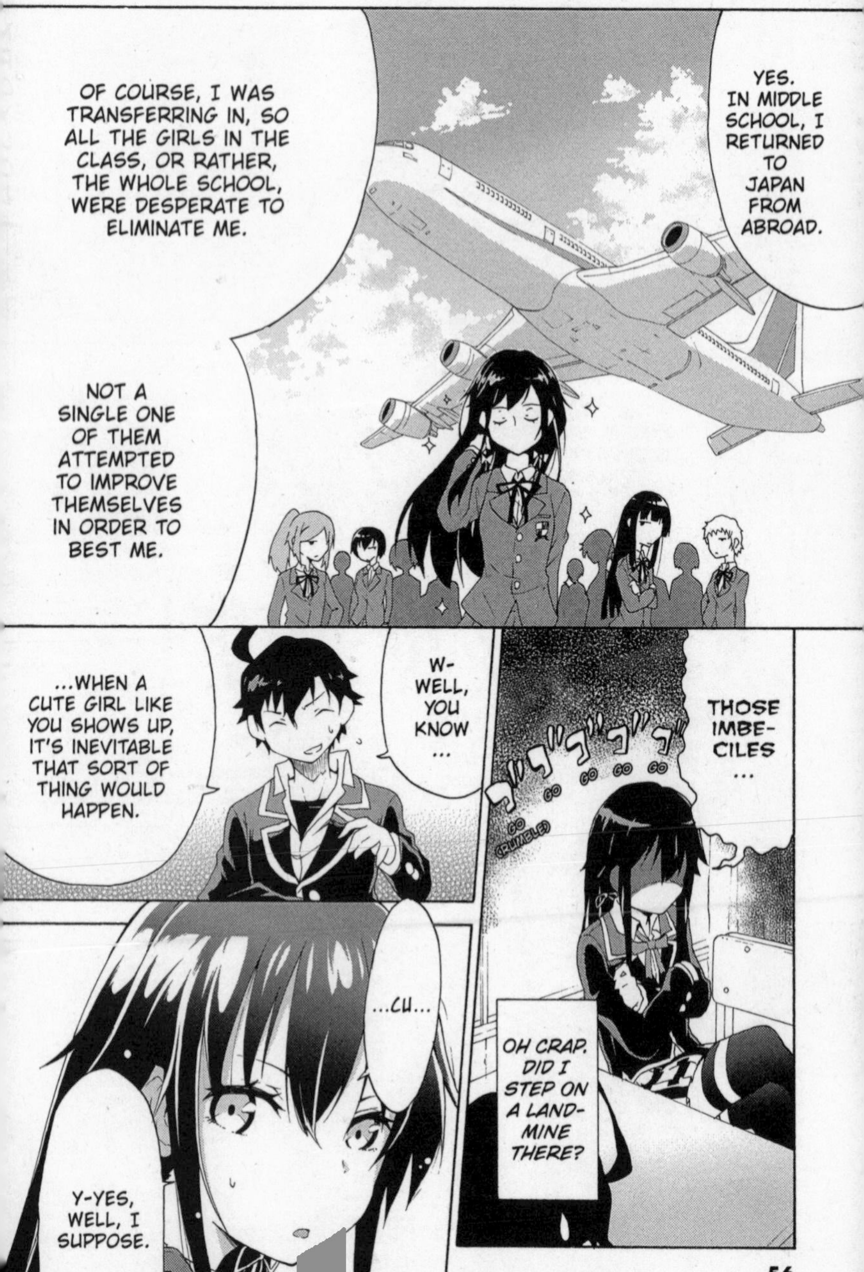
YES. IN MIDDLE SCHOOL, I RETURNED TO JAPAN FROM ABROAD.
OF COURSE, I WAS TRANSFERRING IN, SO ALL THE GIRLS IN THE CLASS, OR RATHER, THE WHOLE SCHOOL, WERE DESPERATE TO ELIMINATE ME.
NOT A SINGLE ONE OF THEM ATTEMPTED TO IMPROVE THEMSELVES IN ORDER TO BEST ME.
THOSE IMBECILES...
GO GO GO GO GO (RUMBLE)
OH CRAP. DID I STEP ON A LANDMINE THERE?
W-WELL, YOU KNOW...
...WHEN A CUTE GIRL LIKE YOU SHOWS UP, IT'S INEVITABLE THAT SORT OF THING WOULD HAPPEN.
...CU...
Y-YES, WELL, I SUPPOSE.

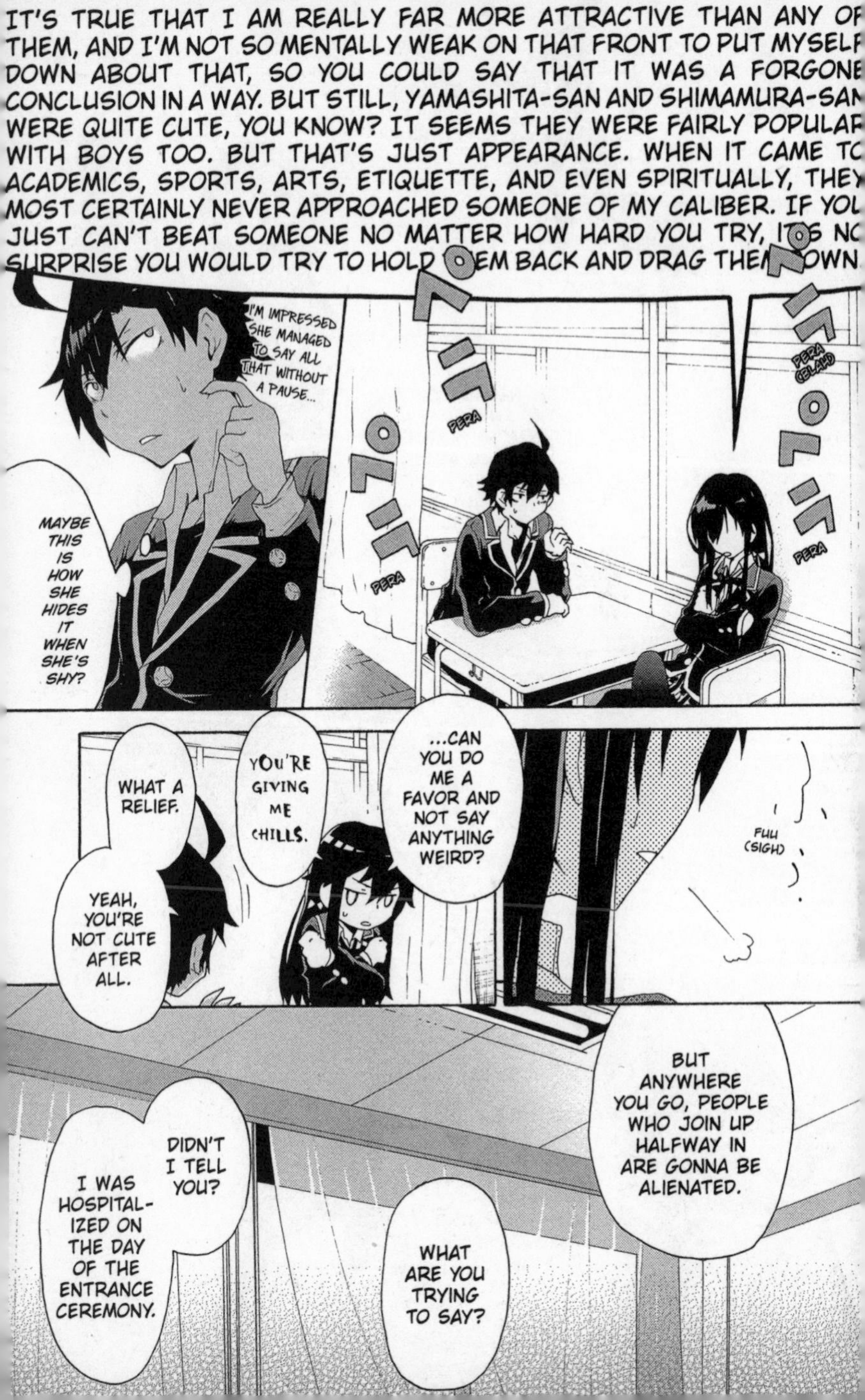
IT'S TRUE THAT I AM REALLY FAR MORE ATTRACTIVE THAN ANY OF THEM, AND I'M NOT SO MENTALLY WEAK ON THAT FRONT TO PUT MYSELF DOWN ABOUT THAT, SO YOU COULD SAY THAT IT WAS A FORGONE CONCLUSION IN A WAY. BUT STILL, YAMASHITA-SAN AND SHIMAMURA-SAN WERE QUITE CUTE, YOU KNOW? IT SEEMS THEY WERE FAIRLY POPULAR WITH BOYS TOO. BUT THAT'S JUST APPEARANCE. WHEN IT CAME TO ACADEMICS, SPORTS, ARTS, ETIQUETTE, AND EVEN SPIRITUALLY, THEY MOST CERTAINLY NEVER APPROACHED SOMEONE OF MY CALIBER. IF YOU JUST CAN'T BEAT SOMEONE NO MATTER HOW HARD YOU TRY, IT'S NO SURPRISE YOU WOULD TRY TO HOLD THEM BACK AND DRAG THEM DOWN.
PERA (BLAH)
PERA
PERA
PERA
I'M IMPRESSED SHE MANAGED TO SAY ALL THAT WITHOUT A PAUSE...
MAYBE THIS IS HOW SHE HIDES IT WHEN SHE'S SHY?
FUU (SIGH)
...CAN YOU DO ME A FAVOR AND NOT SAY ANYTHING WEIRD?
YOU'RE GIVING ME CHILLS.
WHAT A RELIEF.
YEAH, YOU'RE NOT CUTE AFTER ALL.
BUT ANYWHERE YOU GO, PEOPLE WHO JOIN UP HALFWAY IN ARE GONNA BE ALIENATED.
WHAT ARE YOU TRYING TO SAY?
DIDN'T I TELL YOU?
I WAS HOSPITAL-IZED ON THE DAY OF THE ENTRANCE CEREMONY.

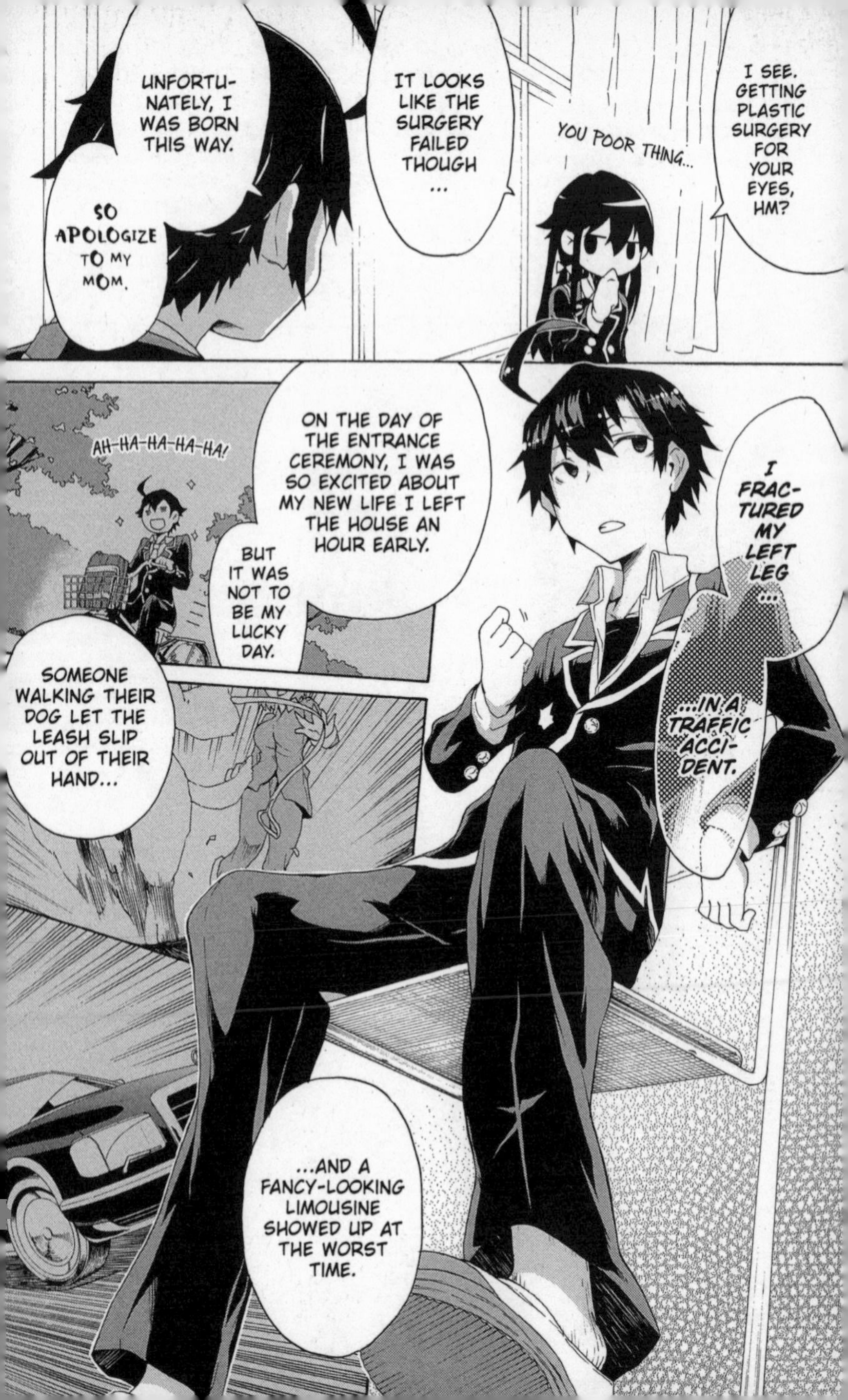
I SEE. GETTING PLASTIC SURGERY FOR YOUR EYES, HM?
YOU POOR THING...
IT LOOKS LIKE THE SURGERY FAILED THOUGH ...
UNFORTUNATELY, I WAS BORN THIS WAY.
SO APOLOGIZE TO MY MOM.
I FRACTURED MY LEFT LEG ...
...IN A TRAFFIC ACCIDENT.
ON THE DAY OF THE ENTRANCE CEREMONY, I WAS SO EXCITED ABOUT MY NEW LIFE I LEFT THE HOUSE AN HOUR EARLY.
AH-HA-HA-HA-HA!
BUT IT WAS NOT TO BE MY LUCKY DAY.
SOMEONE WALKING THEIR DOG LET THE LEASH SLIP OUT OF THEIR HAND...
...AND A FANCY-LOOKING LIMOUSINE SHOWED UP AT THE WORST TIME.

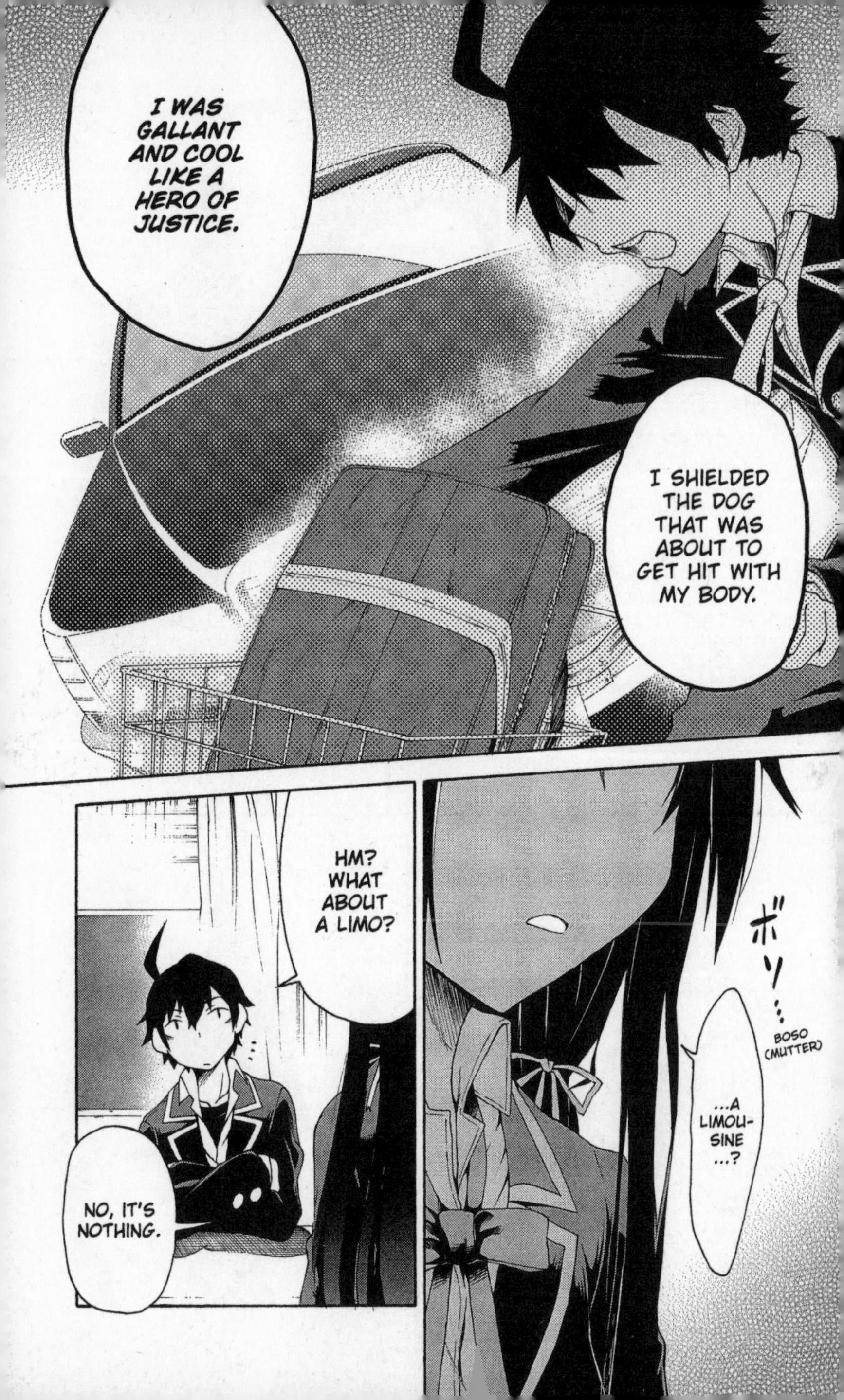
I SHIELDED THE DOG THAT WAS ABOUT TO GET HIT WITH MY BODY.
I WAS GALLANT AND COOL LIKE A HERO OF JUSTICE.
ボソッ
BOSO (MUTTER)
...A LIMOU-SINE ...?
HM? WHAT ABOUT A LIMO?
NO, IT'S NOTHING.

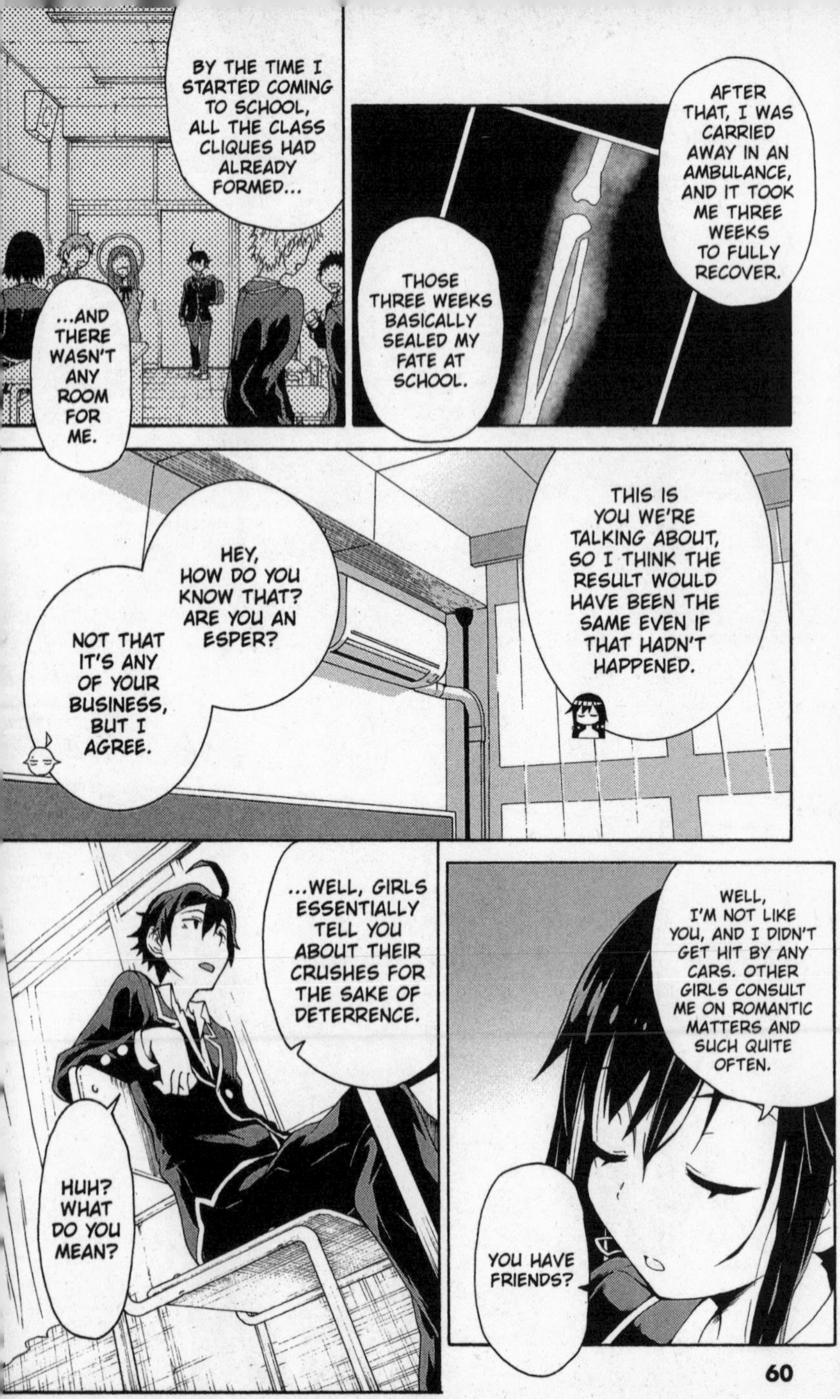
AFTER THAT, I WAS CARRIED AWAY IN AN AMBULANCE, AND IT TOOK ME THREE WEEKS TO FULLY RECOVER.
THOSE THREE WEEKS BASICALLY SEALED MY FATE AT SCHOOL.
BY THE TIME I STARTED COMING TO SCHOOL, ALL THE CLASS CLIQUES HAD ALREADY FORMED...
...AND THERE WASN'T ANY ROOM FOR ME.
THIS IS YOU WE'RE TALKING ABOUT, SO I THINK THE RESULT WOULD HAVE BEEN THE SAME EVEN IF THAT HADN'T HAPPENED.
HEY, HOW DO YOU KNOW THAT? ARE YOU AN ESPER?
NOT THAT IT'S ANY OF YOUR BUSINESS, BUT I AGREE.
WELL, I'M NOT LIKE YOU, AND I DIDN'T GET HIT BY ANY CARS. OTHER GIRLS CONSULT ME ON ROMANTIC MATTERS AND SUCH QUITE OFTEN.
YOU HAVE FRIENDS?
...WELL, GIRLS ESSENTIALLY TELL YOU ABOUT THEIR CRUSHES FOR THE SAKE OF DETERRENCE.
HUH? WHAT DO YOU MEAN?

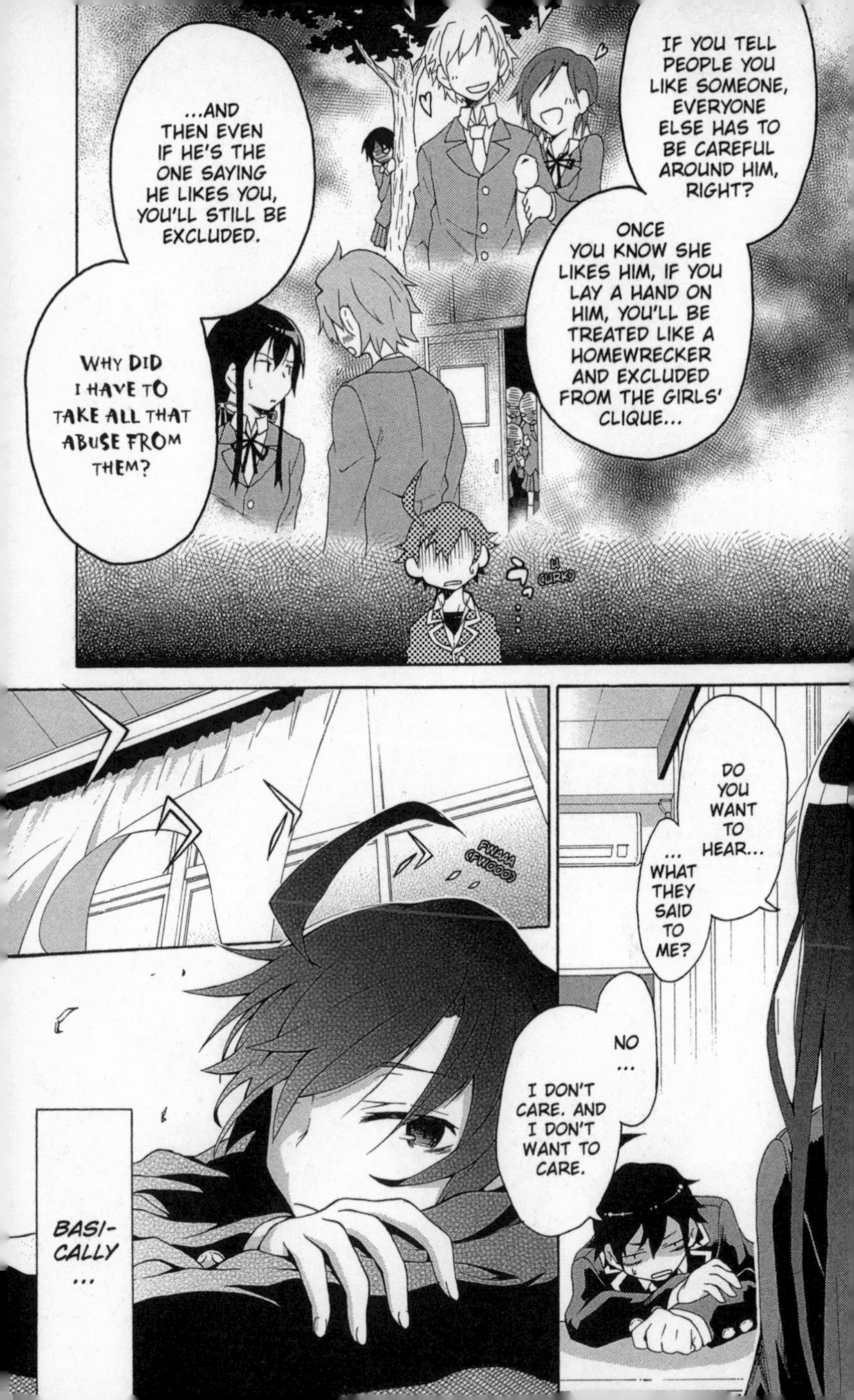
IF YOU TELL PEOPLE YOU LIKE SOMEONE, EVERYONE ELSE HAS TO BE CAREFUL AROUND HIM, RIGHT?
ONCE YOU KNOW SHE LIKES HIM, IF YOU LAY A HAND ON HIM, YOU'LL BE TREATED LIKE A HOMEWRECKER AND EXCLUDED FROM THE GIRLS' CLIQUE...
...AND THEN EVEN IF HE'S THE ONE SAYING HE LIKES YOU, YOU'LL STILL BE EXCLUDED.
WHY DID I HAVE TO TAKE ALL THAT ABUSE FROM THEM?
U (URK)
DO YOU WANT TO HEAR...
... WHAT THEY SAID TO ME?
NO ...
I DON'T CARE. AND I DON'T WANT TO CARE.
FWAAA (FWOOO)
BASI-CALLY ...

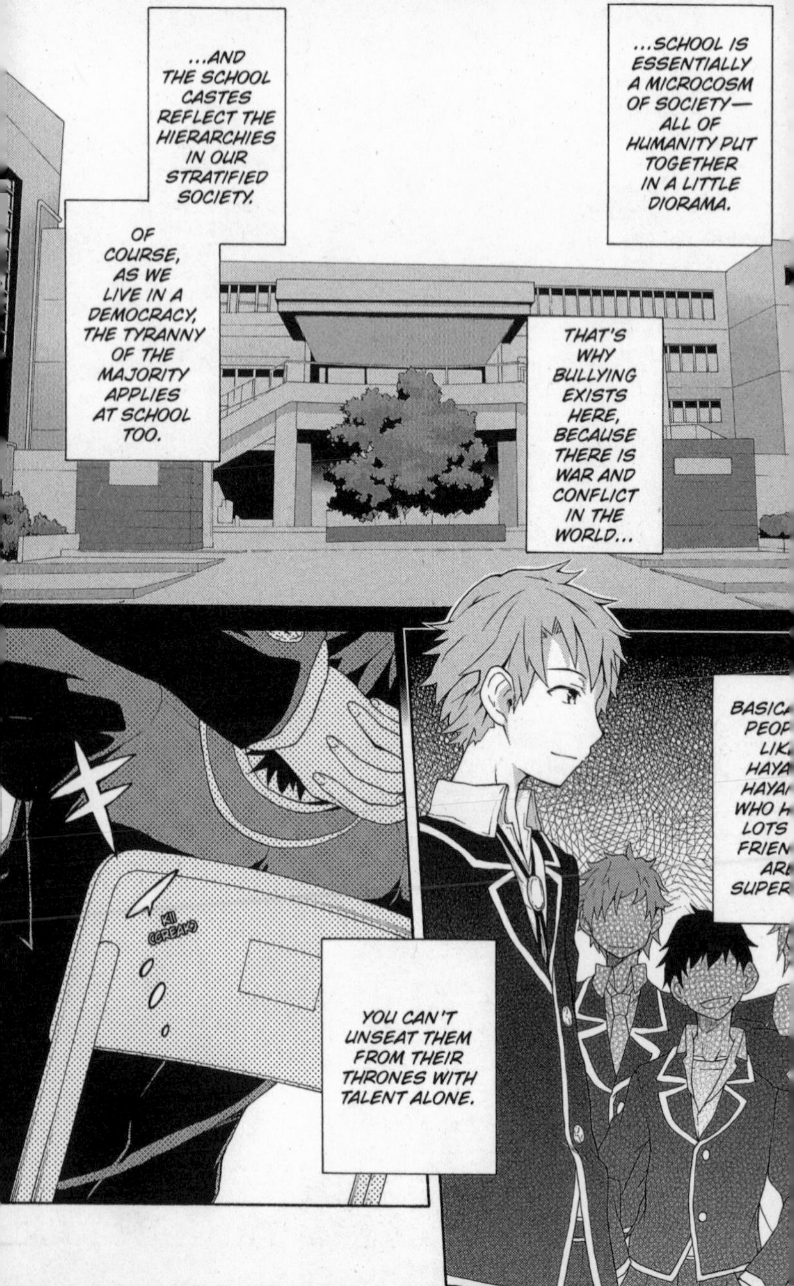
...SCHOOL IS ESSENTIALLY A MICROCOSM OF SOCIETY—ALL OF HUMANITY PUT TOGETHER IN A LITTLE DIORAMA.
THAT'S WHY BULLYING EXISTS HERE, BECAUSE THERE IS WAR AND CONFLICT IN THE WORLD...
...AND THE SCHOOL CASTES REFLECT THE HIERARCHIES IN OUR STRATIFIED SOCIETY.
OF COURSE, AS WE LIVE IN A DEMOCRACY, THE TYRANNY OF THE MAJORITY APPLIES AT SCHOOL TOO.
BASICA PEOP LIK HAYA HAYA WHO H LOTS FRIEN AR SUPER
YOU CAN'T UNSEAT THEM FROM THEIR THRONES WITH TALENT ALONE.
KII (CREAK)

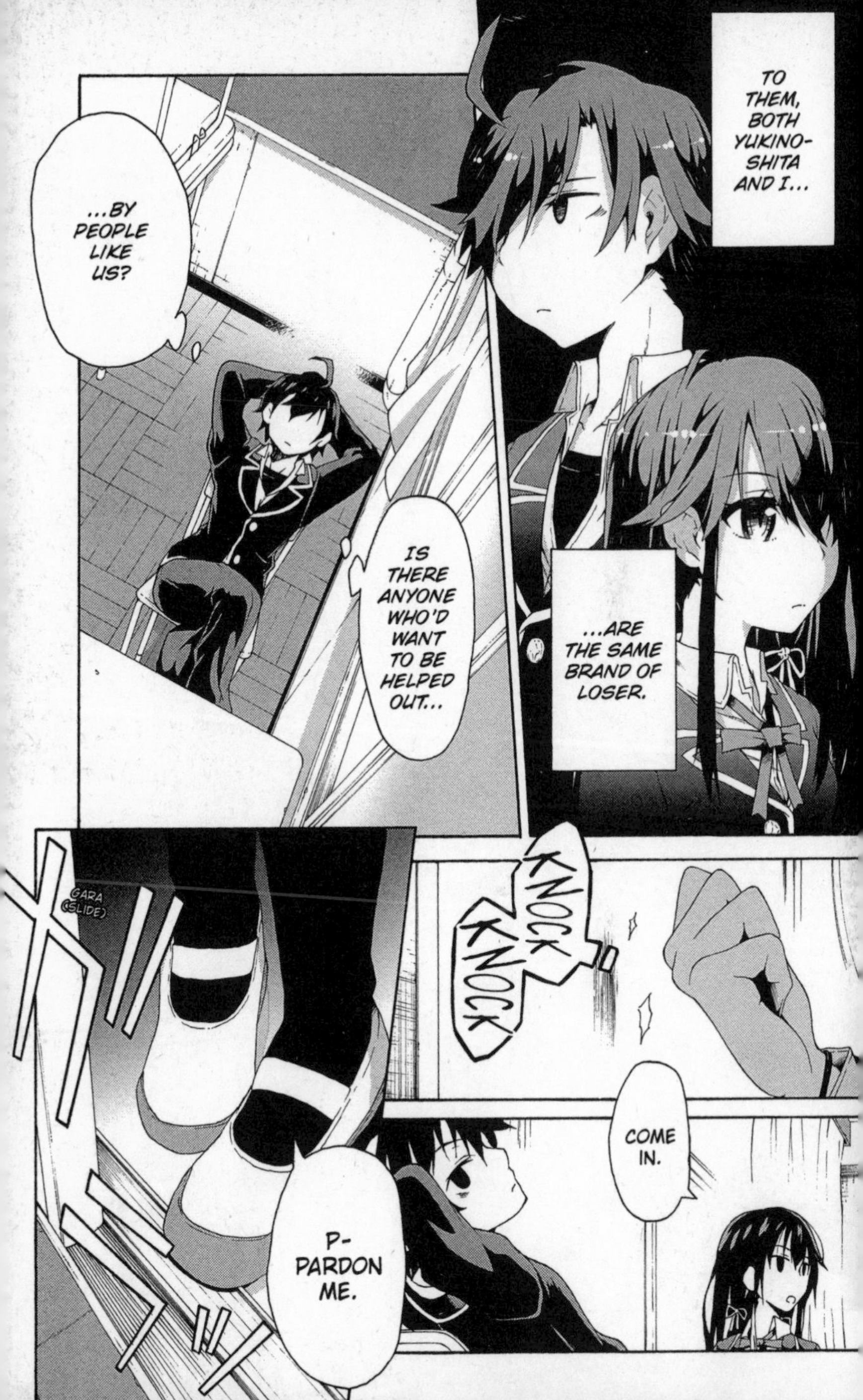
TO THEM, BOTH YUKINO-SHITA AND I...
...ARE THE SAME BRAND OF LOSER.
IS THERE ANYONE WHO'D WANT TO BE HELPED OUT...
...BY PEOPLE LIKE US?
KNOCK KNOCK
COME IN.
GARA (SLIDE)
P-PARDON ME.

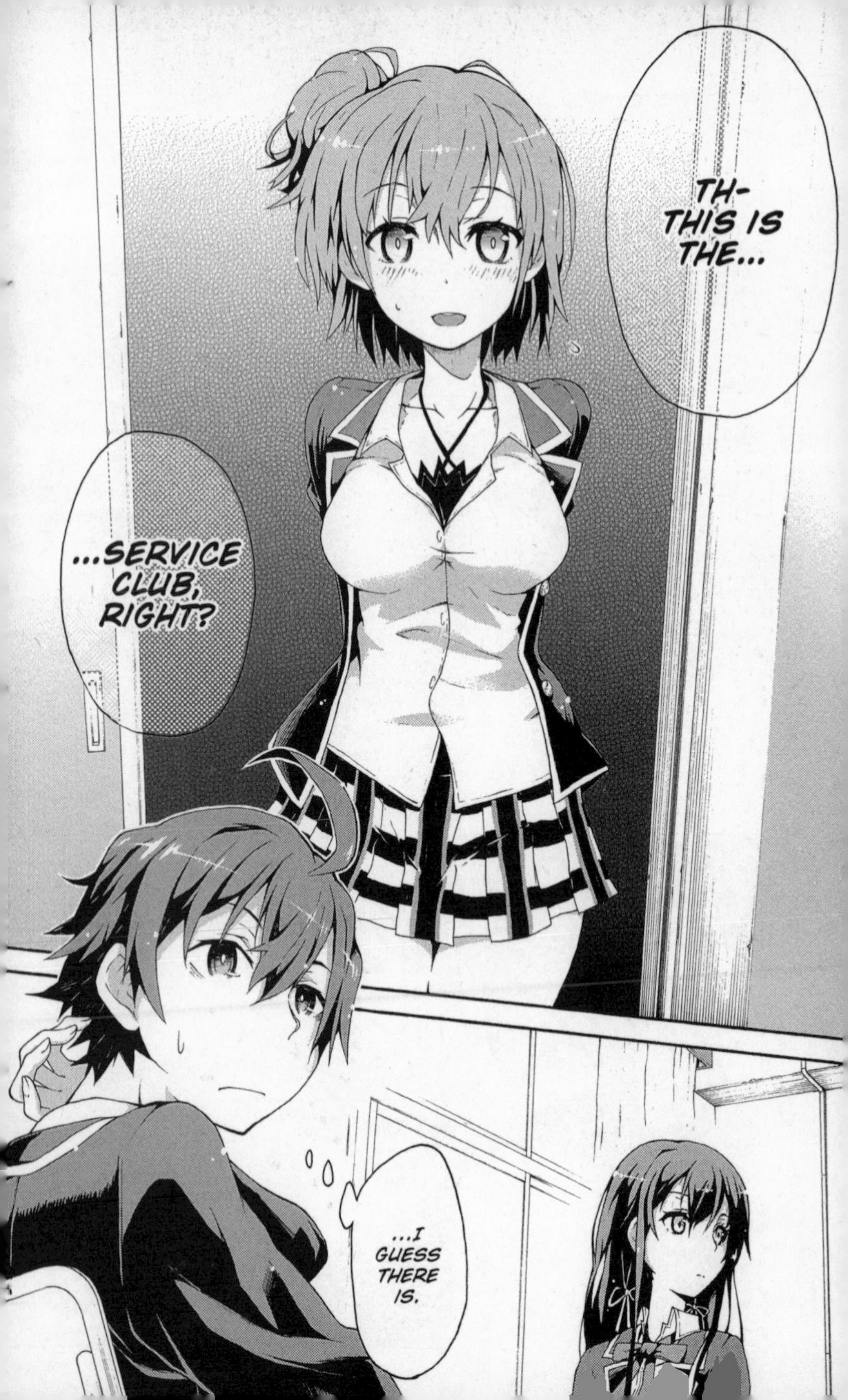
TH- THIS IS THE...
...SERVICE CLUB, RIGHT?
...I GUESS THERE IS.

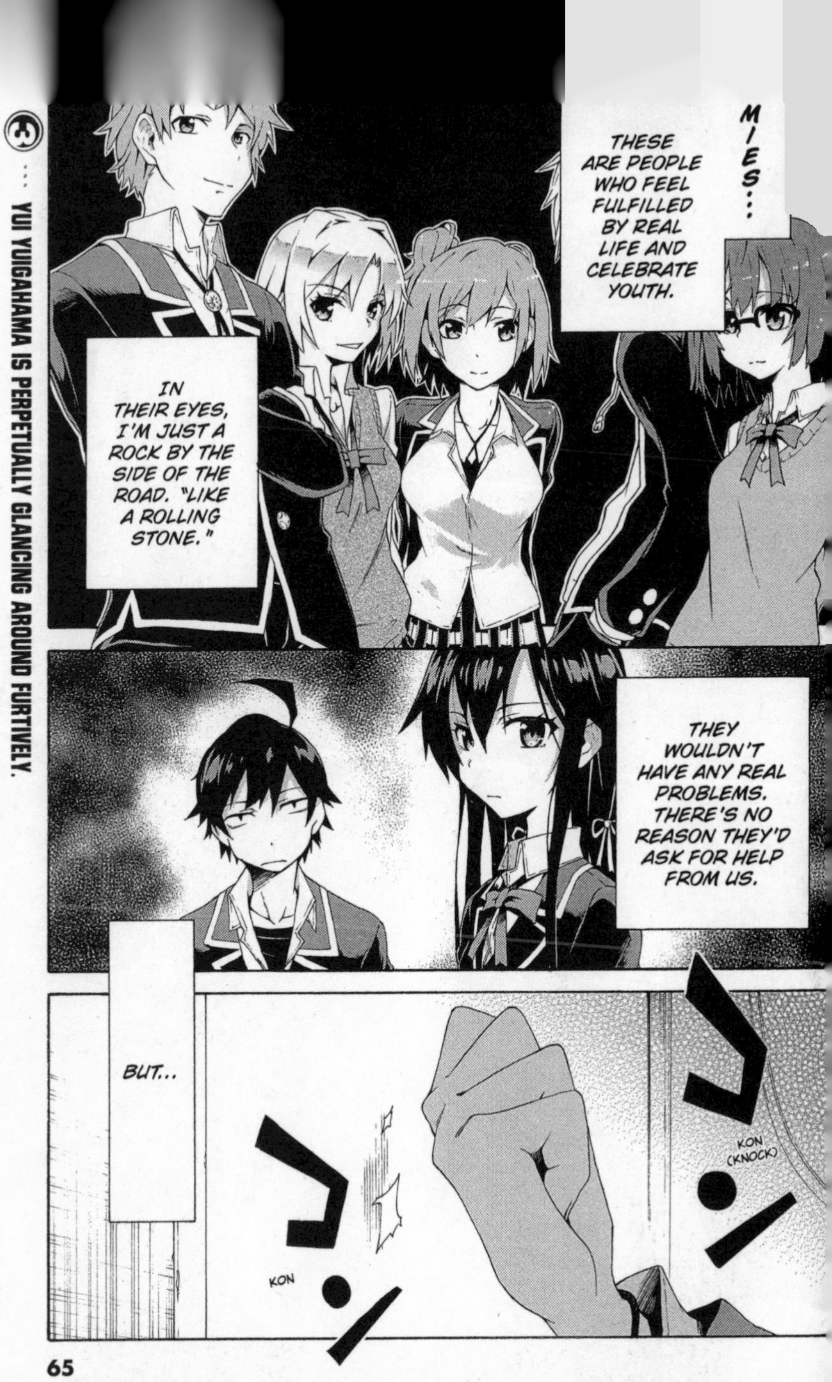
MIES...
THESE ARE PEOPLE WHO FEEL FULFILLED BY REAL LIFE AND CELEBRATE YOUTH.
IN THEIR EYES, I'M JUST A ROCK BY THE SIDE OF THE ROAD. "LIKE A ROLLING STONE."
THEY WOULDN'T HAVE ANY REAL PROBLEMS. THERE'S NO REASON THEY'D ASK FOR HELP FROM US.
BUT...
KON (KNOCK)
KON

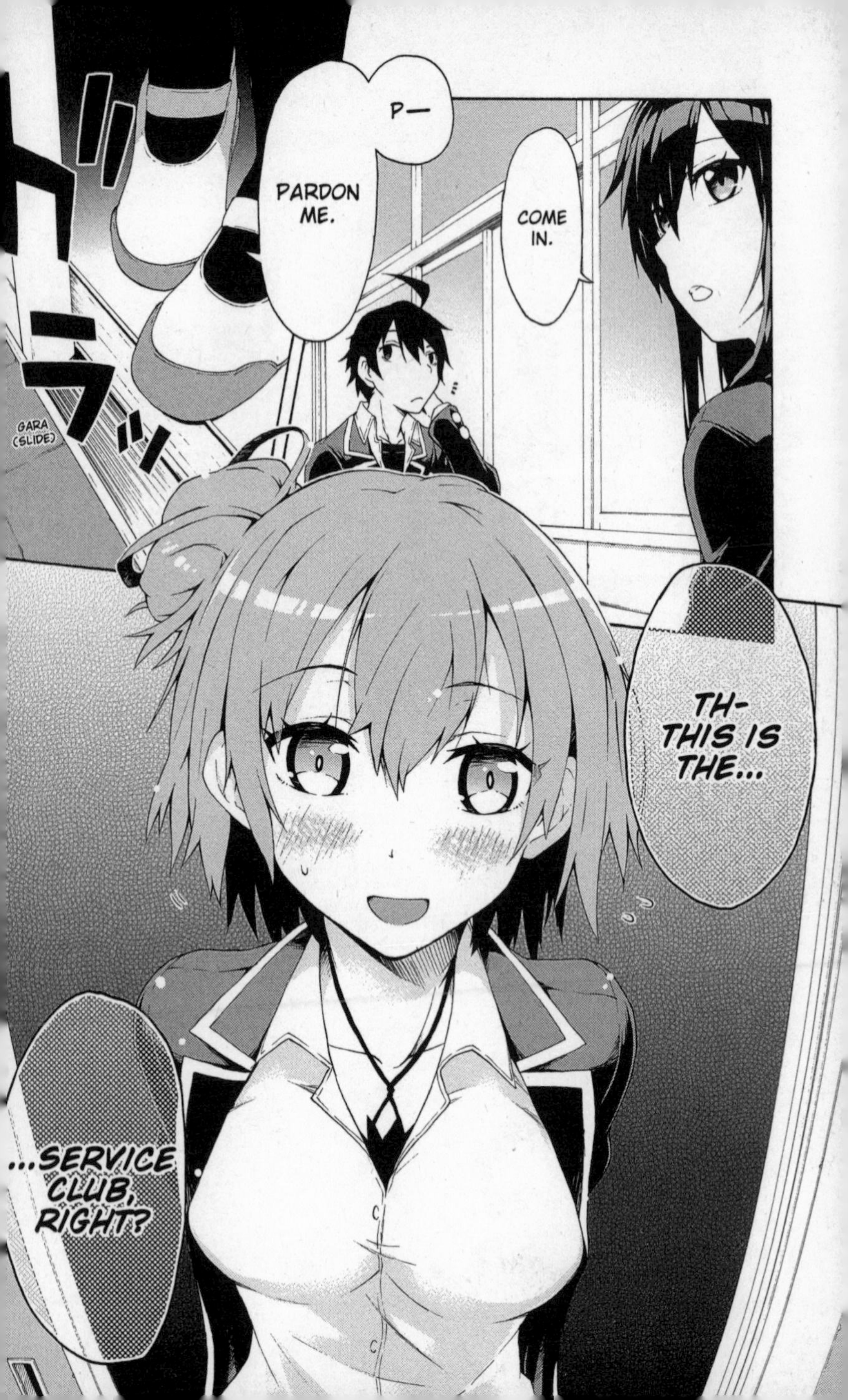
GARA (SLIDE)
P— PARDON ME.
COME IN.
TH- THIS IS THE...
...SERVICE CLUB, RIGHT?

CHAPTER 3 ··· YUI YUIGAHAMA IS PERPETUALLY GLANCING AROUND FURTIVELY.

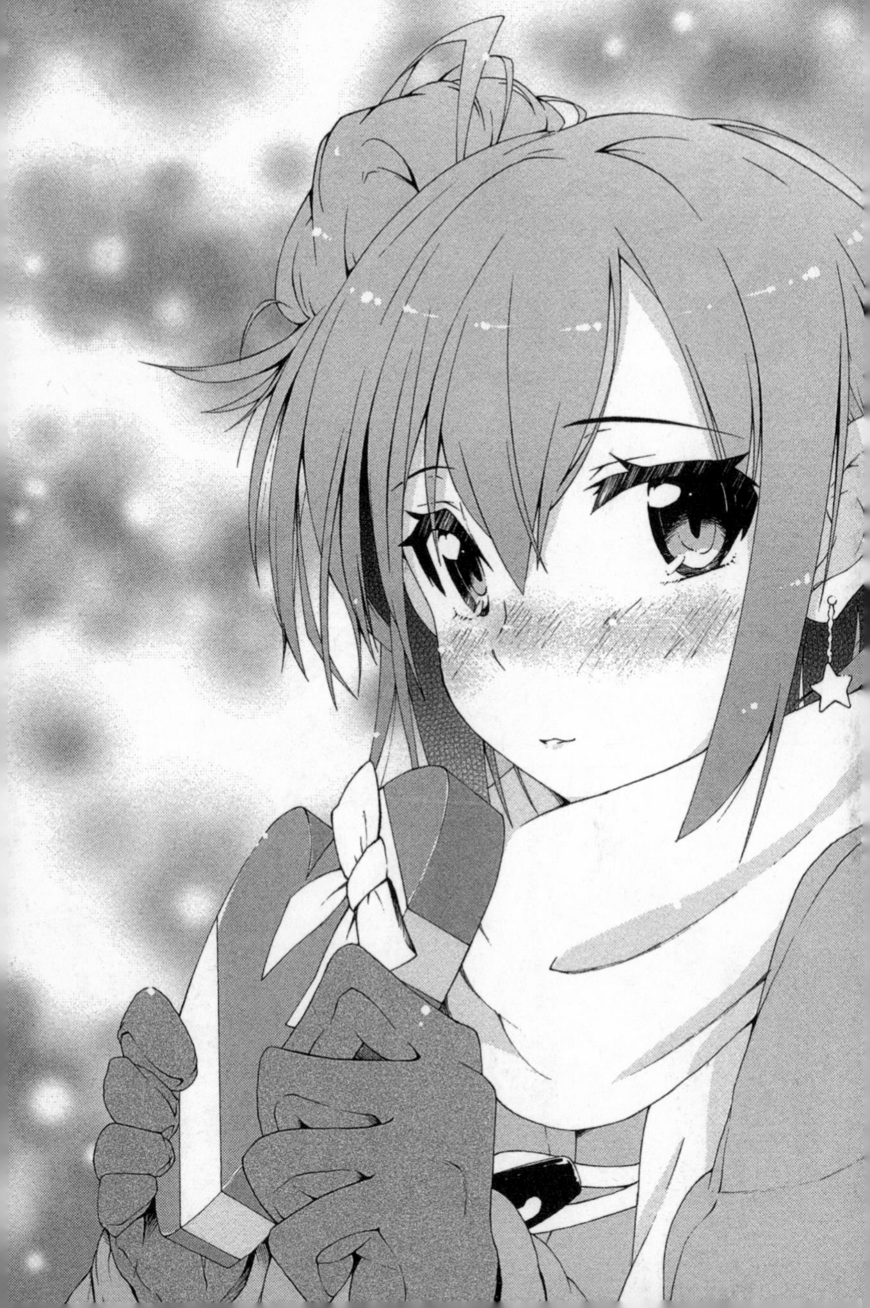

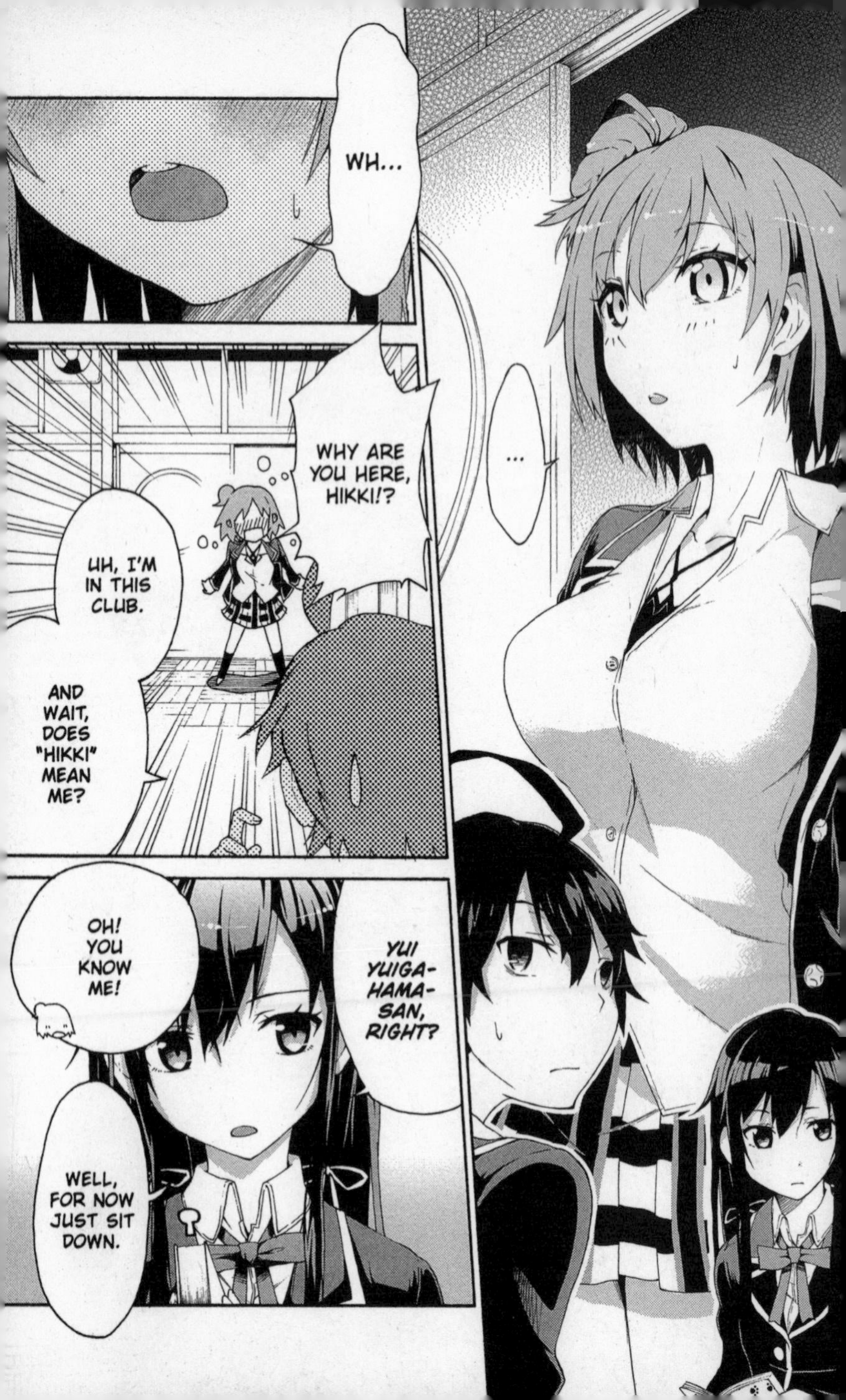
...
WH...
WHY ARE YOU HERE, HIKKI!?
UH, I'M IN THIS CLUB.
AND WAIT, DOES "HIKKI" MEAN ME?
YUI YUIGAHAMA-SAN, RIGHT?
OH! YOU KNOW ME!
WELL, FOR NOW JUST SIT DOWN.

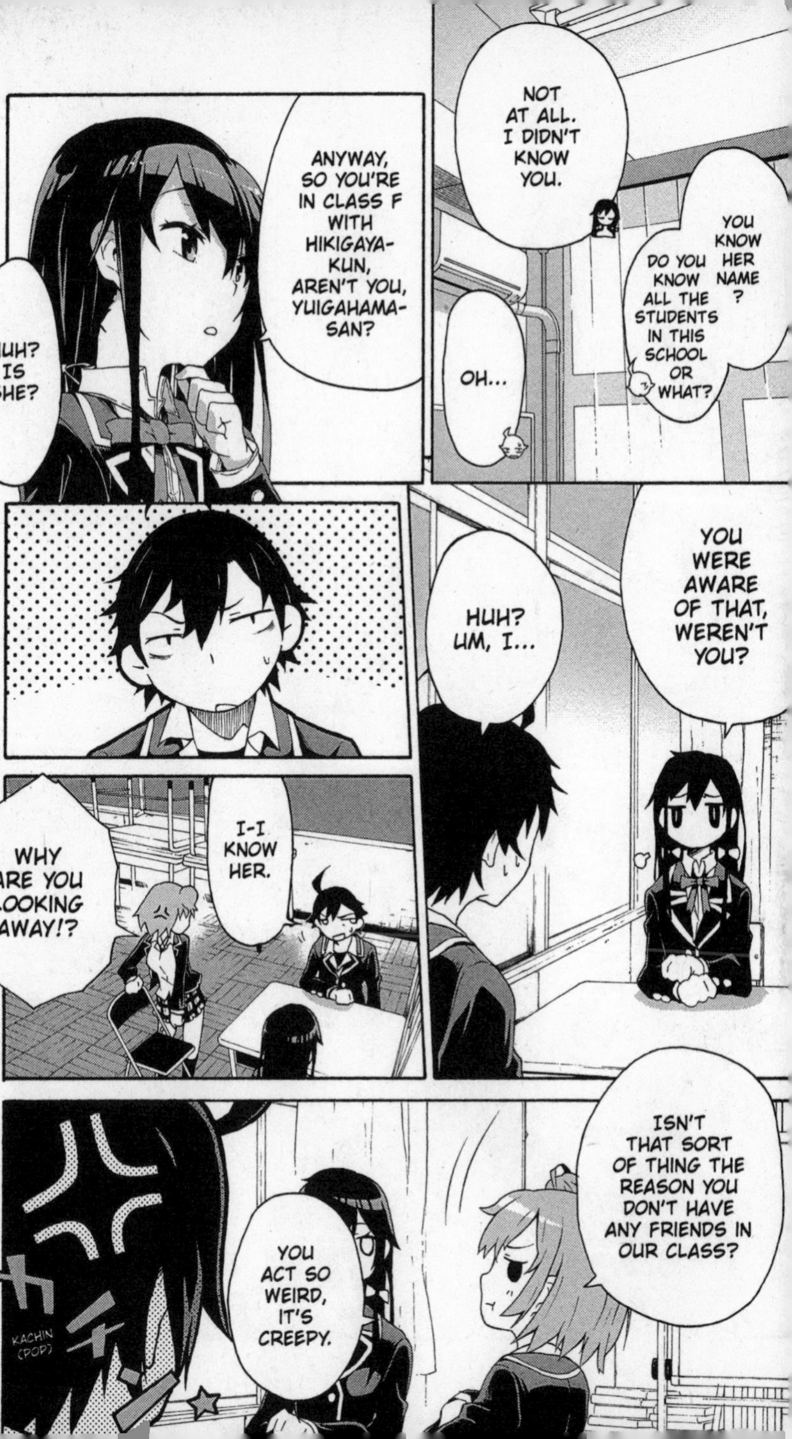
YOU KNOW HER NAME?
DO YOU KNOW ALL THE STUDENTS IN THIS SCHOOL OR WHAT?
NOT AT ALL. I DIDN'T KNOW YOU.
OH...
ANYWAY, SO YOU'RE IN CLASS F WITH HIKIGAYA-KUN, AREN'T YOU, YUIGAHAMA-SAN?
HUH? IS SHE?
YOU WERE AWARE OF THAT, WEREN'T YOU?
HUH? UM, I...
I-I KNOW HER.
WHY ARE YOU LOOKING AWAY!?
ISN'T THAT SORT OF THING THE REASON YOU DON'T HAVE ANY FRIENDS IN OUR CLASS?
YOU ACT SO WEIRD, IT'S CREEPY.
KACHIN (POP)

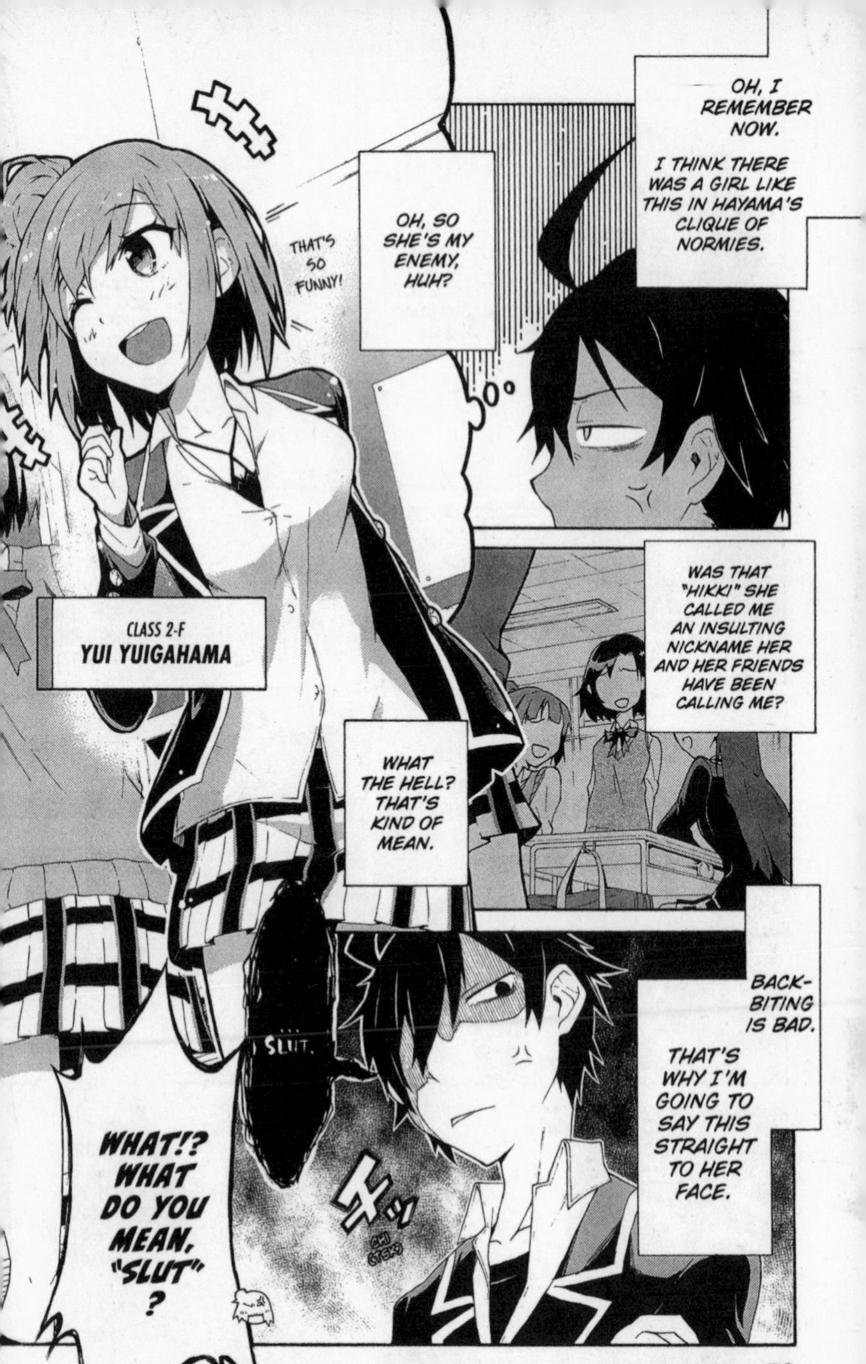
OH, I REMEMBER NOW.
I THINK THERE WAS A GIRL LIKE THIS IN HAYAMA'S CLIQUE OF NORMIES.
OH, SO SHE'S MY ENEMY, HUH?
WAS THAT "HIKKI" SHE CALLED ME AN INSULTING NICKNAME HER AND HER FRIENDS HAVE BEEN CALLING ME?
WHAT THE HELL? THAT'S KIND OF MEAN.
BACK-BITING IS BAD.
THAT'S WHY I'M GOING TO SAY THIS STRAIGHT TO HER FACE.
CHI (TSK)
...SLUT.
THAT'S SO FUNNY!
CLASS 2-F
YUI YUIGAHAMA
WHAT!? WHAT DO YOU MEAN, "SLUT"?

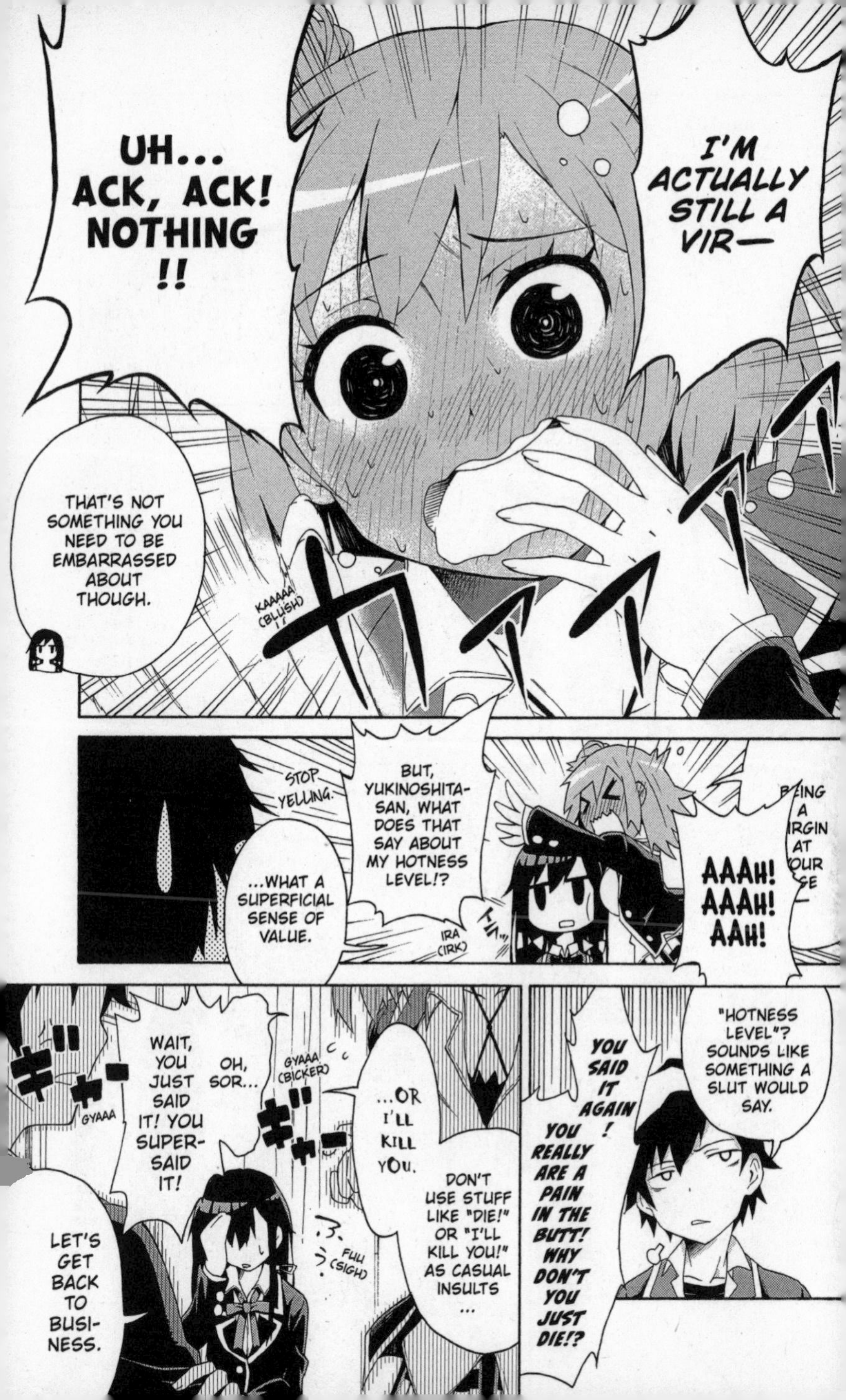
I'M ACTUALLY STILL A VIR—
UH... ACK, ACK! NOTHING !!
KAAAAA (BLUSH)
THAT'S NOT SOMETHING YOU NEED TO BE EMBARRASSED ABOUT THOUGH.
AAAH! AAAH! AAH!
BUT, YUKINOSHITA-SAN, WHAT DOES THAT SAY ABOUT MY HOTNESS LEVEL!?
IRA (IRK)
STOP YELLING.
...WHAT A SUPERFICIAL SENSE OF VALUE.
"HOTNESS LEVEL"? SOUNDS LIKE SOMETHING A SLUT WOULD SAY.
YOU SAID IT AGAIN!
YOU REALLY ARE A PAIN IN THE BUTT! WHY DON'T YOU JUST DIE!?
...OR I'LL KILL YOU.
DON'T USE STUFF LIKE "DIE!" OR "I'LL KILL YOU!" AS CASUAL INSULTS ...
GYAAA (BICKER)
OH, SOR...
WAIT, YOU JUST SAID IT! YOU SUPER-SAID IT!
GYAAA
FUU (SIGH)
LET'S GET BACK TO BUSINESS.

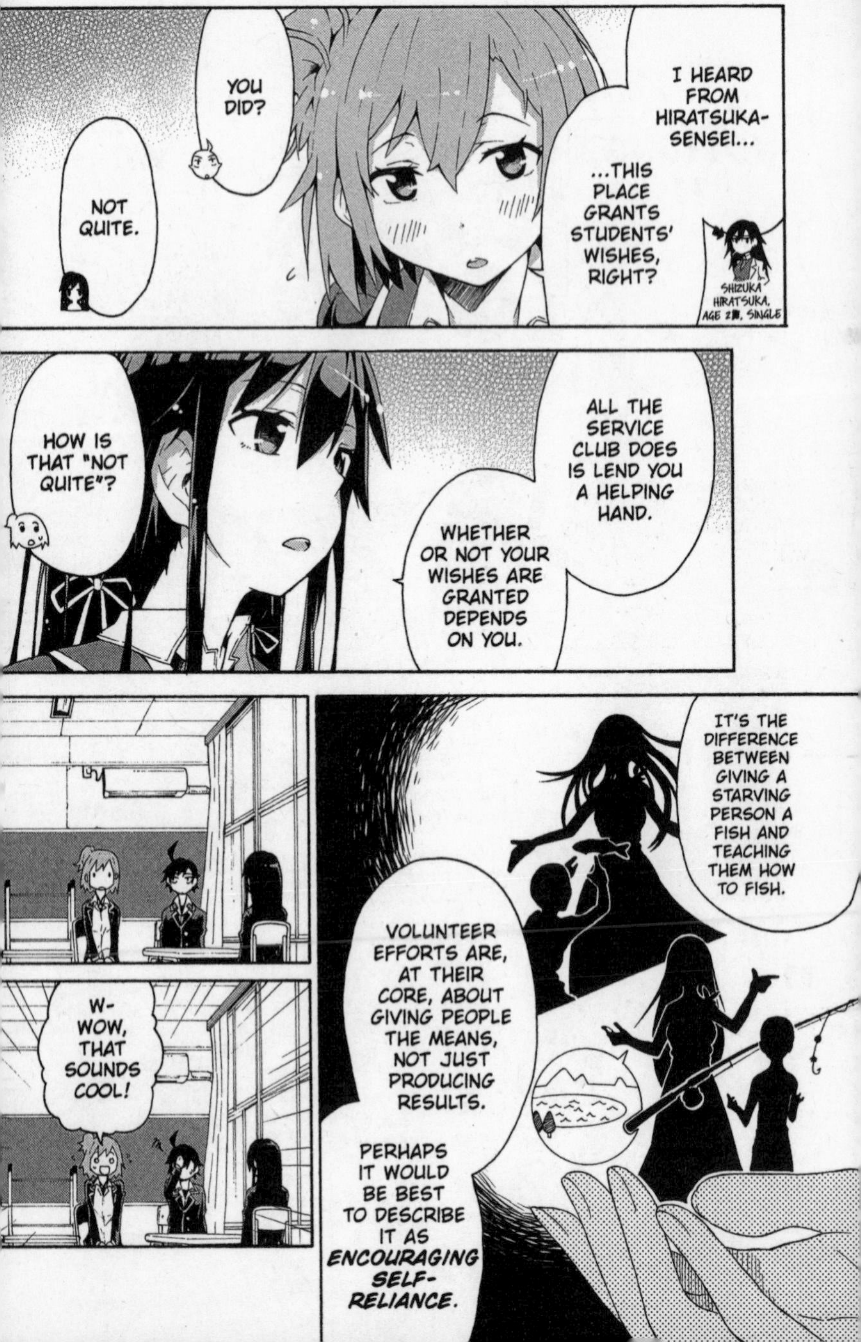
I HEARD FROM HIRATSUKA-SENSEI...
...THIS PLACE GRANTS STUDENTS' WISHES, RIGHT?
SHIZUKA HIRATSUKA, AGE 2[redacted], SINGLE
YOU DID?
NOT QUITE.
ALL THE SERVICE CLUB DOES IS LEND YOU A HELPING HAND.
WHETHER OR NOT YOUR WISHES ARE GRANTED DEPENDS ON YOU.
HOW IS THAT "NOT QUITE"?
IT'S THE DIFFERENCE BETWEEN GIVING A STARVING PERSON A FISH AND TEACHING THEM HOW TO FISH.
VOLUNTEER EFFORTS ARE, AT THEIR CORE, ABOUT GIVING PEOPLE THE MEANS, NOT JUST PRODUCING RESULTS.
PERHAPS IT WOULD BE BEST TO DESCRIBE IT AS *ENCOURAGING SELF-RELIANCE.*
W-WOW, THAT SOUNDS COOL!

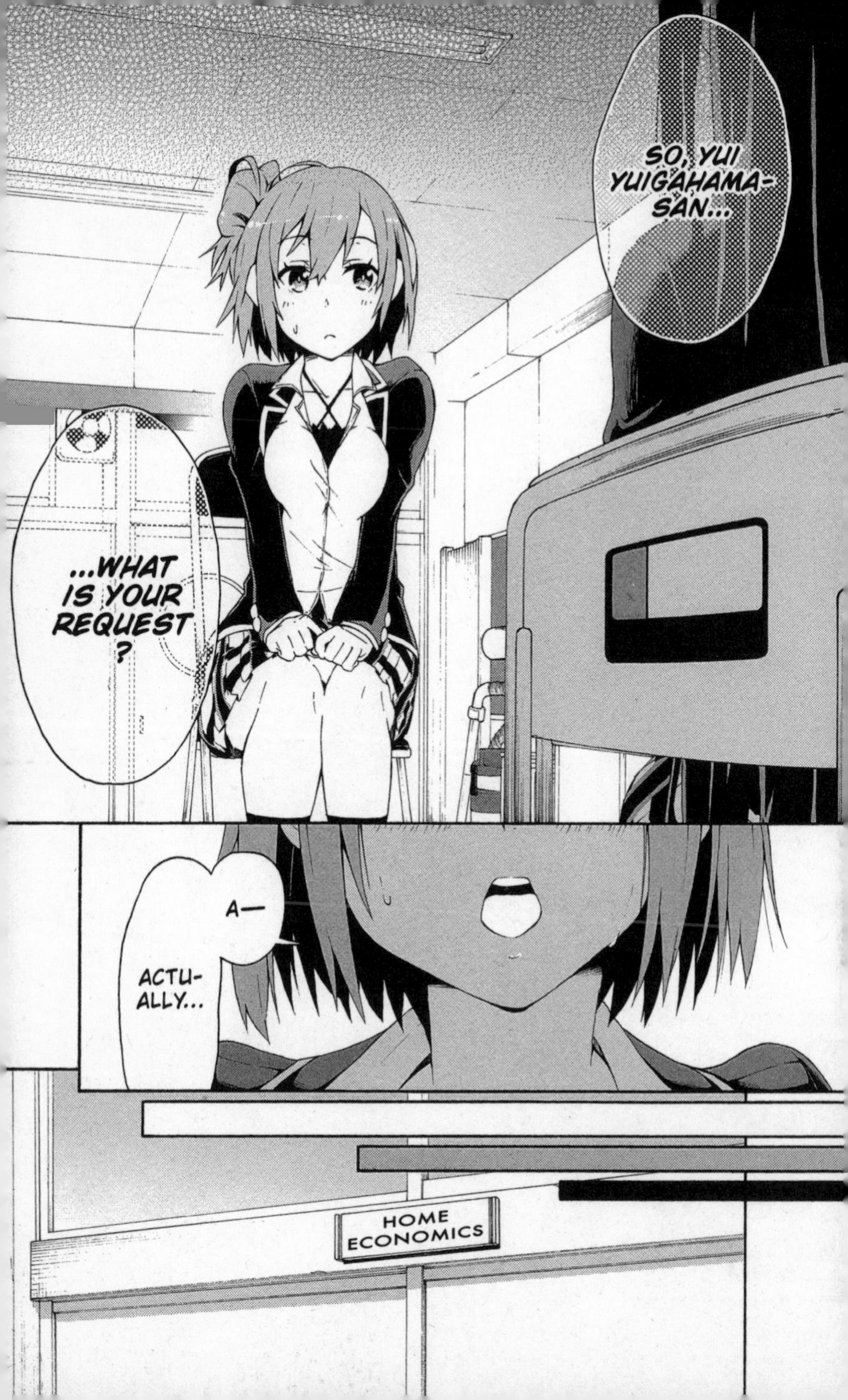
SO, YUI YUIGAHAMA-SAN...
...WHAT IS YOUR REQUEST?
A—
ACTU-ALLY...
HOME ECONOMICS

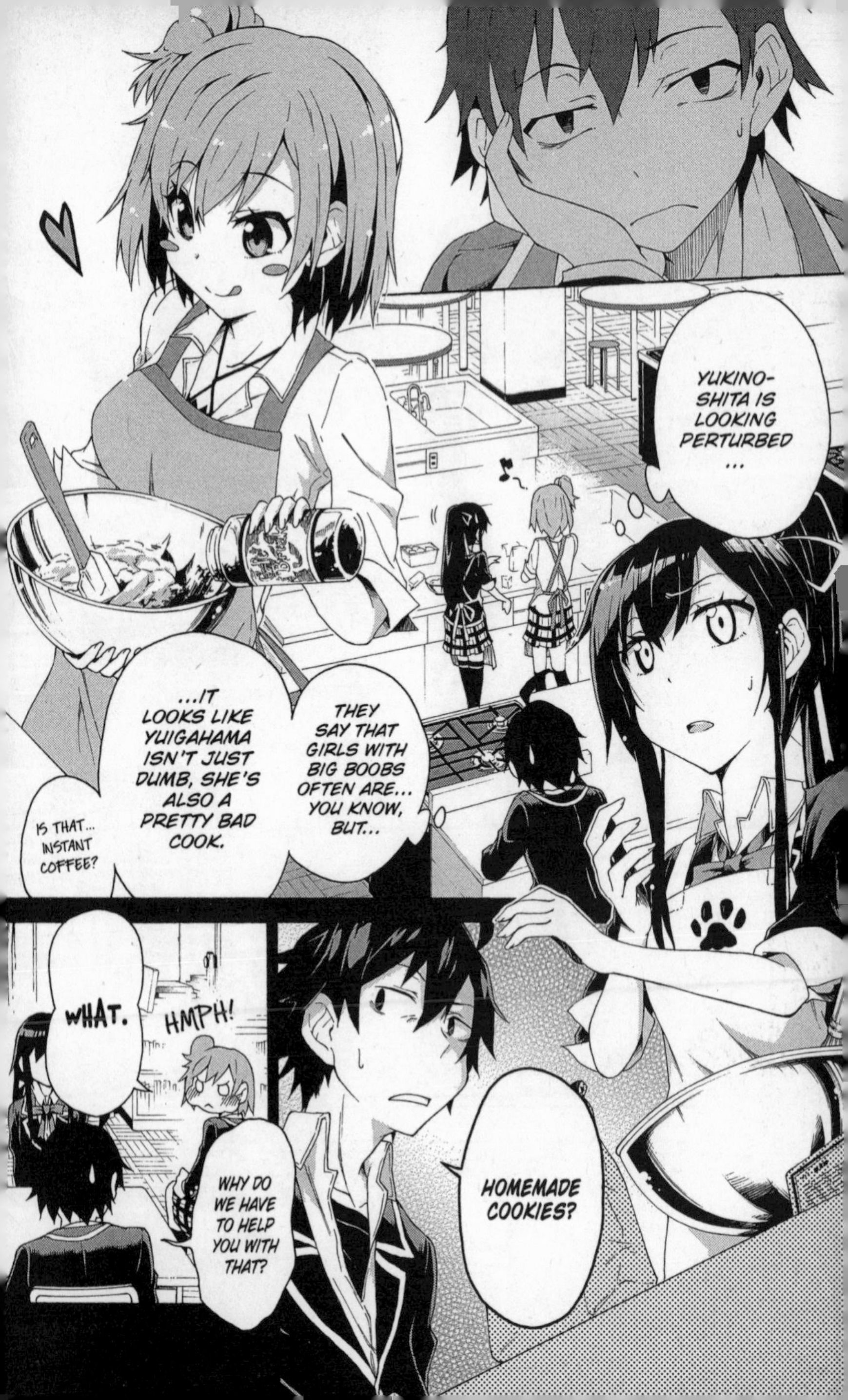
YUKINO-SHITA IS LOOKING PERTURBED...
THEY SAY THAT GIRLS WITH BIG BOOBS OFTEN ARE... YOU KNOW, BUT...
...IT LOOKS LIKE YUIGAHAMA ISN'T JUST DUMB, SHE'S ALSO A PRETTY BAD COOK.
IS THAT... INSTANT COFFEE?
HOMEMADE COOKIES?
WHY DO WE HAVE TO HELP YOU WITH THAT?
HMPH!
WHAT.

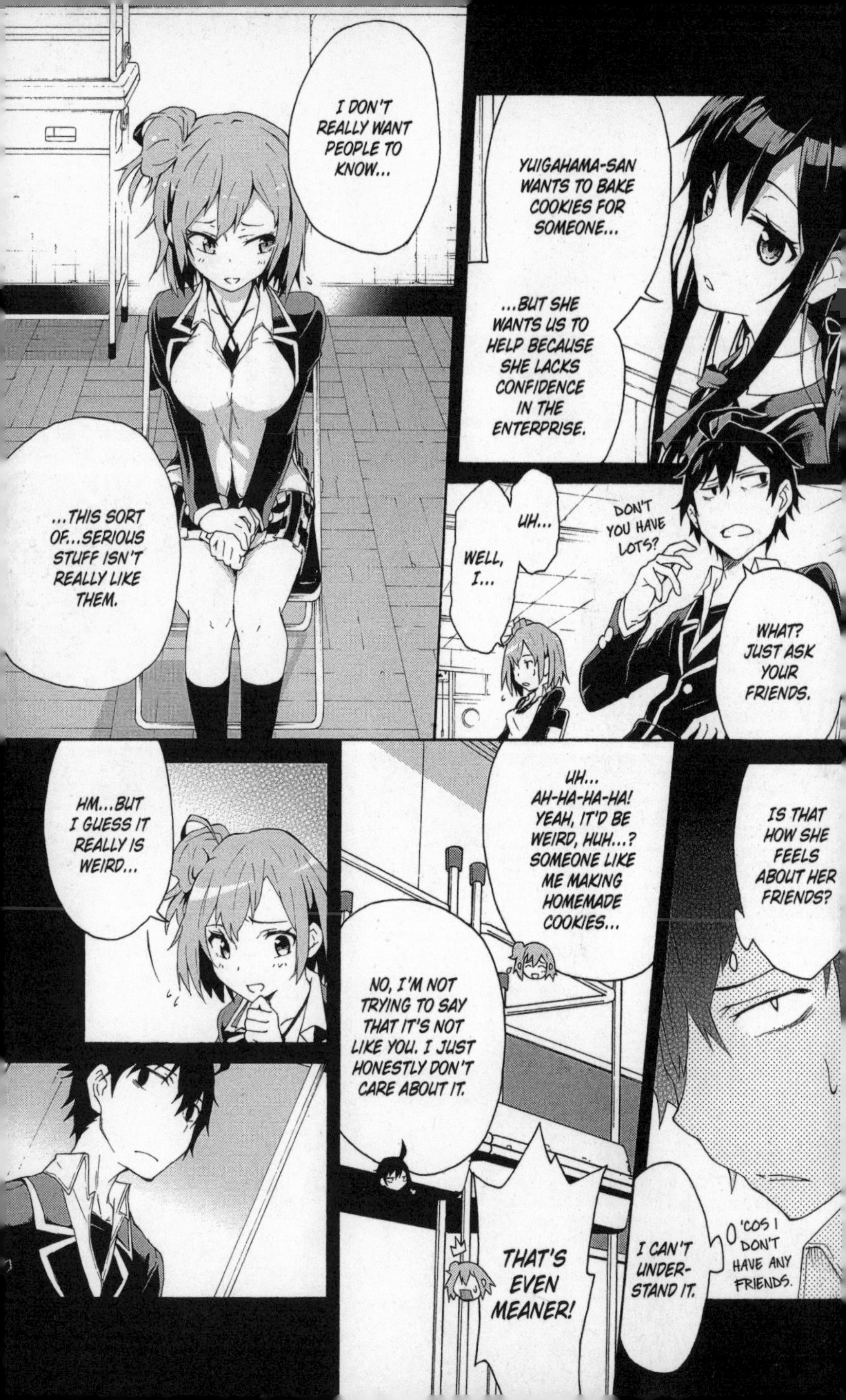
YUIGAHAMA-SAN WANTS TO BAKE COOKIES FOR SOMEONE...
...BUT SHE WANTS US TO HELP BECAUSE SHE LACKS CONFIDENCE IN THE ENTERPRISE.
WHAT? JUST ASK YOUR FRIENDS.
DON'T YOU HAVE LOTS?
UH...
WELL, I...
I DON'T REALLY WANT PEOPLE TO KNOW...
...THIS SORT OF...SERIOUS STUFF ISN'T REALLY LIKE THEM.
IS THAT HOW SHE FEELS ABOUT HER FRIENDS?
'COS I DON'T HAVE ANY FRIENDS.
I CAN'T UNDER-STAND IT.
UH... AH-HA-HA-HA! YEAH, IT'D BE WEIRD, HUH...? SOMEONE LIKE ME MAKING HOMEMADE COOKIES...
NO, I'M NOT TRYING TO SAY THAT IT'S NOT LIKE YOU. I JUST HONESTLY DON'T CARE ABOUT IT.
THAT'S EVEN MEANER!
HM...BUT I GUESS IT REALLY IS WEIRD...

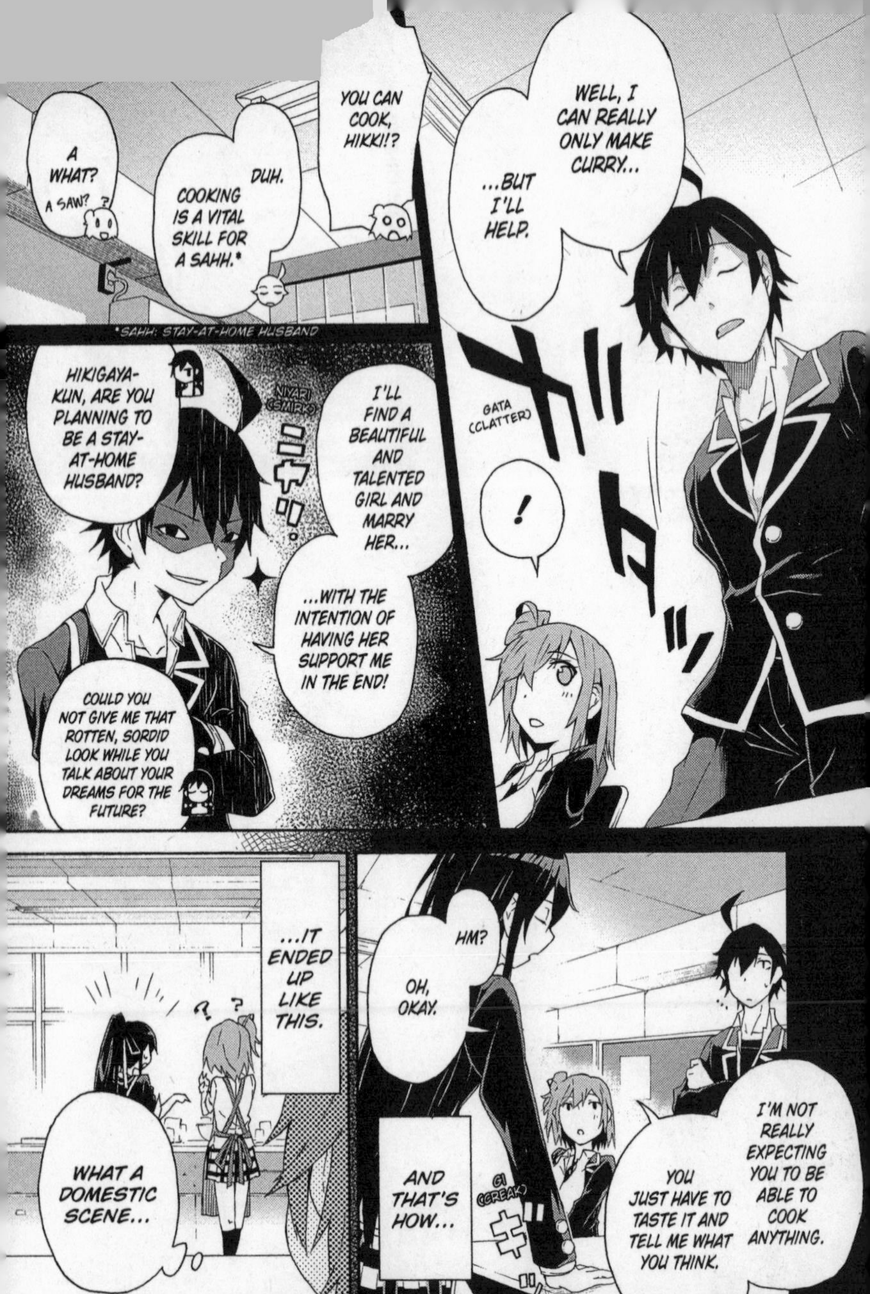
WELL, I CAN REALLY ONLY MAKE CURRY...
...BUT I'LL HELP.
GATA (CLATTER)
!
YOU CAN COOK, HIKKI!?
DUH. COOKING IS A VITAL SKILL FOR A SAHH.*
A WHAT?
A SAW? ?
*SAHH: STAY-AT-HOME HUSBAND
I'LL FIND A BEAUTIFUL AND TALENTED GIRL AND MARRY HER...
NIYARI (SMIRK)
HIKIGAYA-KUN, ARE YOU PLANNING TO BE A STAY-AT-HOME HUSBAND?
...WITH THE INTENTION OF HAVING HER SUPPORT ME IN THE END!
COULD YOU NOT GIVE ME THAT ROTTEN, SORDID LOOK WHILE YOU TALK ABOUT YOUR DREAMS FOR THE FUTURE?
HM?
OH, OKAY.
I'M NOT REALLY EXPECTING YOU TO BE ABLE TO COOK ANYTHING.
YOU JUST HAVE TO TASTE IT AND TELL ME WHAT YOU THINK.
AND THAT'S HOW...
GI (CREAK)
...IT ENDED UP LIKE THIS.
? ?
WHAT A DOMESTIC SCENE...

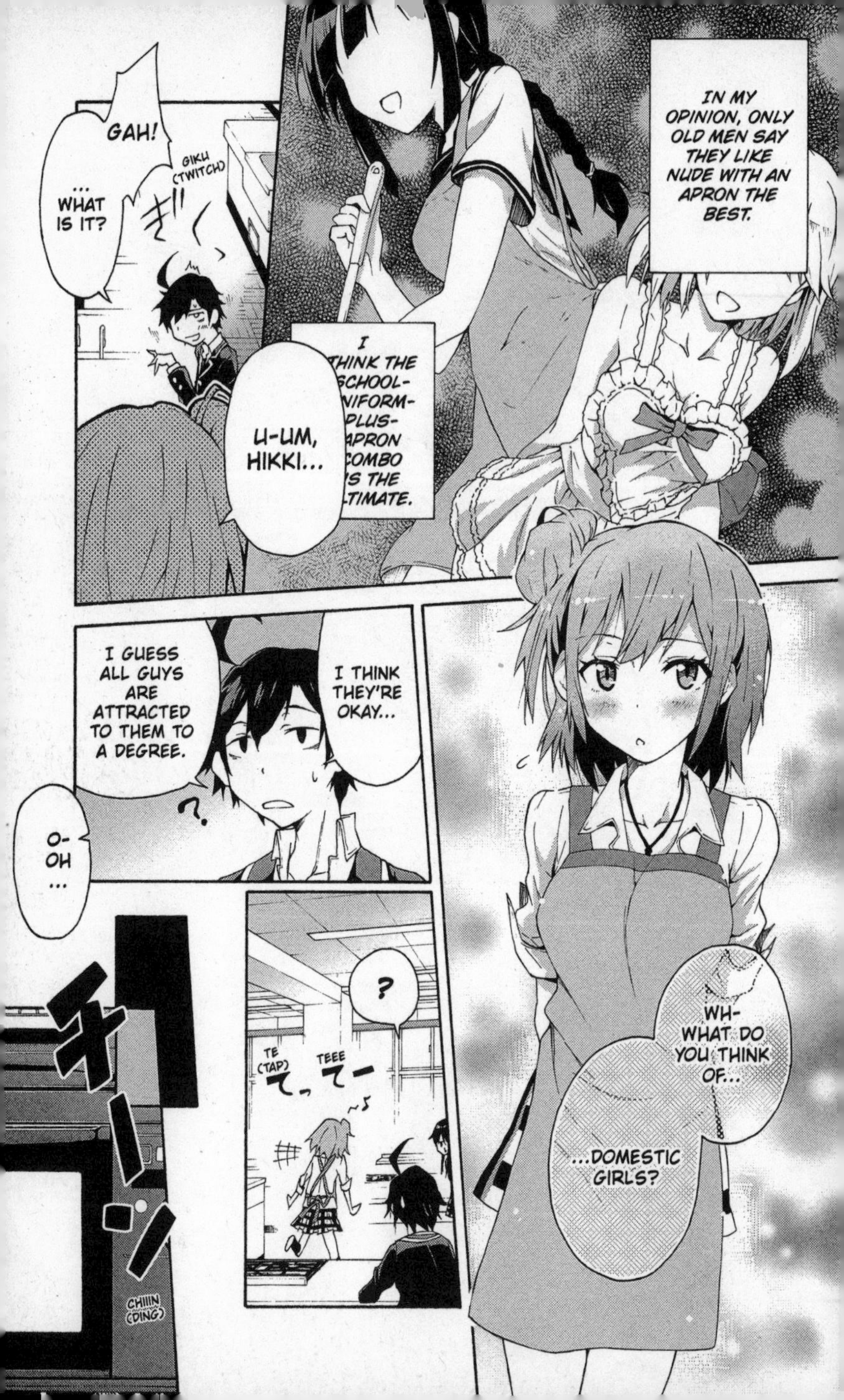
IN MY OPINION, ONLY OLD MEN SAY THEY LIKE NUDE WITH AN APRON THE BEST.
I THINK THE SCHOOL-UNIFORM-PLUS-APRON COMBO IS THE ULTIMATE.
U-UM, HIKKI...
GAH!
GIKU (TWITCH)
... WHAT IS IT?
WH- WHAT DO YOU THINK OF...
...DOMESTIC GIRLS?
I THINK THEY'RE OKAY...
I GUESS ALL GUYS ARE ATTRACTED TO THEM TO A DEGREE.
?
O-OH ...
?
TE (TAP)
TEEE
CHIIIN (DING)

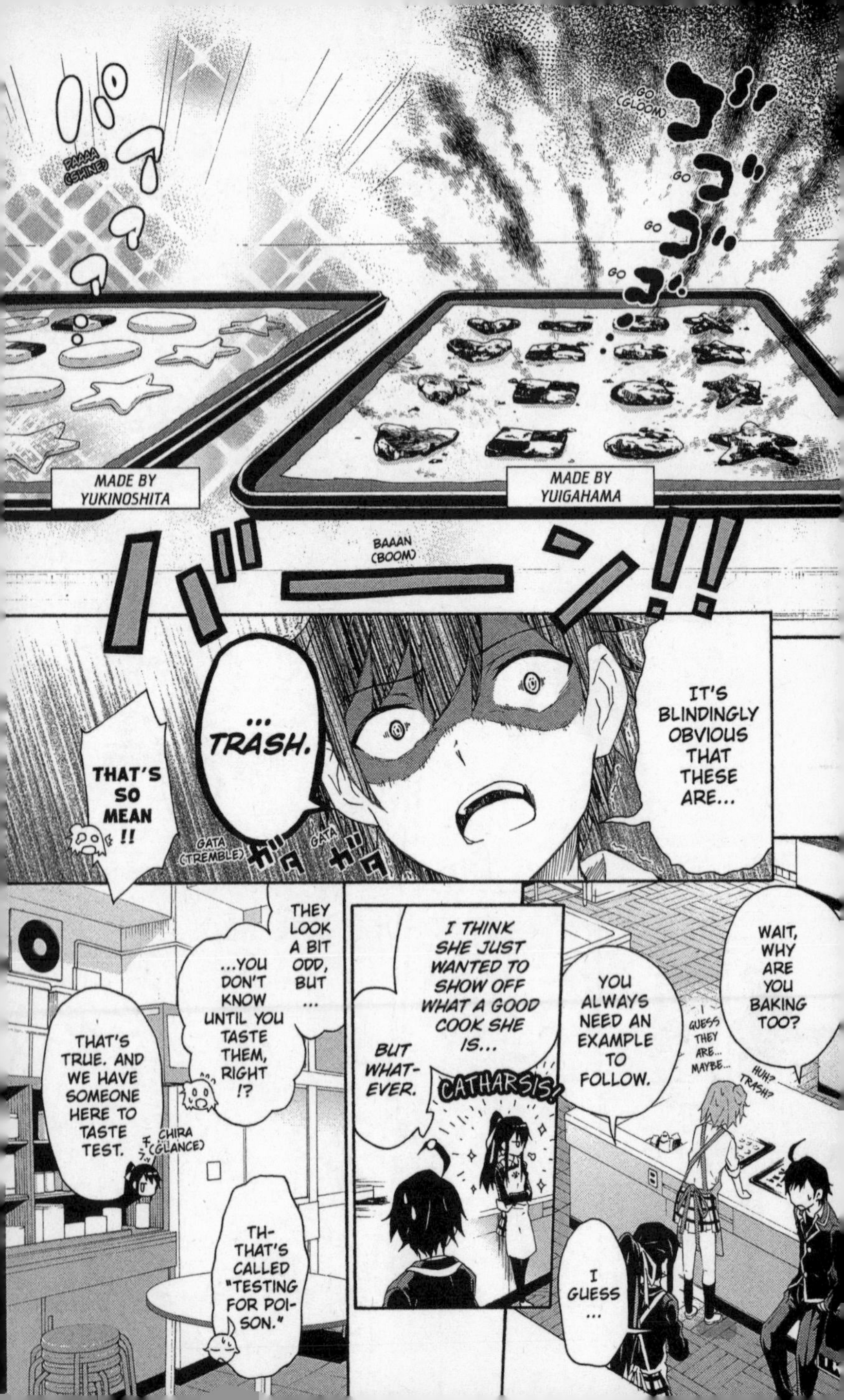
GO (GLOOM)
GO
GO
GO
MADE BY YUIGAHAMA
PAAAA (SHINE)
MADE BY YUKINOSHITA
BAAAN (BOOM)
IT'S BLINDINGLY OBVIOUS THAT THESE ARE...
...TRASH.
GATA GATA (TREMBLE)
THAT'S SO MEAN!!
WAIT, WHY ARE YOU BAKING TOO?
HUH? TRASH?
I GUESS THEY ARE... MAYBE...
YOU ALWAYS NEED AN EXAMPLE TO FOLLOW.
I GUESS...
I THINK SHE JUST WANTED TO SHOW OFF WHAT A GOOD COOK SHE IS...
BUT WHATEVER.
CATHARSIS!
THEY LOOK A BIT ODD, BUT...
...YOU DON'T KNOW UNTIL YOU TASTE THEM, RIGHT!?
THAT'S TRUE. AND WE HAVE SOMEONE HERE TO TASTE TEST.
CHIRA (GLANCE)
TH-THAT'S CALLED "TESTING FOR POISON."

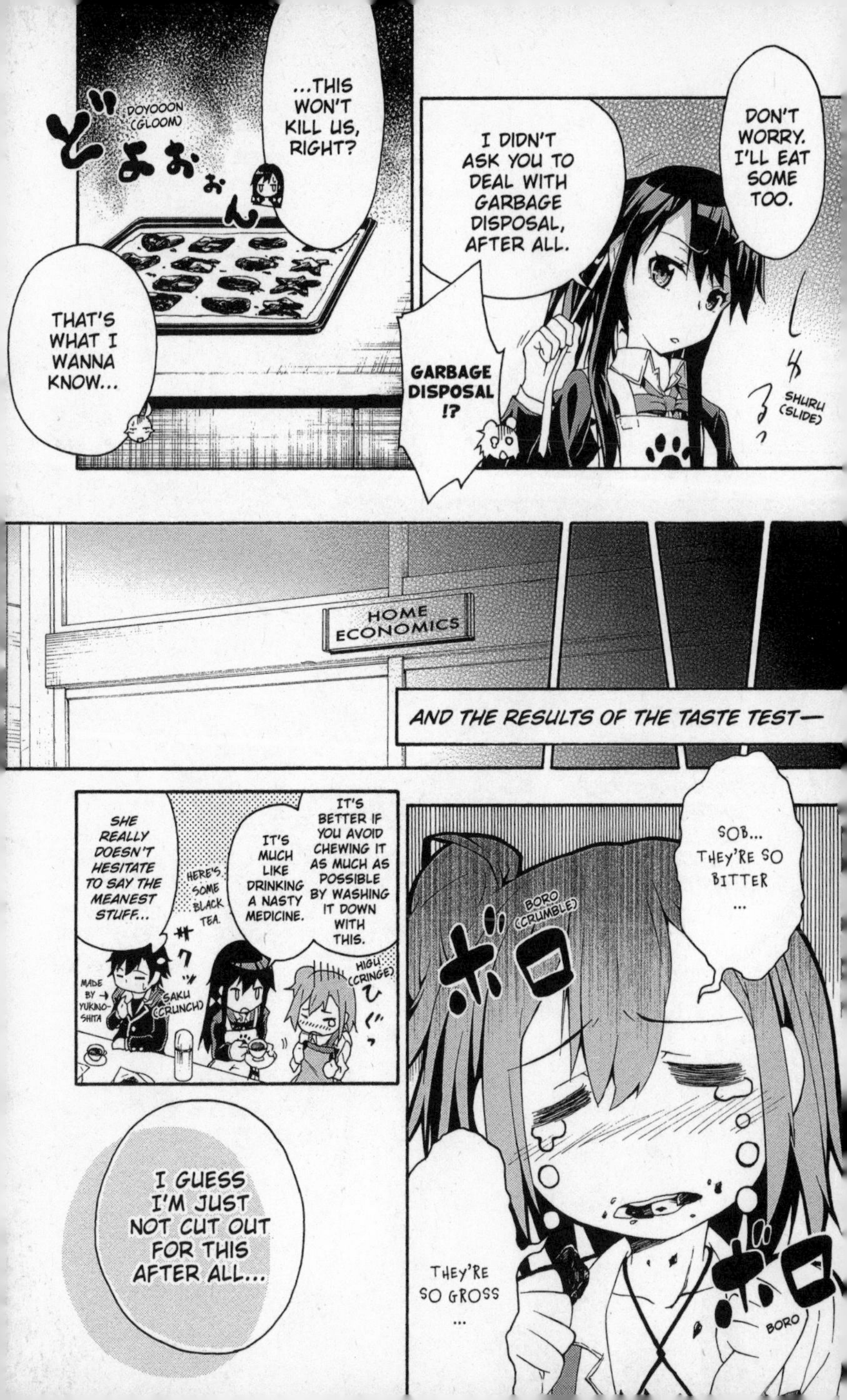
DON'T WORRY. I'LL EAT SOME TOO.
SHURU (SLIDE)
I DIDN'T ASK YOU TO DEAL WITH GARBAGE DISPOSAL, AFTER ALL.
GARBAGE DISPOSAL !?
...THIS WON'T KILL US, RIGHT?
DOYOOON (GLOOM)
THAT'S WHAT I WANNA KNOW...
HOME ECONOMICS
AND THE RESULTS OF THE TASTE TEST—
SOB... THEY'RE SO BITTER ...
BORO (CRUMBLE)
THEY'RE SO GROSS ...
BORO
IT'S BETTER IF YOU AVOID CHEWING IT AS MUCH AS POSSIBLE BY WASHING IT DOWN WITH THIS.
IT'S MUCH LIKE DRINKING A NASTY MEDICINE.
HERE'S SOME BLACK TEA.
SHE REALLY DOESN'T HESITATE TO SAY THE MEANEST STUFF...
HIGU (CRINGE)
SAKU (CRUNCH)
MADE BY → YUKINOSHITA
I GUESS I'M JUST NOT CUT OUT FOR THIS AFTER ALL...

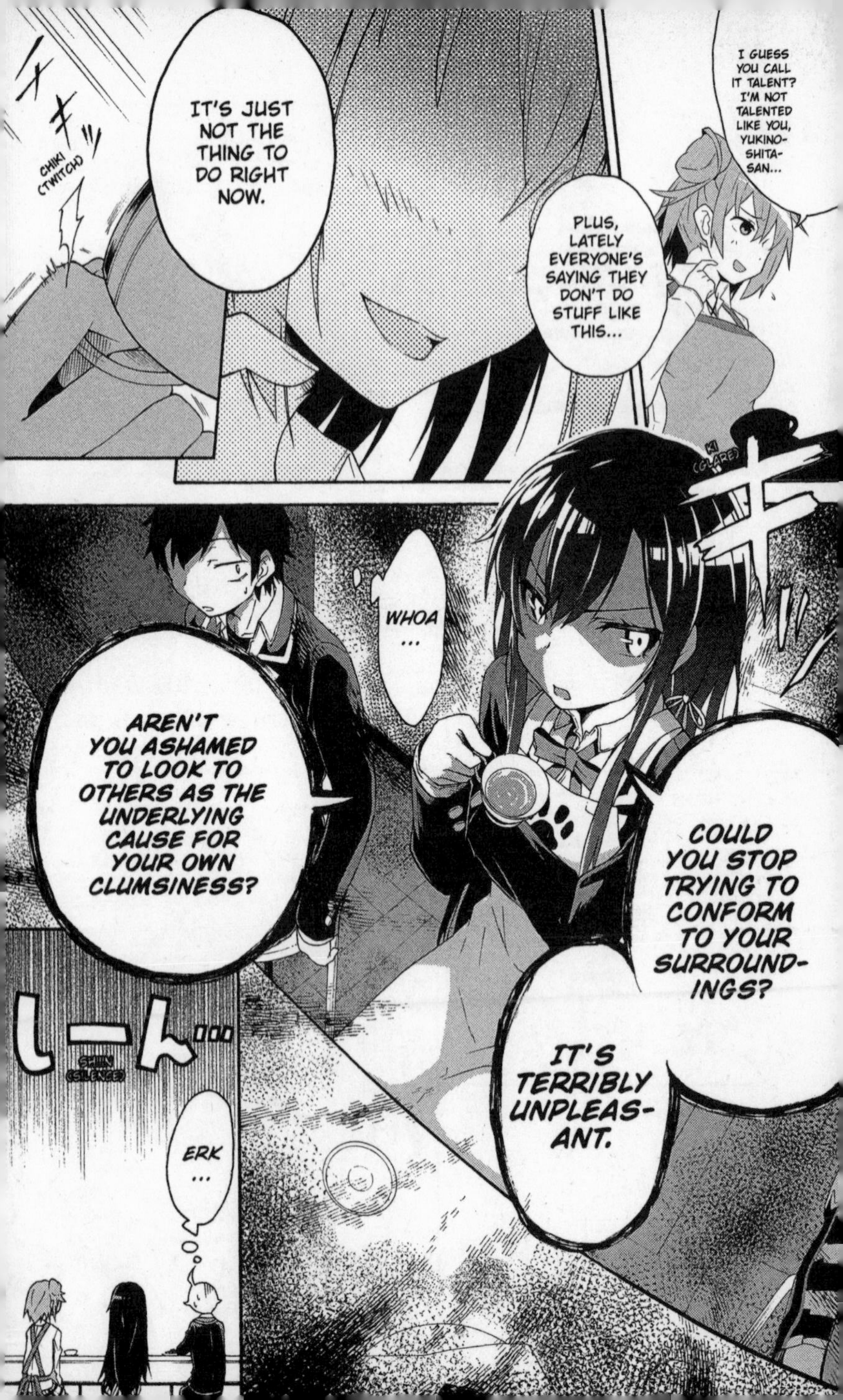
I GUESS YOU CALL IT TALENT? I'M NOT TALENTED LIKE YOU, YUKINO-SHITA-SAN...
PLUS, LATELY EVERYONE'S SAYING THEY DON'T DO STUFF LIKE THIS...
IT'S JUST NOT THE THING TO DO RIGHT NOW.
CHIKI (TWITCH)
KI (GLARE)
COULD YOU STOP TRYING TO CONFORM TO YOUR SURROUND-INGS?
IT'S TERRIBLY UNPLEAS-ANT.
AREN'T YOU ASHAMED TO LOOK TO OTHERS AS THE UNDERLYING CAUSE FOR YOUR OWN CLUMSINESS?
WHOA...
SHIIN (SILENCE)
ERK...

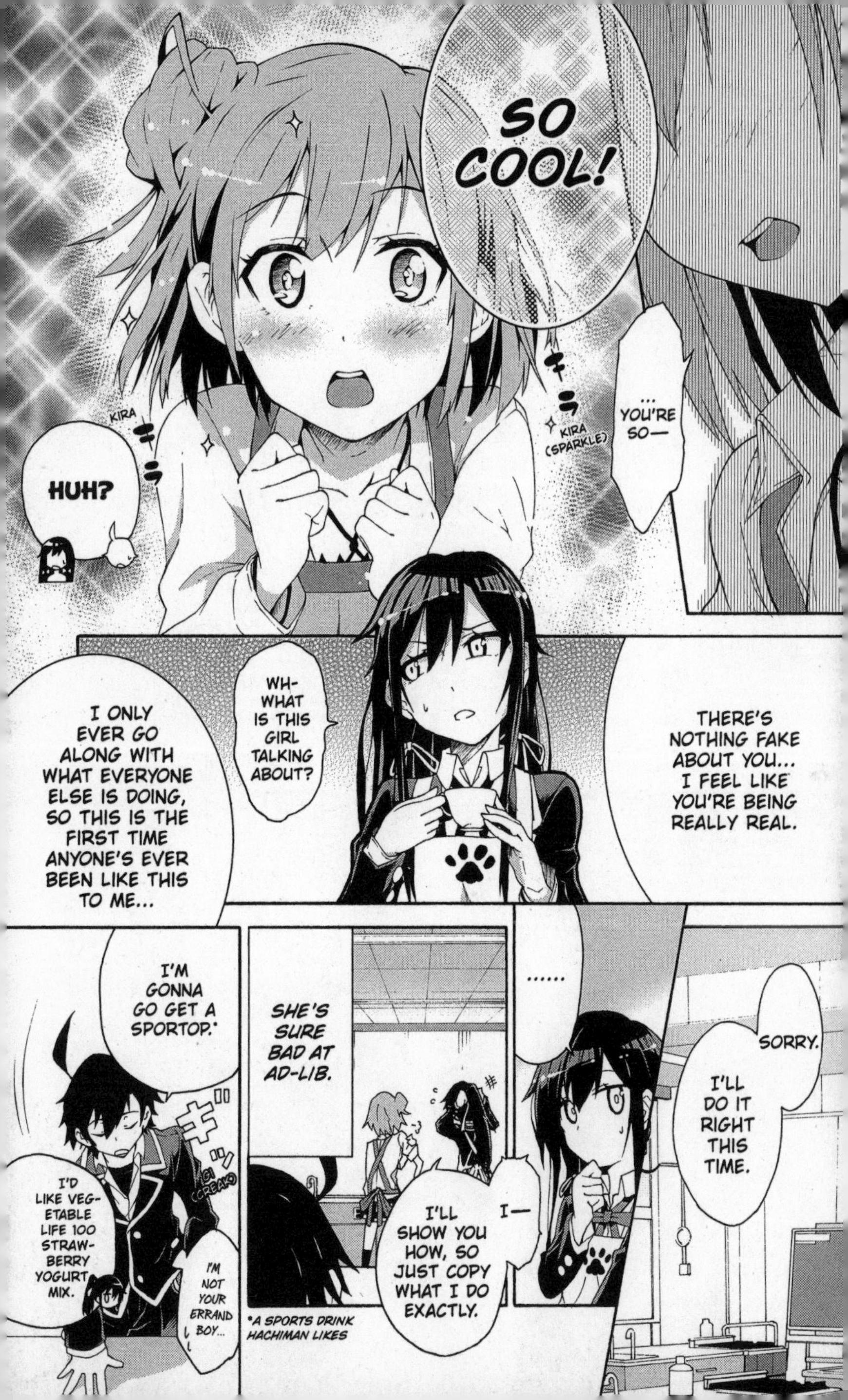
... YOU'RE SO—
SO COOL!
KIRA KIRA (SPARKLE)
HUH?
THERE'S NOTHING FAKE ABOUT YOU... I FEEL LIKE YOU'RE BEING REALLY REAL.
WH-WHAT IS THIS GIRL TALKING ABOUT?
I ONLY EVER GO ALONG WITH WHAT EVERYONE ELSE IS DOING, SO THIS IS THE FIRST TIME ANYONE'S EVER BEEN LIKE THIS TO ME...
SORRY.
I'LL DO IT RIGHT THIS TIME.
......
SHE'S SURE BAD AT AD-LIB.
I—
I'LL SHOW YOU HOW, SO JUST COPY WHAT I DO EXACTLY.
I'M GONNA GO GET A SPORTOP.*
GI (CREAK)
I'D LIKE VEG-ETABLE LIFE 100 STRAW-BERRY YOGURT MIX.
I'M NOT YOUR ERRAND BOY...
*A SPORTS DRINK HACHIMAN LIKES

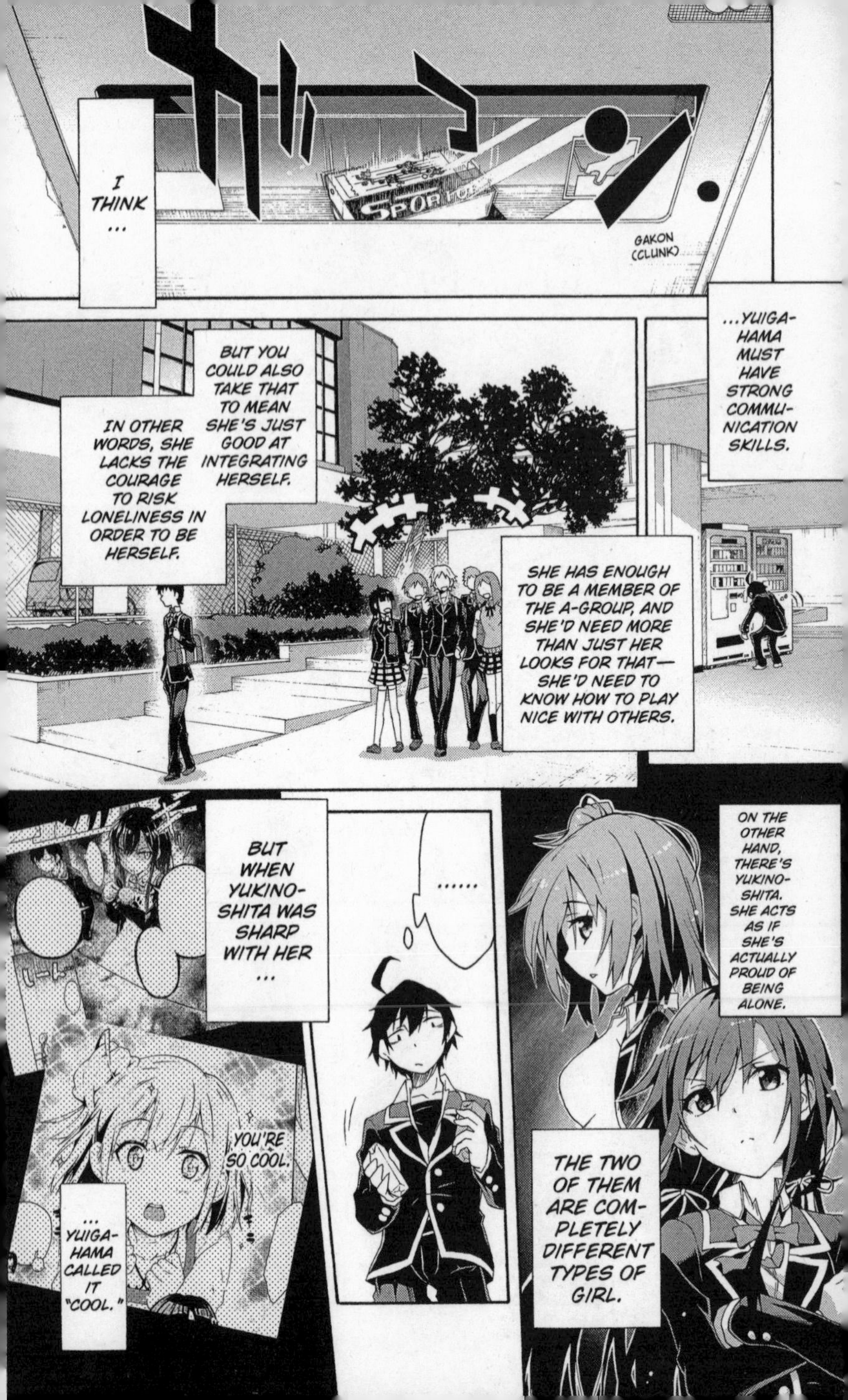
I THINK ...
GAKON (CLUNK)
...YUIGAHAMA MUST HAVE STRONG COMMUNICATION SKILLS.
BUT YOU COULD ALSO TAKE THAT TO MEAN SHE'S JUST GOOD AT INTEGRATING HERSELF.
SHE HAS ENOUGH TO BE A MEMBER OF THE A-GROUP, AND SHE'D NEED MORE THAN JUST HER LOOKS FOR THAT—SHE'D NEED TO KNOW HOW TO PLAY NICE WITH OTHERS.
IN OTHER WORDS, SHE LACKS THE COURAGE TO RISK LONELINESS IN ORDER TO BE HERSELF.
ON THE OTHER HAND, THERE'S YUKINOSHITA. SHE ACTS AS IF SHE'S ACTUALLY PROUD OF BEING ALONE.
THE TWO OF THEM ARE COMPLETELY DIFFERENT TYPES OF GIRL.
......
BUT WHEN YUKINOSHITA WAS SHARP WITH HER ...
YOU'RE SO COOL.
... YUIGAHAMA CALLED IT "COOL."

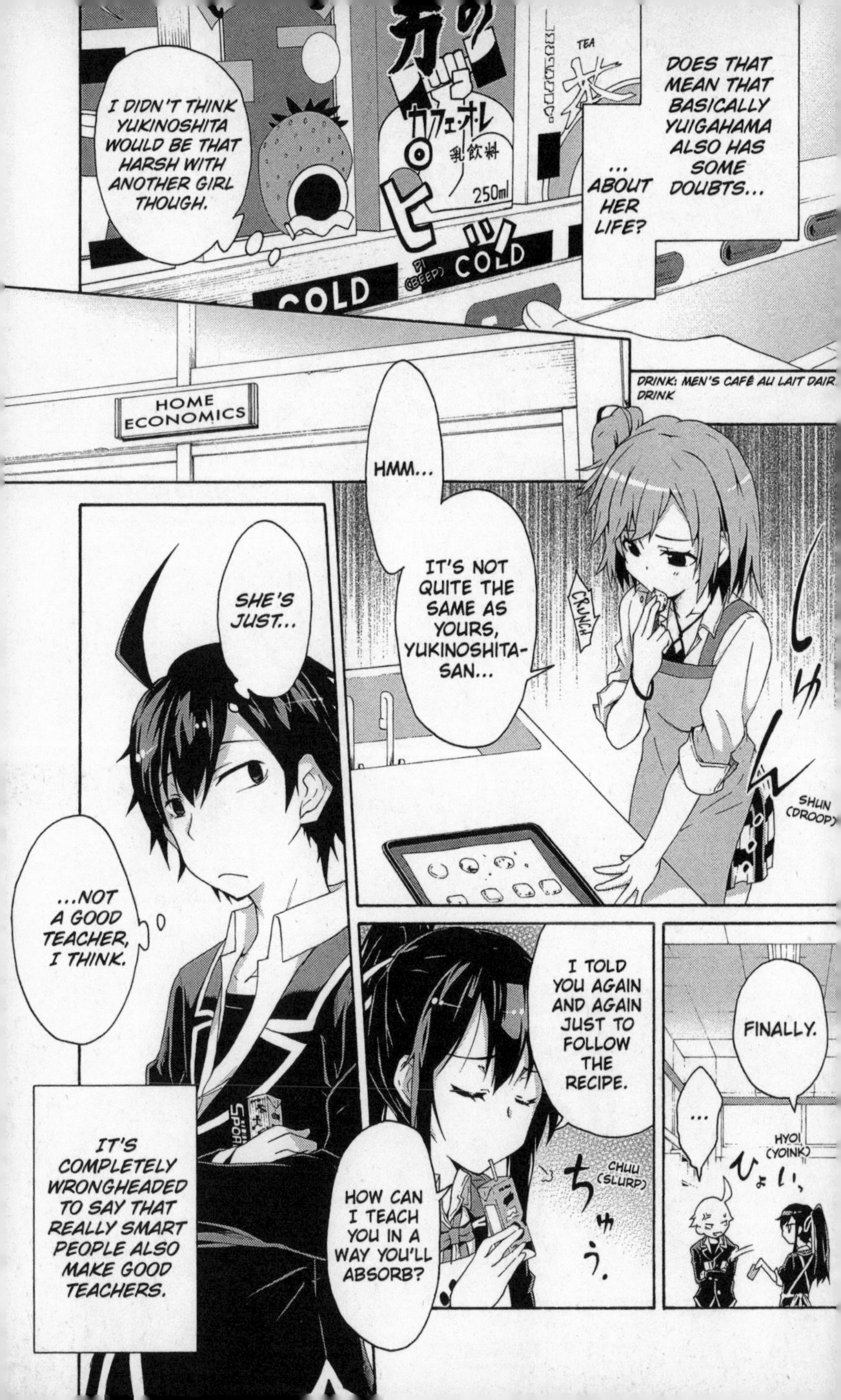
DOES THAT MEAN THAT BASICALLY YUIGAHAMA ALSO HAS SOME DOUBTS...
...ABOUT HER LIFE?
TEA
カフェ・オ・レ
乳飲料
250ml
PI (BEEP)
COLD
COLD
I DIDN'T THINK YUKINOSHITA WOULD BE THAT HARSH WITH ANOTHER GIRL THOUGH.
DRINK: MEN'S CAFÉ AU LAIT DAIR DRINK
HOME ECONOMICS
HMM...
IT'S NOT QUITE THE SAME AS YOURS, YUKINOSHITA-SAN...
CRUNCH
SHUN (DROOP)
FINALLY.
...
HYOI (YOINK)
I TOLD YOU AGAIN AND AGAIN JUST TO FOLLOW THE RECIPE.
CHUU (SLURP)
HOW CAN I TEACH YOU IN A WAY YOU'LL ABSORB?
SHE'S JUST...
...NOT A GOOD TEACHER, I THINK.
IT'S COMPLETELY WRONGHEADED TO SAY THAT REALLY SMART PEOPLE ALSO MAKE GOOD TEACHERS.

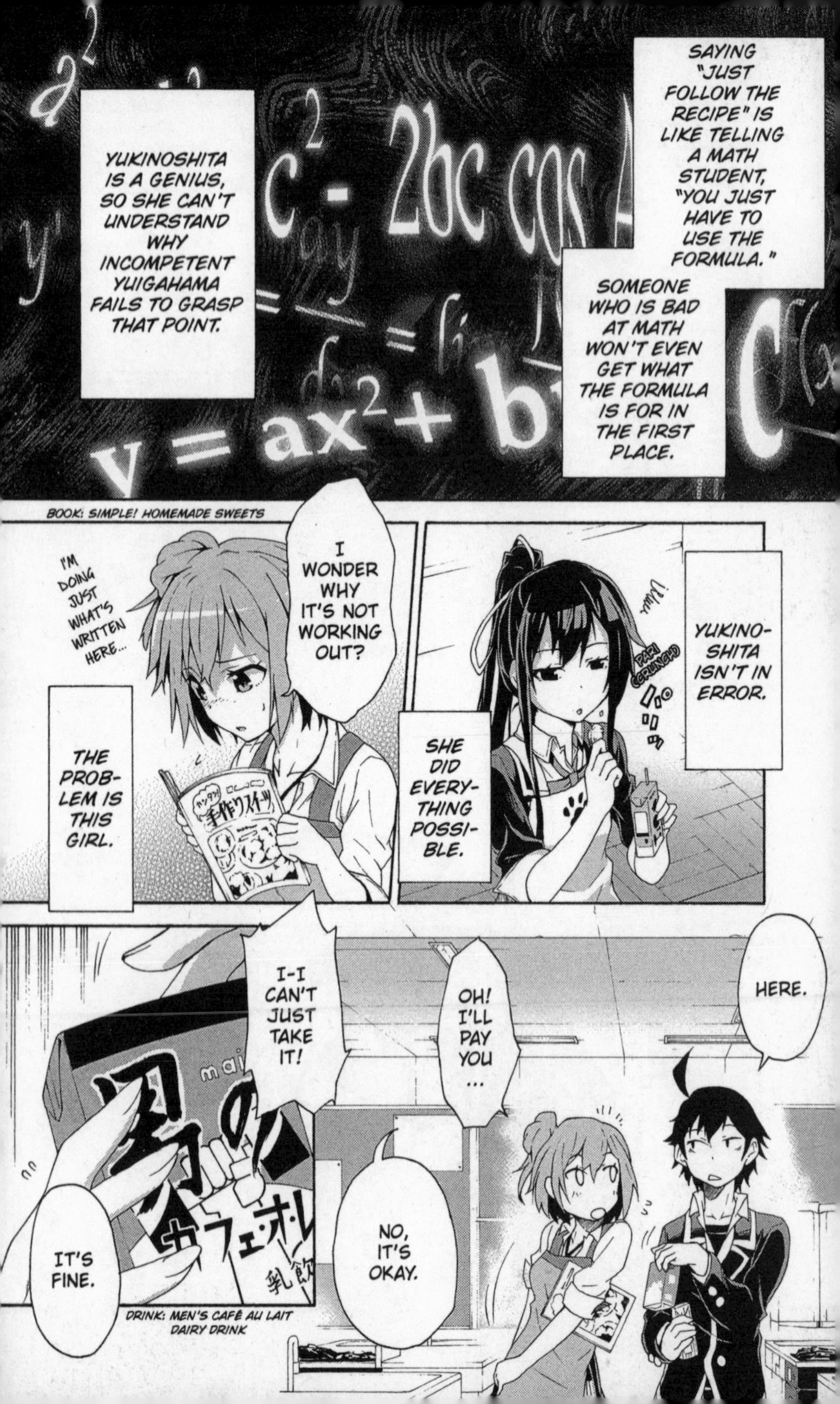
SAYING "JUST FOLLOW THE RECIPE" IS LIKE TELLING A MATH STUDENT, "YOU JUST HAVE TO USE THE FORMULA."
SOMEONE WHO IS BAD AT MATH WON'T EVEN GET WHAT THE FORMULA IS FOR IN THE FIRST PLACE.
YUKINOSHITA IS A GENIUS, SO SHE CAN'T UNDERSTAND WHY INCOMPETENT YUIGAHAMA FAILS TO GRASP THAT POINT.
YUKINO-SHITA ISN'T IN ERROR.
PARI (CRUNCH)
SHE DID EVERY-THING POSSI-BLE.
I WONDER WHY IT'S NOT WORKING OUT?
I'M DOING JUST WHAT'S WRITTEN HERE...
THE PROB-LEM IS THIS GIRL.
BOOK: SIMPLE! HOMEMADE SWEETS
HERE.
OH! I'LL PAY YOU...
I-I CAN'T JUST TAKE IT!
NO, IT'S OKAY.
IT'S FINE.
DRINK: MEN'S CAFÉ AU LAIT DAIRY DRINK

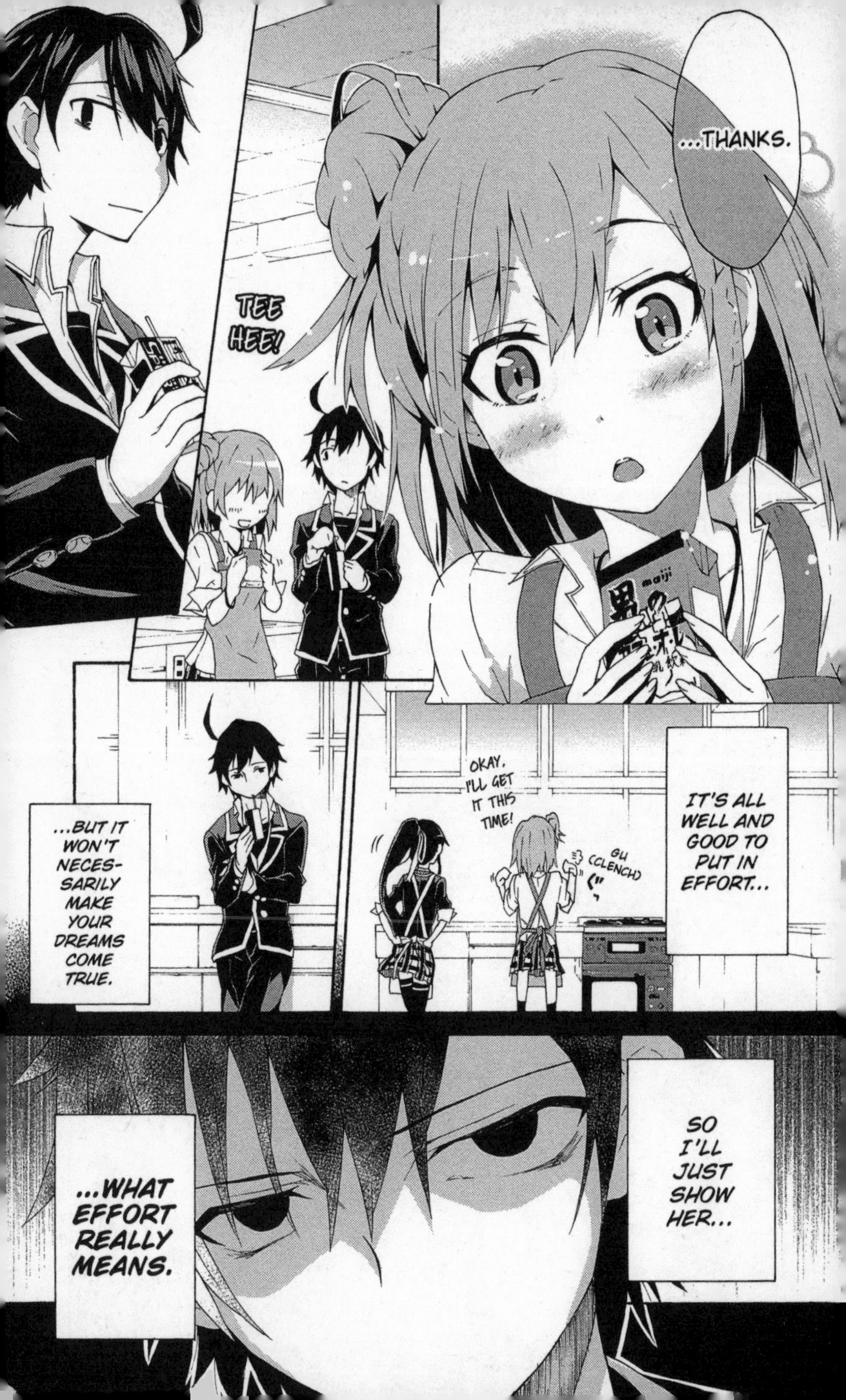
...THANKS.
TEE HEE!
IT'S ALL WELL AND GOOD TO PUT IN EFFORT...
OKAY, I'LL GET IT THIS TIME!
GU (CLENCH)
...BUT IT WON'T NECES-SARILY MAKE YOUR DREAMS COME TRUE.
SO I'LL JUST SHOW HER...
...WHAT EFFORT REALLY MEANS.

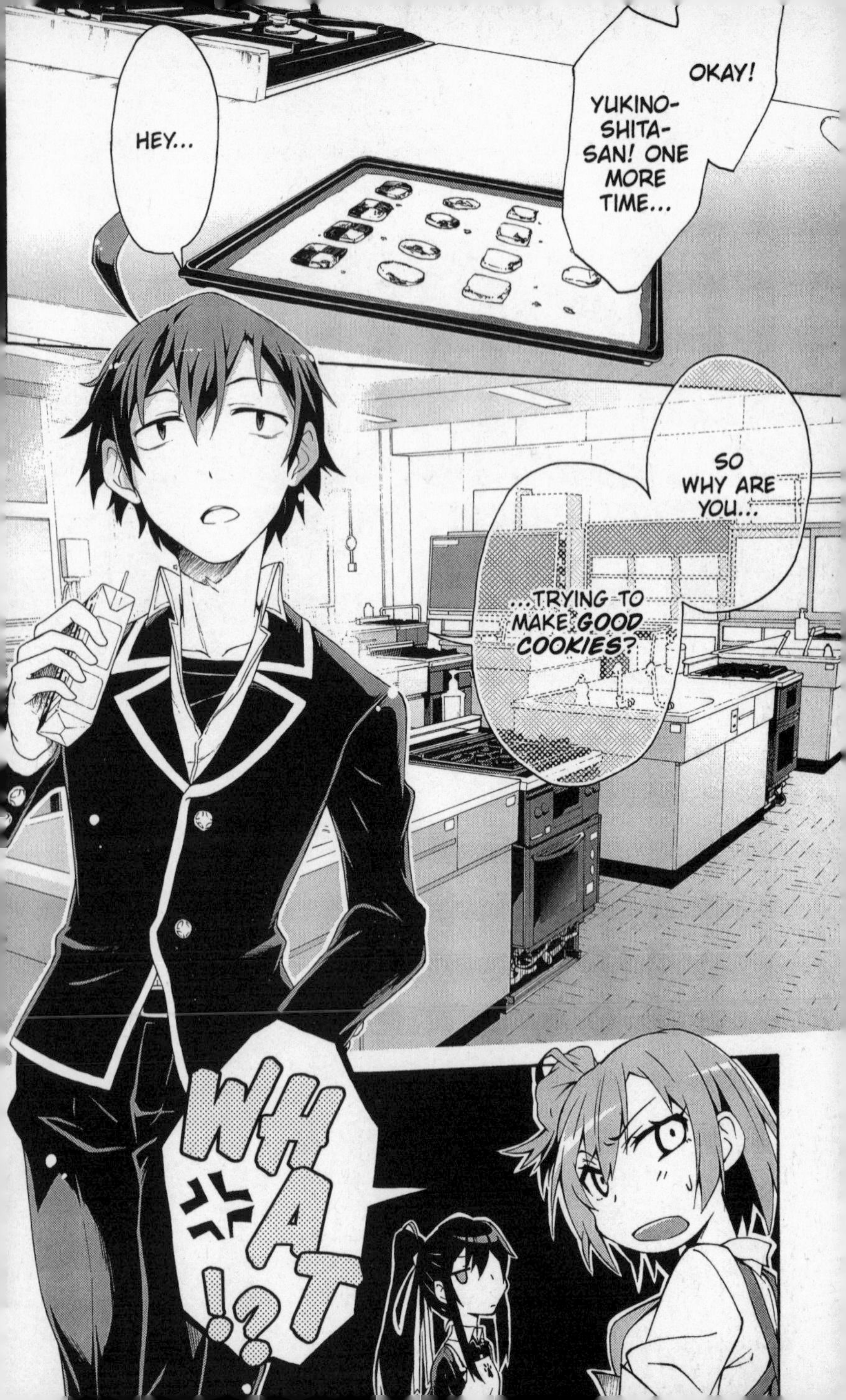

OKAY!
YUKINO-SHITA-SAN! ONE MORE TIME...
HEY...
SO WHY ARE YOU...
...TRYING TO MAKE GOOD COOKIES?
WHAT!?

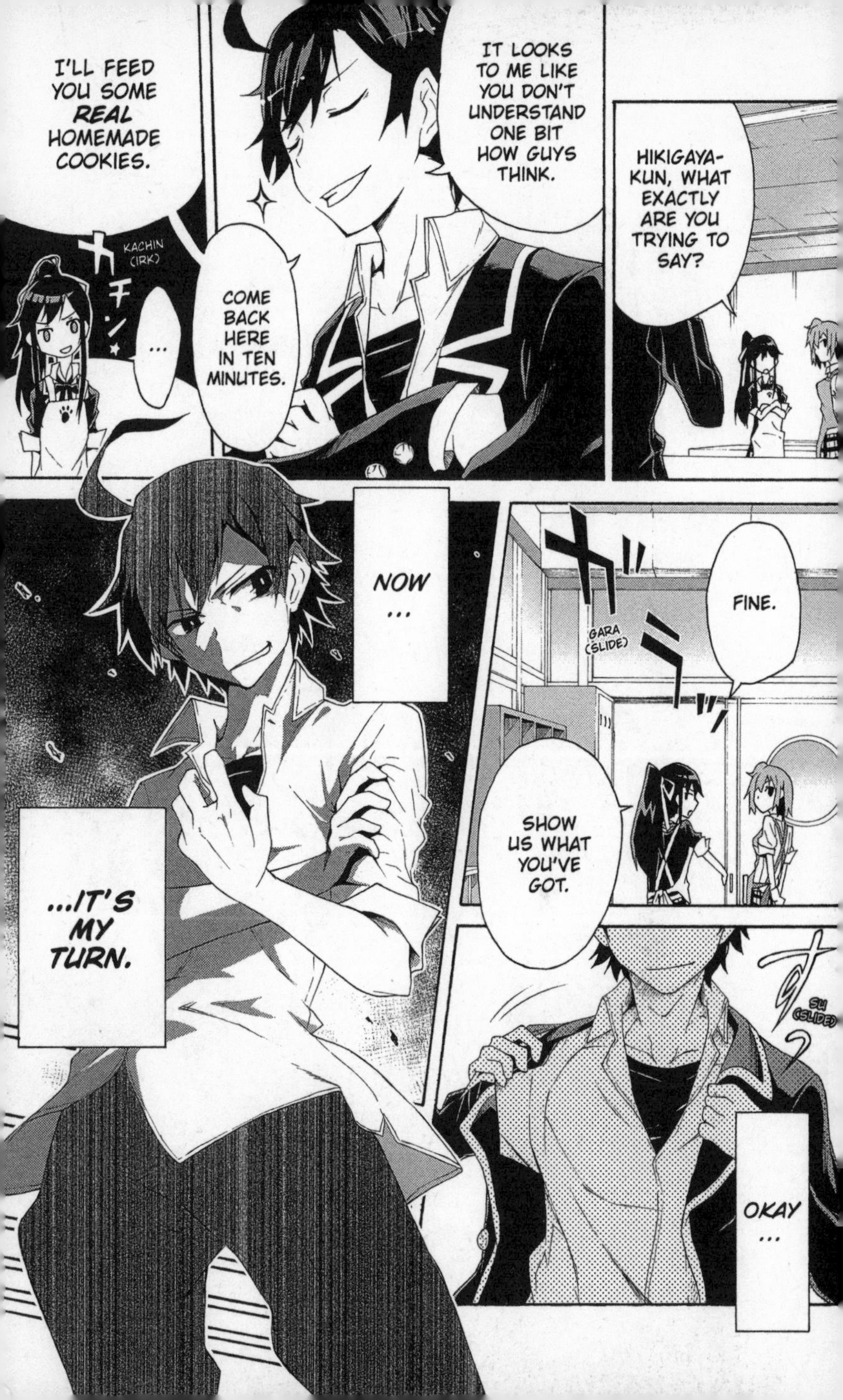
HIKIGAYA-KUN, WHAT EXACTLY ARE YOU TRYING TO SAY?
IT LOOKS TO ME LIKE YOU DON'T UNDERSTAND ONE BIT HOW GUYS THINK.
I'LL FEED YOU SOME REAL HOMEMADE COOKIES.
COME BACK HERE IN TEN MINUTES.
KACHIN (IRK)
...
FINE.
GARA (SLIDE)
SHOW US WHAT YOU'VE GOT.
SU (SLIDE)
OKAY ...
NOW ...
...IT'S MY TURN.

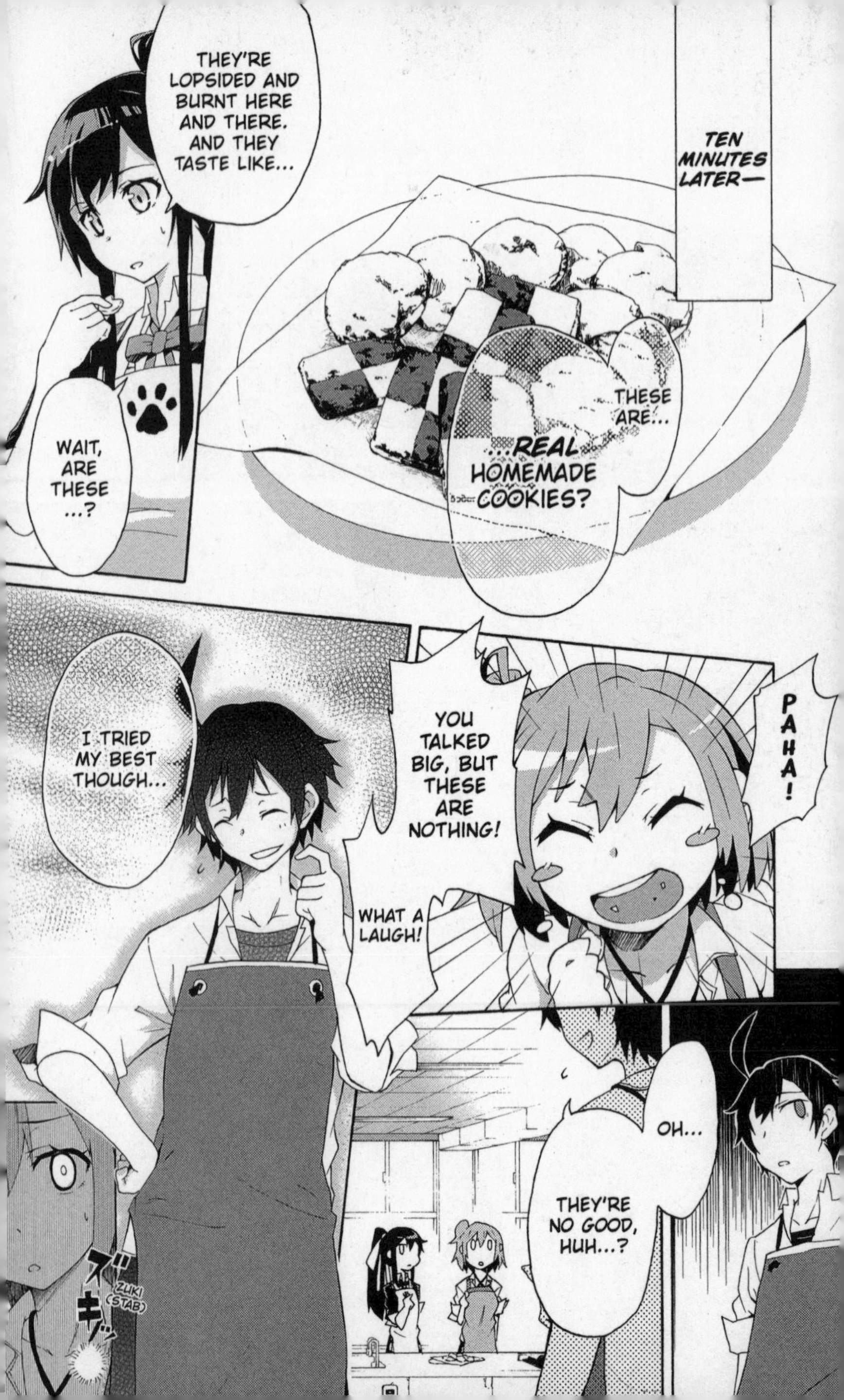
TEN MINUTES LATER—
THEY'RE LOPSIDED AND BURNT HERE AND THERE. AND THEY TASTE LIKE...
THESE ARE... ...REAL HOMEMADE COOKIES?
WAIT, ARE THESE ...?
PAHA!
YOU TALKED BIG, BUT THESE ARE NOTHING!
WHAT A LAUGH!
I TRIED MY BEST THOUGH...
OH...
THEY'RE NO GOOD, HUH...?
ZUKI (STAB)

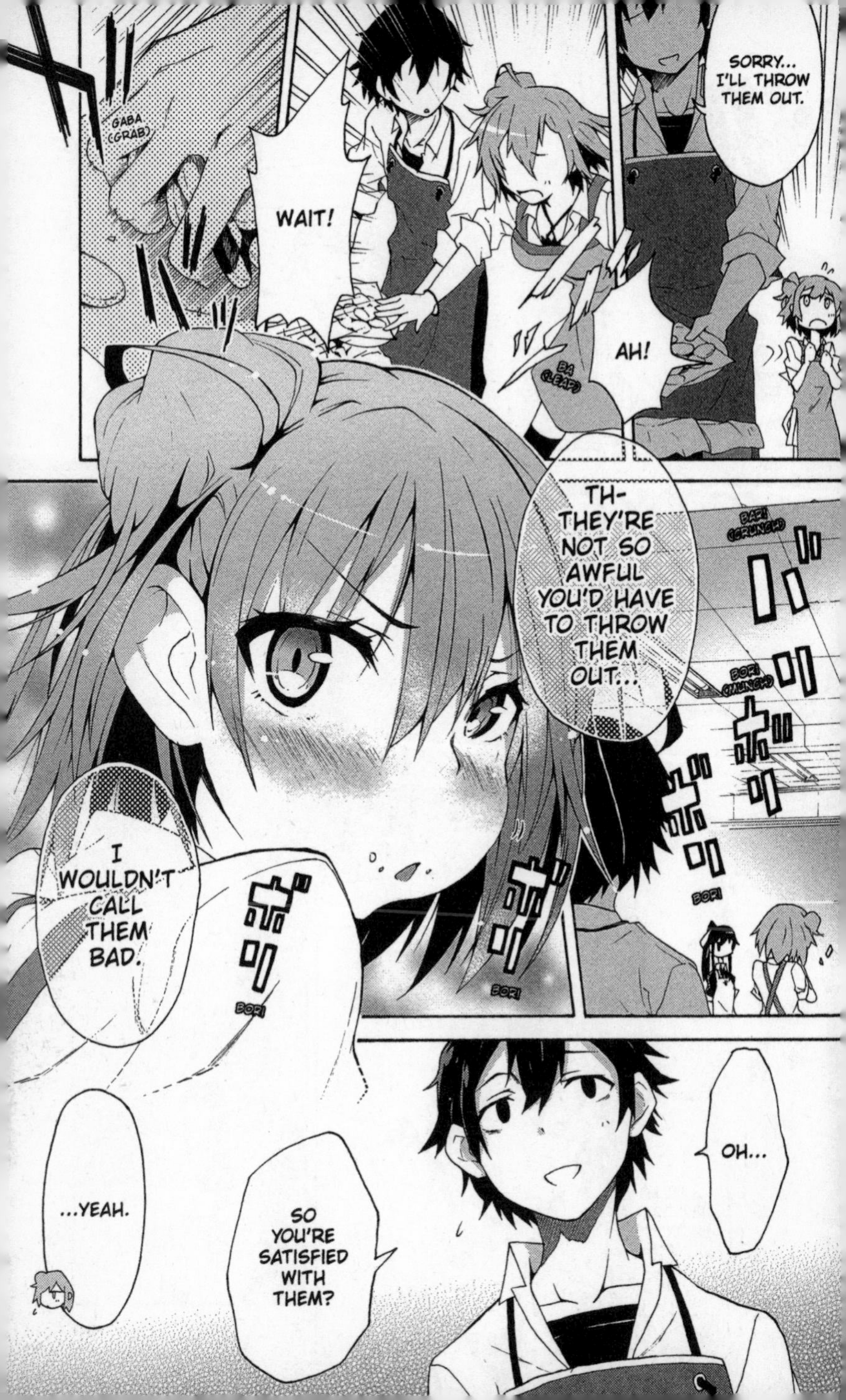
SORRY... I'LL THROW THEM OUT.
AH!
BA (LEAP)
WAIT!
GABA (GRAB)
BARI (CRUNCH)
BORI (MUNCH)
BORI
TH-THEY'RE NOT SO AWFUL YOU'D HAVE TO THROW THEM OUT...
BORI
I WOULDN'T CALL THEM BAD.
BORI
OH...
SO YOU'RE SATISFIED WITH THEM?
...YEAH.

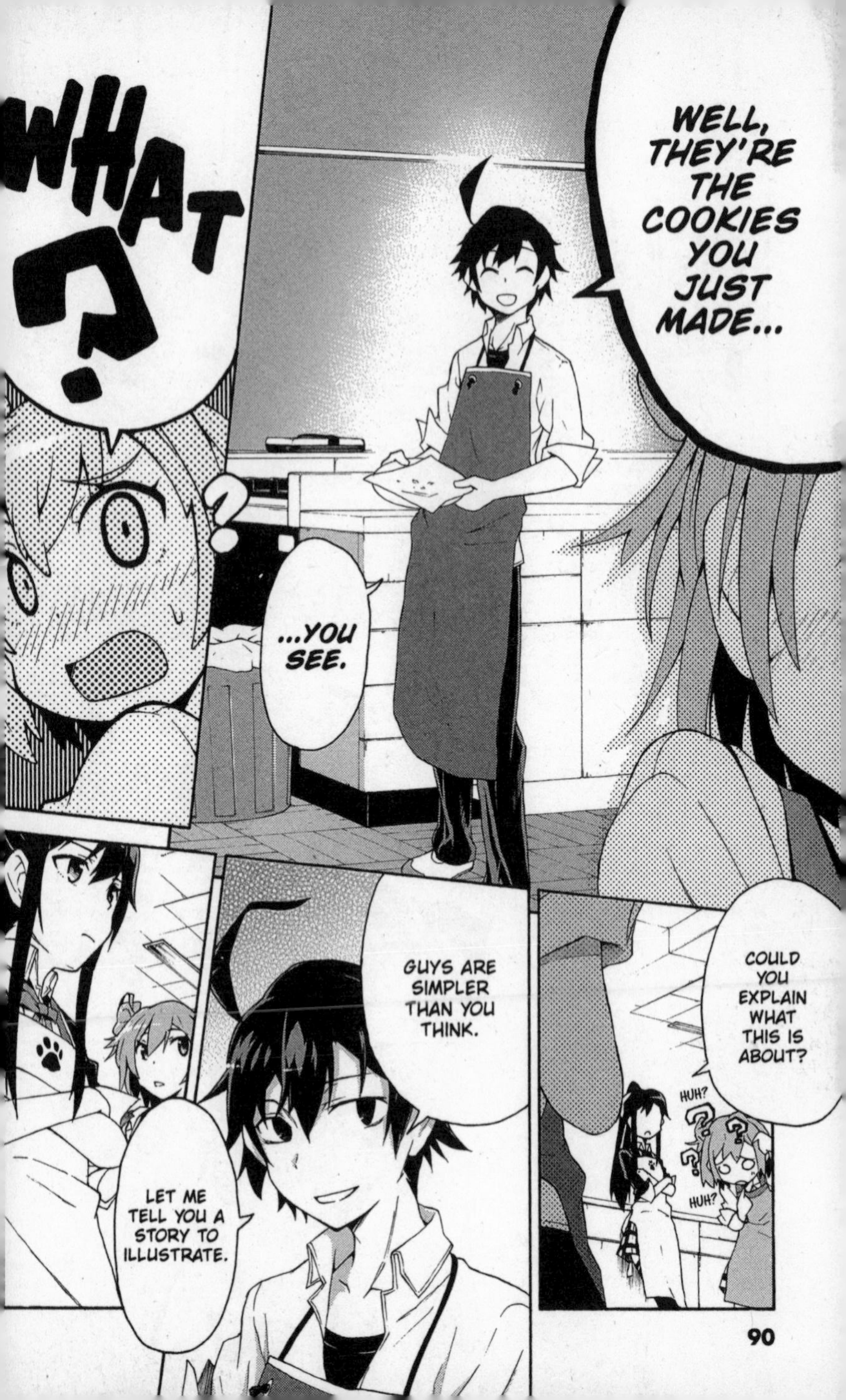
WELL, THEY'RE THE COOKIES YOU JUST MADE...
...YOU SEE.
WHAT??
COULD YOU EXPLAIN WHAT THIS IS ABOUT?
HUH?
HUH?
GUYS ARE SIMPLER THAN YOU THINK.
LET ME TELL YOU A STORY TO ILLUSTRATE.

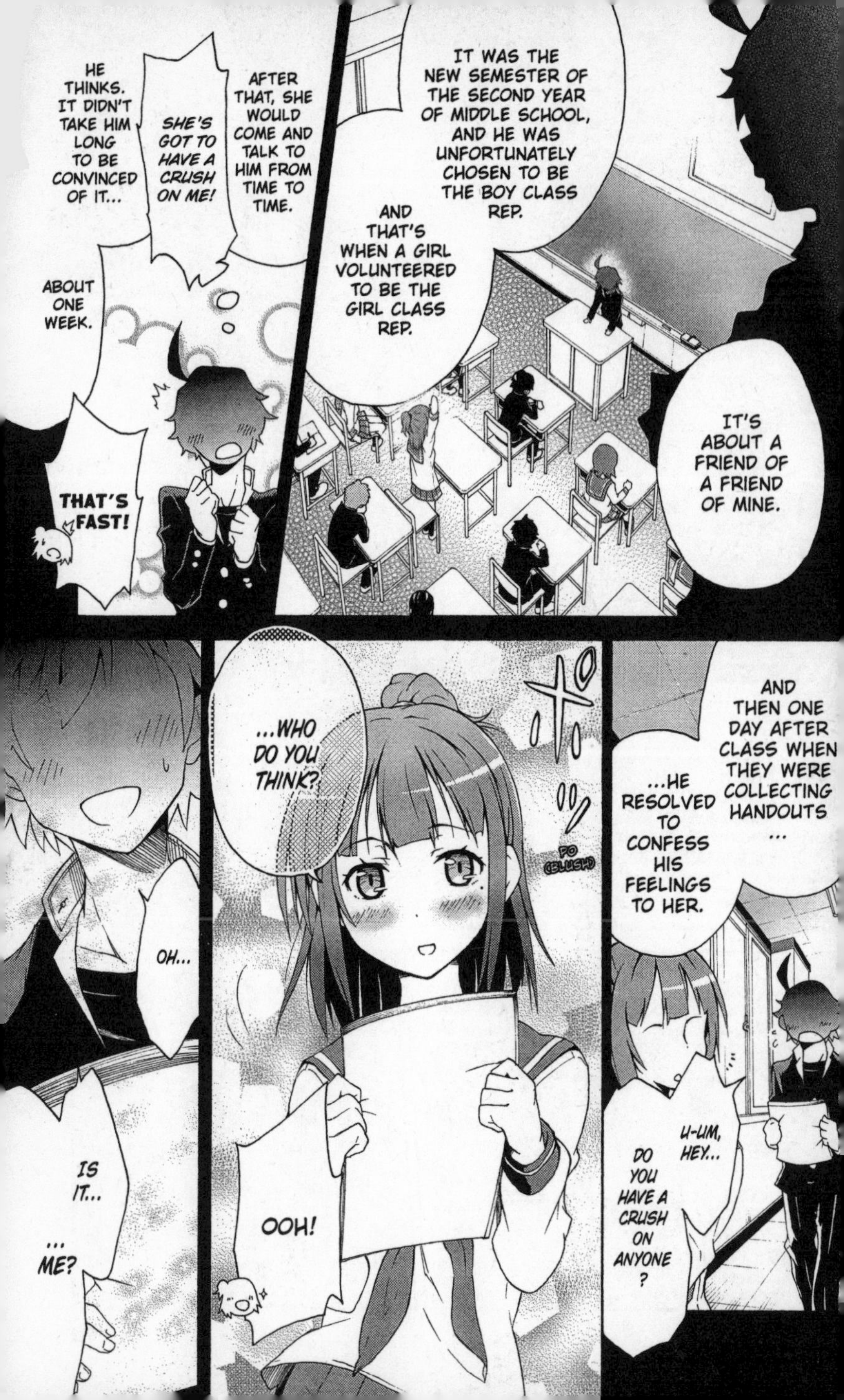
IT'S ABOUT A FRIEND OF A FRIEND OF MINE.
IT WAS THE NEW SEMESTER OF THE SECOND YEAR OF MIDDLE SCHOOL, AND HE WAS UNFORTUNATELY CHOSEN TO BE THE BOY CLASS REP.
AND THAT'S WHEN A GIRL VOLUNTEERED TO BE THE GIRL CLASS REP.
AFTER THAT, SHE WOULD COME AND TALK TO HIM FROM TIME TO TIME.
SHE'S GOT TO HAVE A CRUSH ON ME!
HE THINKS. IT DIDN'T TAKE HIM LONG TO BE CONVINCED OF IT...
ABOUT ONE WEEK.
THAT'S FAST!
AND THEN ONE DAY AFTER CLASS WHEN THEY WERE COLLECTING HANDOUTS...
...HE RESOLVED TO CONFESS HIS FEELINGS TO HER.
U-UM, HEY...
DO YOU HAVE A CRUSH ON ANYONE?
PO (BLUSH)
...WHO DO YOU THINK?
OOH!
OH...
IS IT...
... ME?

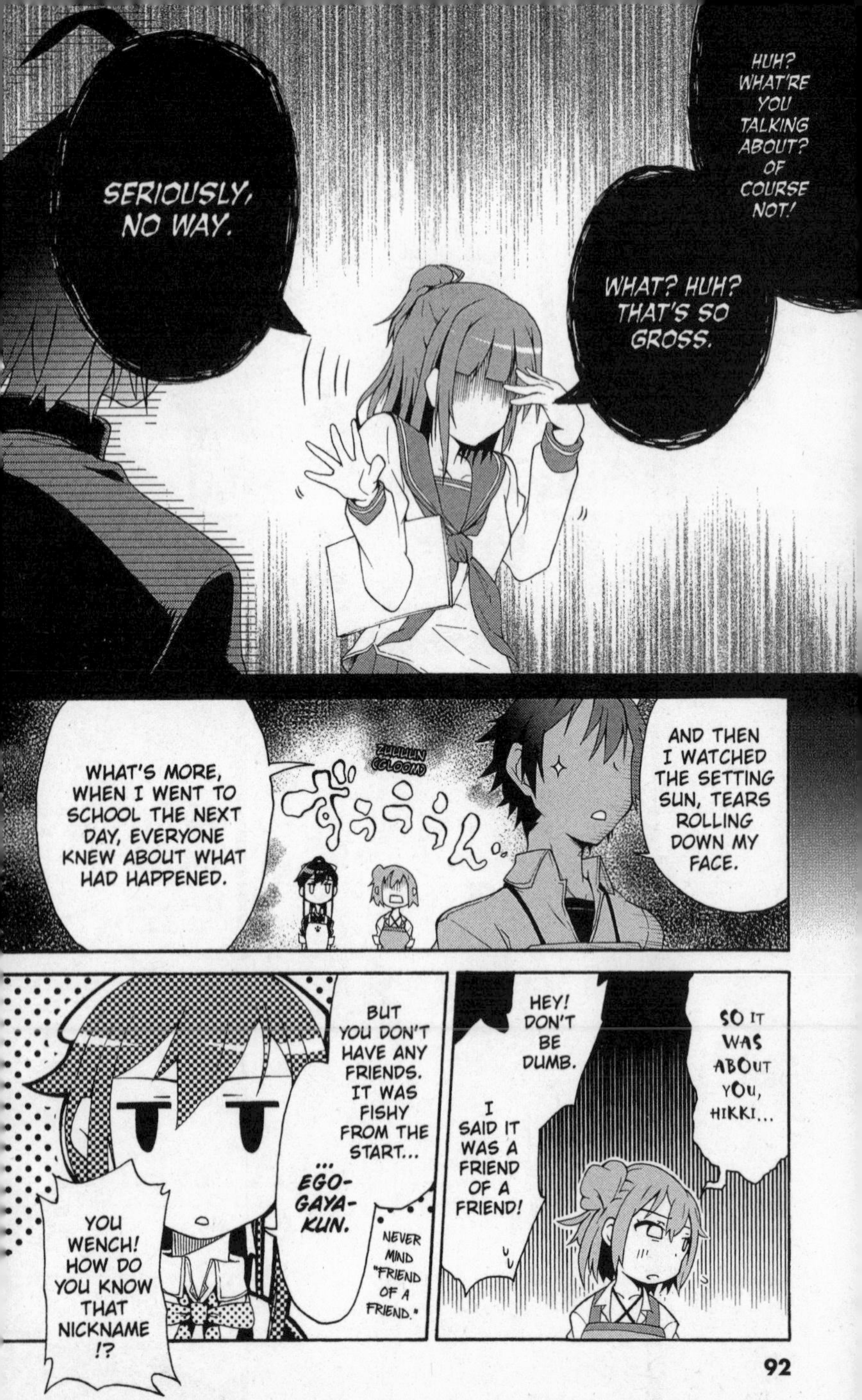
HUH? WHAT'RE YOU TALKING ABOUT? OF COURSE NOT!
WHAT? HUH? THAT'S SO GROSS.
SERIOUSLY, NO WAY.
AND THEN I WATCHED THE SETTING SUN, TEARS ROLLING DOWN MY FACE.
ZUUUUN (GLOOM)
ずううん
WHAT'S MORE, WHEN I WENT TO SCHOOL THE NEXT DAY, EVERYONE KNEW ABOUT WHAT HAD HAPPENED.
SO IT WAS ABOUT YOU, HIKKI...
HEY! DON'T BE DUMB.
I SAID IT WAS A FRIEND OF A FRIEND!
BUT YOU DON'T HAVE ANY FRIENDS. IT WAS FISHY FROM THE START...
...EGO-GAYA-KUN.
NEVER MIND "FRIEND OF A FRIEND."
YOU WENCH! HOW DO YOU KNOW THAT NICKNAME!?

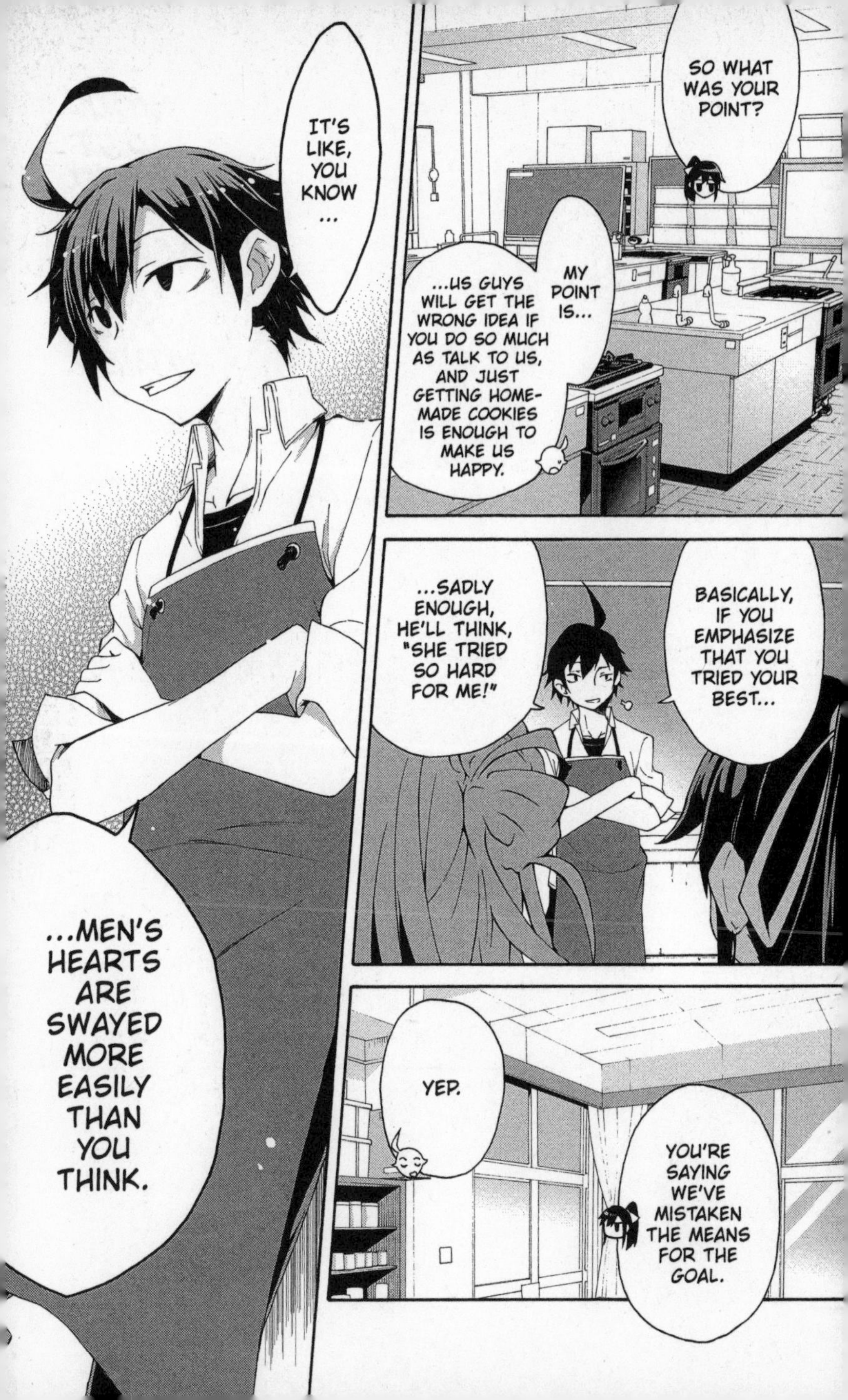
SO WHAT WAS YOUR POINT?
MY POINT IS...
...US GUYS WILL GET THE WRONG IDEA IF YOU DO SO MUCH AS TALK TO US, AND JUST GETTING HOME-MADE COOKIES IS ENOUGH TO MAKE US HAPPY.
BASICALLY, IF YOU EMPHASIZE THAT YOU TRIED YOUR BEST...
...SADLY ENOUGH, HE'LL THINK, "SHE TRIED SO HARD FOR ME!"
YOU'RE SAYING WE'VE MISTAKEN THE MEANS FOR THE GOAL.
YEP.
IT'S LIKE, YOU KNOW...
...MEN'S HEARTS ARE SWAYED MORE EASILY THAN YOU THINK.

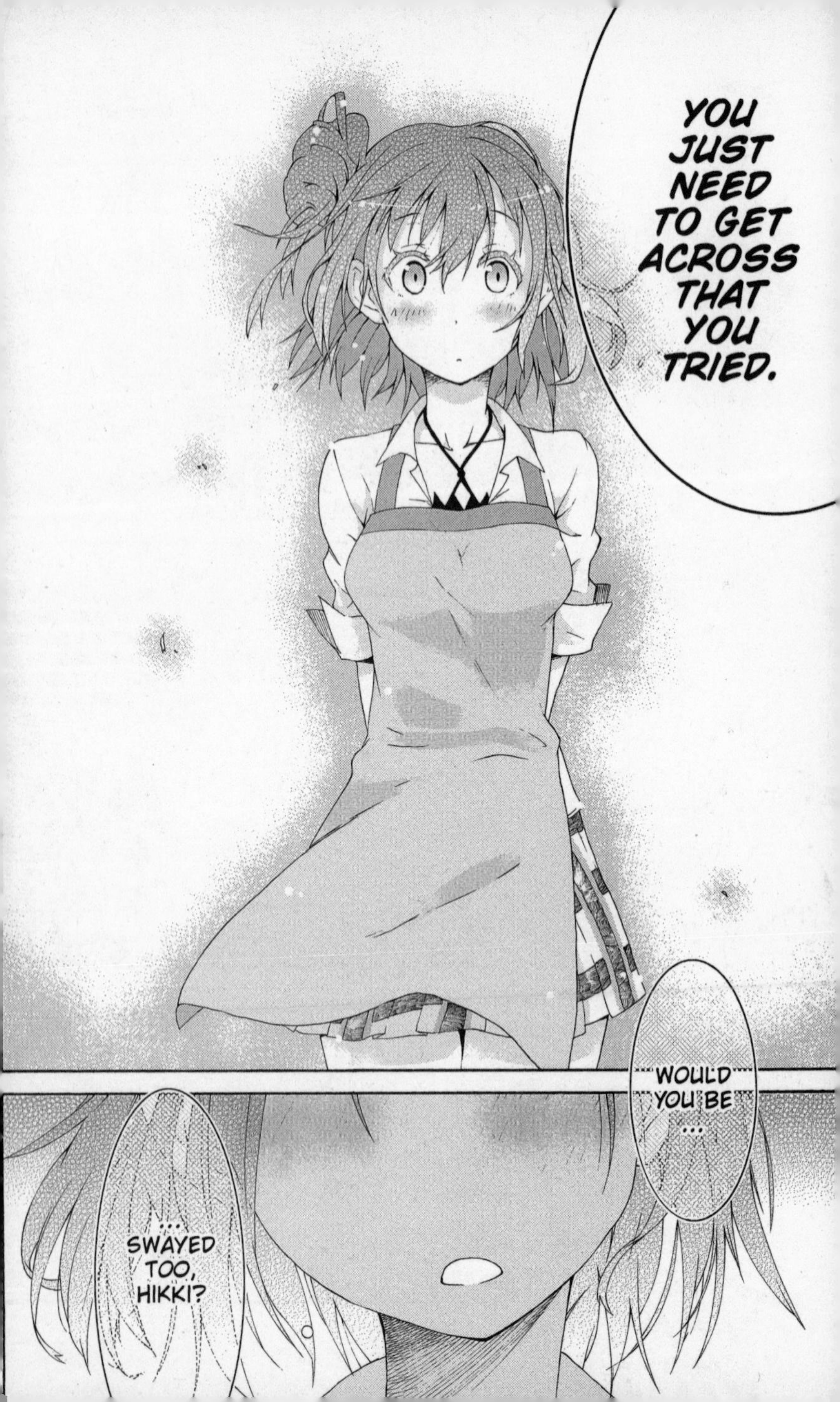
YOU JUST NEED TO GET ACROSS THAT YOU TRIED.
WOULD YOU BE ...
... SWAYED TOO, HIKKI?

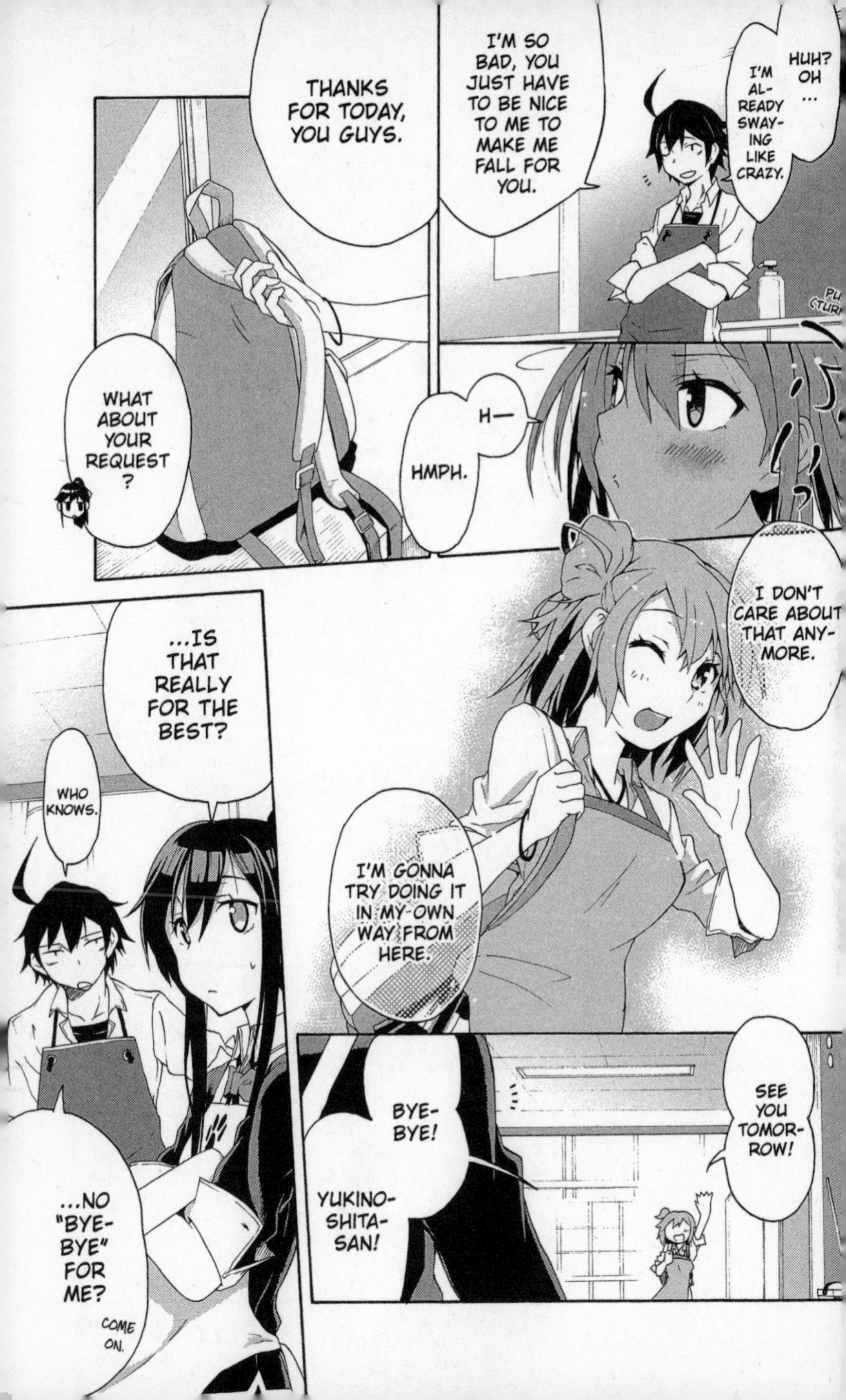
HUH? OH ...
I'M ALREADY SWAYING LIKE CRAZY.
I'M SO BAD, YOU JUST HAVE TO BE NICE TO ME TO MAKE ME FALL FOR YOU.
H—
HMPH.
THANKS FOR TODAY, YOU GUYS.
WHAT ABOUT YOUR REQUEST?
I DON'T CARE ABOUT THAT ANYMORE.
I'M GONNA TRY DOING IT IN MY OWN WAY FROM HERE.
...IS THAT REALLY FOR THE BEST?
WHO KNOWS.
SEE YOU TOMORROW!
BYE-BYE!
YUKINOSHITA-SAN!
...NO "BYE-BYE" FOR ME?
COME ON.

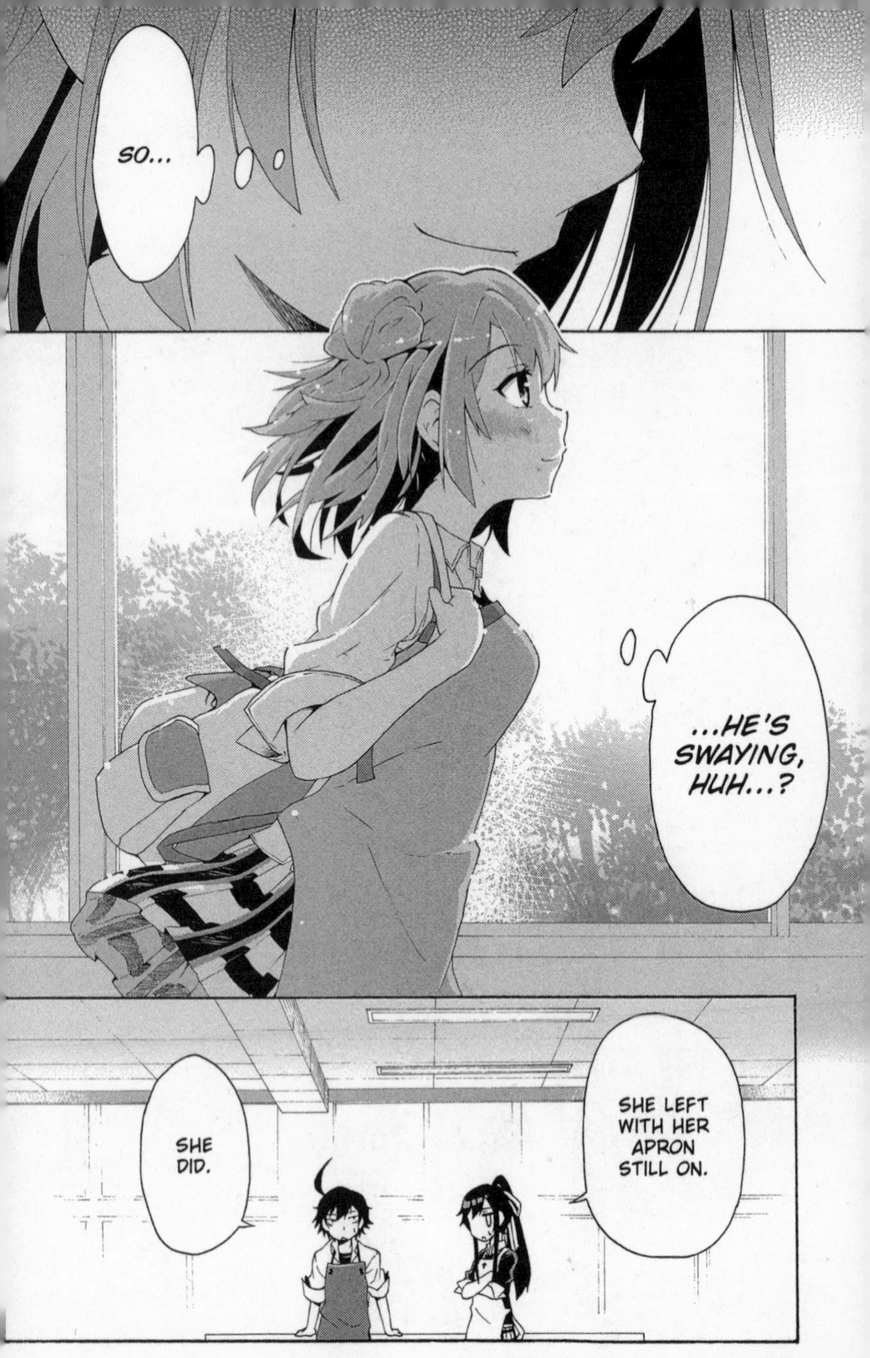
SO...
...HE'S SWAYING, HUH...?
SHE LEFT WITH HER APRON STILL ON.
SHE DID.

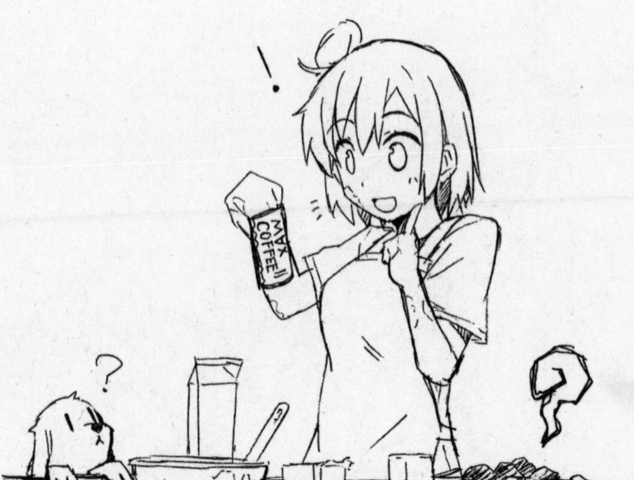
!
MAX COFFEE
?

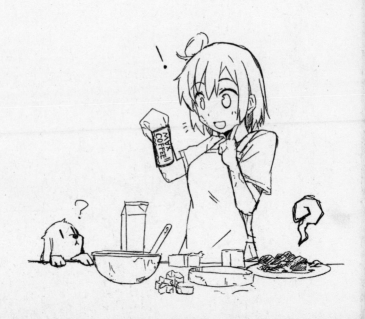

CHAPTER 4 … EVEN SO, THE CLASS IS DOING WELL.

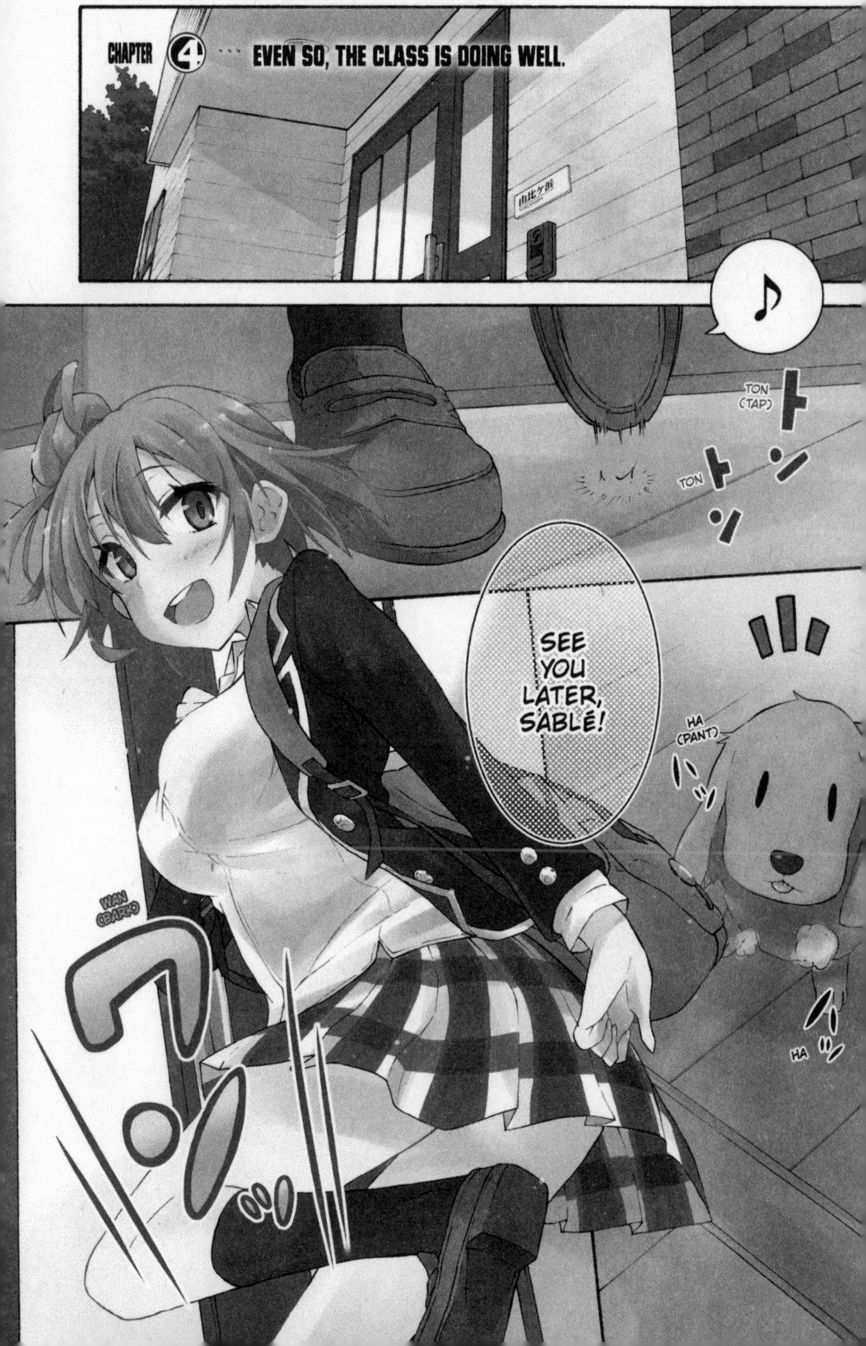
♪
TON (TAP)
TON
SEE YOU LATER, SABLÉ!
HA (PANT)
HA
WAN (BARK)

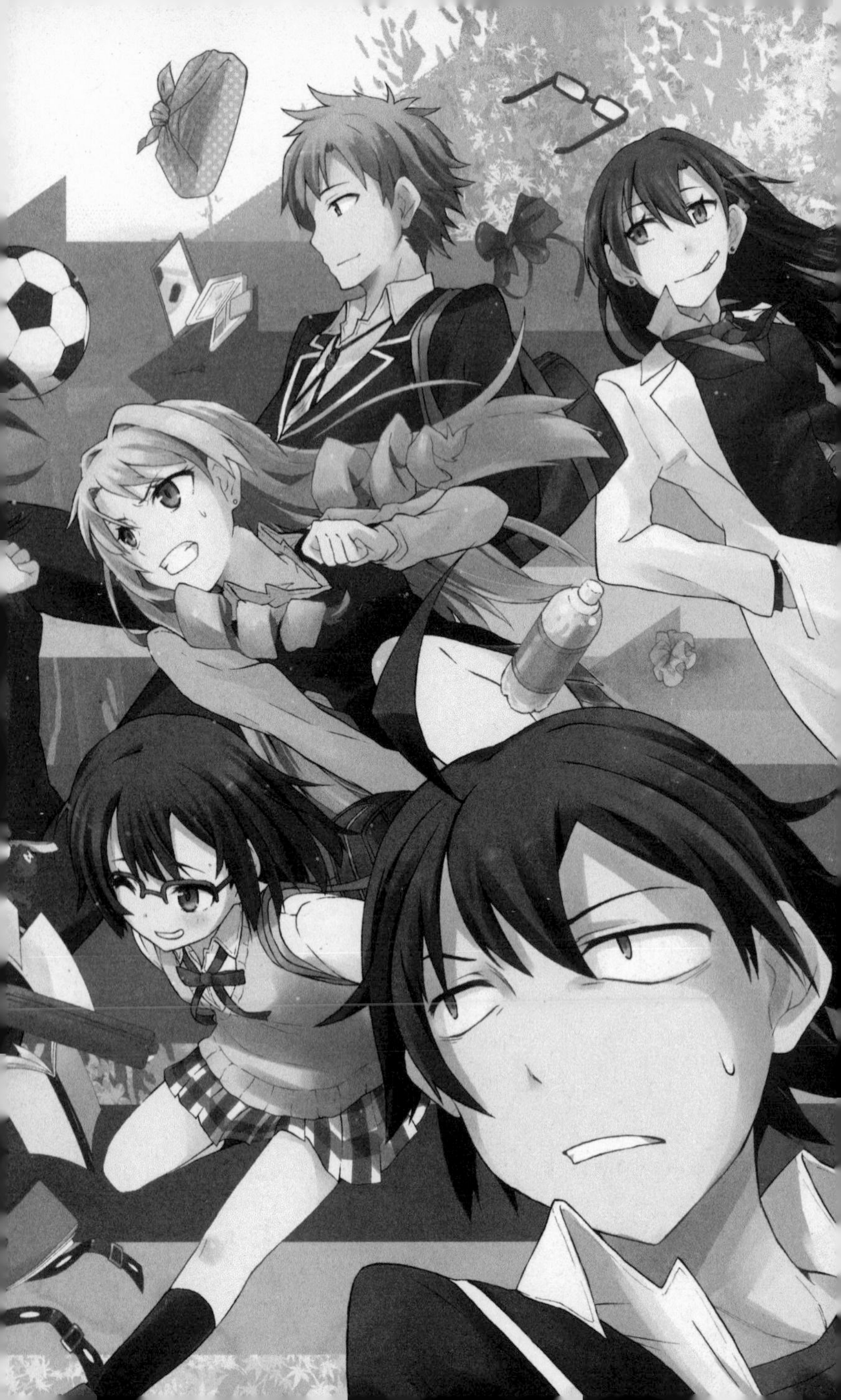

CHAPTER 4 ··· EVEN SO, THE CLASS IS DOING WELL.

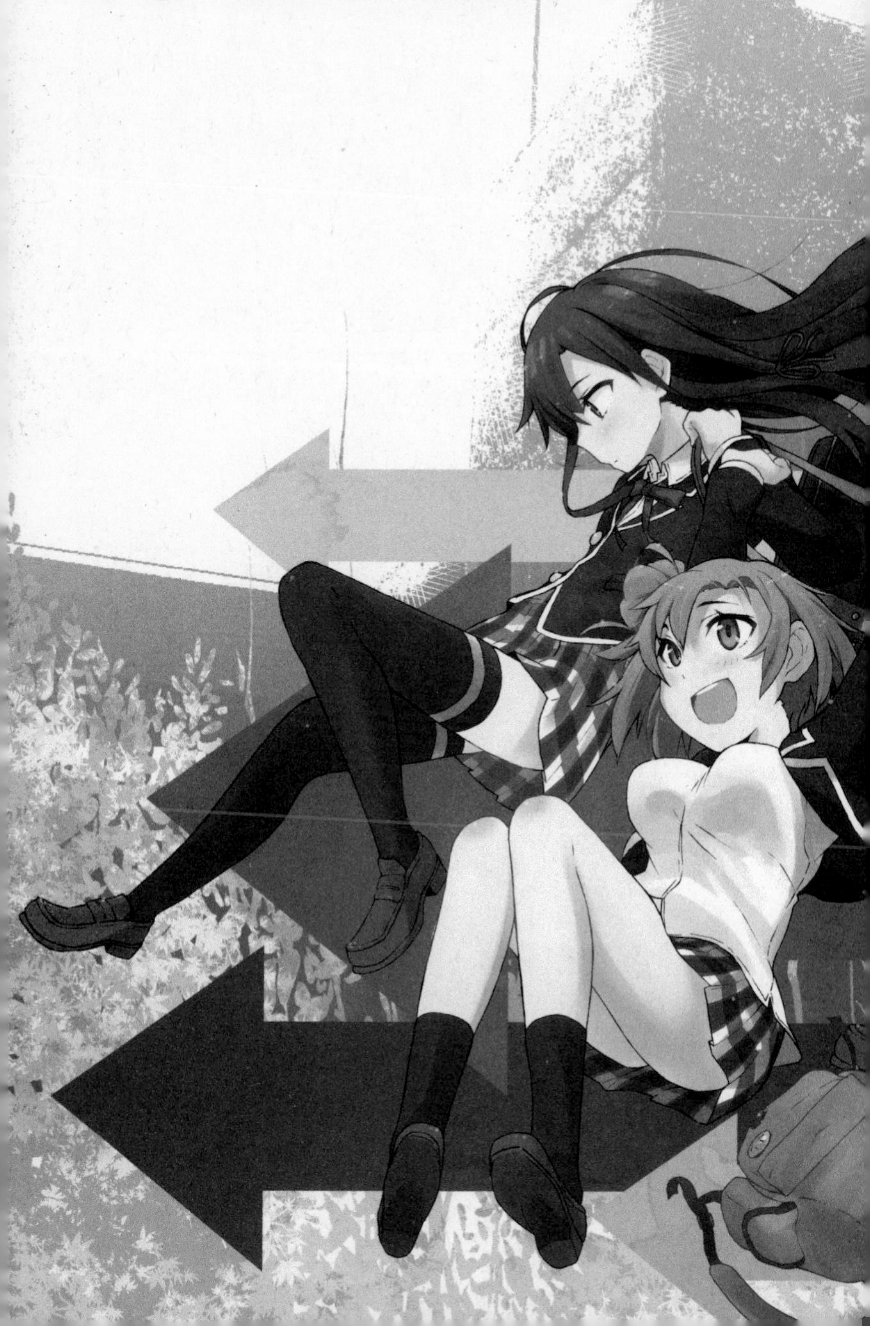

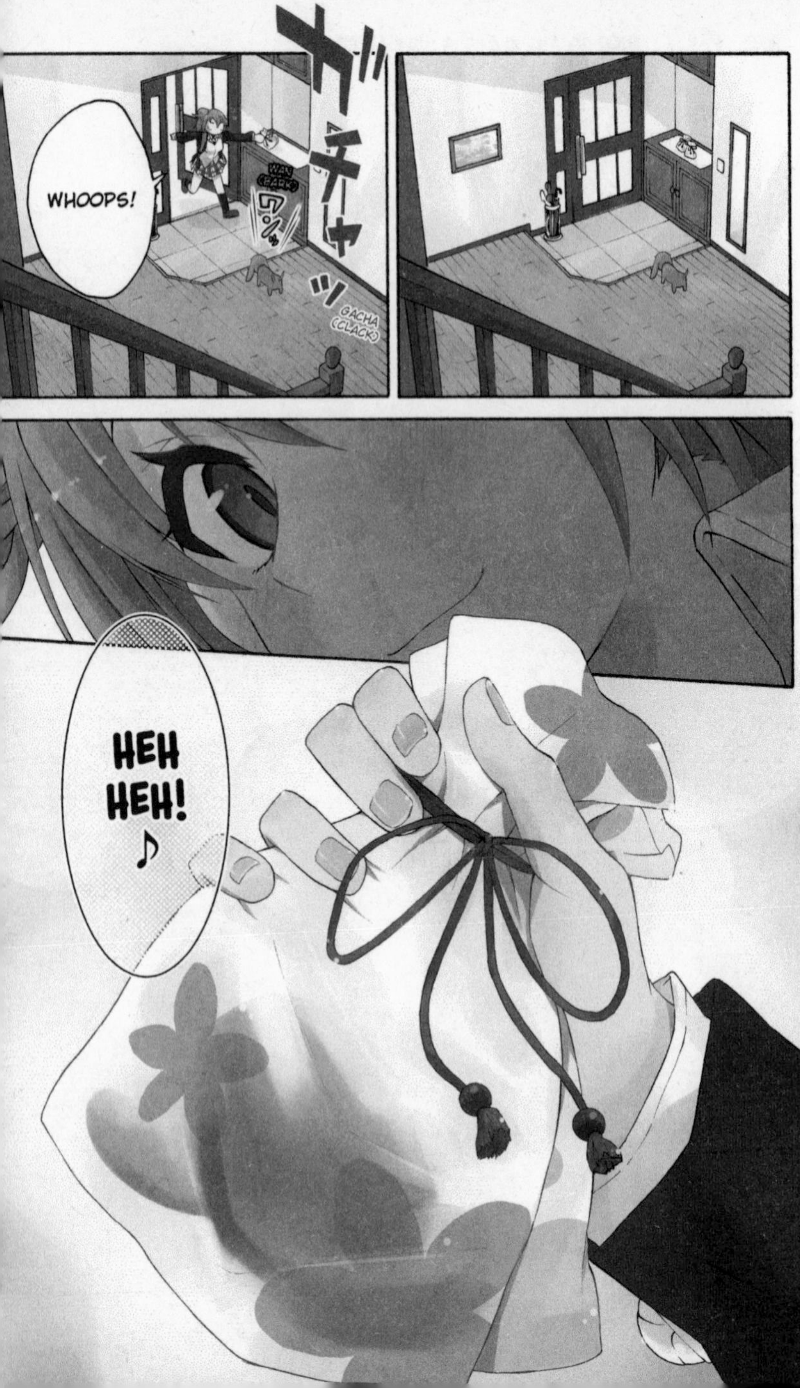
ガチャッ
GACHA (CLACK)
WAN (BARK)
ワン
WHOOPS!
HEH HEH! ♪

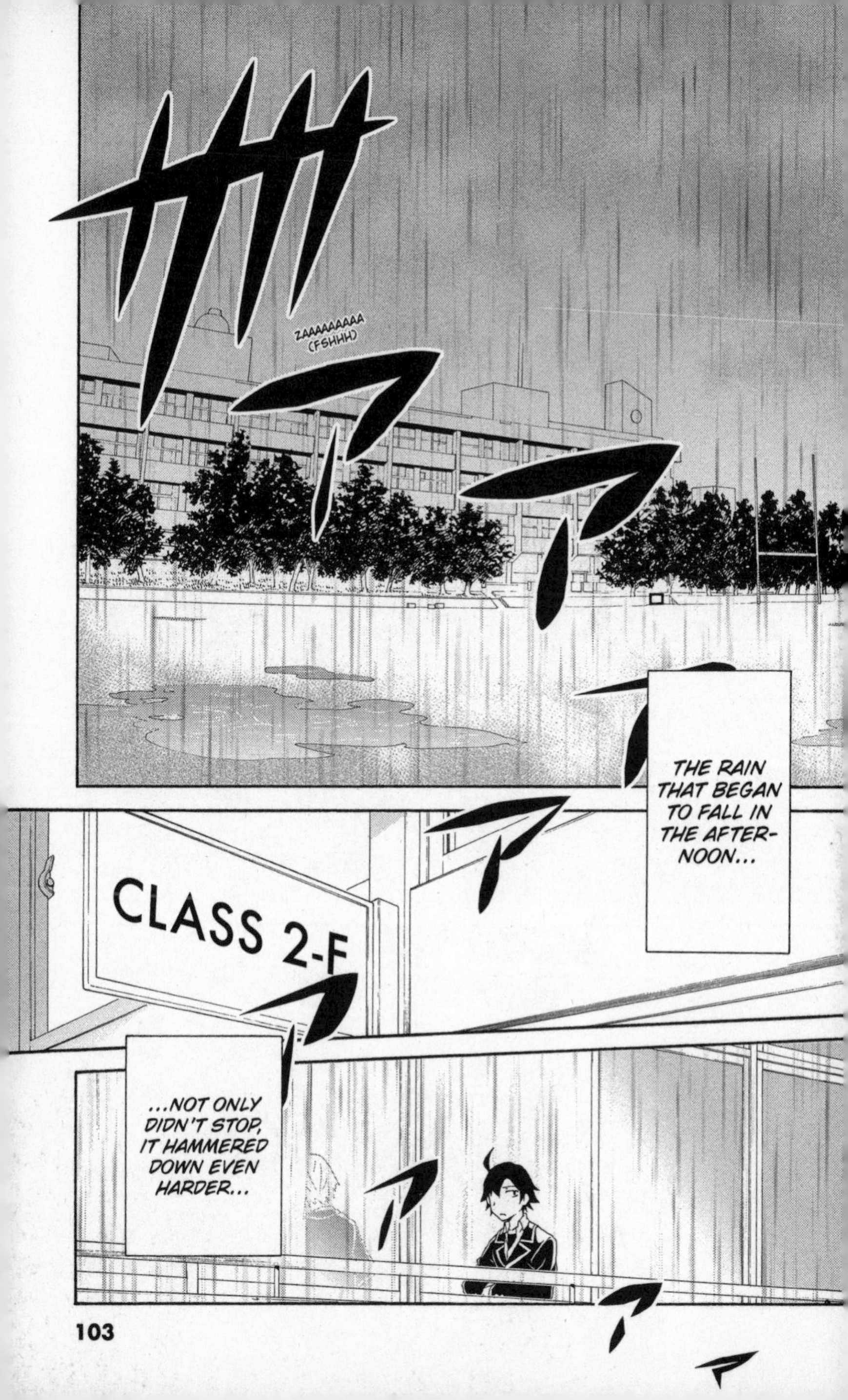
ZAAAAAAAAA
(FSHHH)
THE RAIN THAT BEGAN TO FALL IN THE AFTER-NOON...
CLASS 2-F
...NOT ONLY DIDN'T STOP, IT HAMMERED DOWN EVEN HARDER...

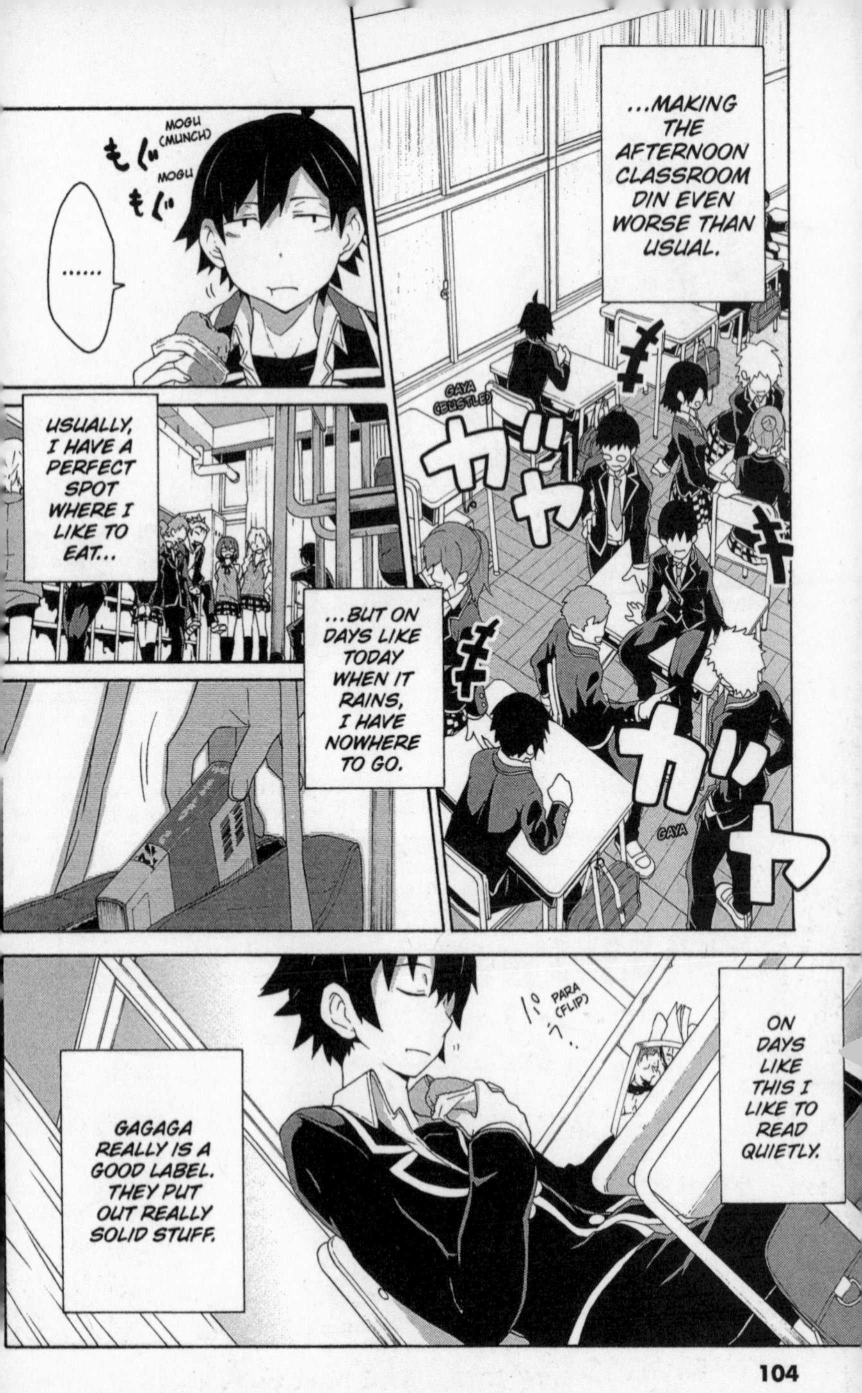
...MAKING THE AFTERNOON CLASSROOM DIN EVEN WORSE THAN USUAL.
GAYA (BUSTLED)
ガヤ
GAYA
ガヤ
MOGU (MUNCH)
もぐ
MOGU
もぐ
......
USUALLY, I HAVE A PERFECT SPOT WHERE I LIKE TO EAT...
...BUT ON DAYS LIKE TODAY WHEN IT RAINS, I HAVE NOWHERE TO GO.
ON DAYS LIKE THIS I LIKE TO READ QUIETLY.
PARA (FLIP)
GAGAGA REALLY IS A GOOD LABEL. THEY PUT OUT REALLY SOLID STUFF.

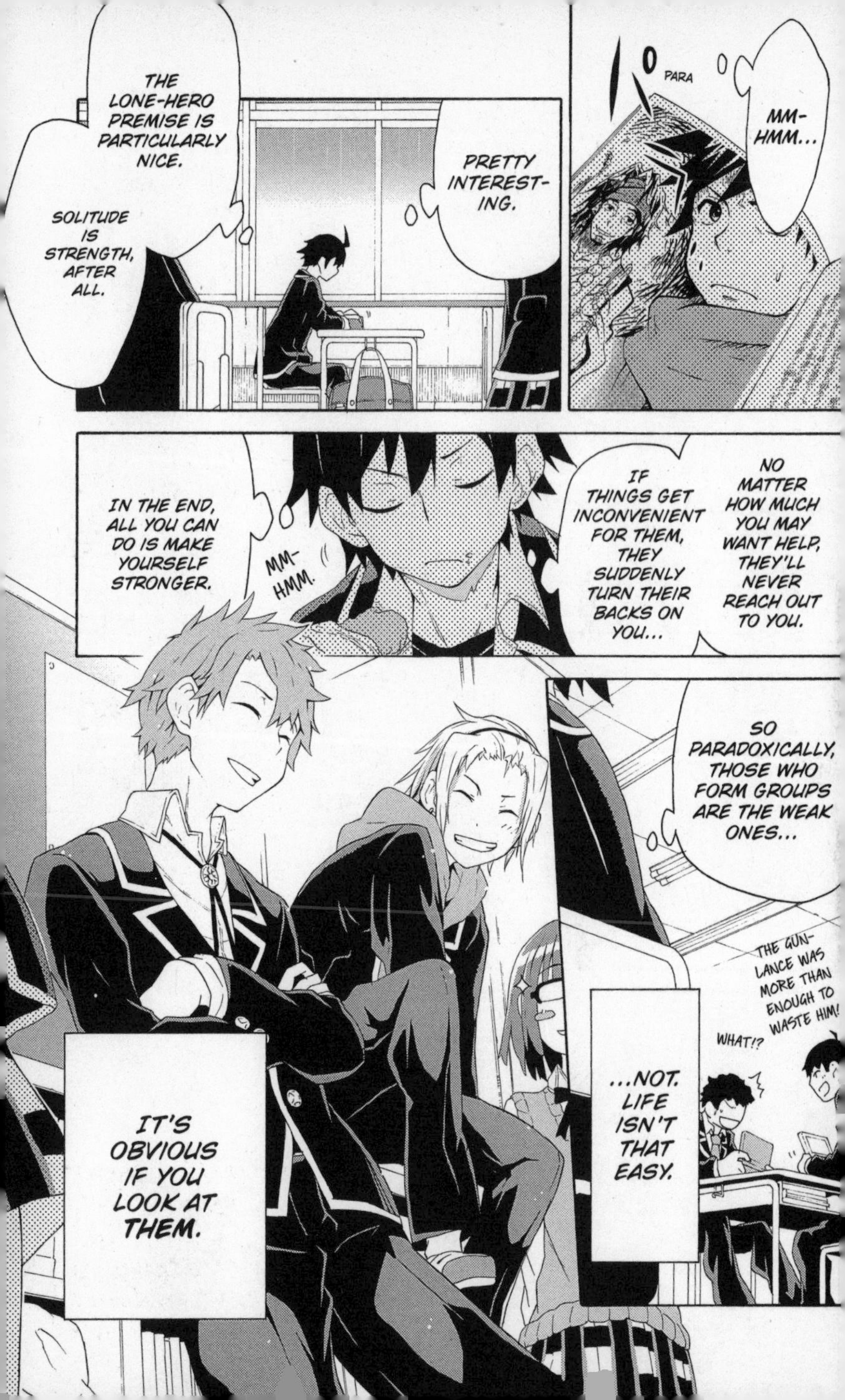
PARA
MM-HMM...
PRETTY INTERESTING.
THE LONE-HERO PREMISE IS PARTICULARLY NICE.
SOLITUDE IS STRENGTH, AFTER ALL.
NO MATTER HOW MUCH YOU MAY WANT HELP, THEY'LL NEVER REACH OUT TO YOU.
IF THINGS GET INCONVENIENT FOR THEM, THEY SUDDENLY TURN THEIR BACKS ON YOU...
MM-HMM.
IN THE END, ALL YOU CAN DO IS MAKE YOURSELF STRONGER.
SO PARADOXICALLY, THOSE WHO FORM GROUPS ARE THE WEAK ONES...
THE GUN-LANCE WAS MORE THAN ENOUGH TO WASTE HIM!
WHAT!?
...NOT. LIFE ISN'T THAT EASY.
IT'S OBVIOUS IF YOU LOOK AT THEM.

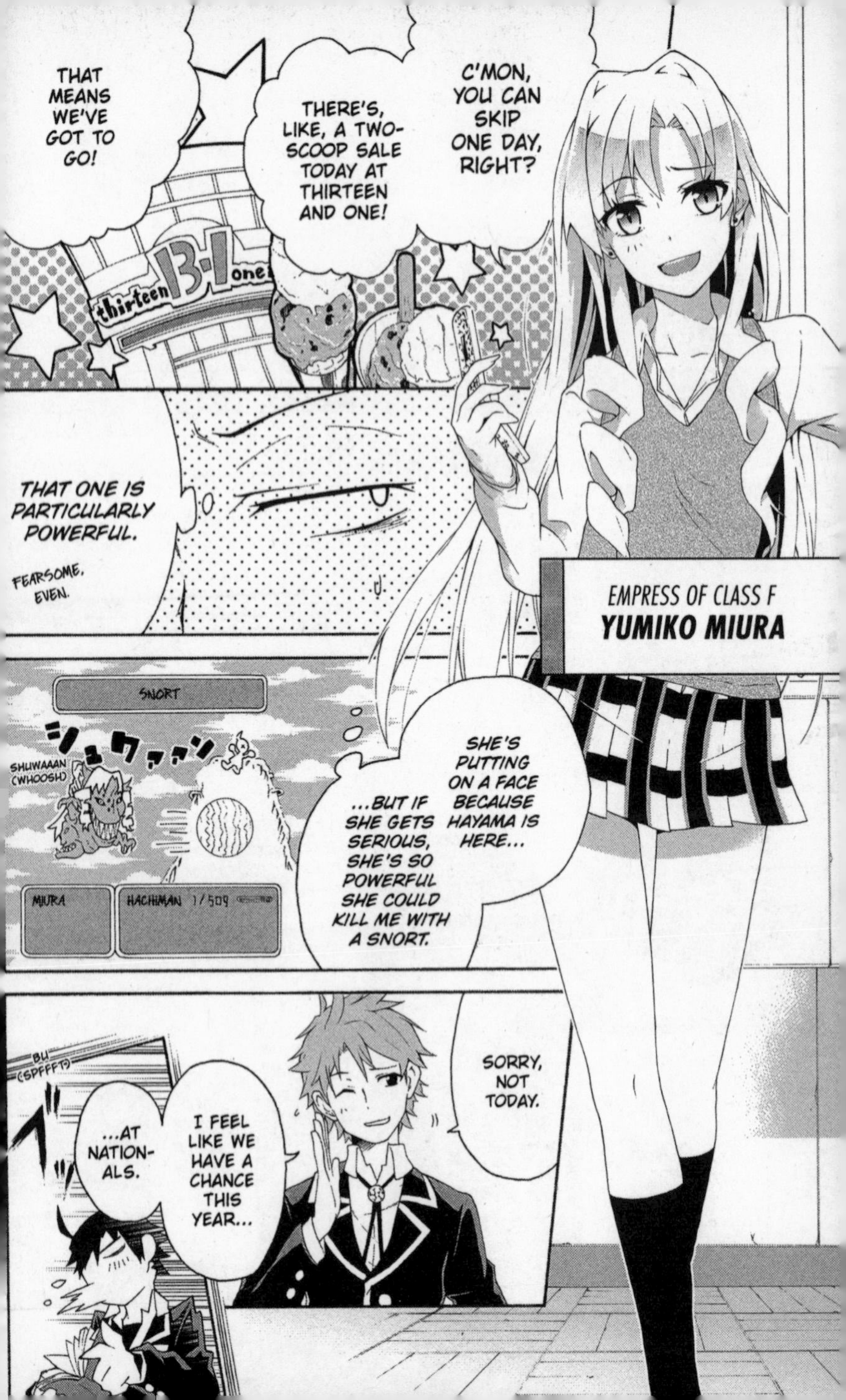
C'MON, YOU CAN SKIP ONE DAY, RIGHT?
THERE'S, LIKE, A TWO-SCOOP SALE TODAY AT THIRTEEN AND ONE!
THAT MEANS WE'VE GOT TO GO!
thirteen 13·1 one
EMPRESS OF CLASS F
YUMIKO MIURA
THAT ONE IS PARTICULARLY POWERFUL.
FEARSOME, EVEN.
SHE'S PUTTING ON A FACE BECAUSE HAYAMA IS HERE...
...BUT IF SHE GETS SERIOUS, SHE'S SO POWERFUL SHE COULD KILL ME WITH A SNORT.
SNORT
SHUWAAAN (WHOOSH)
MIURA
HACHIMAN 1/509
SORRY, NOT TODAY.
I FEEL LIKE WE HAVE A CHANCE THIS YEAR...
...AT NATION-ALS.
BU (SPFFFT)

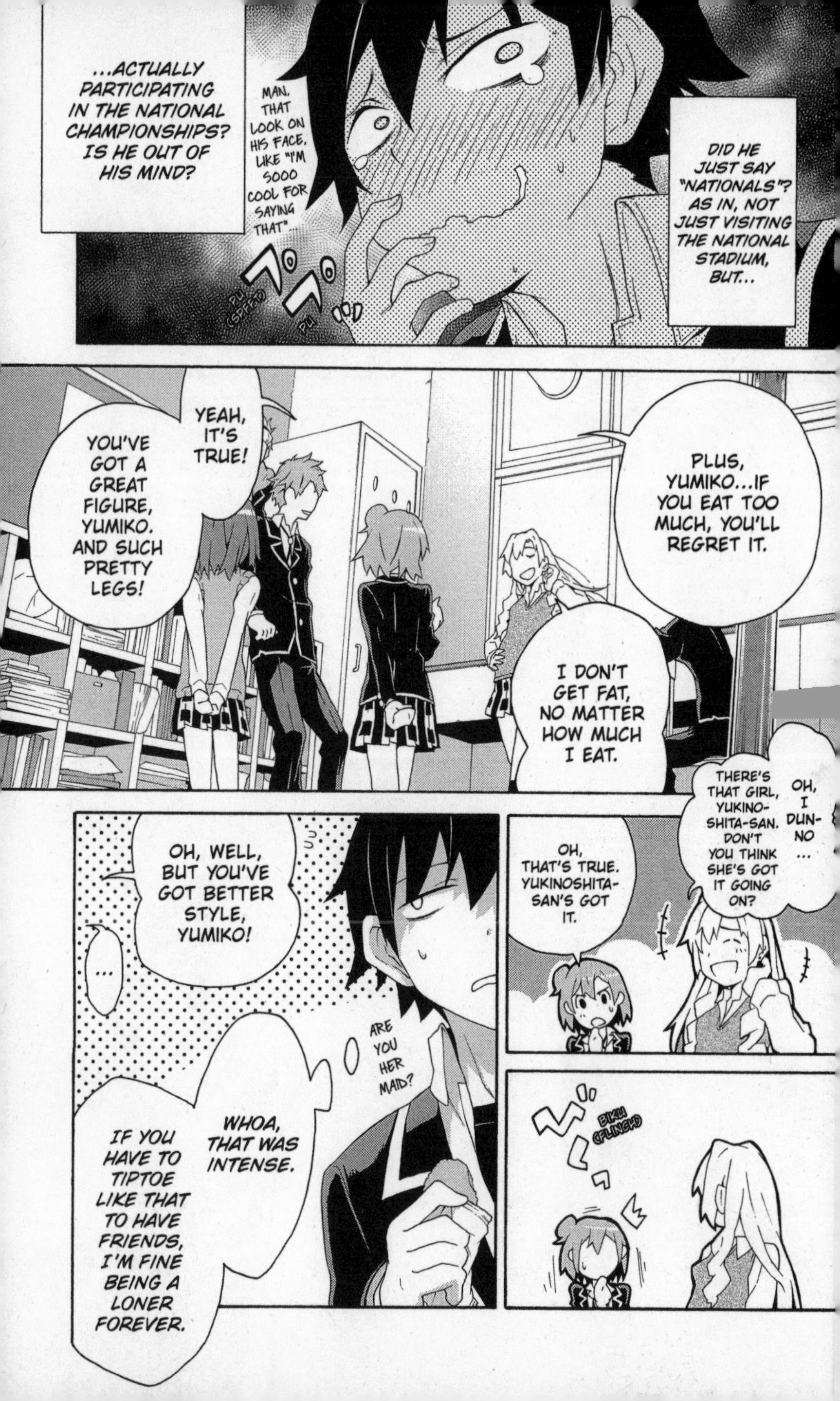
DID HE JUST SAY "NATIONALS"? AS IN, NOT JUST VISITING THE NATIONAL STADIUM, BUT...
MAN, THAT LOOK ON HIS FACE. LIKE "I'M SOOO COOL FOR SAYING THAT"...
...ACTUALLY PARTICIPATING IN THE NATIONAL CHAMPIONSHIPS? IS HE OUT OF HIS MIND?
PU PU (SPFFT)
PLUS, YUMIKO...IF YOU EAT TOO MUCH, YOU'LL REGRET IT.
I DON'T GET FAT, NO MATTER HOW MUCH I EAT.
YEAH, IT'S TRUE!
YOU'VE GOT A GREAT FIGURE, YUMIKO. AND SUCH PRETTY LEGS!
OH, I DUNNO...
THERE'S THAT GIRL, YUKINOSHITA-SAN. DON'T YOU THINK SHE'S GOT IT GOING ON?
OH, THAT'S TRUE. YUKINOSHITA-SAN'S GOT IT.
BIKU (FLINCH)
OH, WELL, BUT YOU'VE GOT BETTER STYLE, YUMIKO!
...
ARE YOU HER MAID?
WHOA, THAT WAS INTENSE.
IF YOU HAVE TO TIPTOE LIKE THAT TO HAVE FRIENDS, I'M FINE BEING A LONER FOREVER.

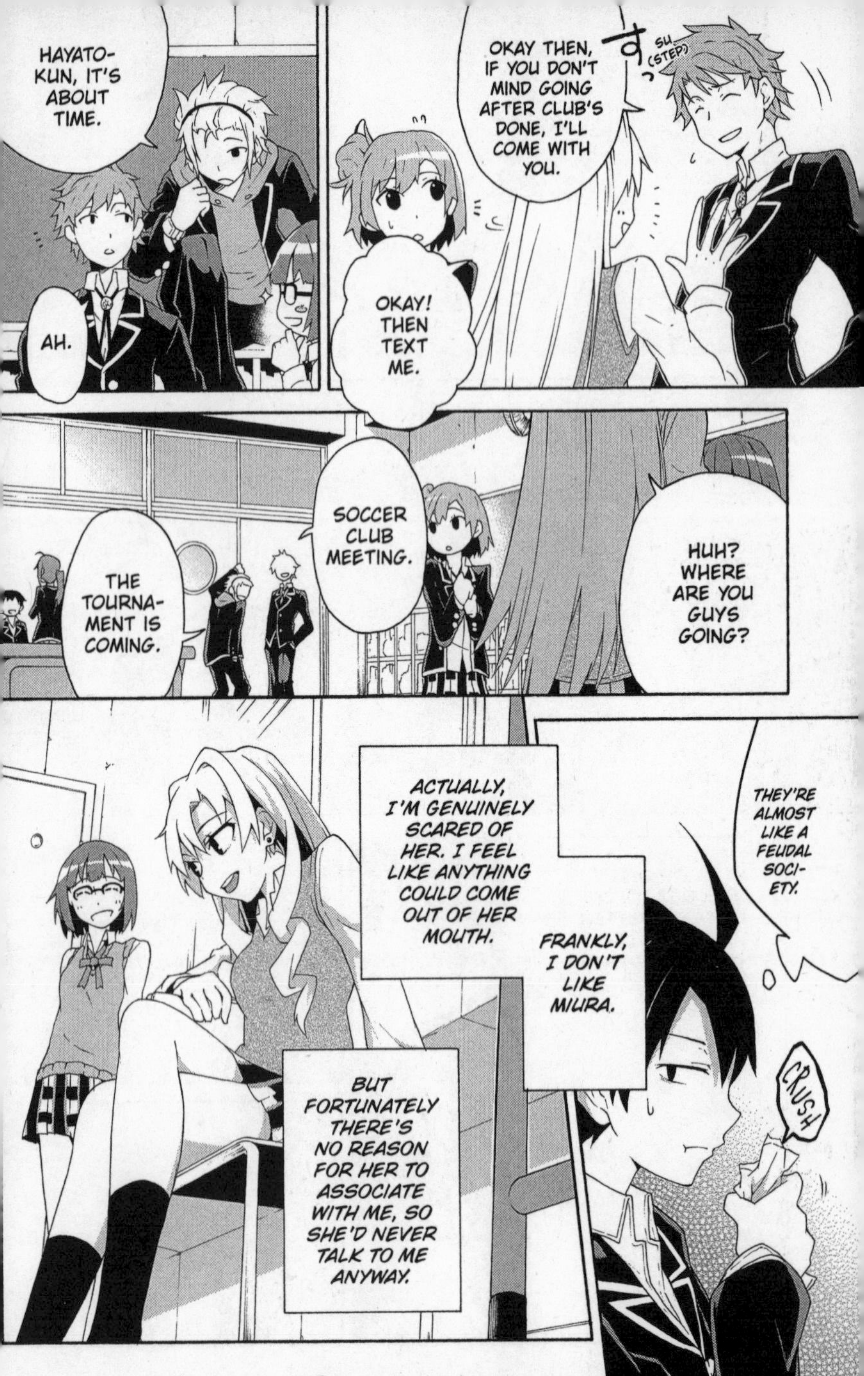
す
SU (STEP)
OKAY THEN, IF YOU DON'T MIND GOING AFTER CLUB'S DONE, I'LL COME WITH YOU.
OKAY! THEN TEXT ME.
HAYATO-KUN, IT'S ABOUT TIME.
AH.
HUH? WHERE ARE YOU GUYS GOING?
SOCCER CLUB MEETING.
THE TOURNAMENT IS COMING.
THEY'RE ALMOST LIKE A FEUDAL SOCIETY.
CRUSH
FRANKLY, I DON'T LIKE MIURA.
ACTUALLY, I'M GENUINELY SCARED OF HER. I FEEL LIKE ANYTHING COULD COME OUT OF HER MOUTH.
BUT FORTUNATELY THERE'S NO REASON FOR HER TO ASSOCIATE WITH ME, SO SHE'D NEVER TALK TO ME ANYWAY.

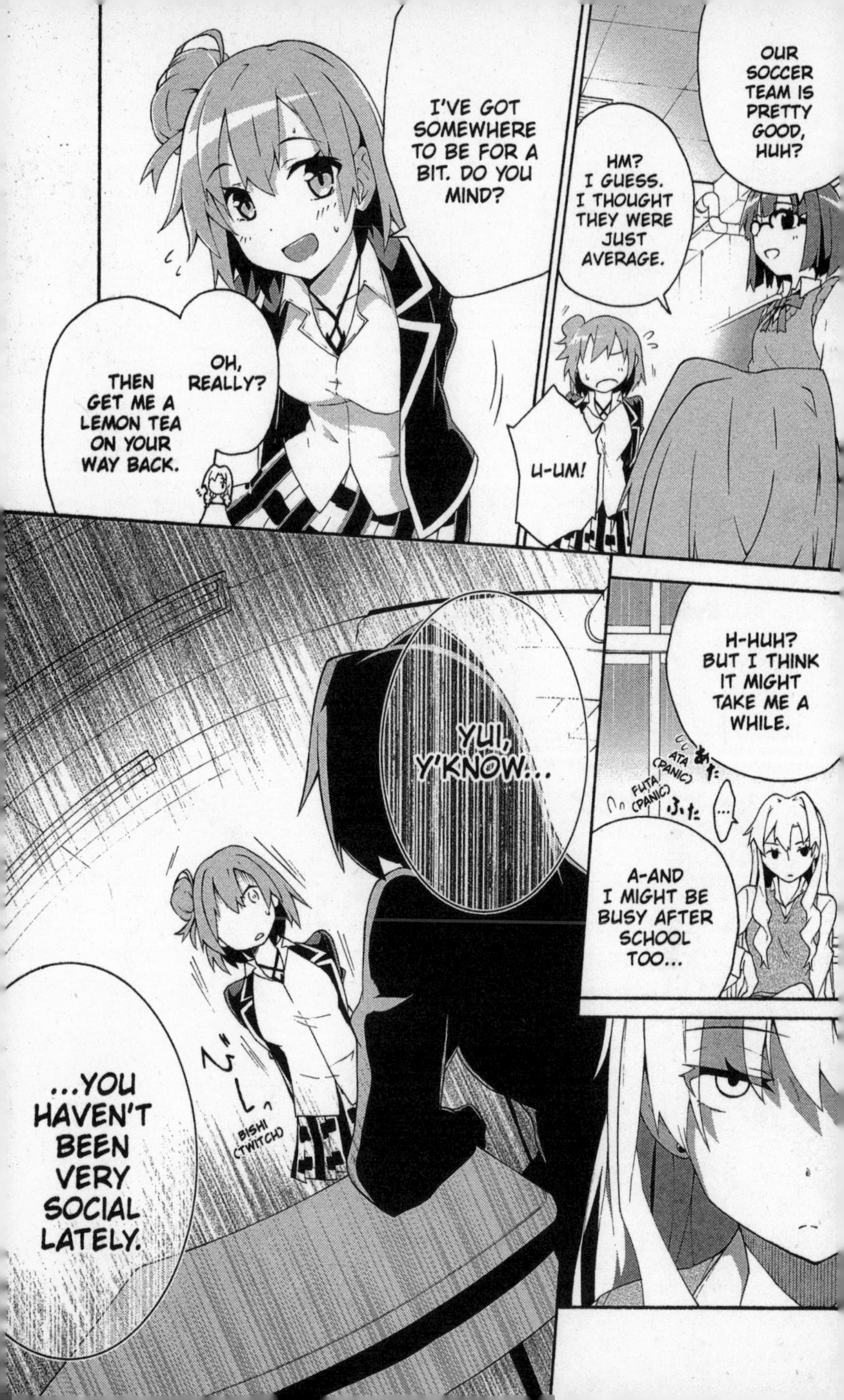
OUR SOCCER TEAM IS PRETTY GOOD, HUH?
HM? I GUESS. I THOUGHT THEY WERE JUST AVERAGE.
U-UM!
I'VE GOT SOMEWHERE TO BE FOR A BIT. DO YOU MIND?
OH, REALLY?
THEN GET ME A LEMON TEA ON YOUR WAY BACK.
H-HUH? BUT I THINK IT MIGHT TAKE ME A WHILE.
ATA (PANIC)
FUTA (PANIC)
...
A-AND I MIGHT BE BUSY AFTER SCHOOL TOO...
YUI, Y'KNOW...
...YOU HAVEN'T BEEN VERY SOCIAL LATELY.
BISHI (TWITCH)

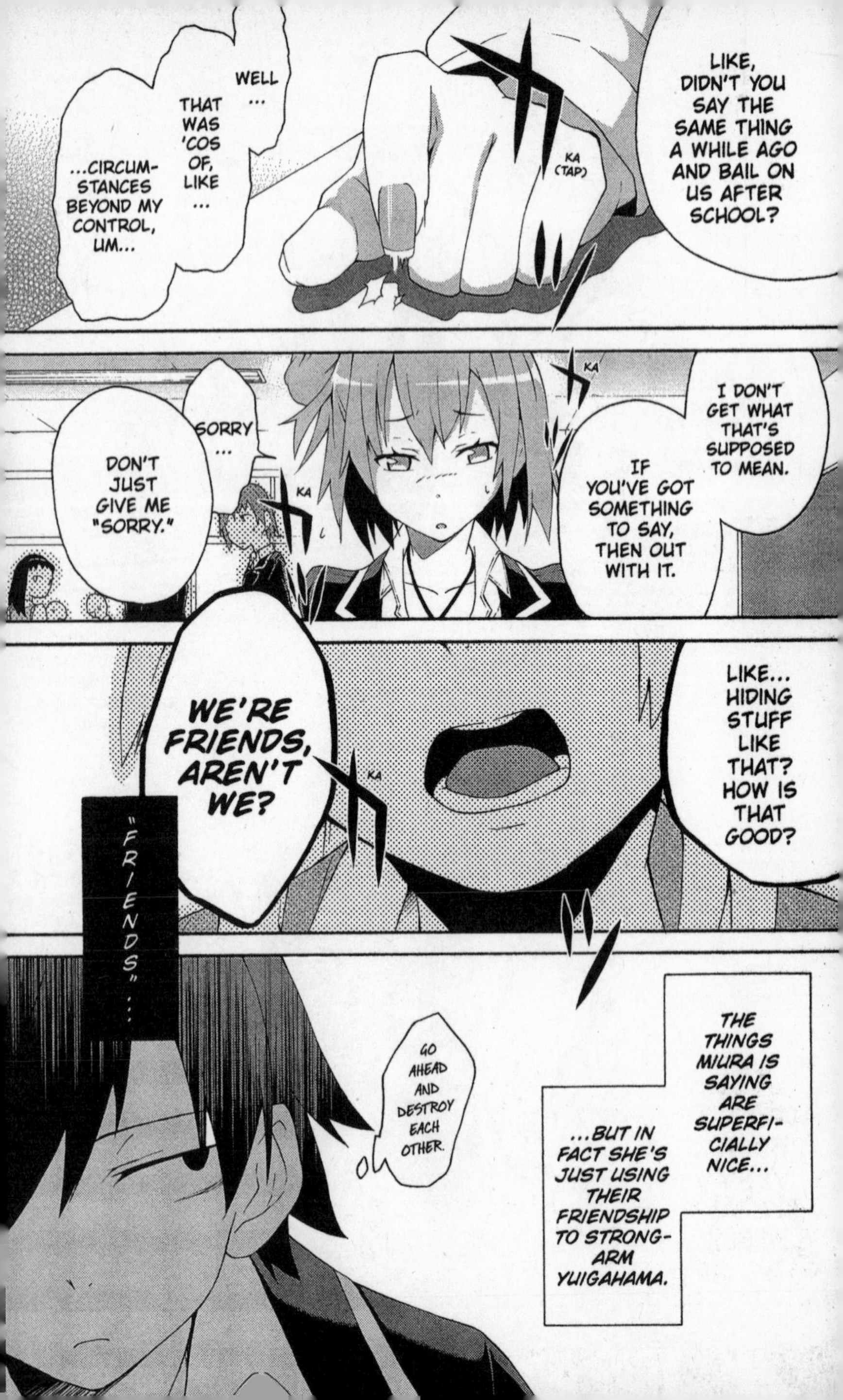
LIKE, DIDN'T YOU SAY THE SAME THING A WHILE AGO AND BAIL ON US AFTER SCHOOL?
KA (TAP)
WELL ... THAT WAS 'COS OF, LIKE ...
...CIRCUM-STANCES BEYOND MY CONTROL, UM...
KA
I DON'T GET WHAT THAT'S SUPPOSED TO MEAN.
IF YOU'VE GOT SOMETHING TO SAY, THEN OUT WITH IT.
KA
SORRY ...
DON'T JUST GIVE ME "SORRY."
LIKE... HIDING STUFF LIKE THAT? HOW IS THAT GOOD?
KA
WE'RE FRIENDS, AREN'T WE?
"FRIENDS"...
THE THINGS MIURA IS SAYING ARE SUPERFI-CIALLY NICE...
...BUT IN FACT SHE'S JUST USING THEIR FRIENDSHIP TO STRONG-ARM YUIGAHAMA.
GO AHEAD AND DESTROY EACH OTHER.

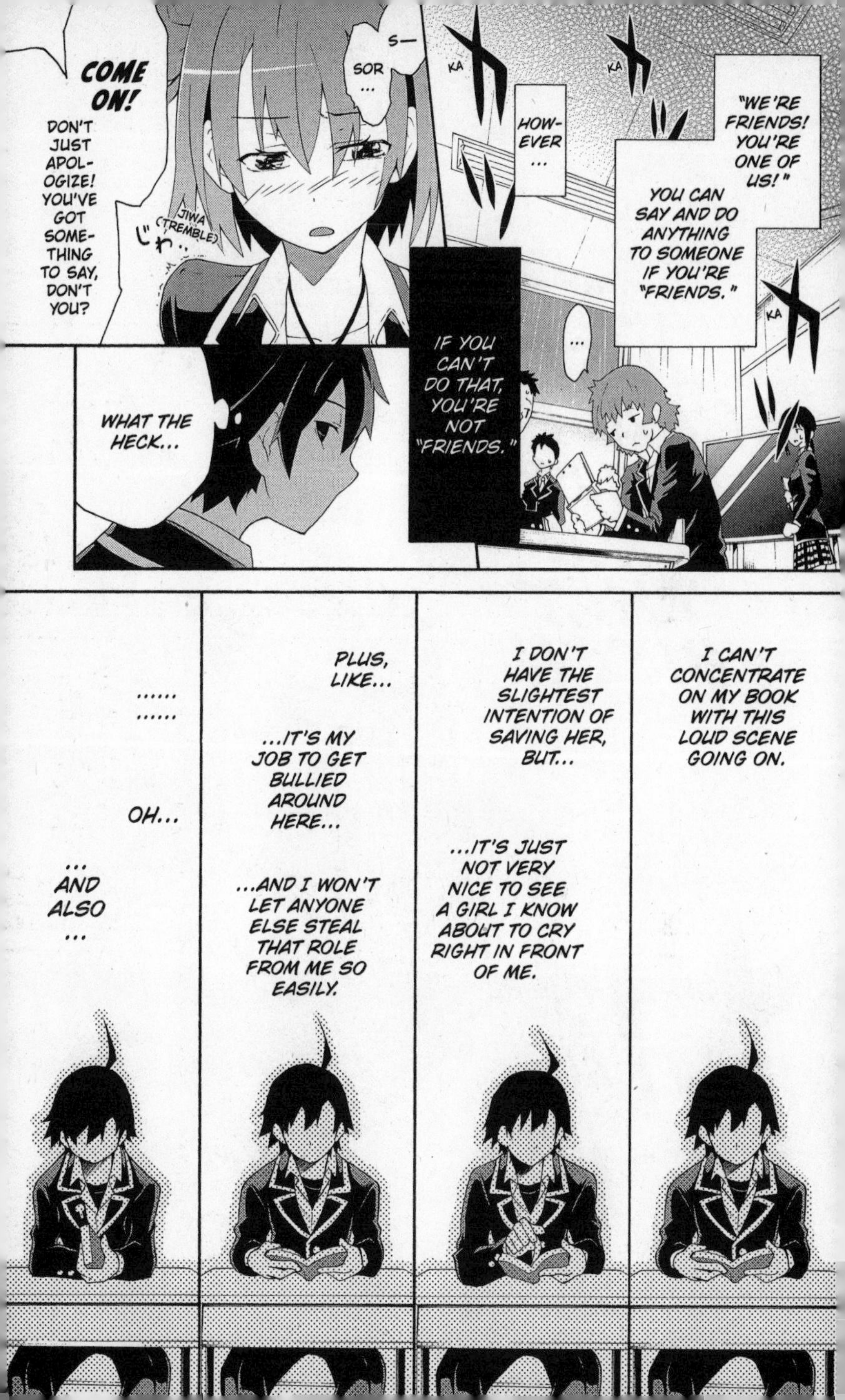

KA
KA
"WE'RE FRIENDS! YOU'RE ONE OF US!"
YOU CAN SAY AND DO ANYTHING TO SOMEONE IF YOU'RE "FRIENDS."
HOW-EVER ...
KA
S— SOR ...
COME ON!
DON'T JUST APOL-OGIZE! YOU'VE GOT SOME-THING TO SAY, DON'T YOU?
JIWA (TREMBLE)
じわ…
...
IF YOU CAN'T DO THAT, YOU'RE NOT "FRIENDS."
WHAT THE HECK...
I CAN'T CONCENTRATE ON MY BOOK WITH THIS LOUD SCENE GOING ON.
I DON'T HAVE THE SLIGHTEST INTENTION OF SAVING HER, BUT...
...IT'S JUST NOT VERY NICE TO SEE A GIRL I KNOW ABOUT TO CRY RIGHT IN FRONT OF ME.
PLUS, LIKE...
...IT'S MY JOB TO GET BULLIED AROUND HERE...
...AND I WON'T LET ANYONE ELSE STEAL THAT ROLE FROM ME SO EASILY.
....
OH...
... AND ALSO ...

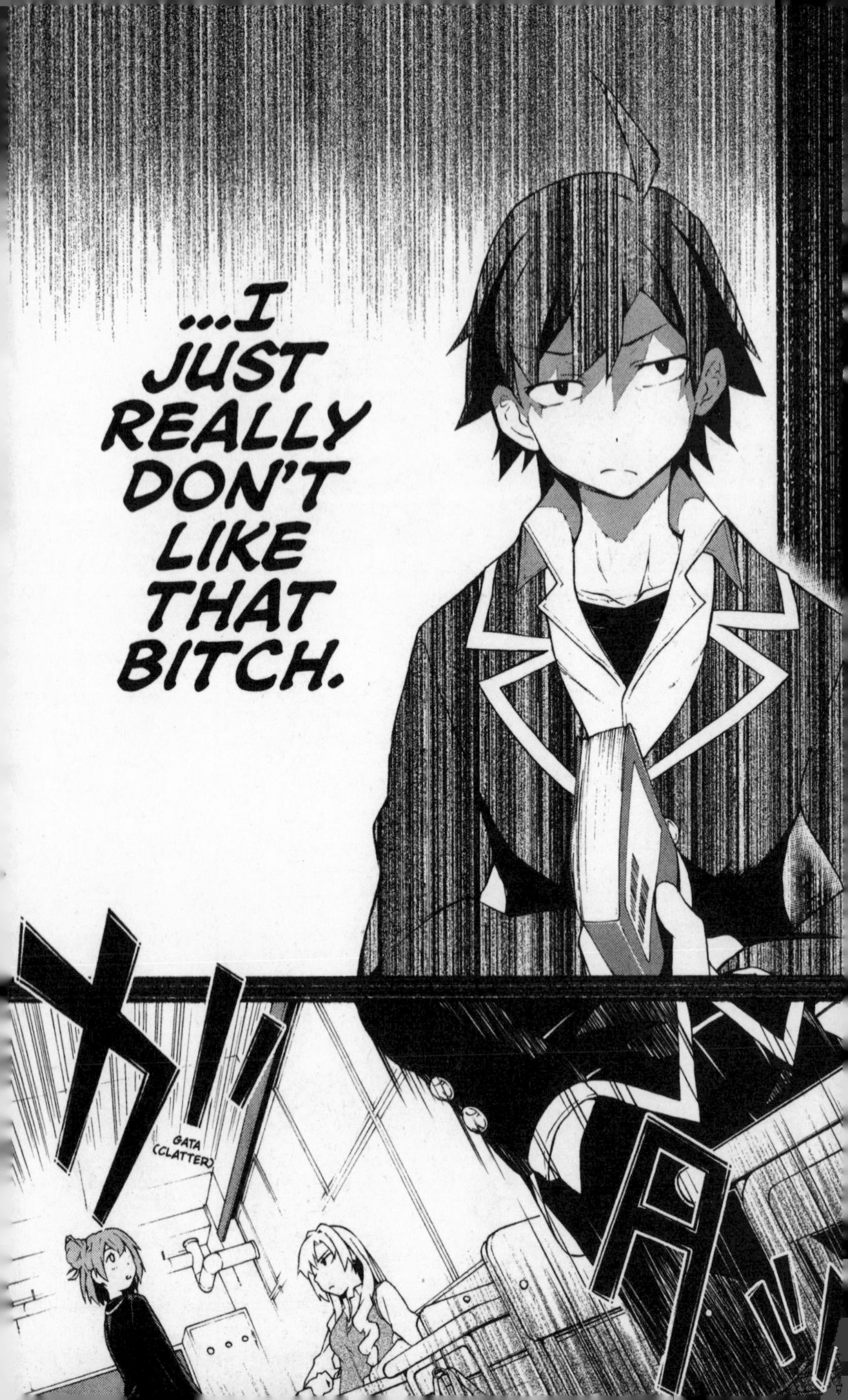
...I JUST REALLY DON'T LIKE THAT BITCH.
GATA (CLATTER)

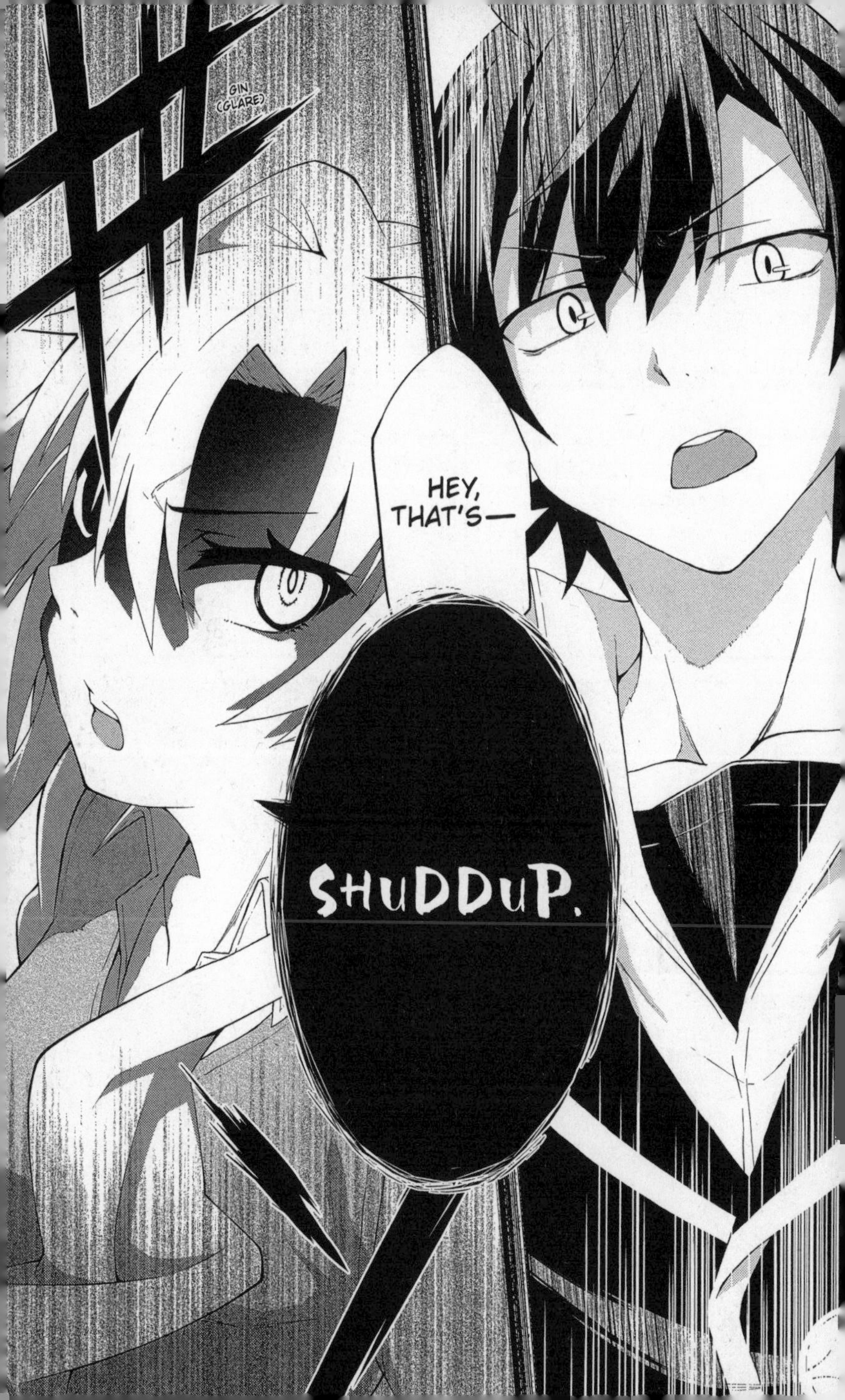
GIN
(GLARE)
HEY, THAT'S—
SHUDDUP.

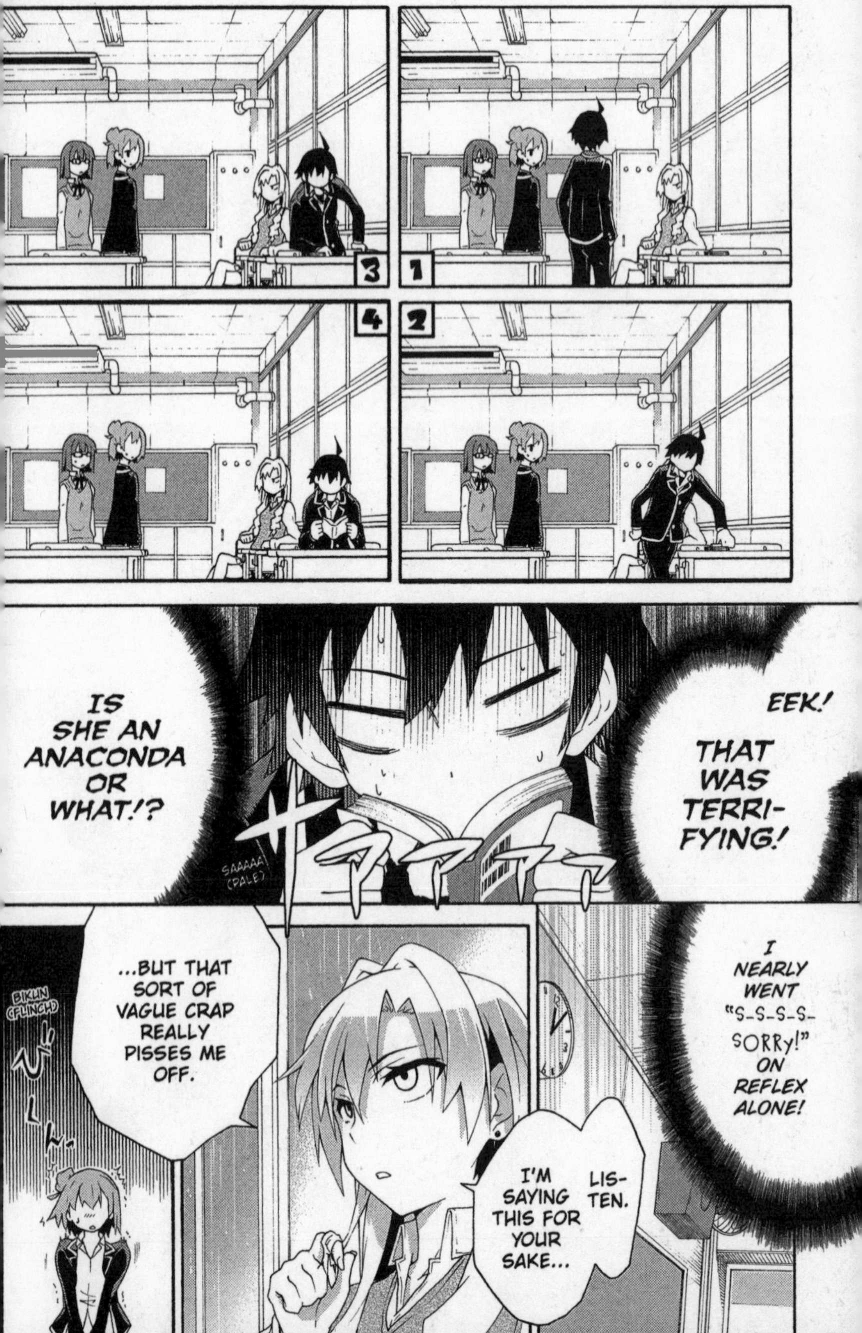
EEK!
THAT WAS TERRI-FYING!
IS SHE AN ANACONDA OR WHAT!?
SAAAAA (PALE)
I NEARLY WENT "S-S-S-S-SORRy!" ON REFLEX ALONE!
LIS-TEN.
I'M SAYING THIS FOR YOUR SAKE...
...BUT THAT SORT OF VAGUE CRAP REALLY PISSES ME OFF.
BIKUN (FLINCH)

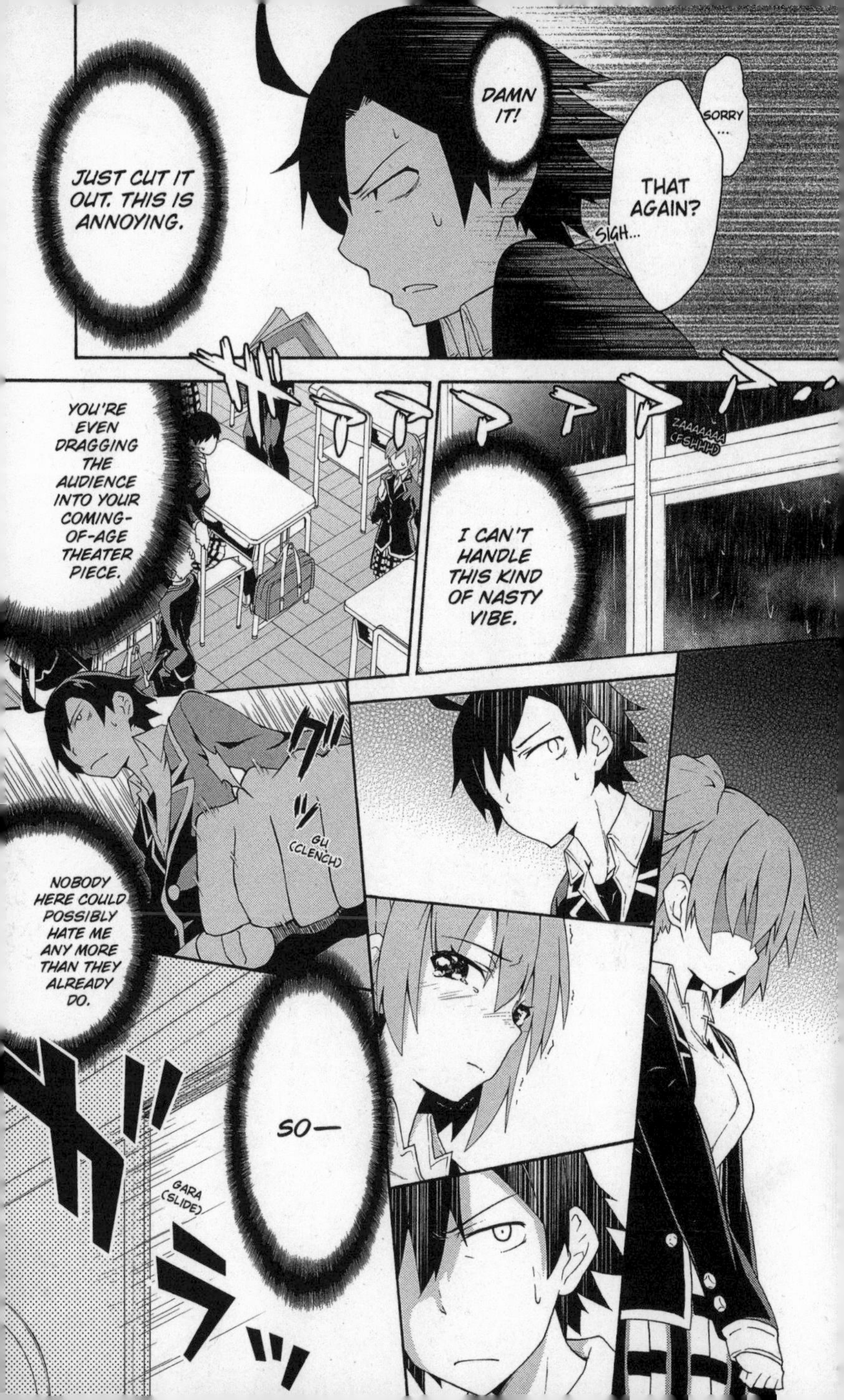
SORRY...
THAT AGAIN?
SIGH...
DAMN IT!
JUST CUT IT OUT. THIS IS ANNOYING.
ZAAAAAAA (FSHHHD)
I CAN'T HANDLE THIS KIND OF NASTY VIBE.
YOU'RE EVEN DRAGGING THE AUDIENCE INTO YOUR COMING-OF-AGE THEATER PIECE.
GU (CLENCH)
NOBODY HERE COULD POSSIBLY HATE ME ANY MORE THAN THEY ALREADY DO.
SO—
GARA (SLIDE)

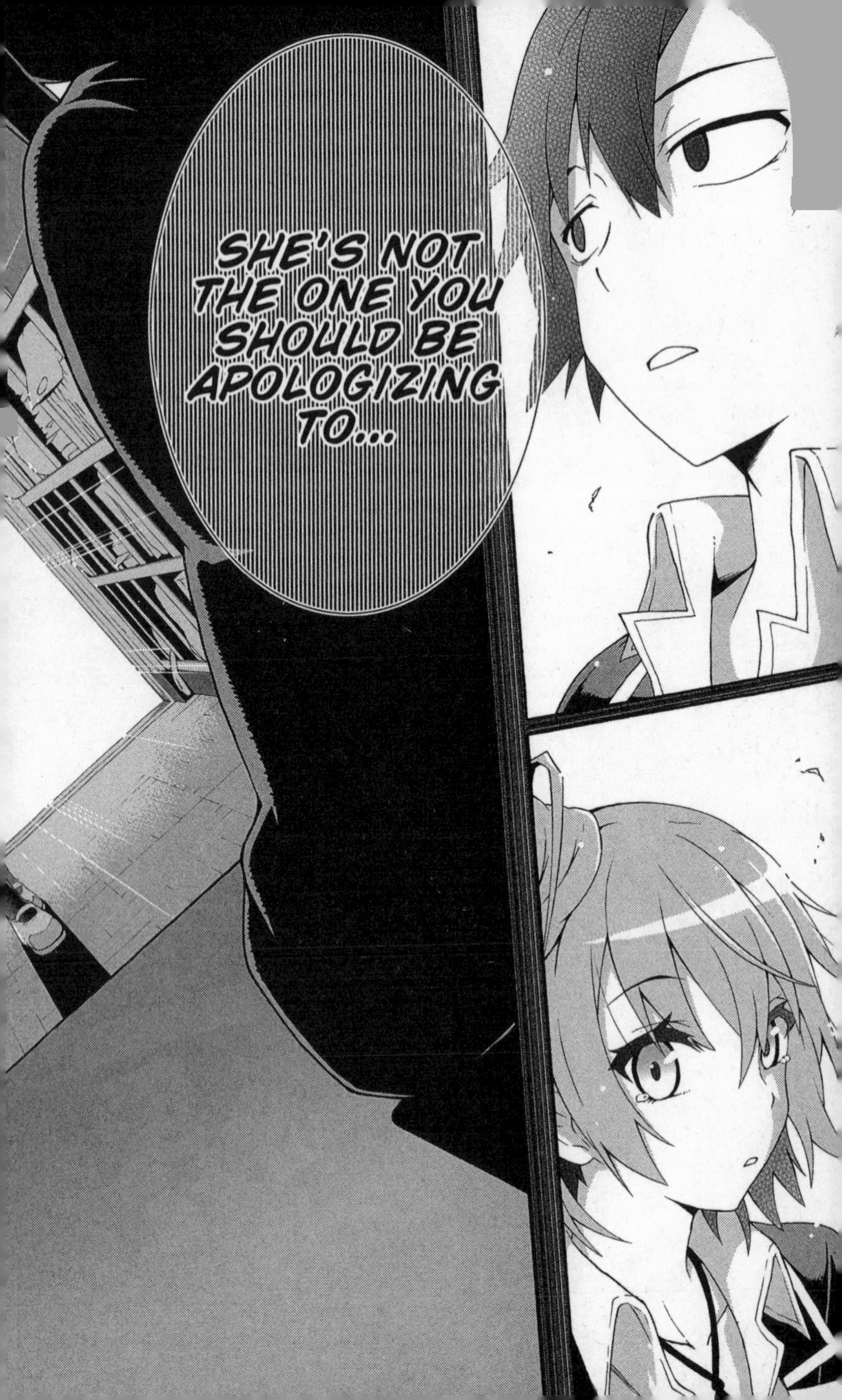
SHE'S NOT THE ONE YOU SHOULD BE APOLOGIZING TO...

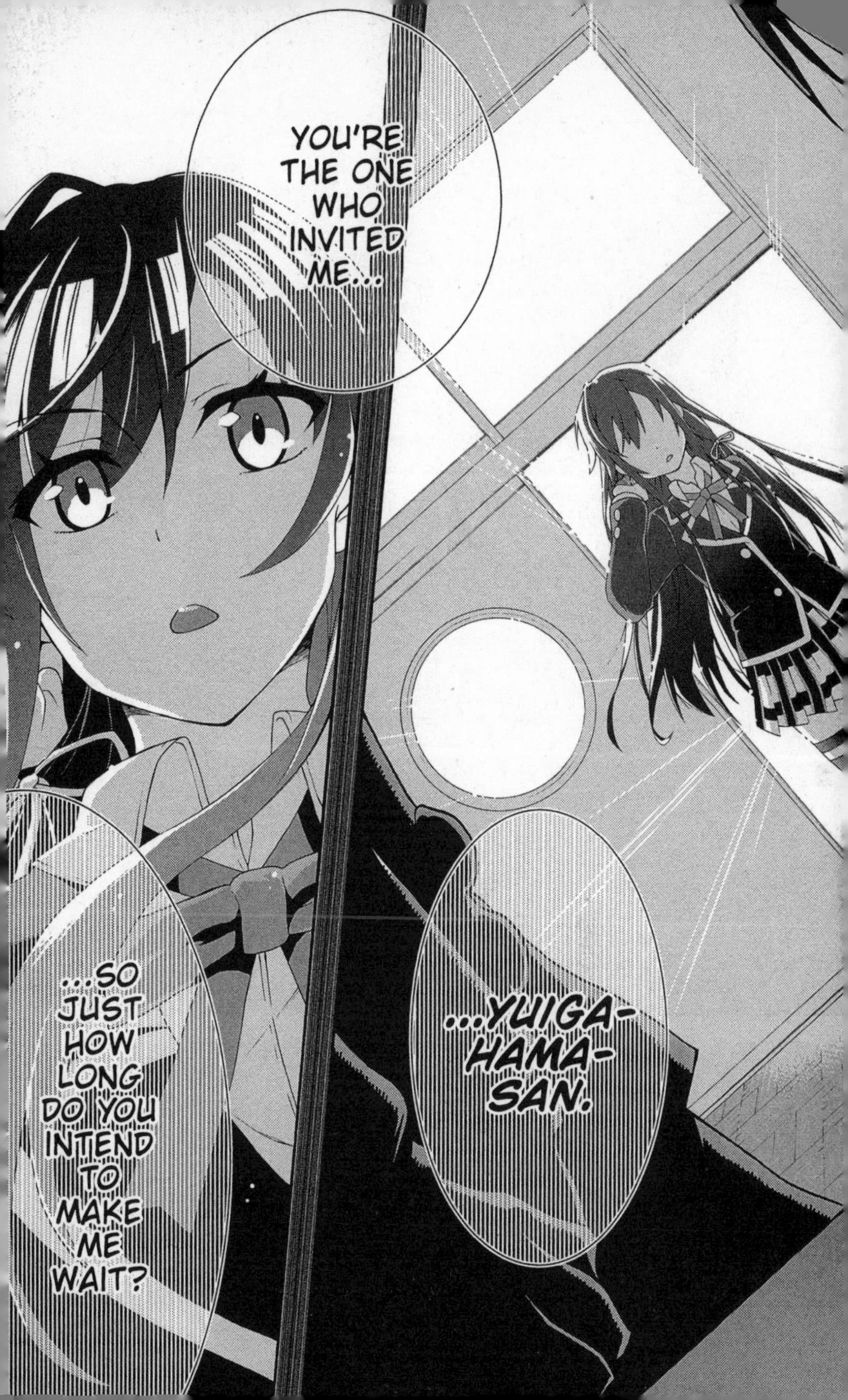
YOU'RE THE ONE WHO INVITED ME...!
...YUIGA-HAMA-SAN.
...SO JUST HOW LONG DO YOU INTEND TO MAKE ME WAIT?

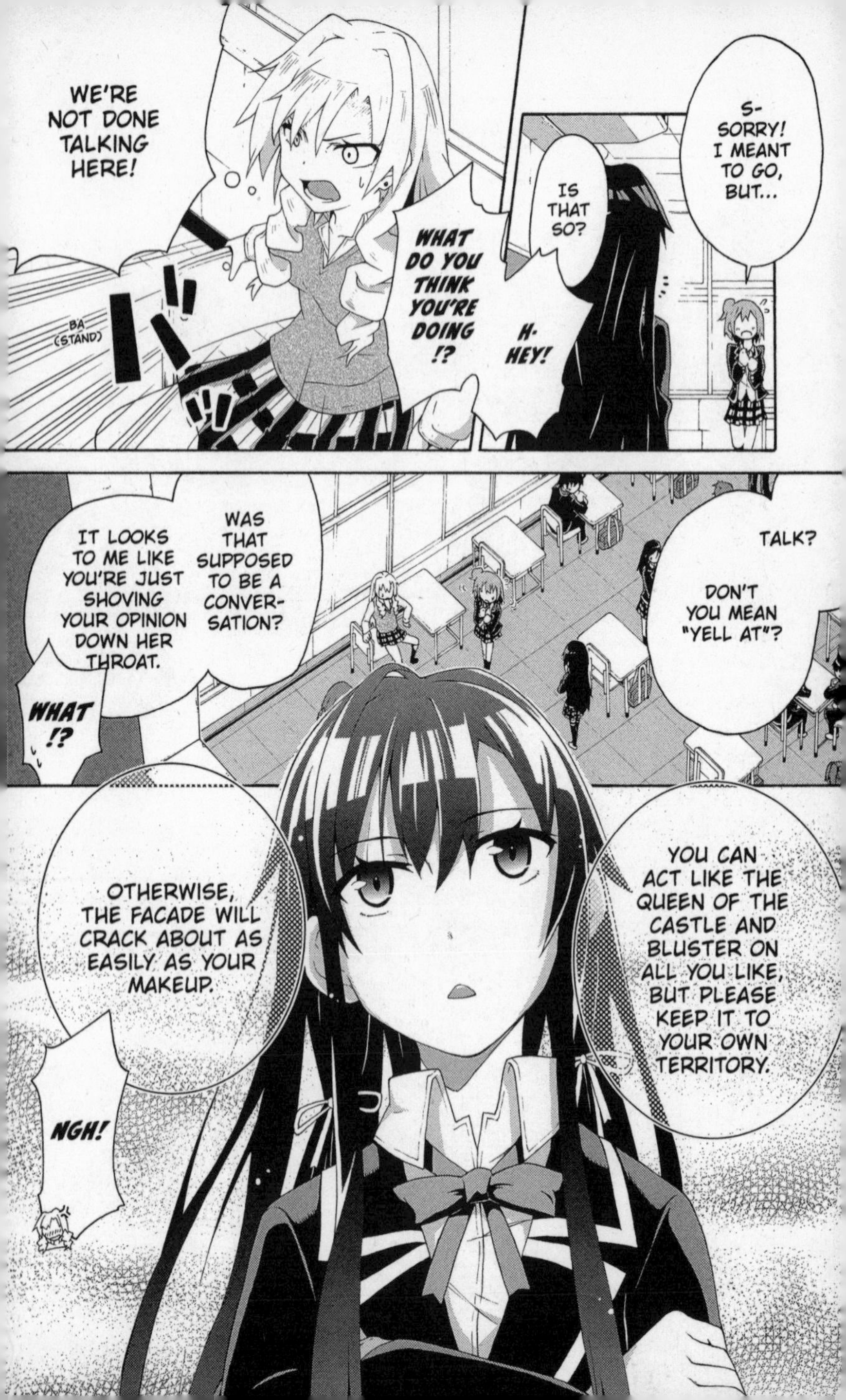
S-SORRY! I MEANT TO GO, BUT...
IS THAT SO?
WHAT DO YOU THINK YOU'RE DOING!?
H-HEY!
WE'RE NOT DONE TALKING HERE!
BA (STAND)
TALK?
DON'T YOU MEAN "YELL AT"?
WAS THAT SUPPOSED TO BE A CONVERSATION?
IT LOOKS TO ME LIKE YOU'RE JUST SHOVING YOUR OPINION DOWN HER THROAT.
WHAT!?
YOU CAN ACT LIKE THE QUEEN OF THE CASTLE AND BLUSTER ON ALL YOU LIKE, BUT PLEASE KEEP IT TO YOUR OWN TERRITORY.
OTHERWISE, THE FACADE WILL CRACK ABOUT AS EASILY AS YOUR MAKEUP.
NGH!

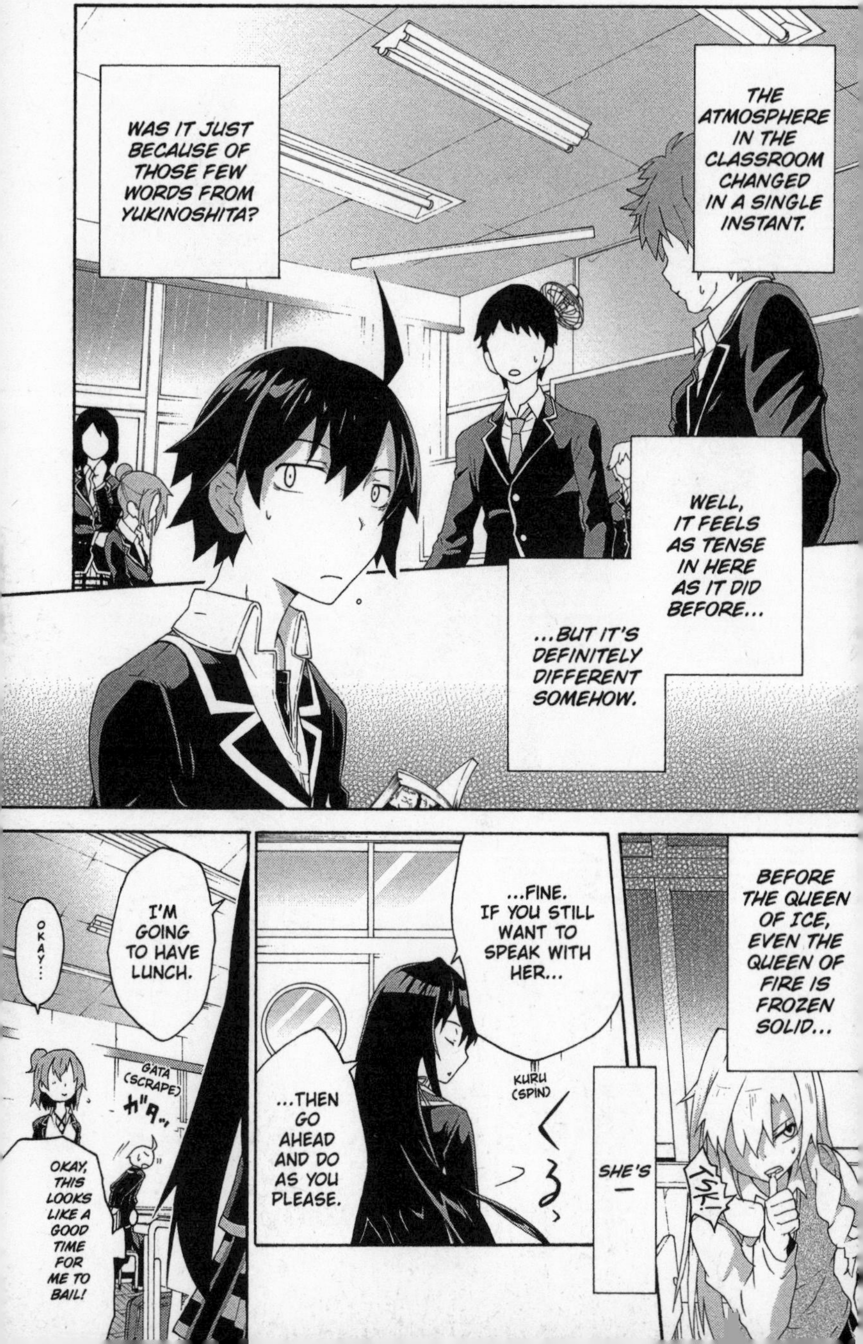
THE ATMOSPHERE IN THE CLASSROOM CHANGED IN A SINGLE INSTANT.
WAS IT JUST BECAUSE OF THOSE FEW WORDS FROM YUKINOSHITA?
WELL, IT FEELS AS TENSE IN HERE AS IT DID BEFORE...
...BUT IT'S DEFINITELY DIFFERENT SOMEHOW.
BEFORE THE QUEEN OF ICE, EVEN THE QUEEN OF FIRE IS FROZEN SOLID...
SHE'S —
TSK!
...FINE. IF YOU STILL WANT TO SPEAK WITH HER...
KURU (SPIN)
...THEN GO AHEAD AND DO AS YOU PLEASE.
I'M GOING TO HAVE LUNCH.
OKAY...
GATA (SCRAPE)
OKAY, THIS LOOKS LIKE A GOOD TIME FOR ME TO BAIL!

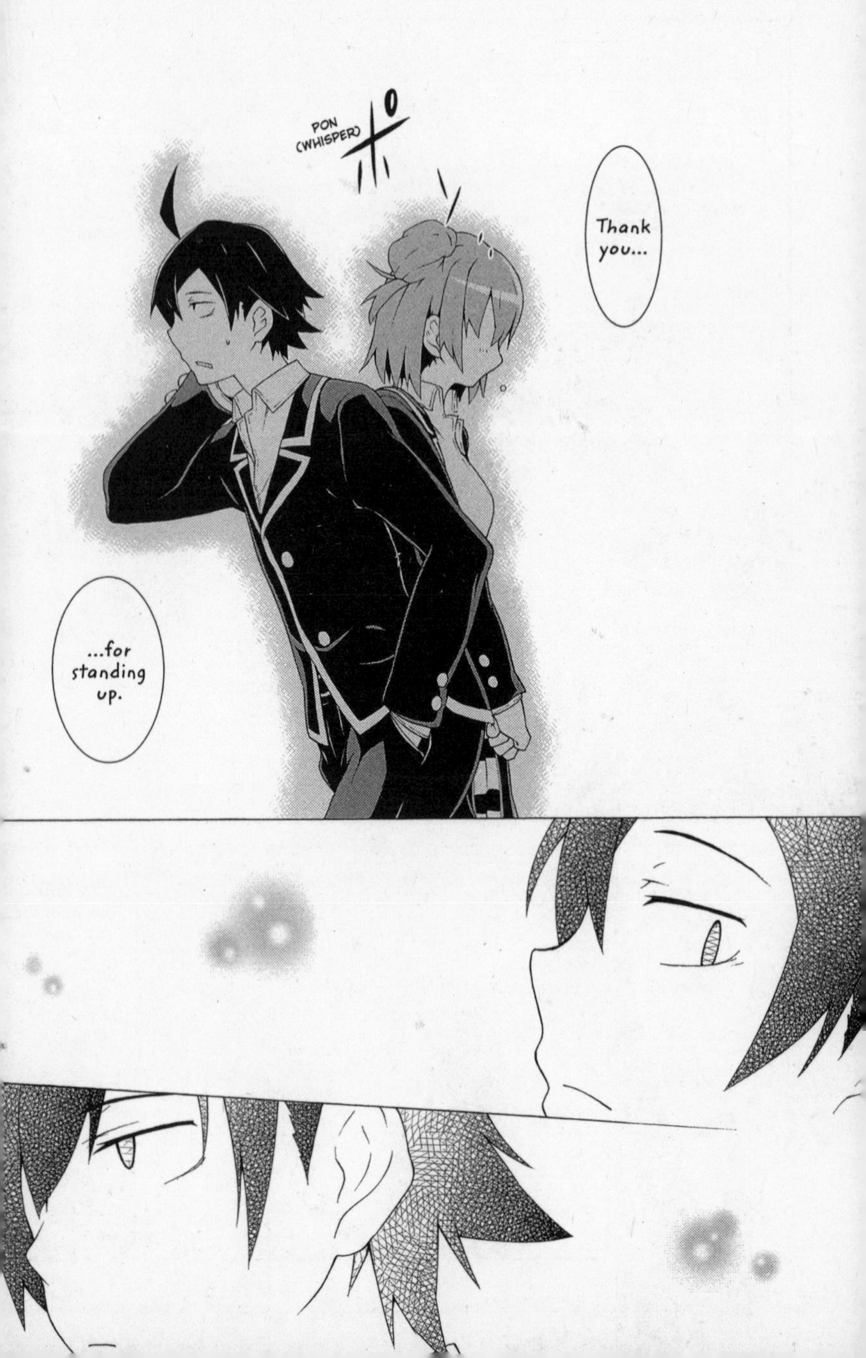
Thank you...
PON (WHISPER)
...for standing up.

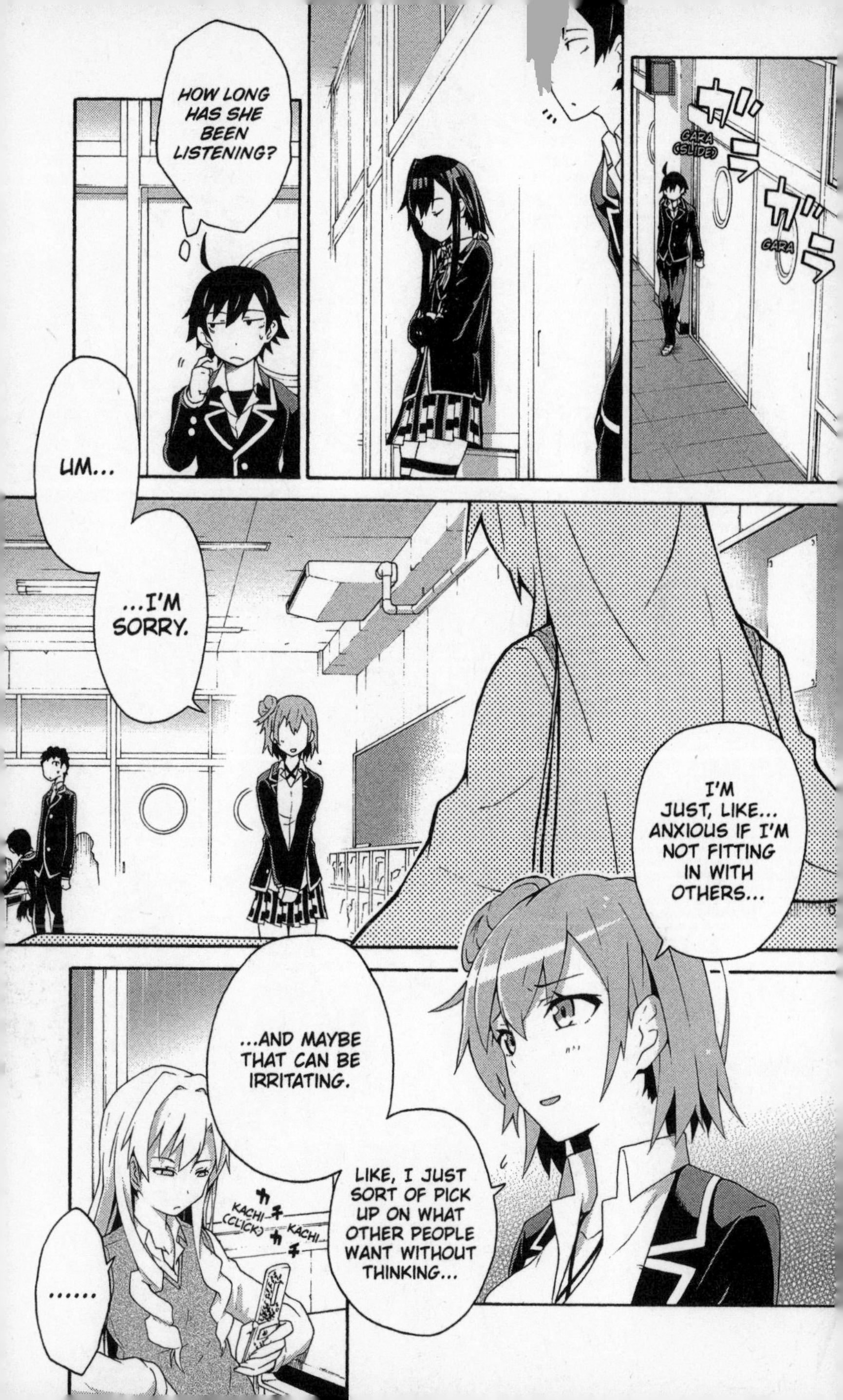

GARA (SLIDE)
GARA
HOW LONG HAS SHE BEEN LISTENING?
UM...
...I'M SORRY.
I'M JUST, LIKE... ANXIOUS IF I'M NOT FITTING IN WITH OTHERS...
...AND MAYBE THAT CAN BE IRRITATING.
LIKE, I JUST SORT OF PICK UP ON WHAT OTHER PEOPLE WANT WITHOUT THINKING...
KACHI (CLICK)
KACHI
......

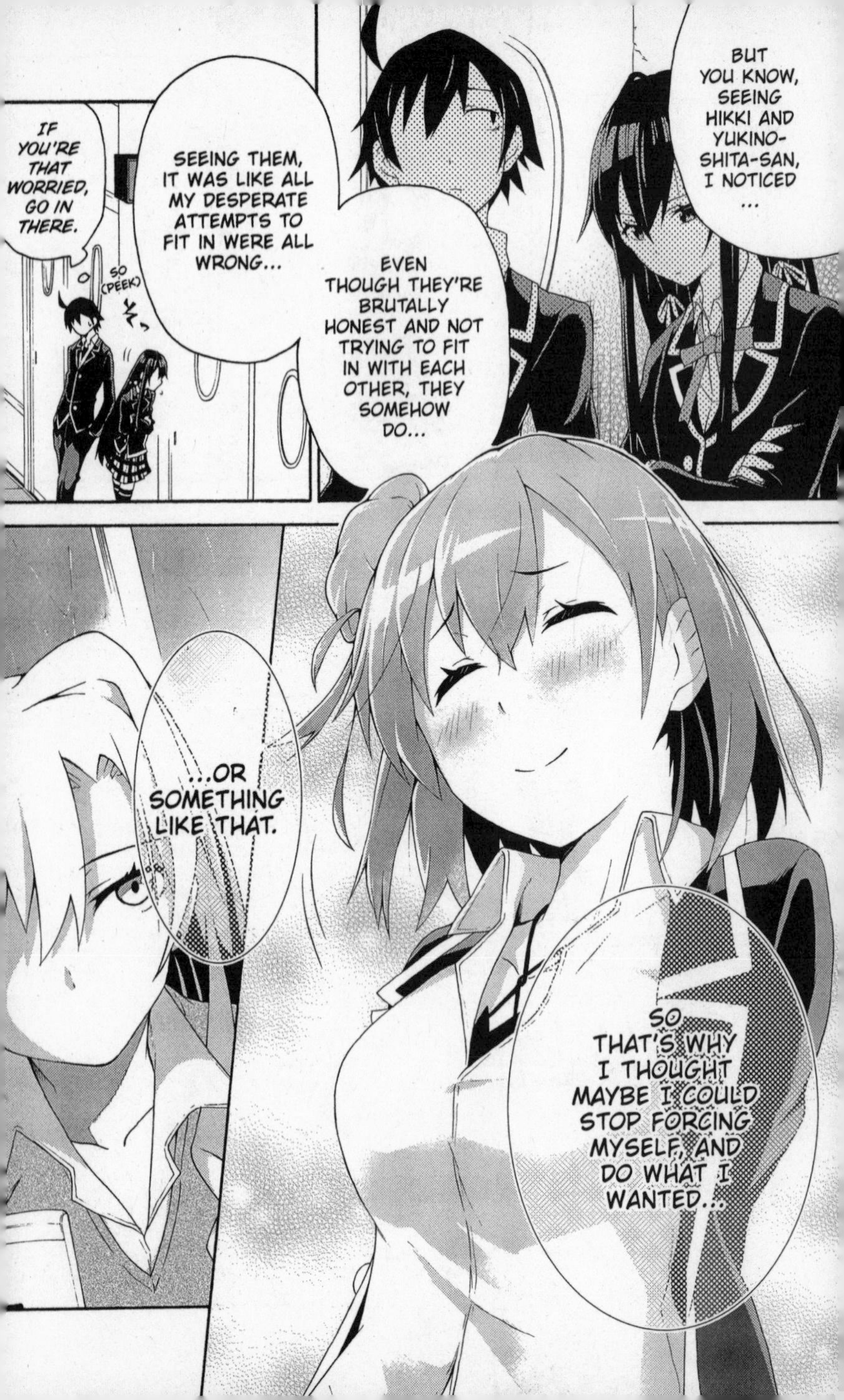
BUT YOU KNOW, SEEING HIKKI AND YUKINO-SHITA-SAN, I NOTICED...
EVEN THOUGH THEY'RE BRUTALLY HONEST AND NOT TRYING TO FIT IN WITH EACH OTHER, THEY SOMEHOW DO...
SEEING THEM, IT WAS LIKE ALL MY DESPERATE ATTEMPTS TO FIT IN WERE ALL WRONG...
IF YOU'RE THAT WORRIED, GO IN THERE.
SO (PEEK)
SO THAT'S WHY I THOUGHT MAYBE I COULD STOP FORCING MYSELF, AND DO WHAT I WANTED...
...OR SOMETHING LIKE THAT.

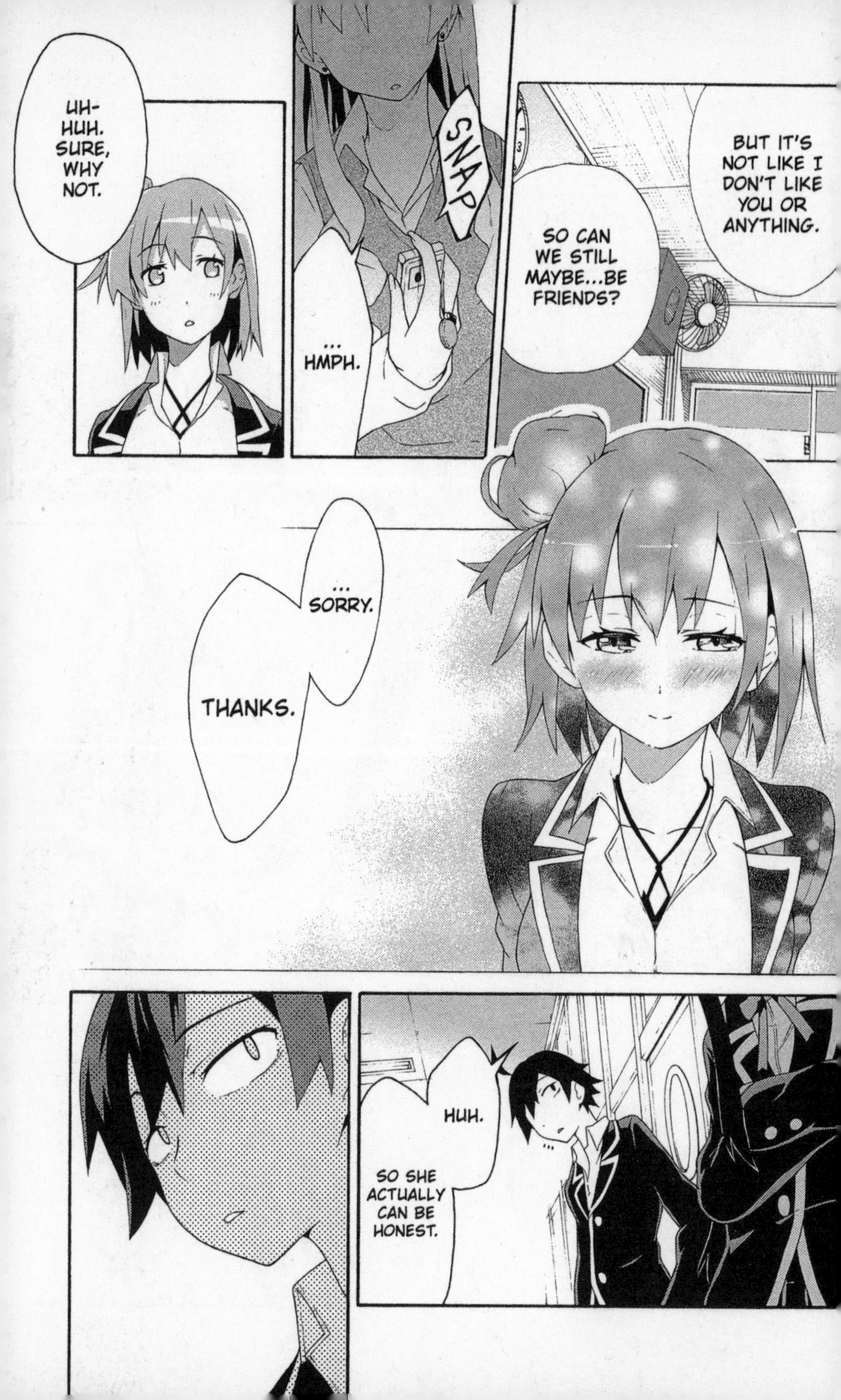
BUT IT'S NOT LIKE I DON'T LIKE YOU OR ANYTHING.
SO CAN WE STILL MAYBE...BE FRIENDS?
SNAP
... HMPH.
UH-HUH. SURE, WHY NOT.
... SORRY.
THANKS.
HUH.
...
SO SHE ACTUALLY CAN BE HONEST.

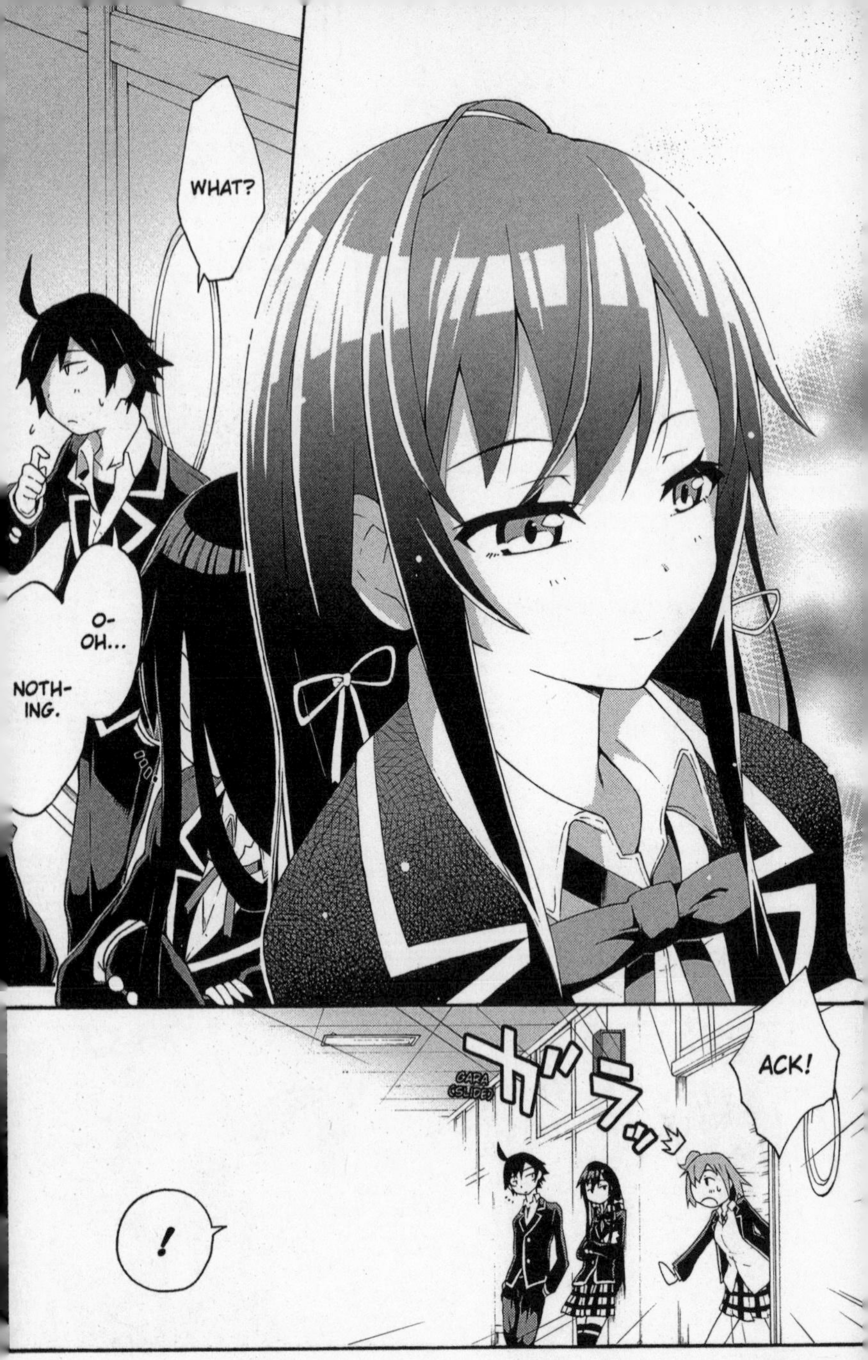
WHAT?
O-OH... NOTHING.
ACK!
GARA (SLIDE)
!

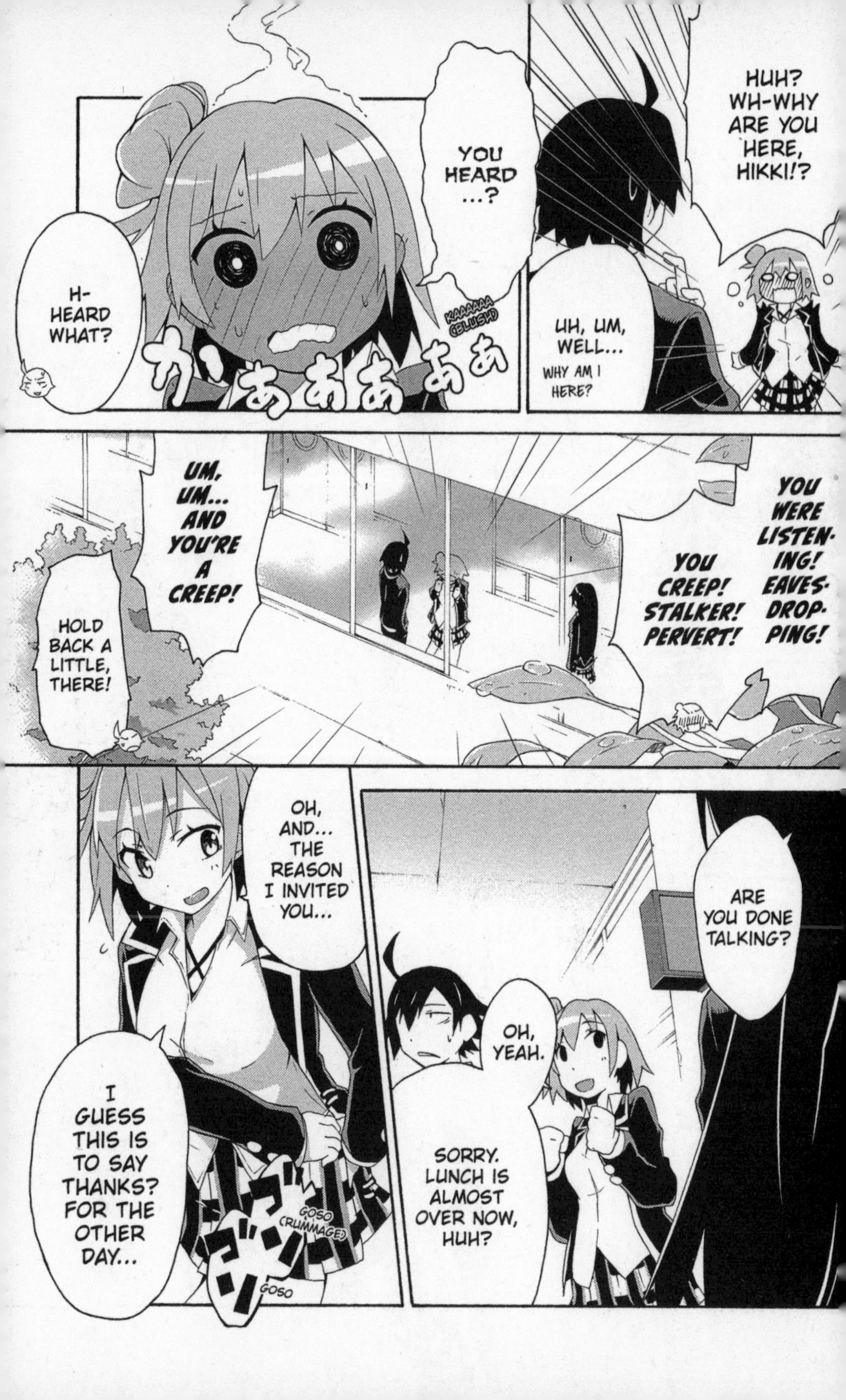
HUH? WH-WHY ARE YOU HERE, HIKKI!?
UH, UM, WELL...
WHY AM I HERE?
YOU HEARD ...?
KAAAAAA (BLUSH)
かぁぁぁぁ
H-HEARD WHAT?
YOU WERE LISTENING! EAVES-DROPPING!
YOU CREEP! STALKER! PERVERT!
UM, UM... AND YOU'RE A CREEP!
HOLD BACK A LITTLE, THERE!
ARE YOU DONE TALKING?
OH, YEAH.
SORRY. LUNCH IS ALMOST OVER NOW, HUH?
OH, AND... THE REASON I INVITED YOU...
I GUESS THIS IS TO SAY THANKS? FOR THE OTHER DAY...
GOSO (RUMMAGE)
GOSO

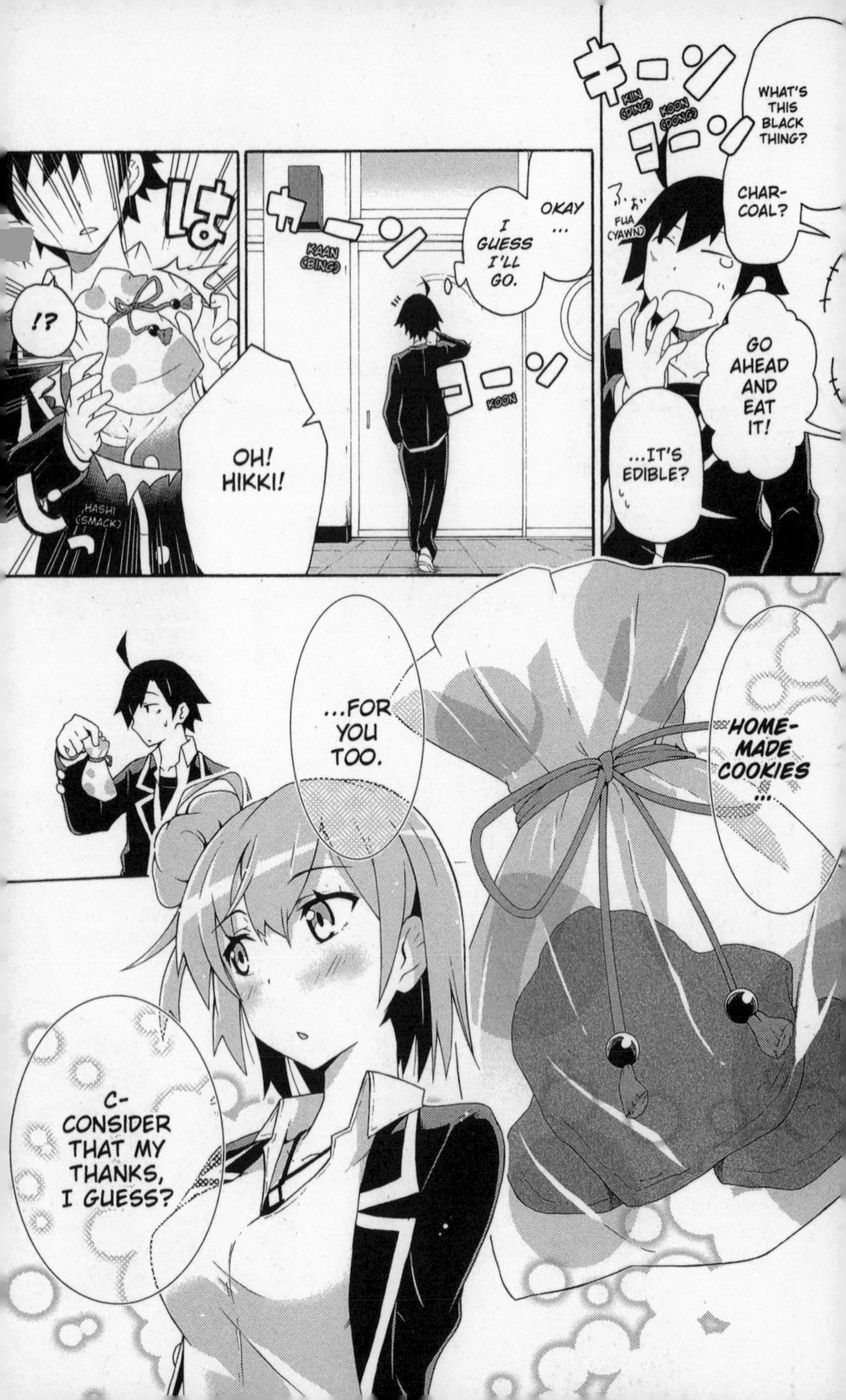
WHAT'S THIS BLACK THING?
KIIN (DING)
KOON (DONG)
CHAR-COAL?
FUA (YAWN)
GO AHEAD AND EAT IT!
...IT'S EDIBLE?
OKAY... I GUESS I'LL GO.
KAAN (BING)
KOON
OH! HIKKI!
HASHI (SMACK)
!?
HOME-MADE COOKIES...
...FOR YOU TOO.
C-CONSIDER THAT MY THANKS, I GUESS?

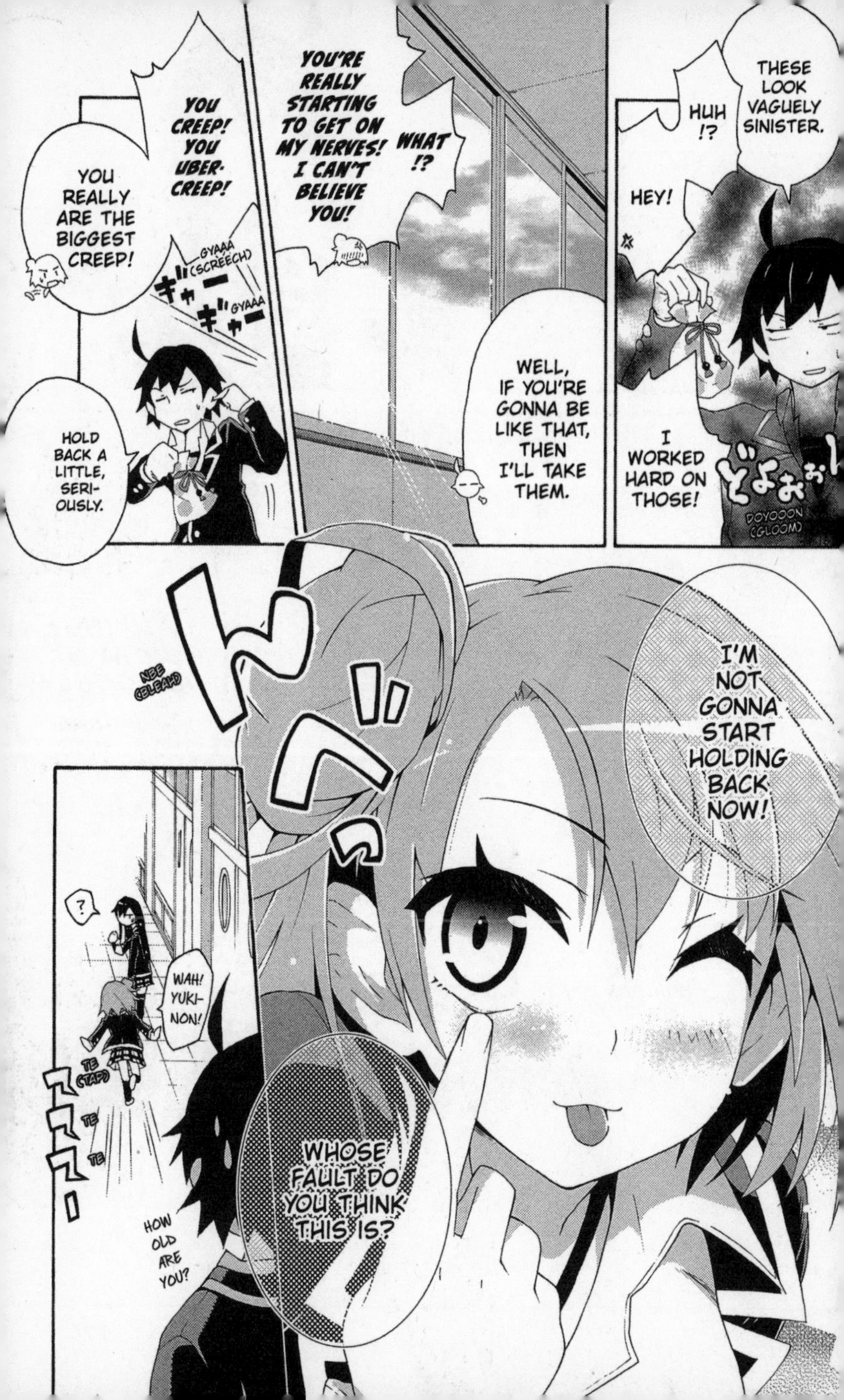
THESE LOOK VAGUELY SINISTER.
HUH!?
HEY!
I WORKED HARD ON THOSE!
DOYOOON (GLOOM)
WELL, IF YOU'RE GONNA BE LIKE THAT, THEN I'LL TAKE THEM.
WHAT!?
YOU'RE REALLY STARTING TO GET ON MY NERVES! I CAN'T BELIEVE YOU!
YOU CREEP! YOU UBER-CREEP!
YOU REALLY ARE THE BIGGEST CREEP!
GYAAA (SCREECH)
GYAAA
HOLD BACK A LITTLE, SERIOUSLY.
I'M NOT GONNA START HOLDING BACK NOW!
NBE (BLEAH)
WHOSE FAULT DO YOU THINK THIS IS?
HOW OLD ARE YOU?
?
WAH! YUKI-NON!
TE (TAP)
TE
TE

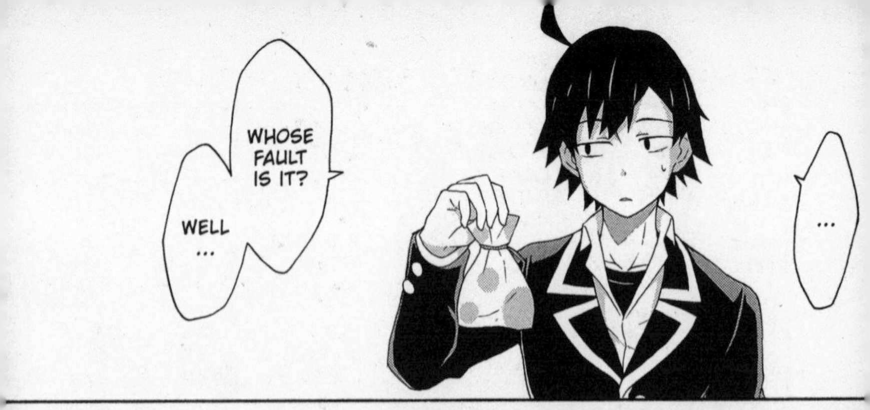
...
WHOSE FAULT IS IT? WELL ...

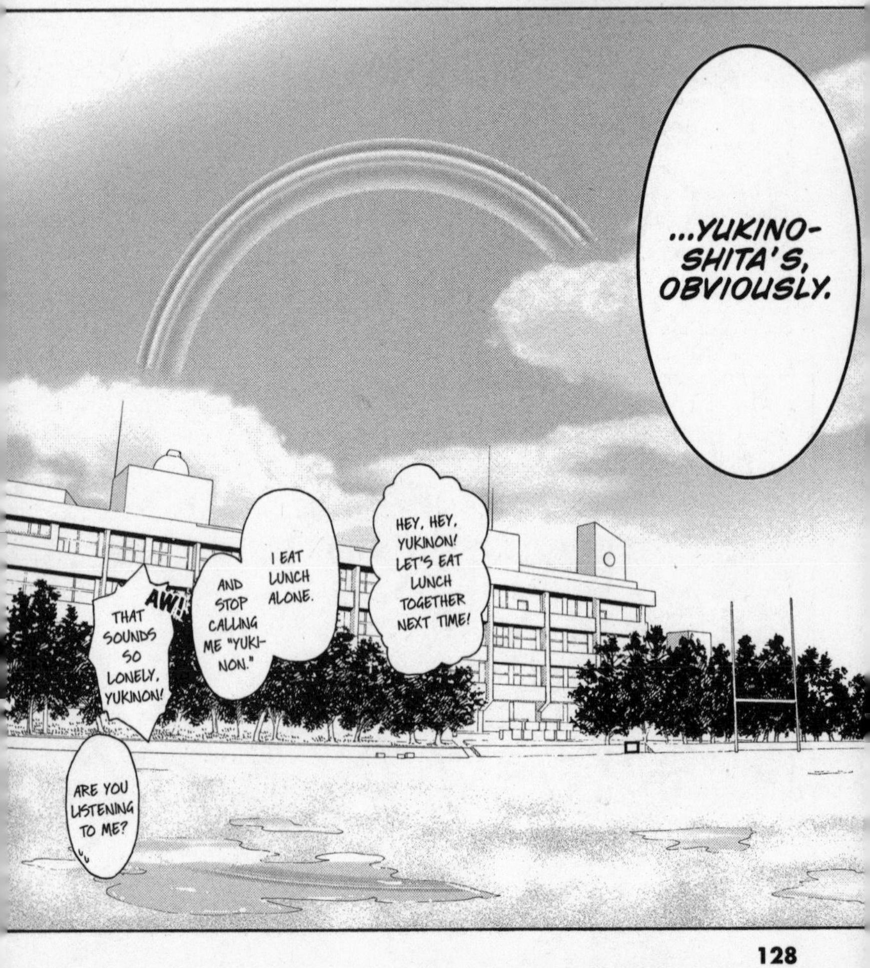
...YUKINO-SHITA'S, OBVIOUSLY.
HEY, HEY, YUKINON! LET'S EAT LUNCH TOGETHER NEXT TIME!
I EAT LUNCH ALONE.
AND STOP CALLING ME "YUKI-NON."
AW!
THAT SOUNDS SO LONELY, YUKINON!
ARE YOU LISTENING TO ME?

CHAPTER 5 ··· IN OTHER WORDS, YOSHITERU ZAIMOKUZA IS RATHER OFF.

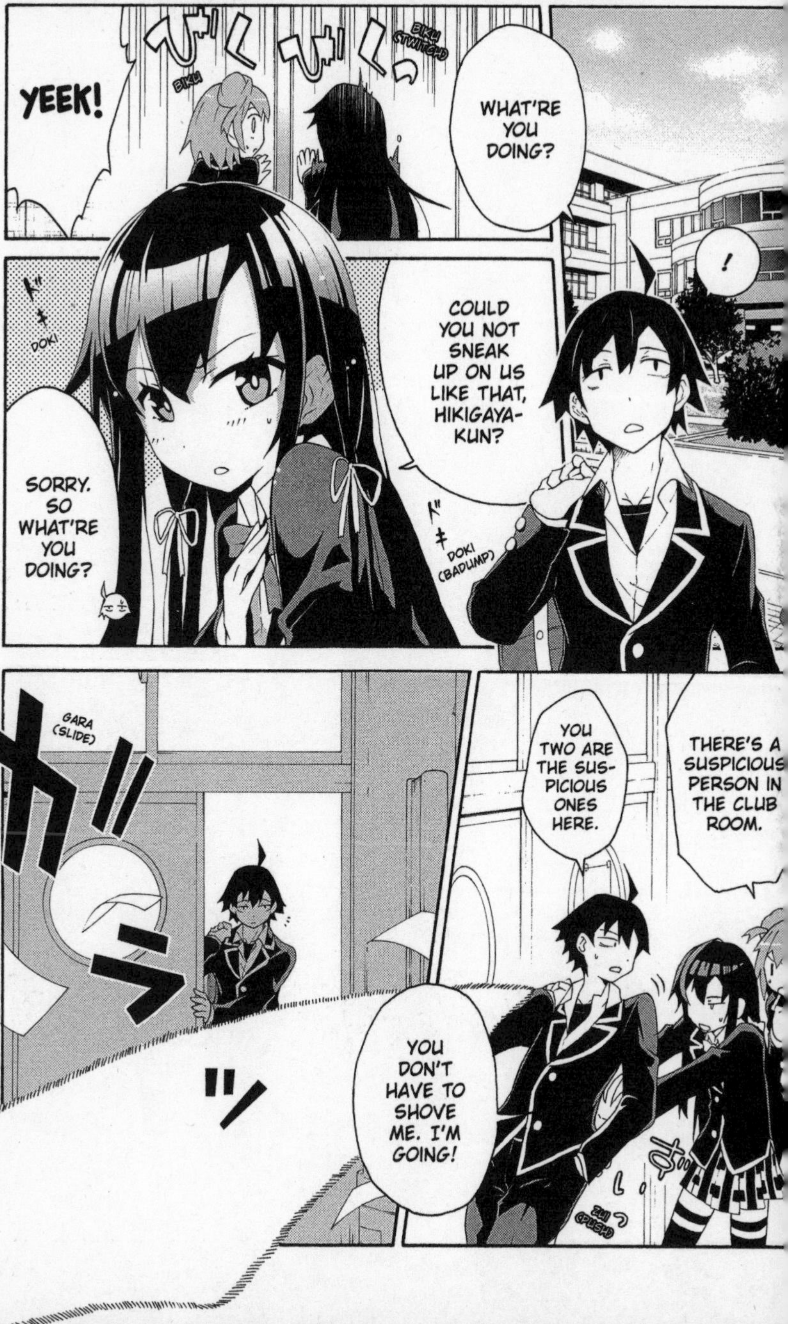
WHAT'RE YOU DOING?
!
BIKU (TWITCH)
BIKU
YEEK!
COULD YOU NOT SNEAK UP ON US LIKE THAT, HIKIGAYA-KUN?
DOKI
DOKI (BADUMP)
SORRY. SO WHAT'RE YOU DOING?
THERE'S A SUSPICIOUS PERSON IN THE CLUB ROOM.
YOU TWO ARE THE SUSPICIOUS ONES HERE.
YOU DON'T HAVE TO SHOVE ME. I'M GOING!
ZUI (PUSH)
GARA (SLIDE)

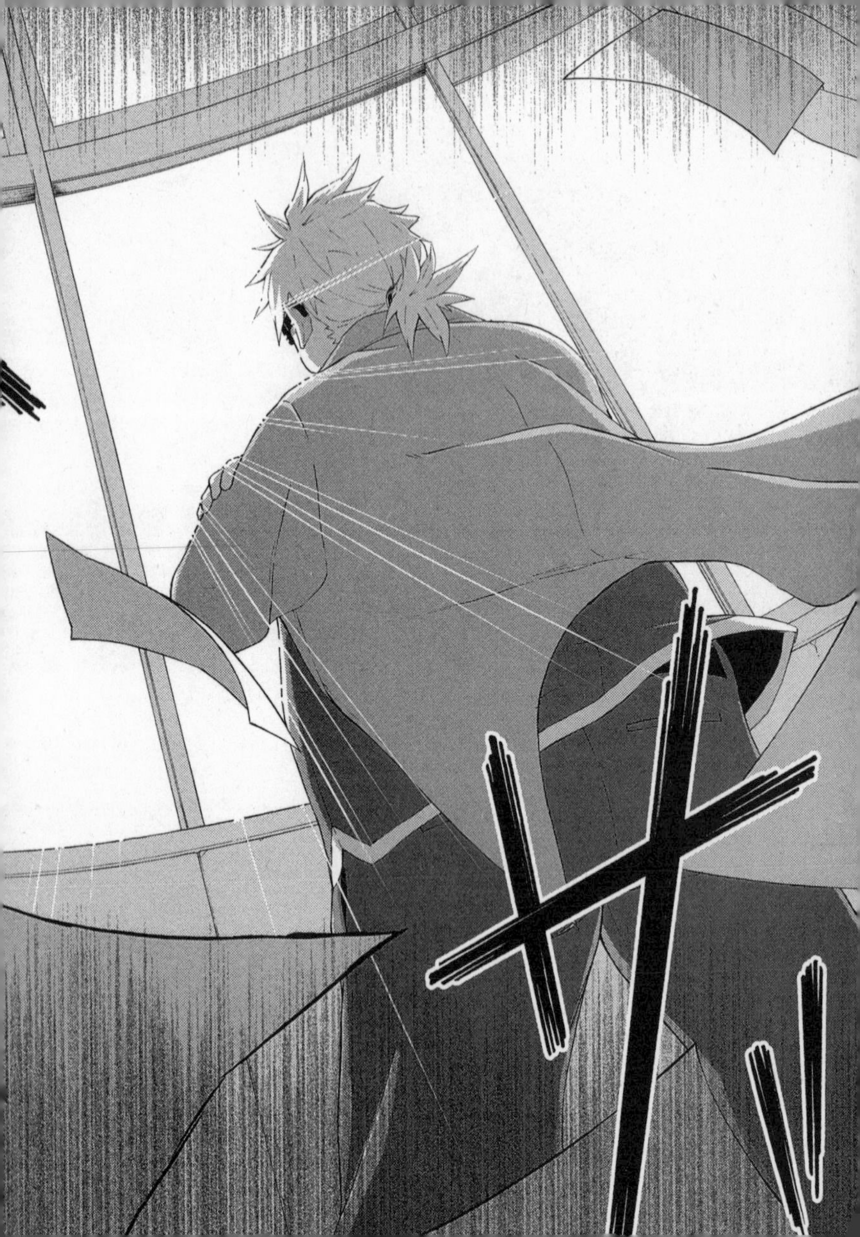

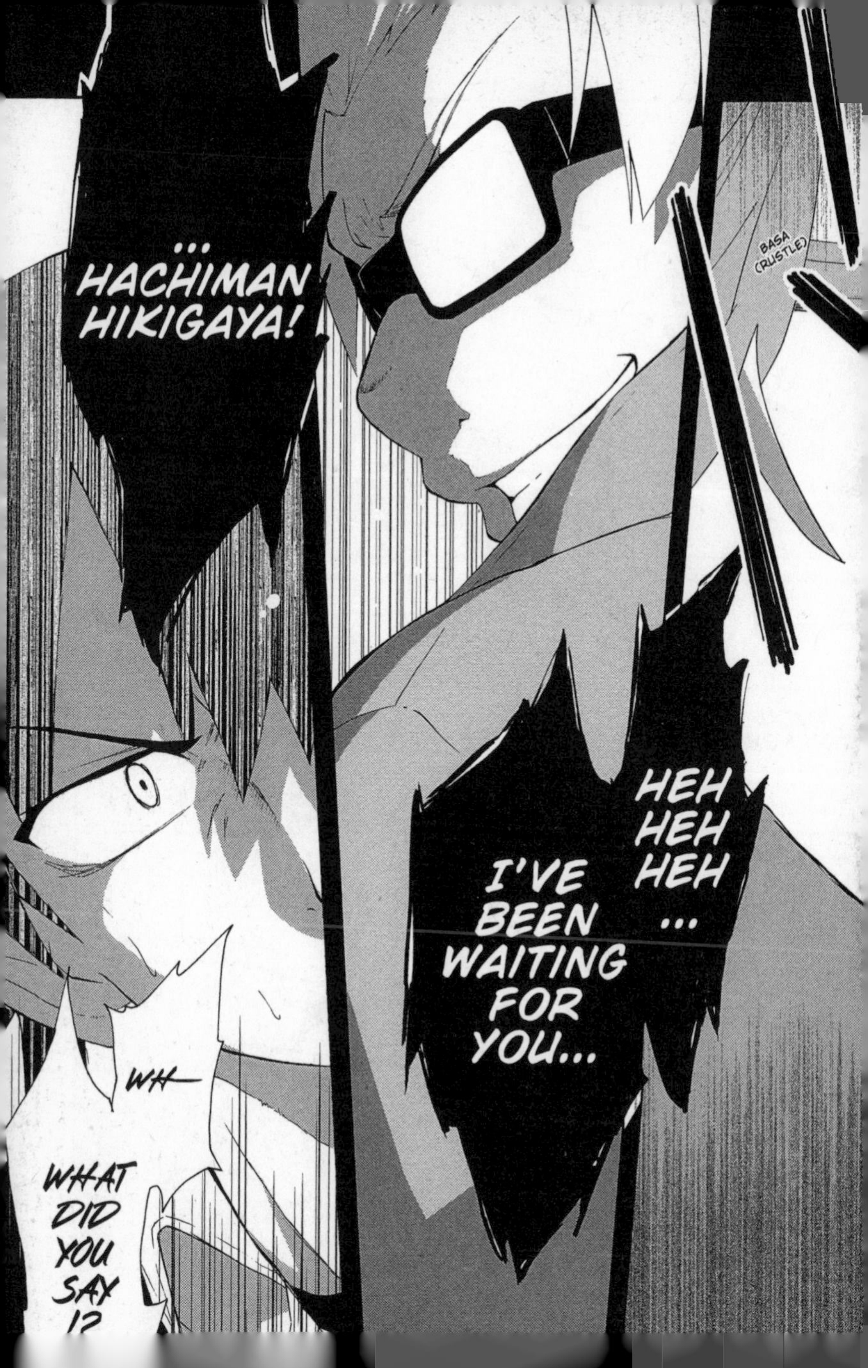
BASA (RUSTLE)
...HACHIMAN HIKIGAYA!
HEH HEH HEH...
I'VE BEEN WAITING FOR YOU...
WH
WHAT DID YOU SAY!?

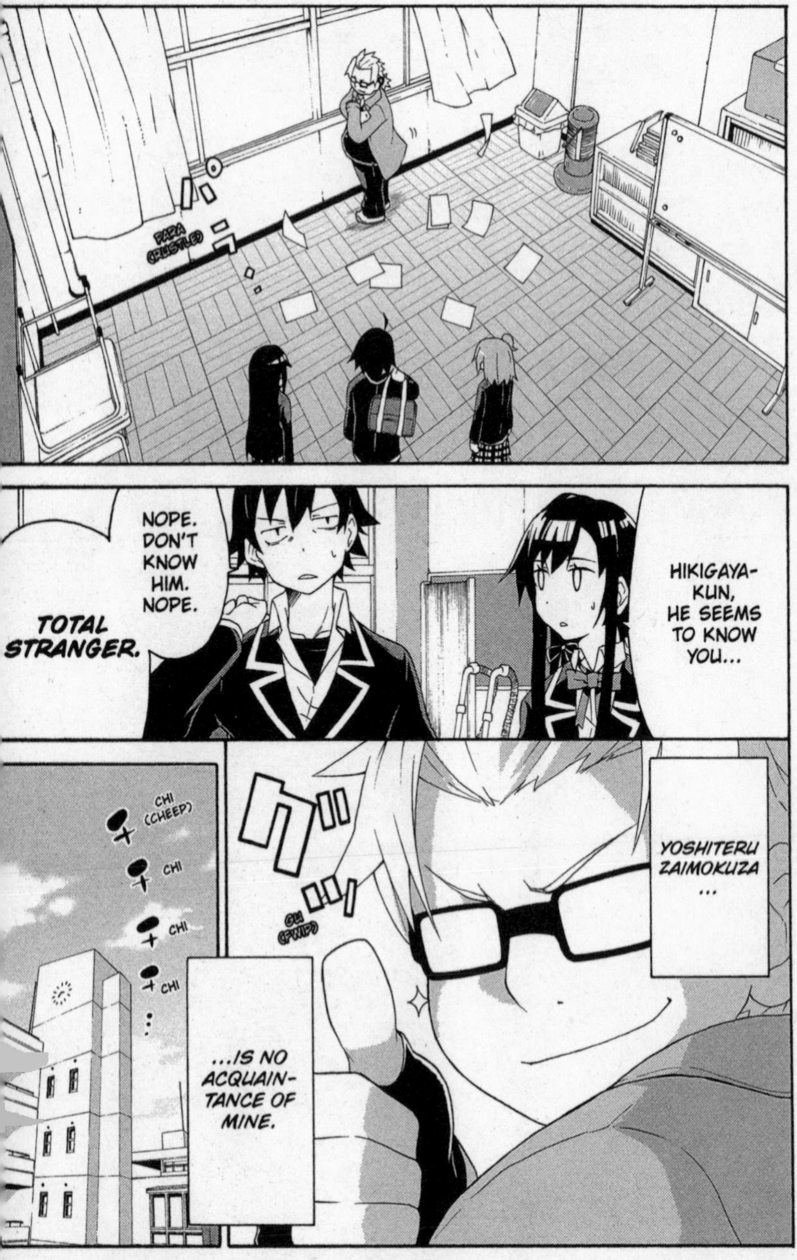
PARA
(RUSTLE)
HIKIGAYA-KUN, HE SEEMS TO KNOW YOU...
NOPE. DON'T KNOW HIM. NOPE.
TOTAL STRANGER.
YOSHITERU ZAIMOKUZA ...
GU
(FWIP)
...IS NO ACQUAINTANCE OF MINE.
CHI
(CHEEP)
CHI
CHI
CHI

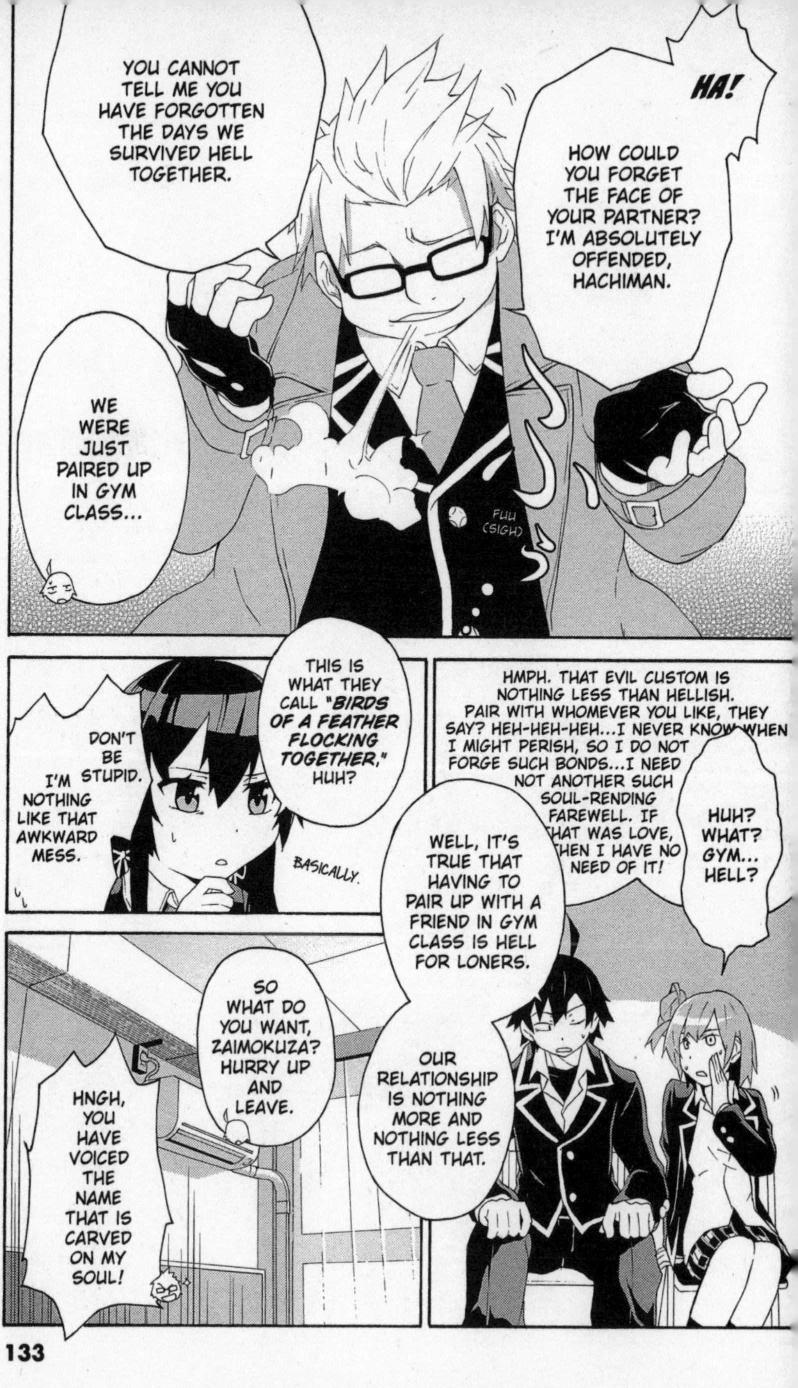
HA!
HOW COULD YOU FORGET THE FACE OF YOUR PARTNER? I'M ABSOLUTELY OFFENDED, HACHIMAN.
YOU CANNOT TELL ME YOU HAVE FORGOTTEN THE DAYS WE SURVIVED HELL TOGETHER.
FUU (SIGH)
WE WERE JUST PAIRED UP IN GYM CLASS...
HMPH. THAT EVIL CUSTOM IS NOTHING LESS THAN HELLISH. PAIR WITH WHOMEVER YOU LIKE, THEY SAY? HEH-HEH-HEH...I NEVER KNOW WHEN I MIGHT PERISH, SO I DO NOT FORGE SUCH BONDS...I NEED NOT ANOTHER SUCH SOUL-RENDING FAREWELL. IF THAT WAS LOVE, THEN I HAVE NO NEED OF IT!
HUH? WHAT? GYM... HELL?
THIS IS WHAT THEY CALL "BIRDS OF A FEATHER FLOCKING TOGETHER," HUH?
BASICALLY.
DON'T BE STUPID.
I'M NOTHING LIKE THAT AWKWARD MESS.
WELL, IT'S TRUE THAT HAVING TO PAIR UP WITH A FRIEND IN GYM CLASS IS HELL FOR LONERS.
OUR RELATIONSHIP IS NOTHING MORE AND NOTHING LESS THAN THAT.
SO WHAT DO YOU WANT, ZAIMOKUZA? HURRY UP AND LEAVE.
HNGH, YOU HAVE VOICED THE NAME THAT IS CARVED ON MY SOUL!

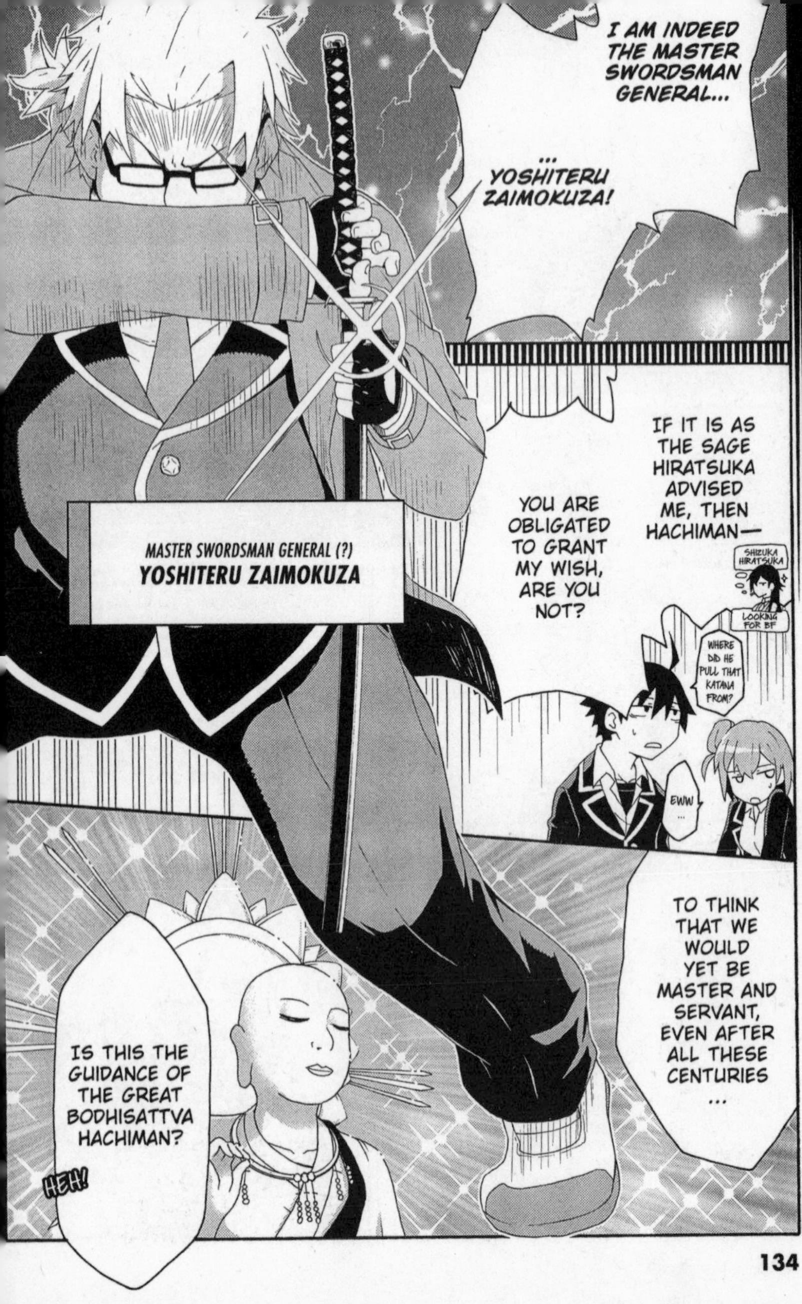

I AM INDEED THE MASTER SWORDSMAN GENERAL...
... YOSHITERU ZAIMOKUZA!
IF IT IS AS THE SAGE HIRATSUKA ADVISED ME, THEN HACHIMAN—
YOU ARE OBLIGATED TO GRANT MY WISH, ARE YOU NOT?
SHIZUKA HIRATSUKA
LOOKING FOR BF
WHERE DID HE PULL THAT KATANA FROM?
EWW ...
MASTER SWORDSMAN GENERAL (?)
YOSHITERU ZAIMOKUZA
TO THINK THAT WE WOULD YET BE MASTER AND SERVANT, EVEN AFTER ALL THESE CENTURIES ...
IS THIS THE GUIDANCE OF THE GREAT BODHISATTVA HACHIMAN?
HEH!

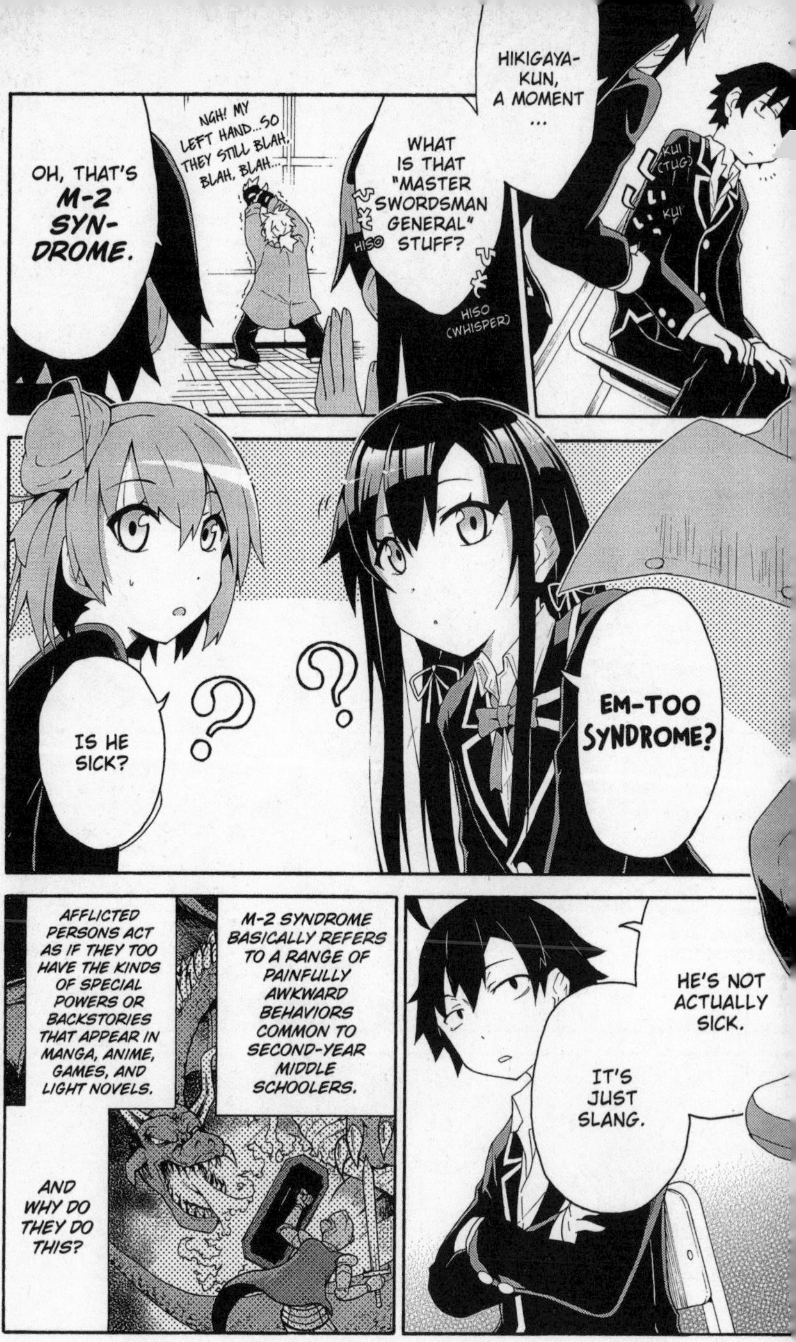
HIKIGAYA-KUN, A MOMENT...
KUI (TUG)
KUI
WHAT IS THAT "MASTER SWORDSMAN GENERAL" STUFF?
HISO (WHISPER)
HISO
NGH! MY LEFT HAND...SO THEY STILL BLAH, BLAH, BLAH...
OH, THAT'S M-2 SYNDROME.
EM-TOO SYNDROME?
IS HE SICK?
HE'S NOT ACTUALLY SICK.
IT'S JUST SLANG.
M-2 SYNDROME BASICALLY REFERS TO A RANGE OF PAINFULLY AWKWARD BEHAVIORS COMMON TO SECOND-YEAR MIDDLE SCHOOLERS.
AFFLICTED PERSONS ACT AS IF THEY TOO HAVE THE KINDS OF SPECIAL POWERS OR BACKSTORIES THAT APPEAR IN MANGA, ANIME, GAMES, AND LIGHT NOVELS.
AND WHY DO THEY DO THIS?

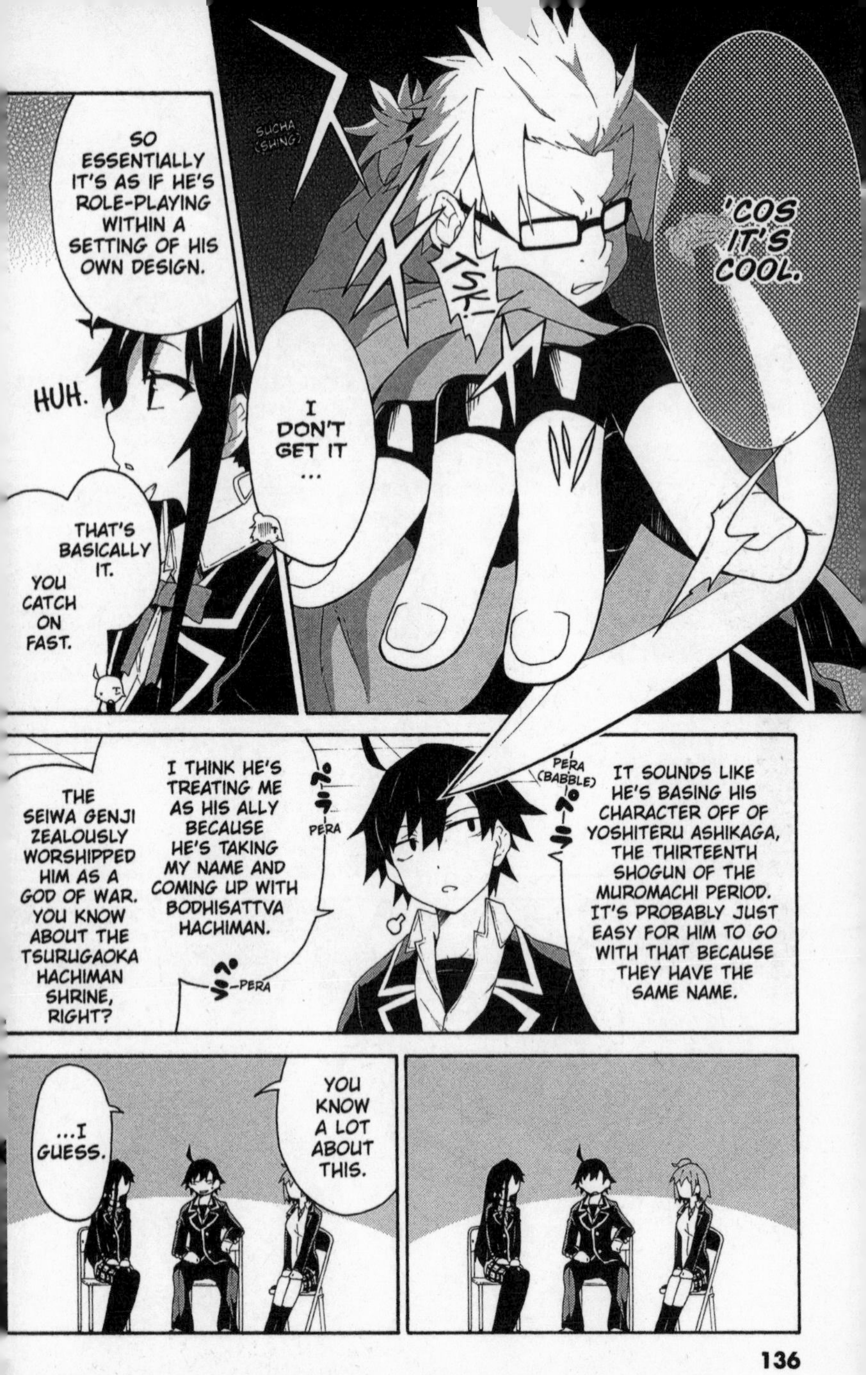
SUCHA (SHING)
'COS IT'S COOL.
TSK!
I DON'T GET IT ...
SO ESSENTIALLY IT'S AS IF HE'S ROLE-PLAYING WITHIN A SETTING OF HIS OWN DESIGN.
HUH.
THAT'S BASICALLY IT.
YOU CATCH ON FAST.
PERA (BABBLE)
IT SOUNDS LIKE HE'S BASING HIS CHARACTER OFF OF YOSHITERU ASHIKAGA, THE THIRTEENTH SHOGUN OF THE MUROMACHI PERIOD. IT'S PROBABLY JUST EASY FOR HIM TO GO WITH THAT BECAUSE THEY HAVE THE SAME NAME.
PERA
I THINK HE'S TREATING ME AS HIS ALLY BECAUSE HE'S TAKING MY NAME AND COMING UP WITH BODHISATTVA HACHIMAN.
PERA
THE SEIWA GENJI ZEALOUSLY WORSHIPPED HIM AS A GOD OF WAR. YOU KNOW ABOUT THE TSURUGAOKA HACHIMAN SHRINE, RIGHT?
YOU KNOW A LOT ABOUT THIS.
...I GUESS.

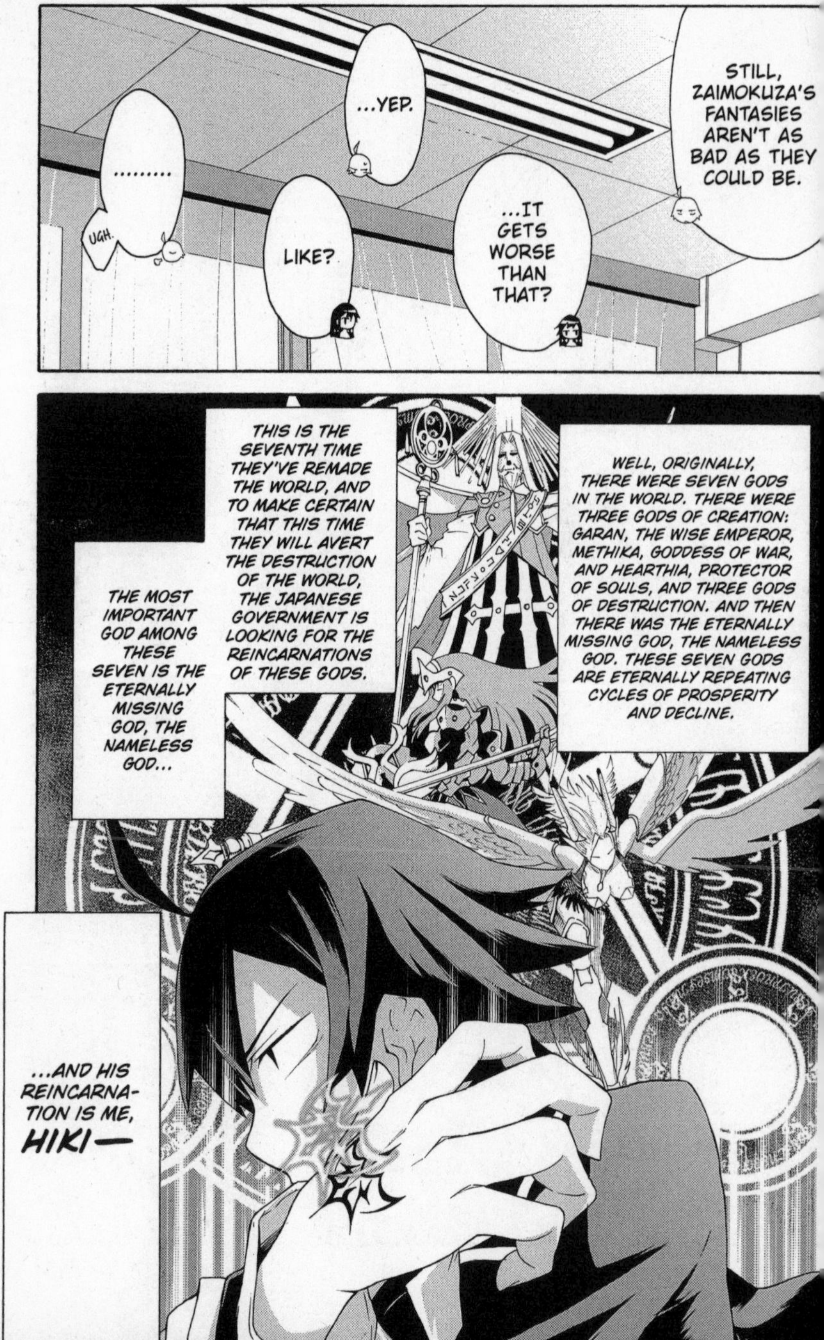
STILL, ZAIMOKUZA'S FANTASIES AREN'T AS BAD AS THEY COULD BE.
...IT GETS WORSE THAN THAT?
...YEP.
LIKE?
....
UGH.
WELL, ORIGINALLY, THERE WERE SEVEN GODS IN THE WORLD. THERE WERE THREE GODS OF CREATION: GARAN, THE WISE EMPEROR, METHIKA, GODDESS OF WAR, AND HEARTHIA, PROTECTOR OF SOULS, AND THREE GODS OF DESTRUCTION. AND THEN THERE WAS THE ETERNALLY MISSING GOD, THE NAMELESS GOD. THESE SEVEN GODS ARE ETERNALLY REPEATING CYCLES OF PROSPERITY AND DECLINE.
THIS IS THE SEVENTH TIME THEY'VE REMADE THE WORLD, AND TO MAKE CERTAIN THAT THIS TIME THEY WILL AVERT THE DESTRUCTION OF THE WORLD, THE JAPANESE GOVERNMENT IS LOOKING FOR THE REINCARNATIONS OF THESE GODS.
THE MOST IMPORTANT GOD AMONG THESE SEVEN IS THE ETERNALLY MISSING GOD, THE NAMELESS GOD...
...AND HIS REINCARNATION IS ME, HIKI—

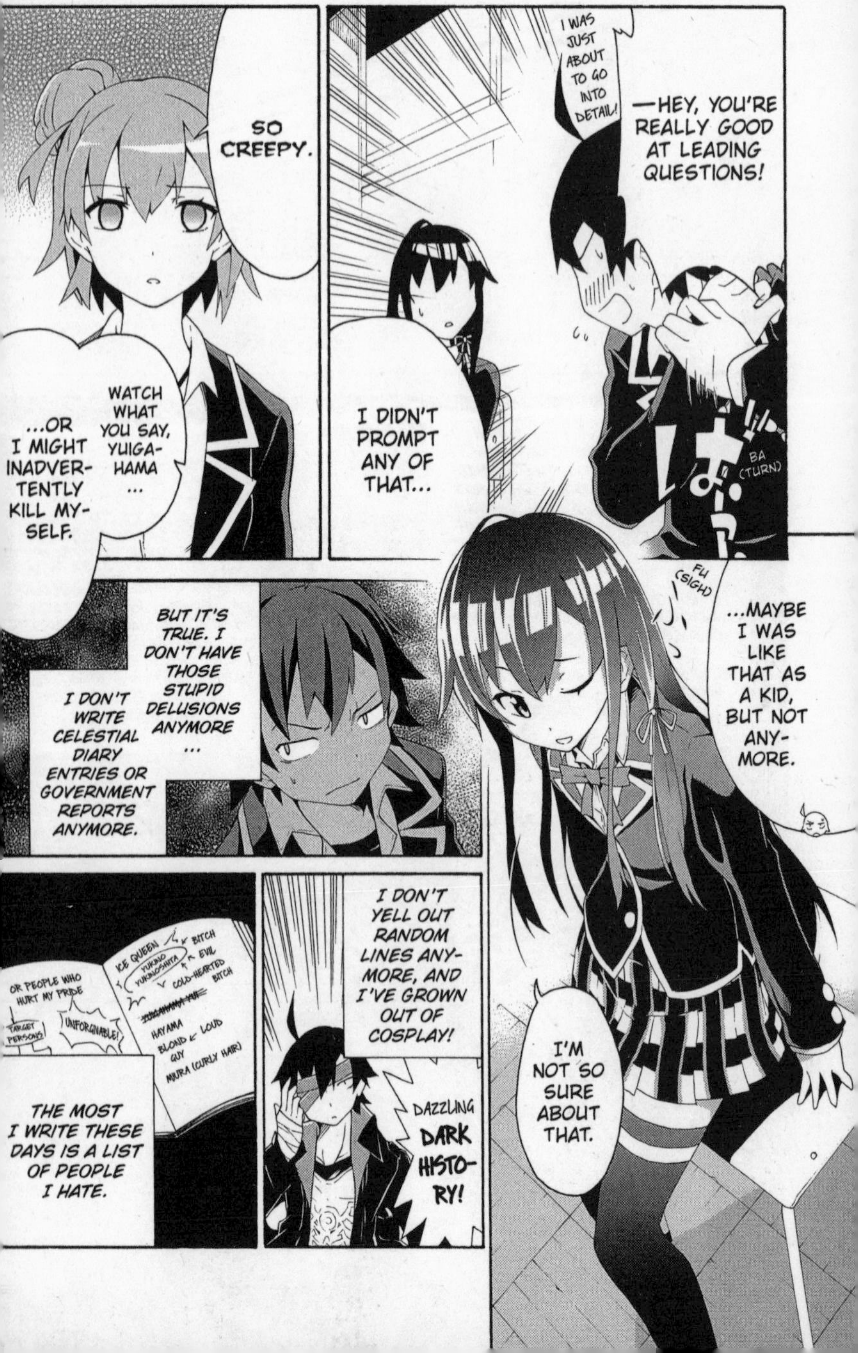

I WAS JUST ABOUT TO GO INTO DETAIL!
—HEY, YOU'RE REALLY GOOD AT LEADING QUESTIONS!
I DIDN'T PROMPT ANY OF THAT...
BA (TURN)
SO CREEPY.
WATCH WHAT YOU SAY, YUIGAHAMA...
...OR I MIGHT INADVERTENTLY KILL MYSELF.
FU (SIGH)
...MAYBE I WAS LIKE THAT AS A KID, BUT NOT ANYMORE.
I'M NOT SO SURE ABOUT THAT.
BUT IT'S TRUE. I DON'T HAVE THOSE STUPID DELUSIONS ANYMORE...
I DON'T WRITE CELESTIAL DIARY ENTRIES OR GOVERNMENT REPORTS ANYMORE.
I DON'T YELL OUT RANDOM LINES ANYMORE, AND I'VE GROWN OUT OF COSPLAY!
DAZZLING DARK HISTORY!
ICE QUEEN
YUKINO YUKINOSHITA
BITCH
EVIL
COLD-HEARTED BITCH
YUIGAHAMA YUI
HAYAMA
BLOND GUY
LOUD
MIURA (CURLY HAIR)
OR PEOPLE WHO HURT MY PRIDE
TARGET PERSONS!
UNFORGIVABLE!
THE MOST I WRITE THESE DAYS IS A LIST OF PEOPLE I HATE.

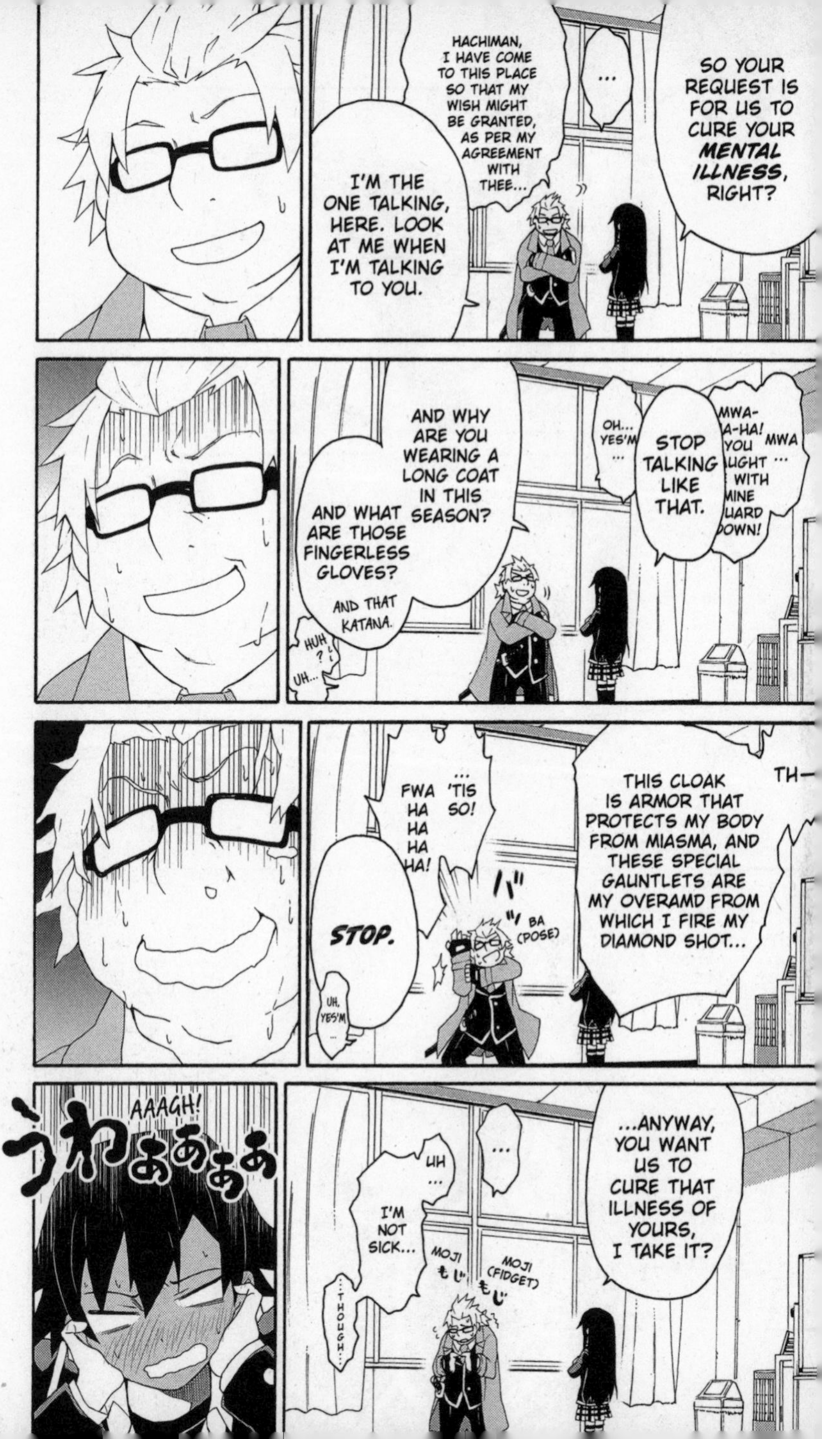
SO YOUR REQUEST IS FOR US TO CURE YOUR ***MENTAL ILLNESS***, RIGHT?
...
HACHIMAN, I HAVE COME TO THIS PLACE SO THAT MY WISH MIGHT BE GRANTED, AS PER MY AGREEMENT WITH THEE...
I'M THE ONE TALKING, HERE. LOOK AT ME WHEN I'M TALKING TO YOU.
MWA ...
MWA-A-HA! YOU UGHT WITH MINE UARD DOWN!
STOP TALKING LIKE THAT.
OH... YES'M ...
AND WHY ARE YOU WEARING A LONG COAT IN THIS SEASON?
AND WHAT ARE THOSE FINGERLESS GLOVES?
AND THAT KATANA.
HUH?
UH...
TH—
THIS CLOAK IS ARMOR THAT PROTECTS MY BODY FROM MIASMA, AND THESE SPECIAL GAUNTLETS ARE MY OVERAMD FROM WHICH I FIRE MY DIAMOND SHOT...
...'TIS SO!
FWA HA HA HA HA!
バ BA (POSE)
STOP.
UH, YES'M ...
...ANYWAY, YOU WANT US TO CURE THAT ILLNESS OF YOURS, I TAKE IT?
...
UH ...
I'M NOT SICK...
もじ MOJI (FIDGET)
もじ MOJI
...THOUGH...
うわぁぁぁぁ AAAGH!

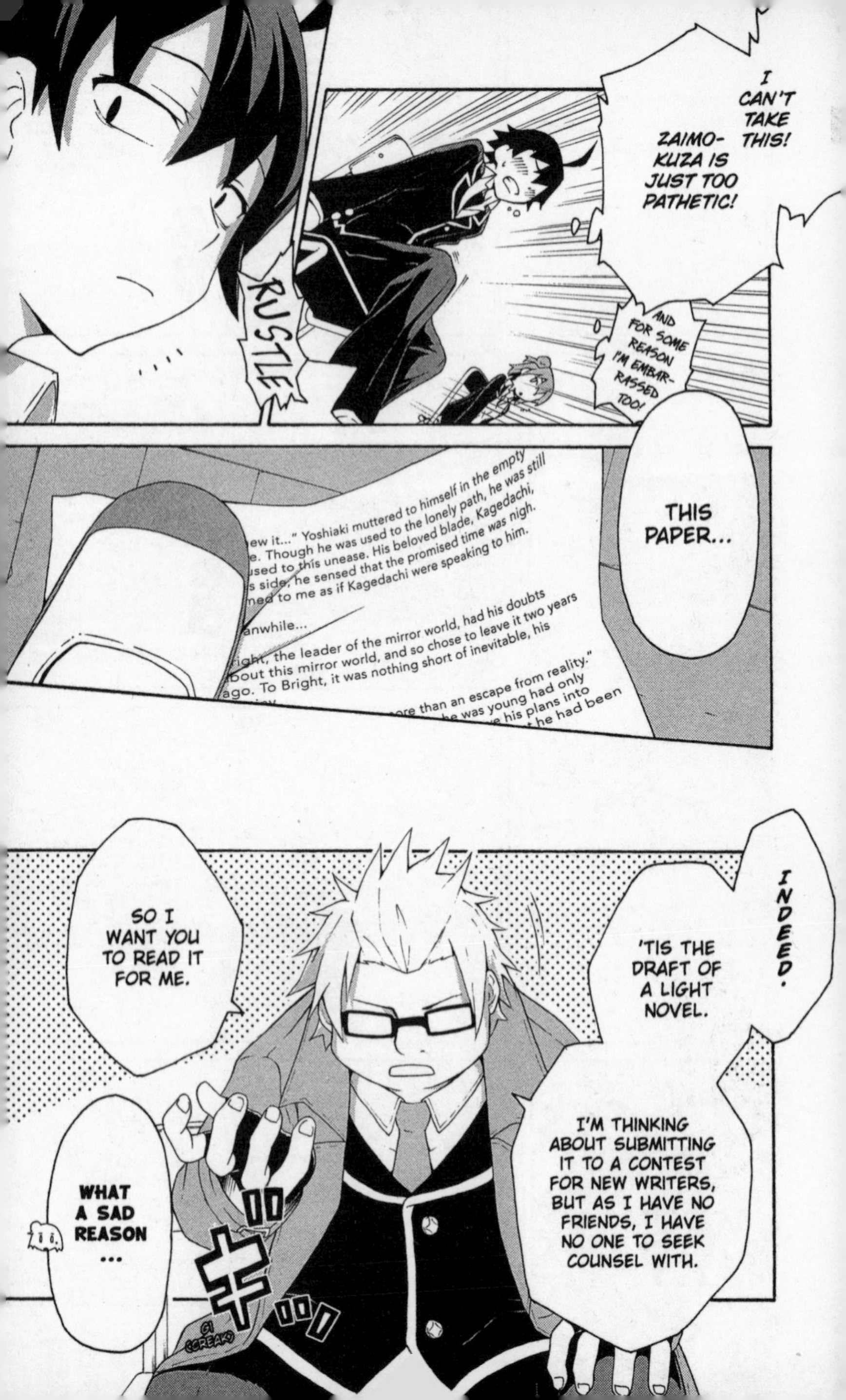
I CAN'T TAKE THIS!
ZAIMOKUZA IS JUST TOO PATHETIC!
AND FOR SOME REASON I'M EMBARRASSED TOO!
RUSTLE
...
THIS PAPER...
ew it..." Yoshiaki muttered to himself in the empty
e. Though he was used to the lonely path, he was still
used to this unease. His beloved blade, Kagedachi,
s side, he sensed that the promised time was nigh.
med to me as if Kagedachi were speaking to him.
anwhile...
right, the leader of the mirror world, had his doubts
bout this mirror world, and so chose to leave it two years
ago. To Bright, it was nothing short of inevitable, his
ore than an escape from reality."
INDEED.
'TIS THE DRAFT OF A LIGHT NOVEL.
I'M THINKING ABOUT SUBMITTING IT TO A CONTEST FOR NEW WRITERS, BUT AS I HAVE NO FRIENDS, I HAVE NO ONE TO SEEK COUNSEL WITH.
SO I WANT YOU TO READ IT FOR ME.
WHAT A SAD REASON...
GI (CREAK)

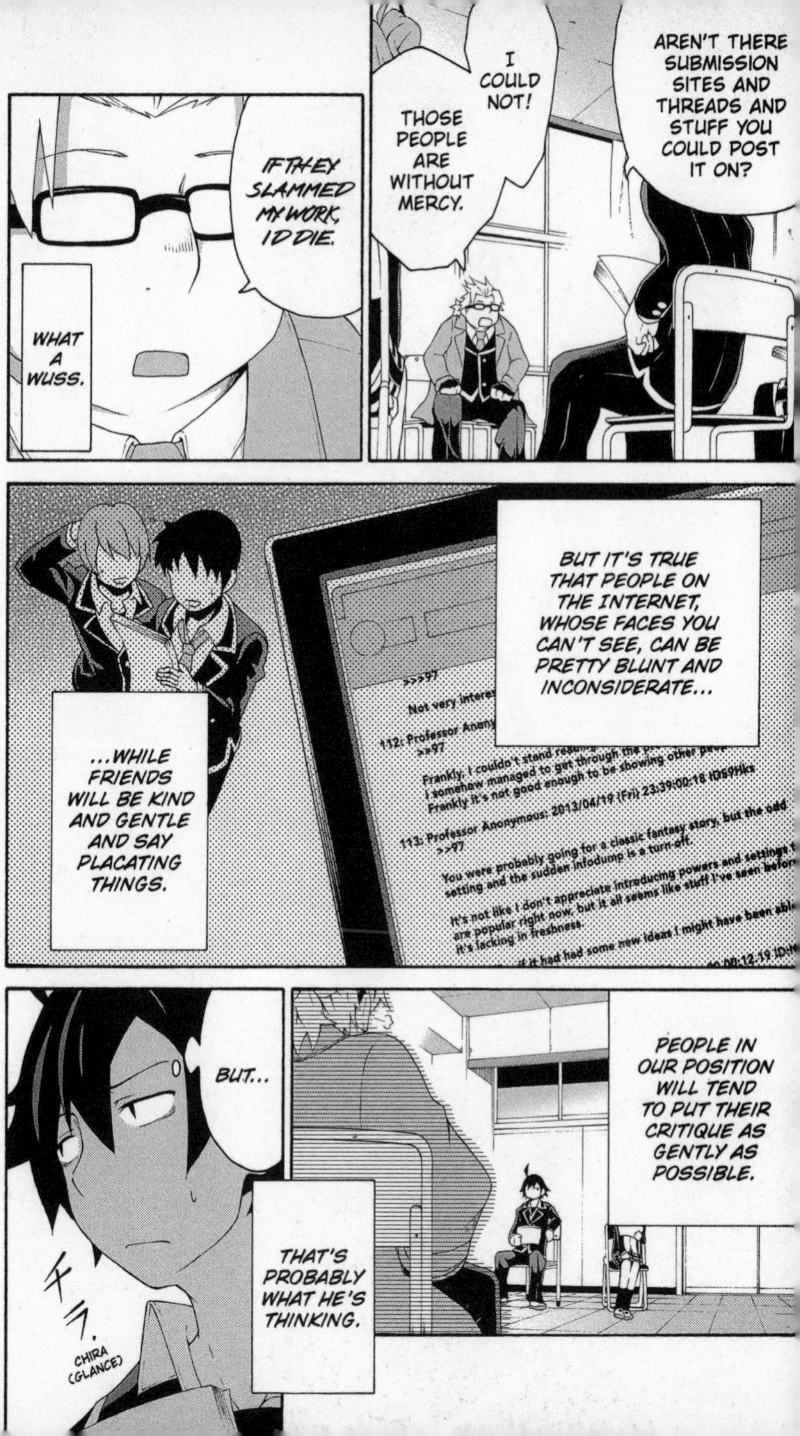

AREN'T THERE SUBMISSION SITES AND THREADS AND STUFF YOU COULD POST IT ON?
I COULD NOT!
THOSE PEOPLE ARE WITHOUT MERCY.
IF THEY SLAMMED MY WORK, I'D DIE.
WHAT A WUSS.
BUT IT'S TRUE THAT PEOPLE ON THE INTERNET, WHOSE FACES YOU CAN'T SEE, CAN BE PRETTY BLUNT AND INCONSIDERATE...
>>97
Not very interes
112: Professor Anony
>>97
Frankly, I couldn't stand readi
I somehow managed to get through the
Frankly it's not good enough to be showing other peo
113: Professor Anonymous: 2013/04/19 (Fri) 23:39:00.18
>>97
You were probably going for a classic fantasy story, but the odd
setting and the sudden infodump is a turn-off.
It's not like I don't appreciate introducing powers and settings
are popular right now, but it all seems like stuff I've seen before
it's lacking in freshness.
...WHILE FRIENDS WILL BE KIND AND GENTLE AND SAY PLACATING THINGS.
PEOPLE IN OUR POSITION WILL TEND TO PUT THEIR CRITIQUE AS GENTLY AS POSSIBLE.
BUT...
THAT'S PROBABLY WHAT HE'S THINKING.
CHIRA (GLANCE)

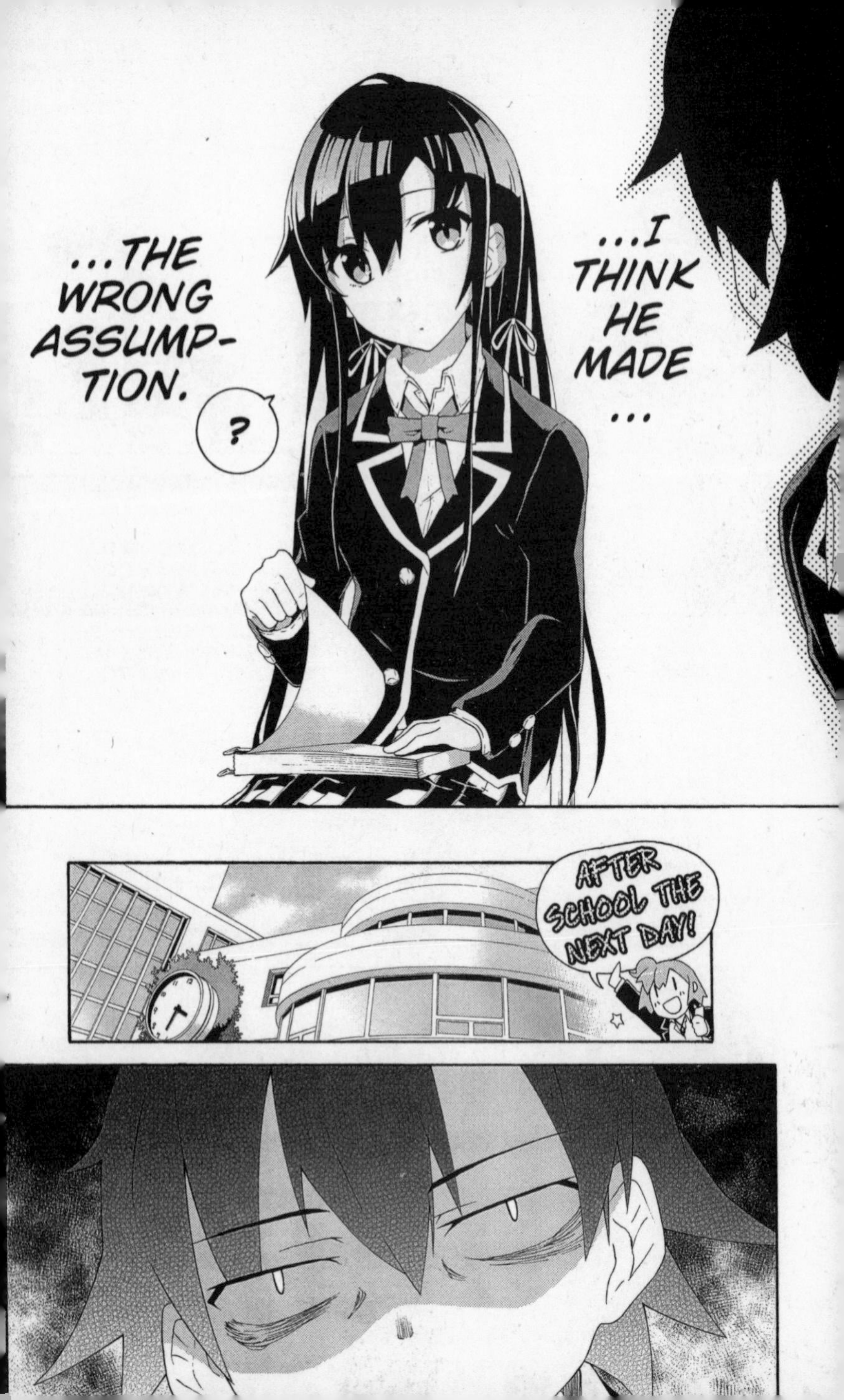
...I THINK HE MADE...
...THE WRONG ASSUMP-TION.
?
AFTER SCHOOL THE NEXT DAY!

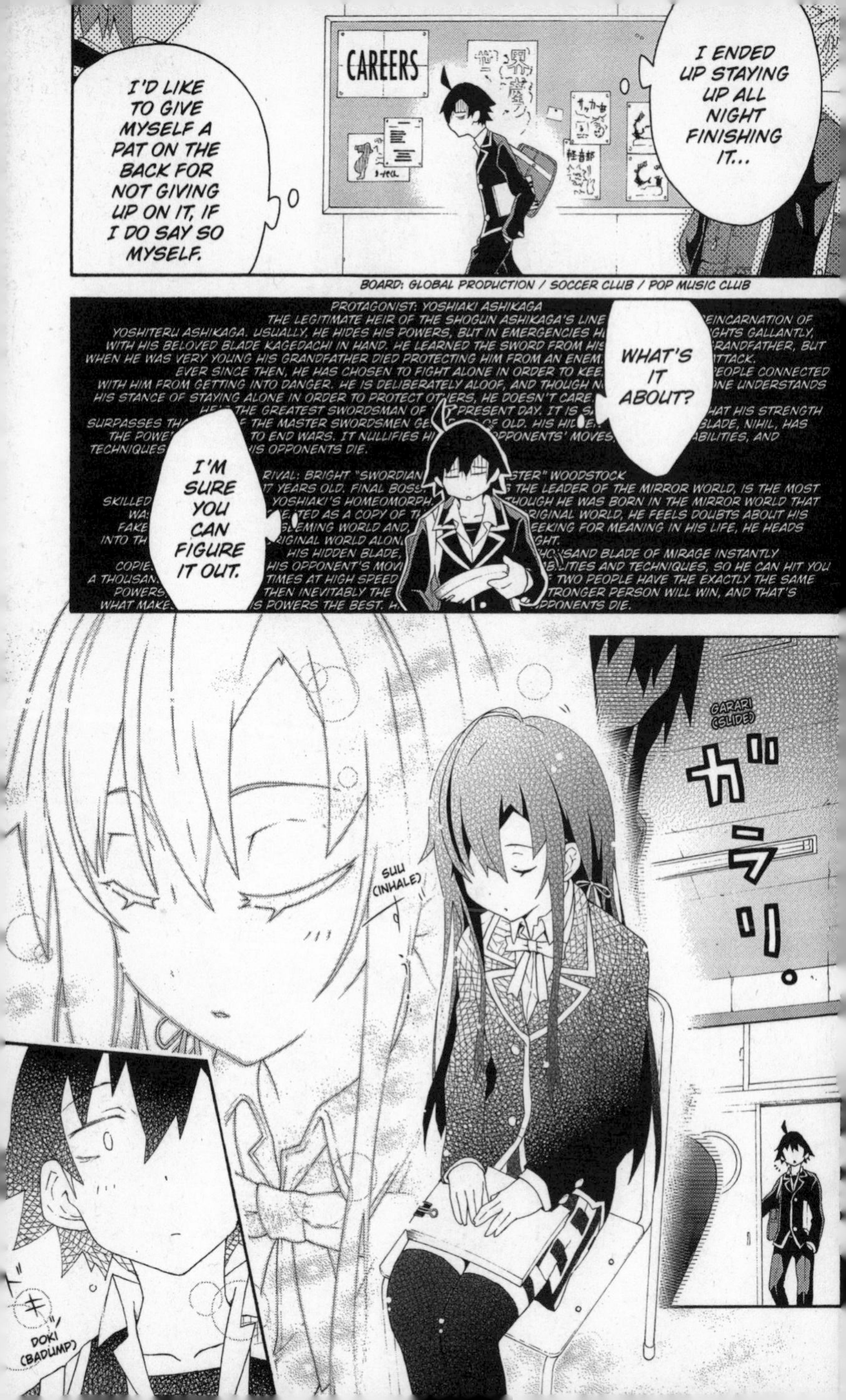

I ENDED UP STAYING UP ALL NIGHT FINISHING IT...
I'D LIKE TO GIVE MYSELF A PAT ON THE BACK FOR NOT GIVING UP ON IT, IF I DO SAY SO MYSELF.
BOARD: GLOBAL PRODUCTION / SOCCER CLUB / POP MUSIC CLUB
CAREERS
WHAT'S IT ABOUT?
I'M SURE YOU CAN FIGURE IT OUT.
GARARI (SLIDE)
ガラリ。
SUU (INHALE)
DOKI (BADUMP)

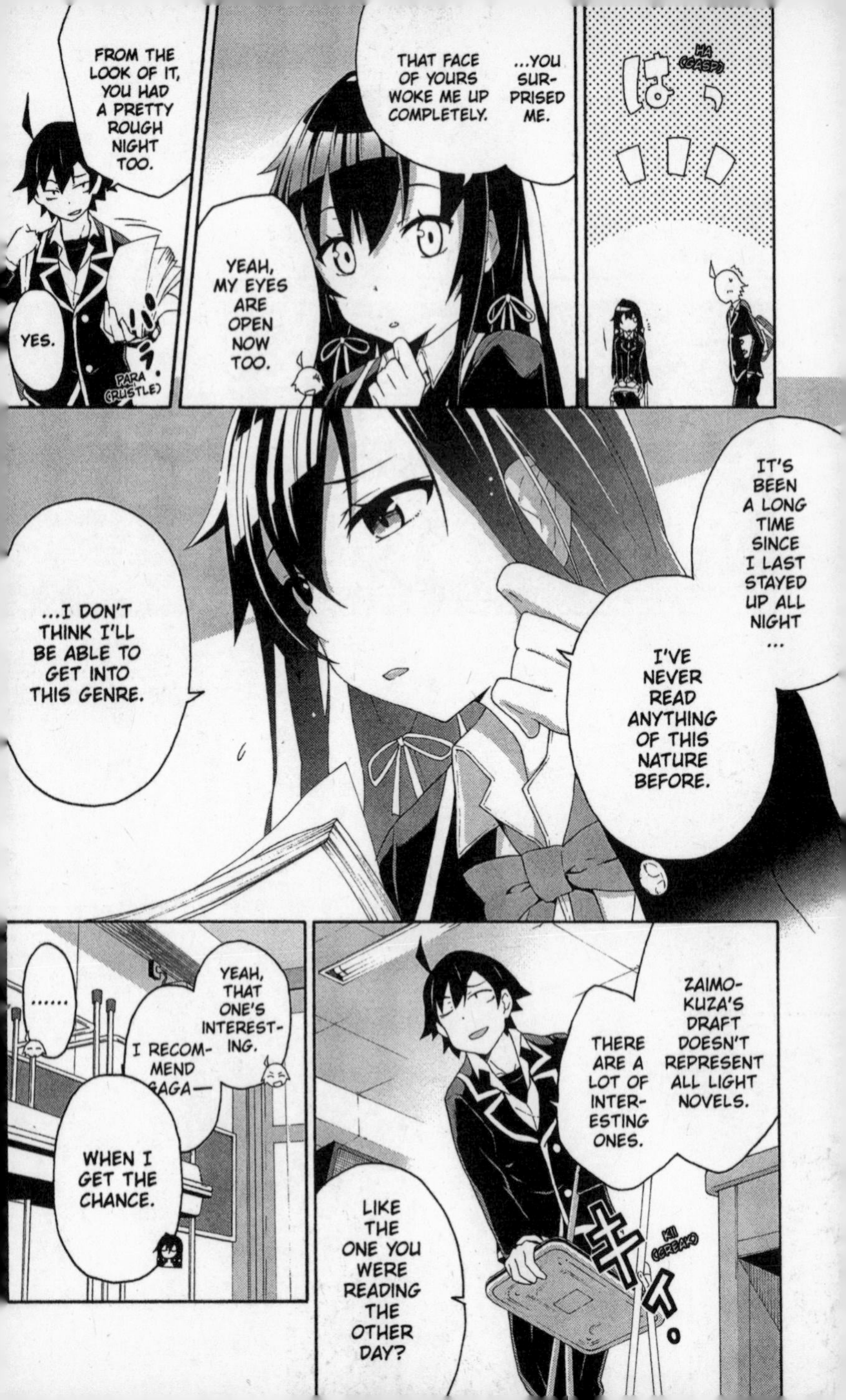
HA (GASP)
...YOU SURPRISED ME.
THAT FACE OF YOURS WOKE ME UP COMPLETELY.
YEAH, MY EYES ARE OPEN NOW TOO.
FROM THE LOOK OF IT, YOU HAD A PRETTY ROUGH NIGHT TOO.
YES.
PARA (RUSTLE)
IT'S BEEN A LONG TIME SINCE I LAST STAYED UP ALL NIGHT...
I'VE NEVER READ ANYTHING OF THIS NATURE BEFORE.
...I DON'T THINK I'LL BE ABLE TO GET INTO THIS GENRE.
ZAIMOKUZA'S DRAFT DOESN'T REPRESENT ALL LIGHT NOVELS.
THERE ARE A LOT OF INTERESTING ONES.
LIKE THE ONE YOU WERE READING THE OTHER DAY?
KII (CREAK)
YEAH, THAT ONE'S INTERESTING.
I RECOMMEND GAGA—
WHEN I GET THE CHANCE.
......

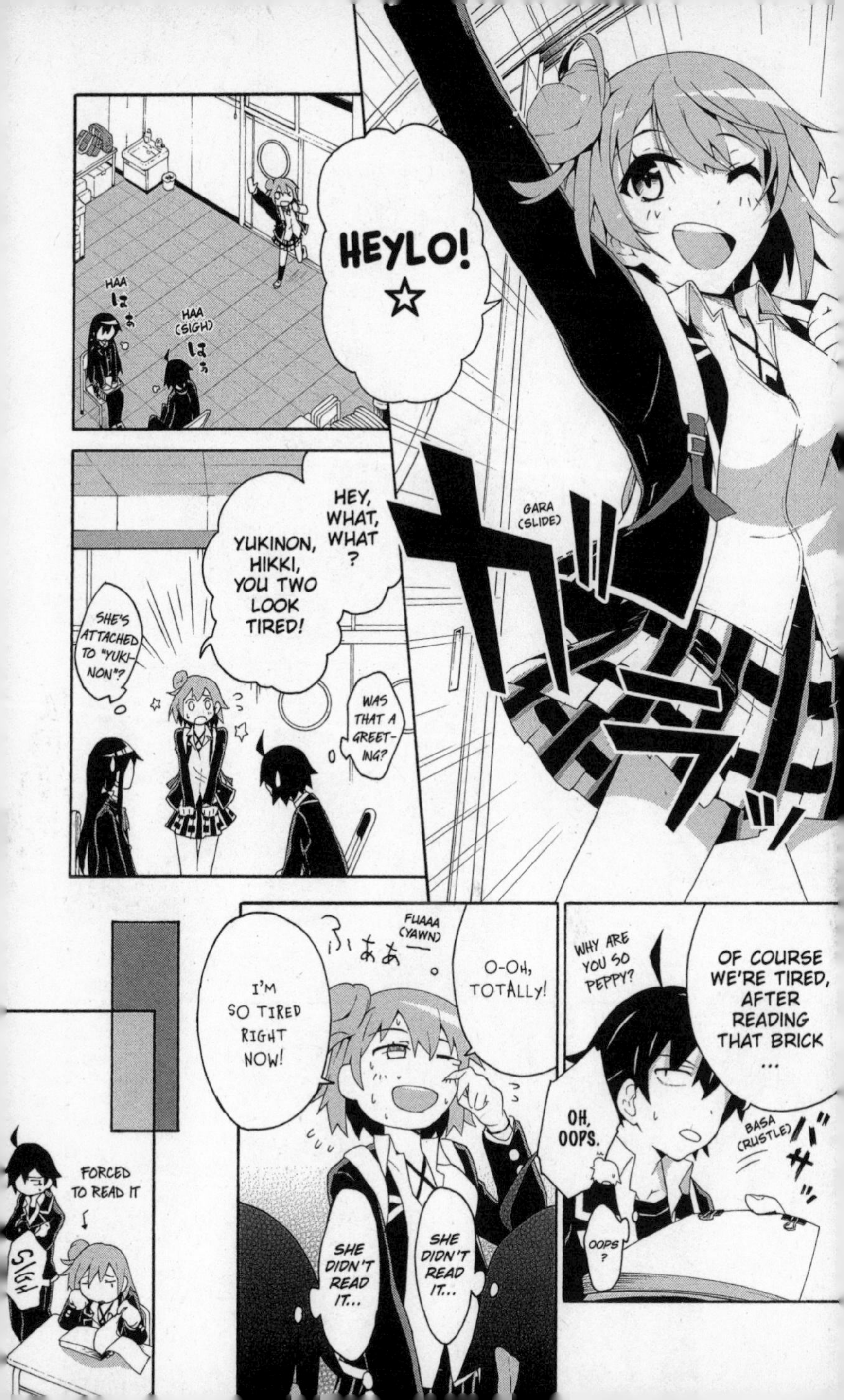
HEYLO! ☆
GARA (SLIDE)
HAA はぁ
HAA (SIGH) はぁ
HEY, WHAT, WHAT?
YUKINON, HIKKI, YOU TWO LOOK TIRED!
WAS THAT A GREETING?
SHE'S ATTACHED TO "YUKI-NON"?
OF COURSE WE'RE TIRED, AFTER READING THAT BRICK ...
WHY ARE YOU SO PEPPY?
BASA (RUSTLE)
OH, OOPS.
OOPS?
O-OH, TOTALLY!
FUAAA (YAWN) ふあぁー
I'M SO TIRED RIGHT NOW!
SHE DIDN'T READ IT...
SHE DIDN'T READ IT...
FORCED TO READ IT
SIGH

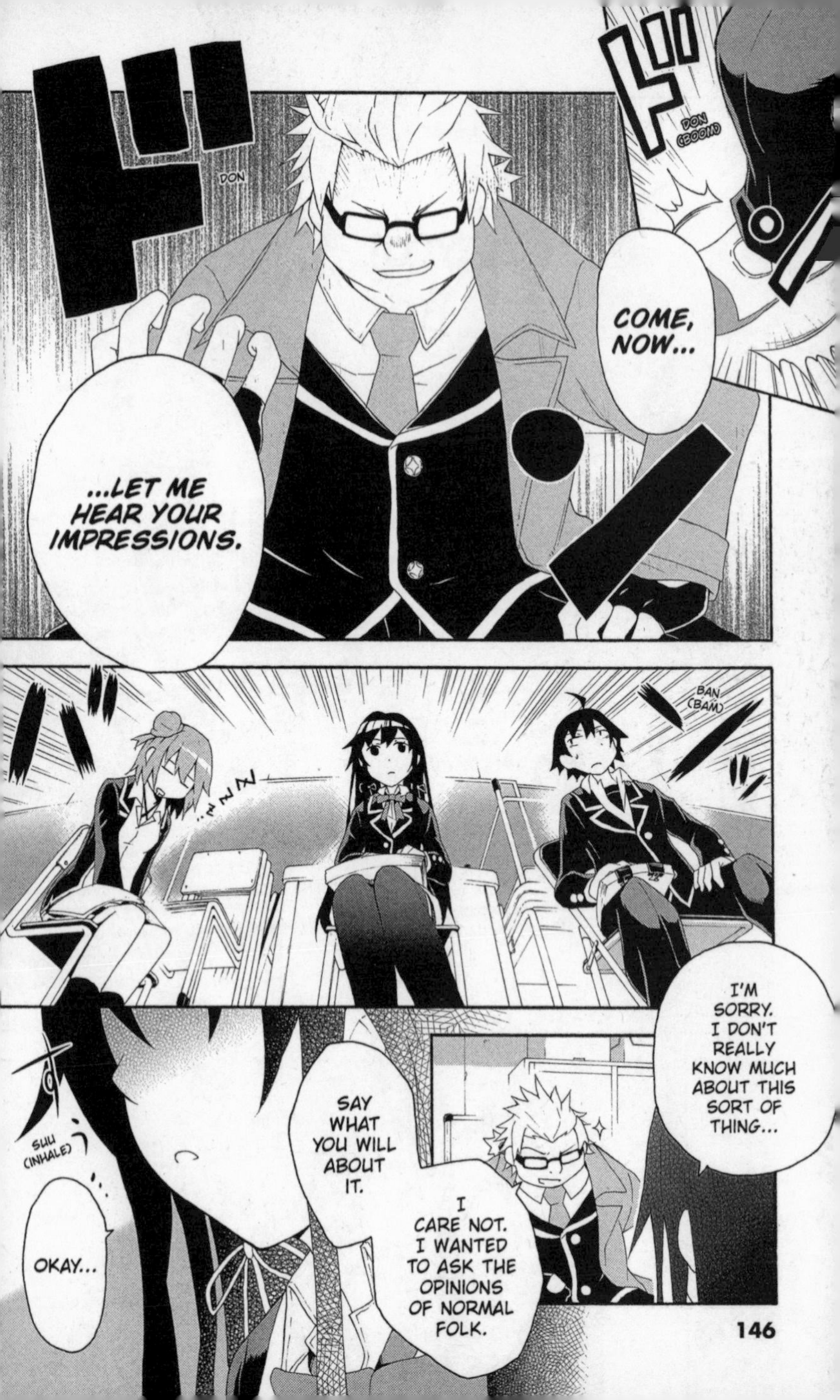
DON (BOOM)
COME, NOW...
DON
...LET ME HEAR YOUR IMPRESSIONS.
BAN (BAM)
I'M SORRY. I DON'T REALLY KNOW MUCH ABOUT THIS SORT OF THING...
I CARE NOT. I WANTED TO ASK THE OPINIONS OF NORMAL FOLK.
SAY WHAT YOU WILL ABOUT IT.
SUU (INHALE)
OKAY...

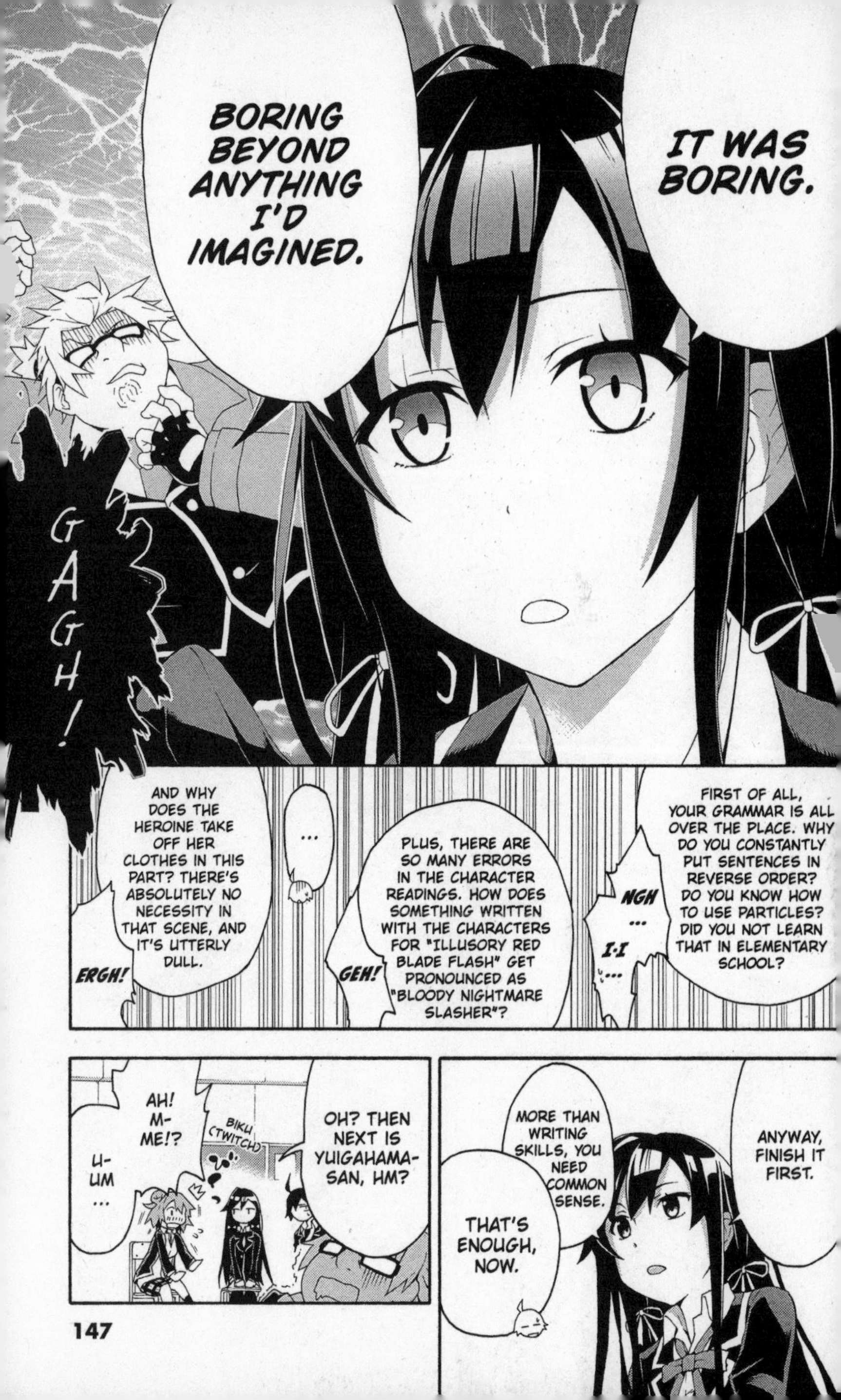
IT WAS BORING.
BORING BEYOND ANYTHING I'D IMAGINED.
GAGH!
FIRST OF ALL, YOUR GRAMMAR IS ALL OVER THE PLACE. WHY DO YOU CONSTANTLY PUT SENTENCES IN REVERSE ORDER? DO YOU KNOW HOW TO USE PARTICLES? DID YOU NOT LEARN THAT IN ELEMENTARY SCHOOL?
NGH ...
I-I ...
PLUS, THERE ARE SO MANY ERRORS IN THE CHARACTER READINGS. HOW DOES SOMETHING WRITTEN WITH THE CHARACTERS FOR "ILLUSORY RED BLADE FLASH" GET PRONOUNCED AS "BLOODY NIGHTMARE SLASHER"?
GEH!
...
AND WHY DOES THE HEROINE TAKE OFF HER CLOTHES IN THIS PART? THERE'S ABSOLUTELY NO NECESSITY IN THAT SCENE, AND IT'S UTTERLY DULL.
ERGH!
ANYWAY, FINISH IT FIRST.
MORE THAN WRITING SKILLS, YOU NEED COMMON SENSE.
THAT'S ENOUGH, NOW.
OH? THEN NEXT IS YUIGAHAMA-SAN, HM?
BIKU (TWITCH)
AH! M-ME!?
U-UM ...

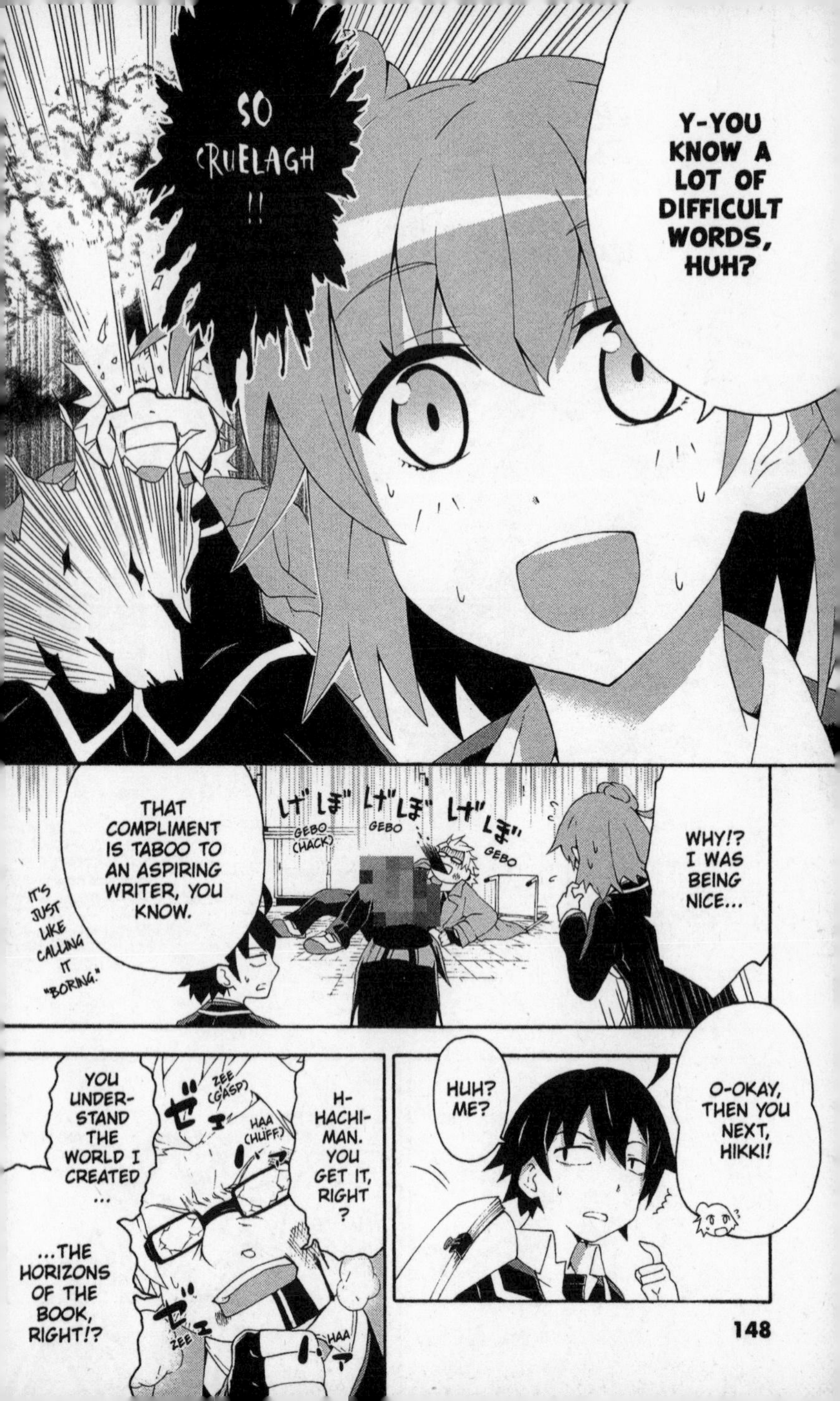

Y-YOU KNOW A LOT OF DIFFICULT WORDS, HUH?
SO CRUELAGH !!
WHY!? I WAS BEING NICE...
GEBO (HACK)
GEBO
GEBO
THAT COMPLIMENT IS TABOO TO AN ASPIRING WRITER, YOU KNOW.
IT'S JUST LIKE CALLING IT "BORING."
O-OKAY, THEN YOU NEXT, HIKKI!
HUH? ME?
H-HACHIMAN. YOU GET IT, RIGHT?
ZEE (GASP)
HAA (HUFF)
YOU UNDERSTAND THE WORLD I CREATED...
...THE HORIZONS OF THE BOOK, RIGHT!?
ZEE
HAA

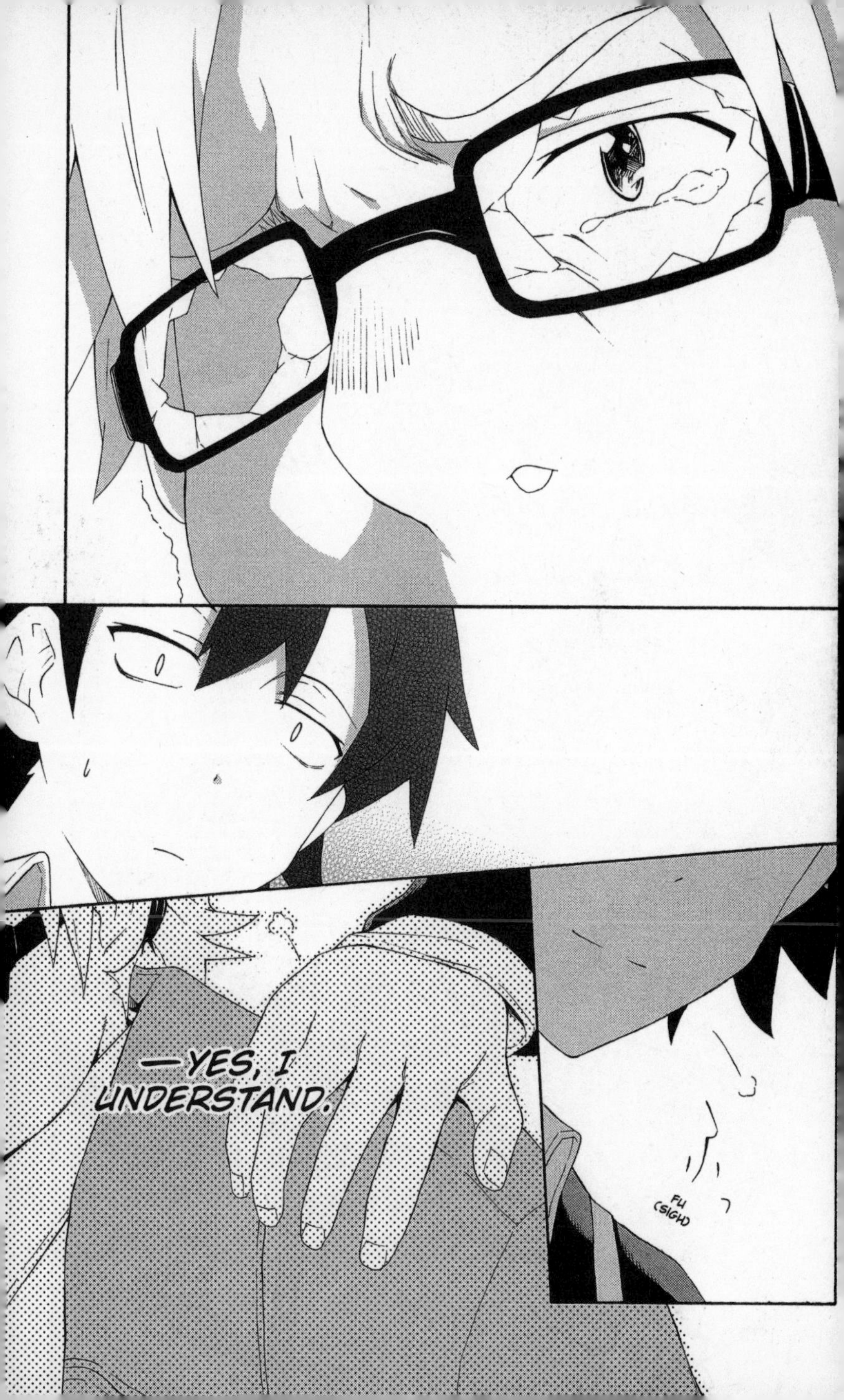
—YES, I UNDERSTAND.
FU (SIGH)

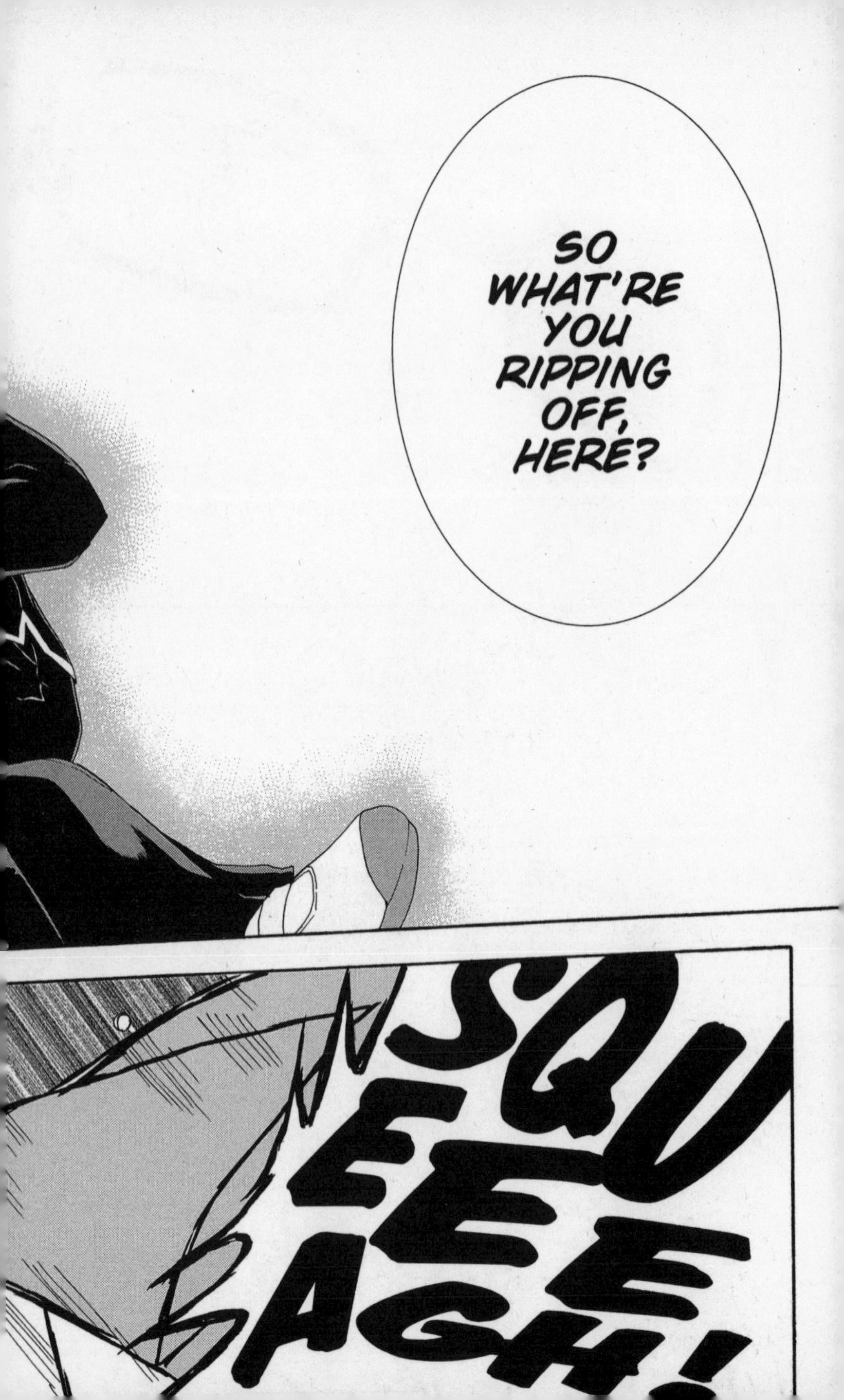
SO WHAT'RE YOU RIPPING OFF, HERE?
SQUEEEAGH!

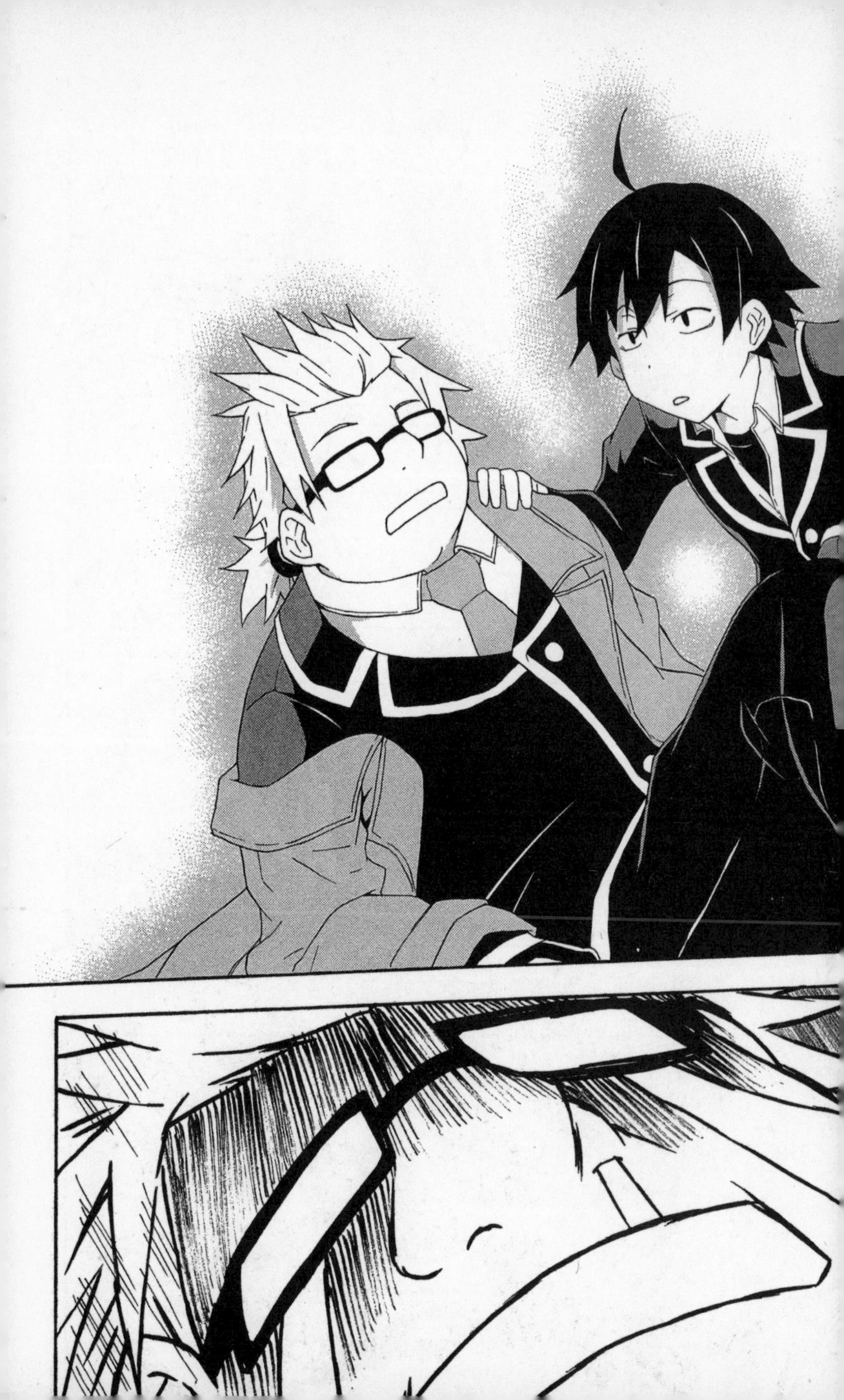

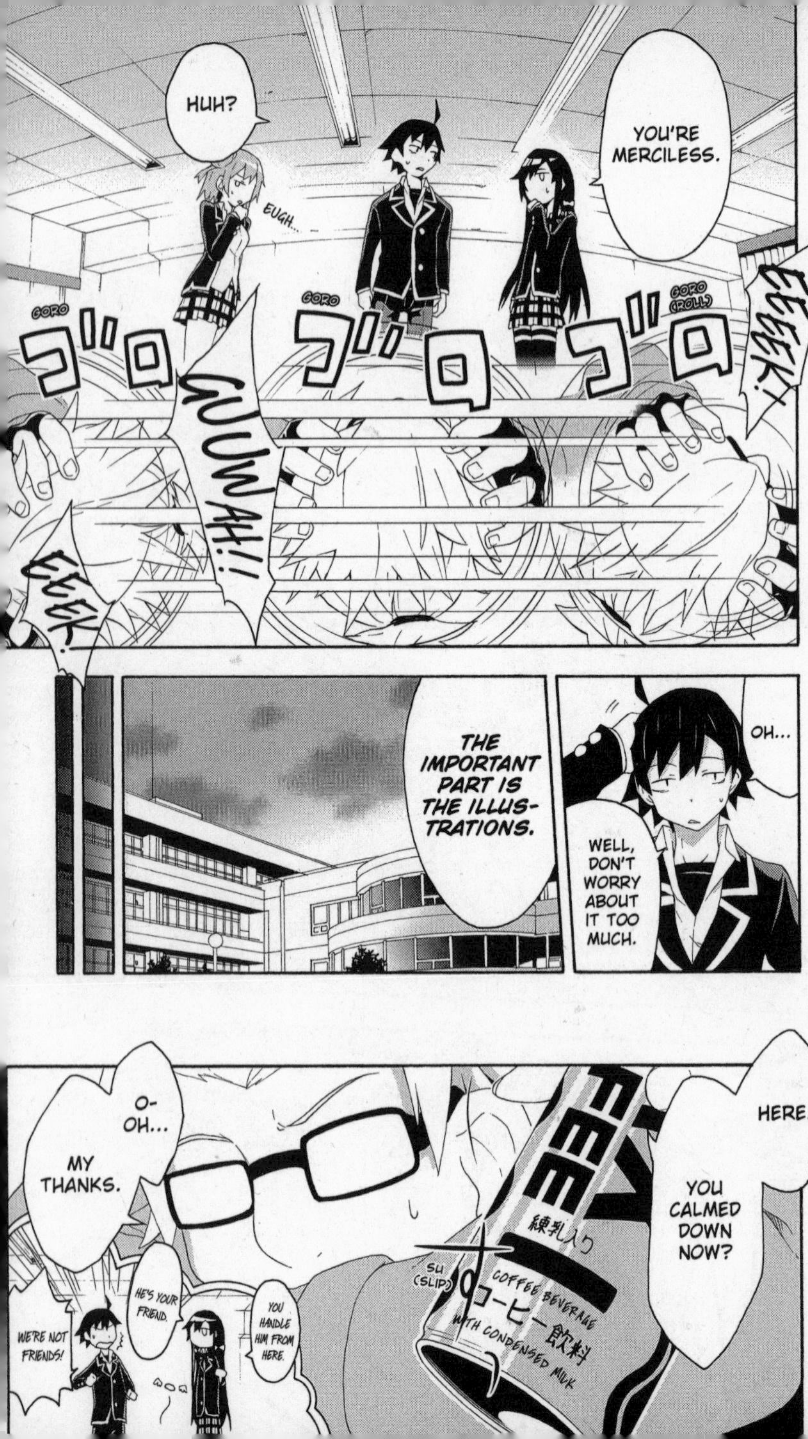
YOU'RE MERCILESS.
HUH?
EUGH...
EEEEK!
GORO (ROLL)
ゴロ
GORO
ゴロ
GORO
ゴロ
GUUWAH!!
EEEEK!
OH...
WELL, DON'T WORRY ABOUT IT TOO MUCH.
THE IMPORTANT PART IS THE ILLUS-TRATIONS.
HERE.
YOU CALMED DOWN NOW?
O-OH...
MY THANKS.
FEE
練乳入り
コーヒー飲料
COFFEE BEVERAGE WITH CONDENSED MILK
SU (SLIP)
YOU HANDLE HIM FROM HERE.
HE'S YOUR FRIEND.
WE'RE NOT FRIENDS!

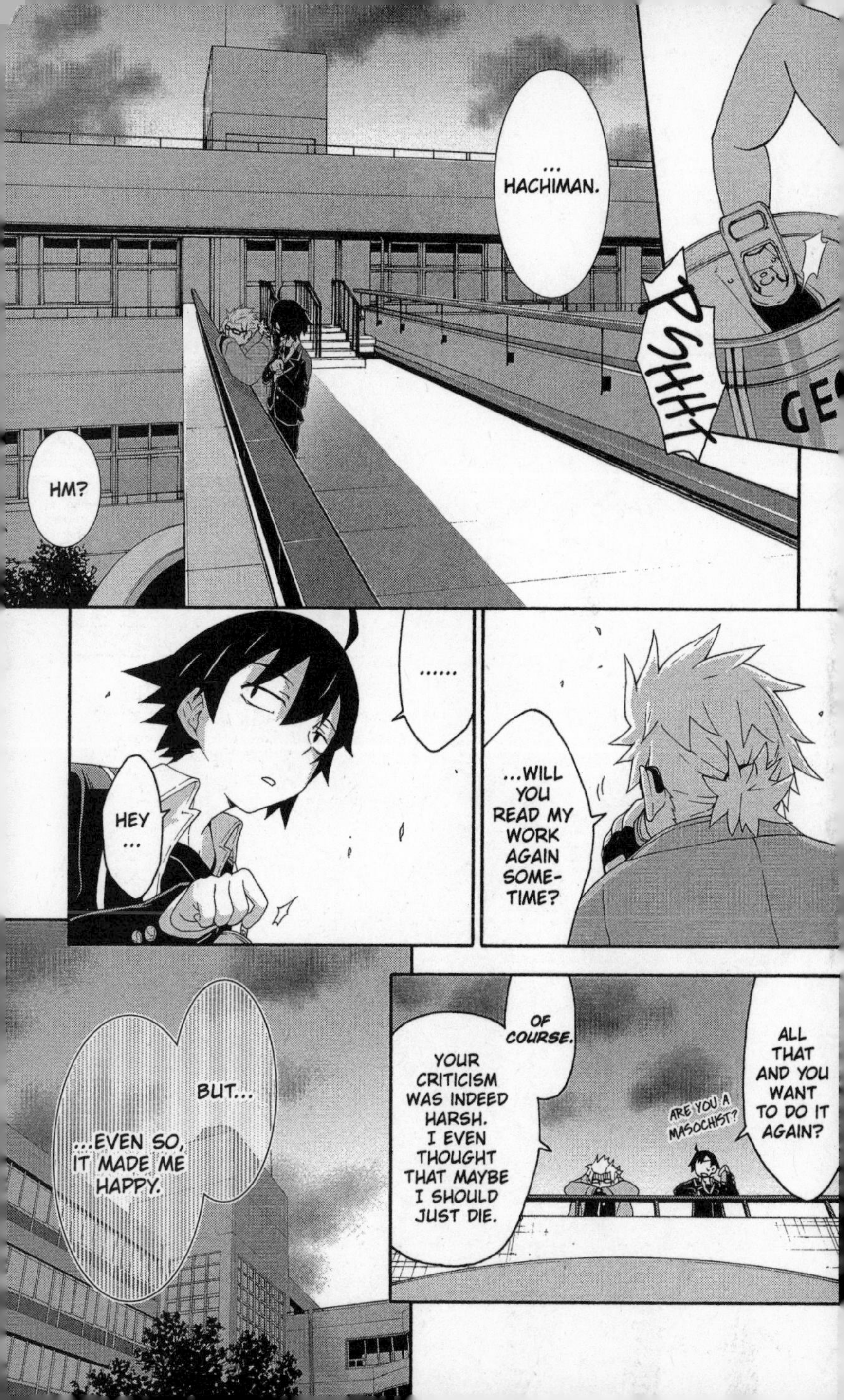
PSHHT
...HACHIMAN.
HM?
...WILL YOU READ MY WORK AGAIN SOMETIME?
......
HEY ...
ALL THAT AND YOU WANT TO DO IT AGAIN?
ARE YOU A MASOCHIST?
OF COURSE.
YOUR CRITICISM WAS INDEED HARSH. I EVEN THOUGHT THAT MAYBE I SHOULD JUST DIE.
BUT...
...EVEN SO, IT MADE ME HAPPY.

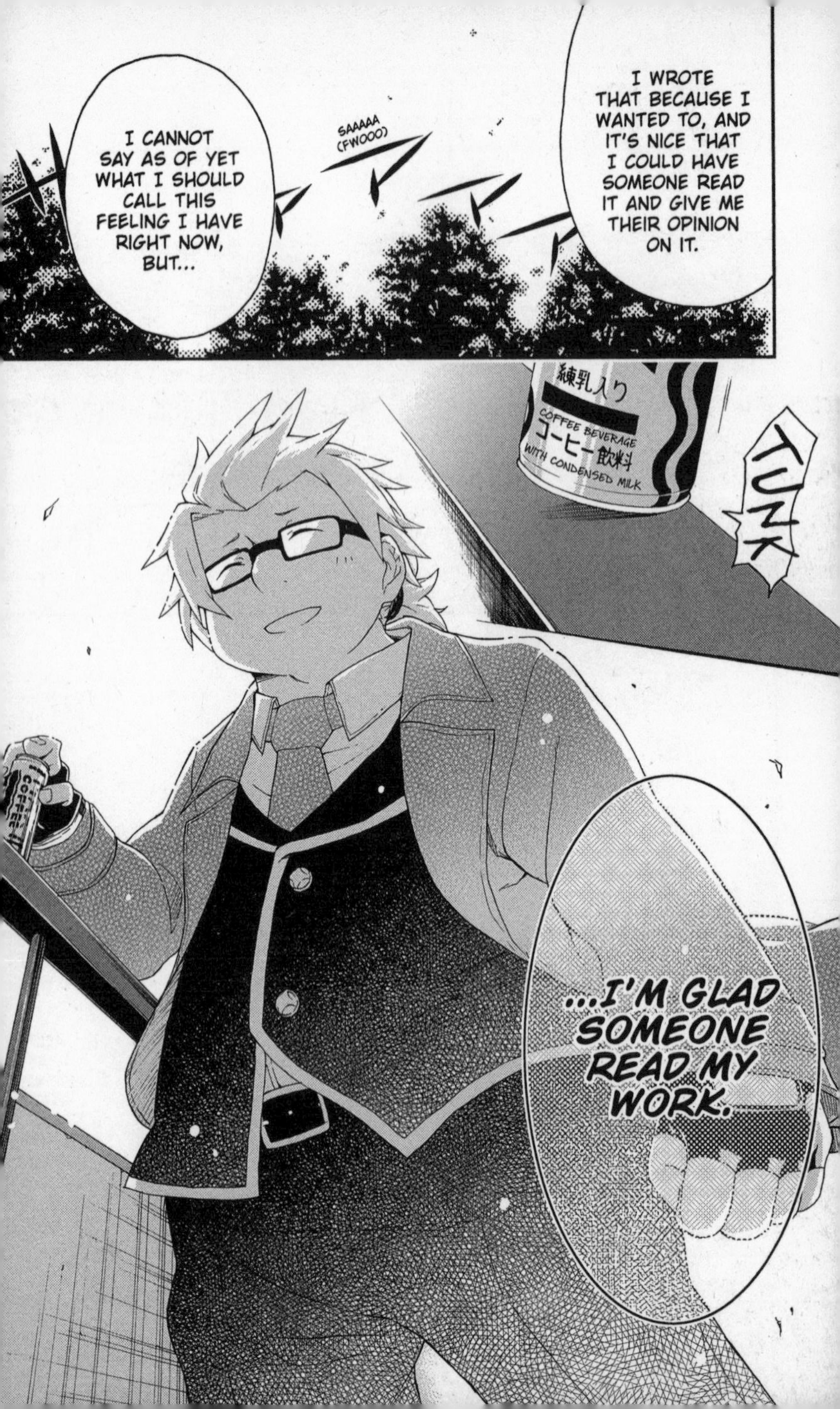
I WROTE THAT BECAUSE I WANTED TO, AND IT'S NICE THAT I COULD HAVE SOMEONE READ IT AND GIVE ME THEIR OPINION ON IT.
SAAAAA (FWOOO)
I CANNOT SAY AS OF YET WHAT I SHOULD CALL THIS FEELING I HAVE RIGHT NOW, BUT...
TUNK
練乳入り
COFFEE BEVERAGE
コーヒー飲料
WITH CONDENSED MILK
...I'M GLAD SOMEONE READ MY WORK.

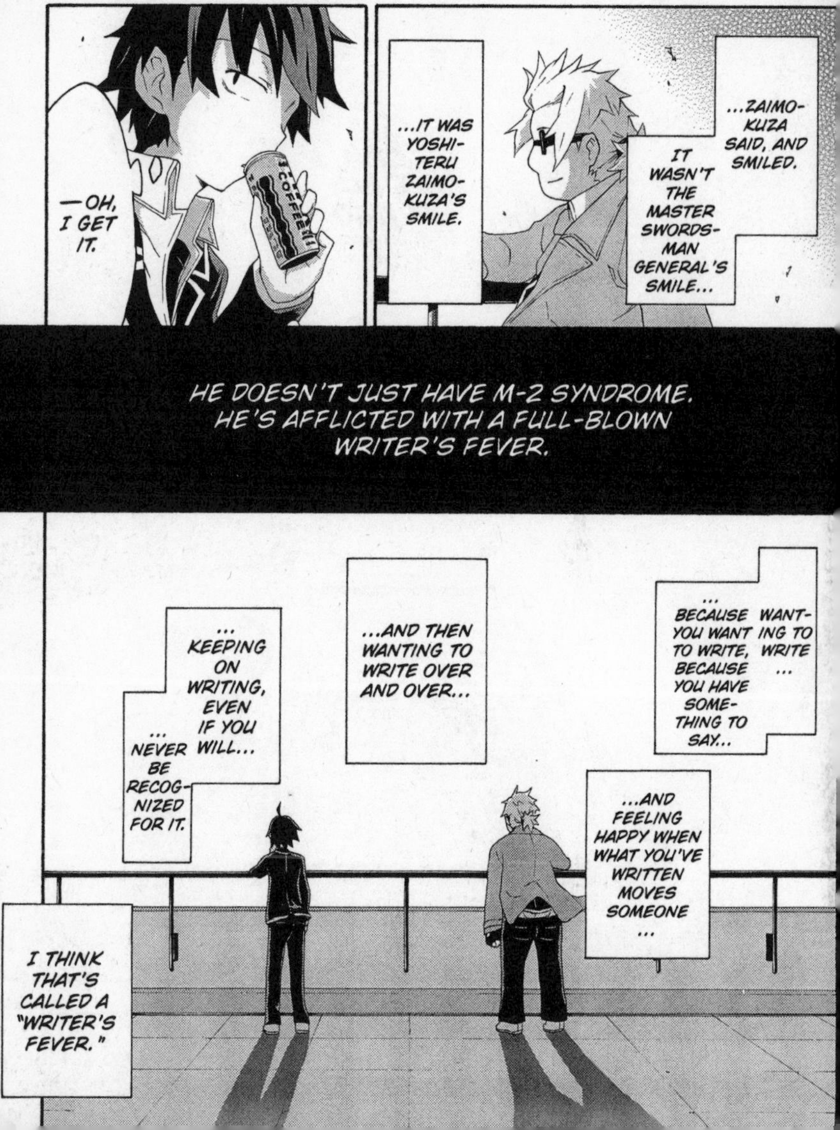
...ZAIMOKUZA SAID, AND SMILED.
IT WASN'T THE MASTER SWORDSMAN GENERAL'S SMILE...
...IT WAS YOSHITERU ZAIMOKUZA'S SMILE.
—OH, I GET IT.
HE DOESN'T JUST HAVE M-2 SYNDROME. HE'S AFFLICTED WITH A FULL-BLOWN WRITER'S FEVER.
...WANTING TO WRITE...
...BECAUSE YOU WANT TO WRITE, BECAUSE YOU HAVE SOMETHING TO SAY...
...AND FEELING HAPPY WHEN WHAT YOU'VE WRITTEN MOVES SOMEONE...
...AND THEN WANTING TO WRITE OVER AND OVER...
...KEEPING ON WRITING, EVEN IF YOU WILL...
...NEVER BE RECOGNIZED FOR IT.
I THINK THAT'S CALLED A "WRITER'S FEVER."

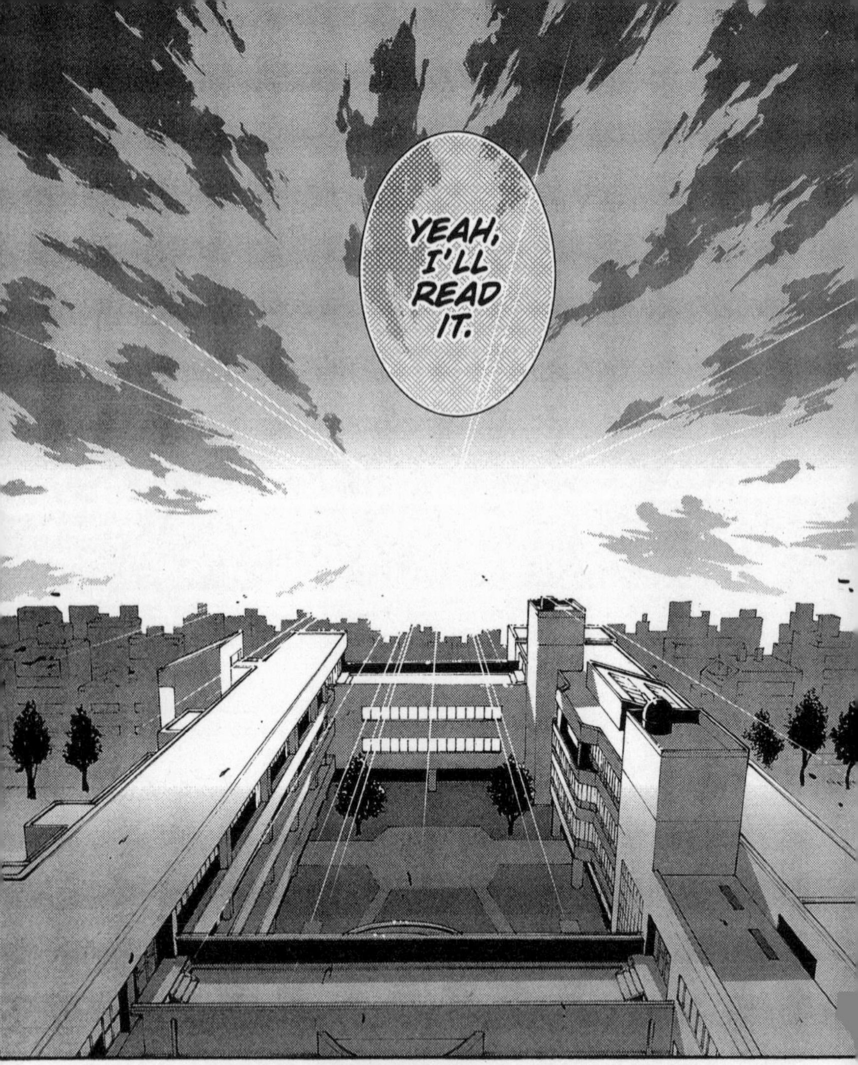
YEAH, I'LL READ IT.
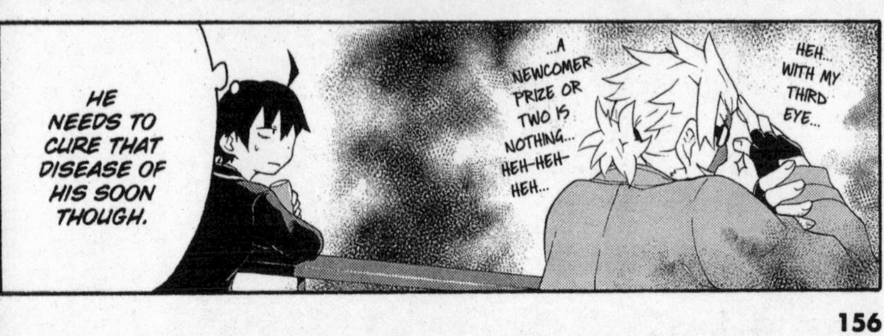
HEH... WITH MY THIRD EYE...
...A NEWCOMER PRIZE OR TWO IS NOTHING... HEH-HEH-HEH...
HE NEEDS TO CURE THAT DISEASE OF HIS SOON THOUGH.

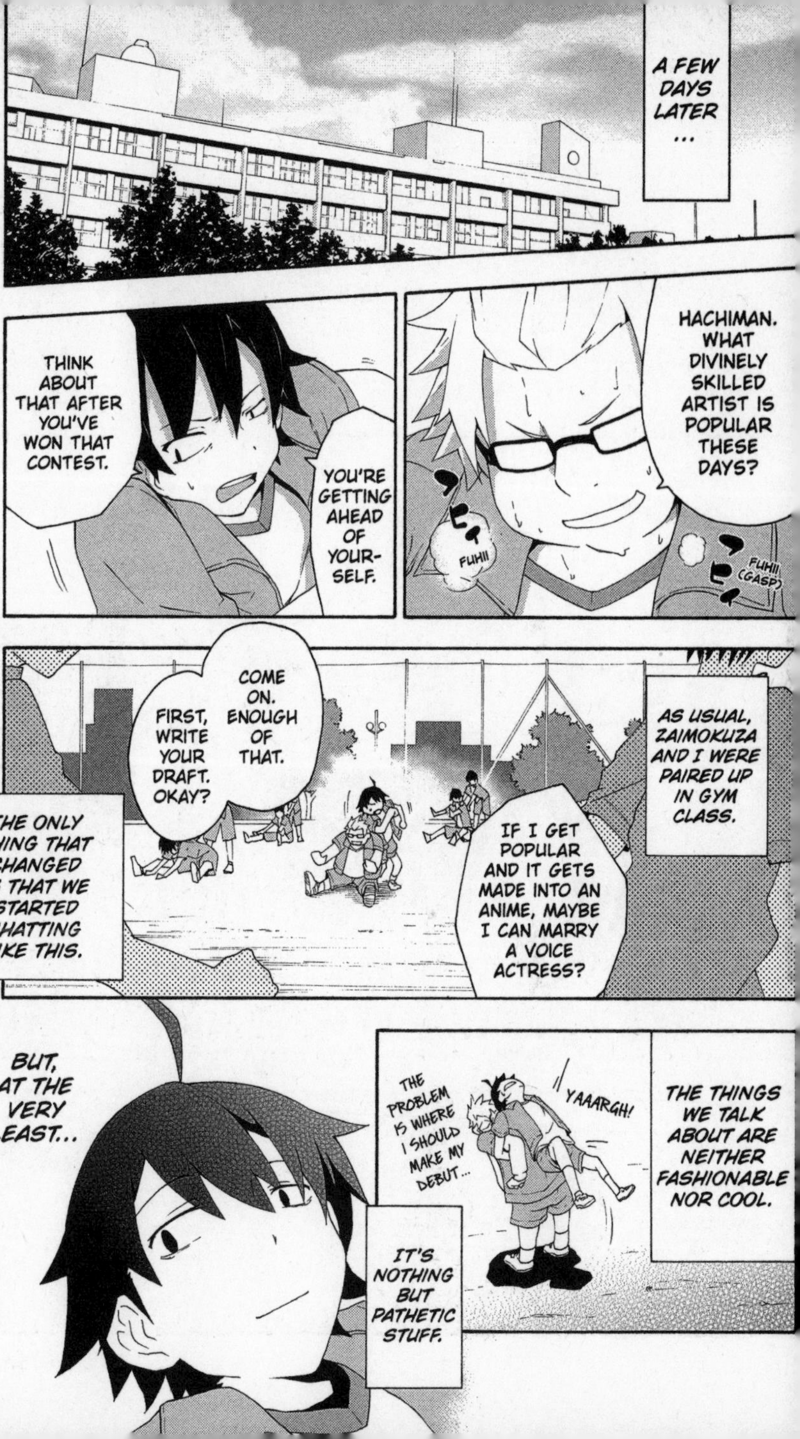
A FEW DAYS LATER...
HACHIMAN. WHAT DIVINELY SKILLED ARTIST IS POPULAR THESE DAYS?
FUHII (GASP)
FUHII
YOU'RE GETTING AHEAD OF YOURSELF.
THINK ABOUT THAT AFTER YOU'VE WON THAT CONTEST.
AS USUAL, ZAIMOKUZA AND I WERE PAIRED UP IN GYM CLASS.
IF I GET POPULAR AND IT GETS MADE INTO AN ANIME, MAYBE I CAN MARRY A VOICE ACTRESS?
COME ON. ENOUGH OF THAT.
FIRST, WRITE YOUR DRAFT. OKAY?
THE ONLY THING THAT CHANGED IS THAT WE STARTED CHATTING LIKE THIS.
THE THINGS WE TALK ABOUT ARE NEITHER FASHIONABLE NOR COOL.
YAAARGH!
THE PROBLEM IS WHERE I SHOULD MAKE MY DEBUT...
IT'S NOTHING BUT PATHETIC STUFF.
BUT, AT THE VERY LEAST...

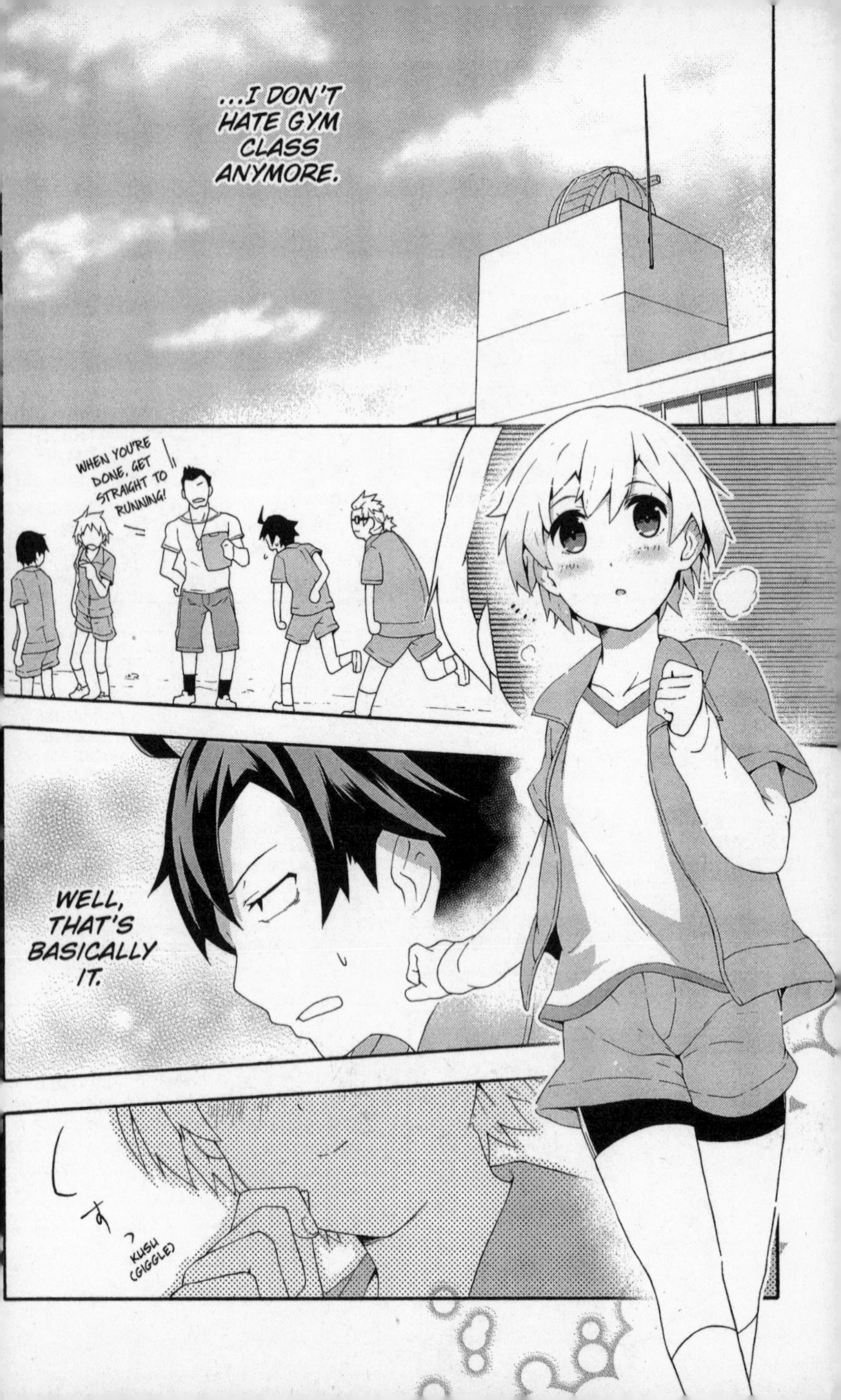
...I DON'T HATE GYM CLASS ANYMORE.
WHEN YOU'RE DONE, GET STRAIGHT TO RUNNING!
WELL, THAT'S BASICALLY IT.
KUSU (GIGGLE)

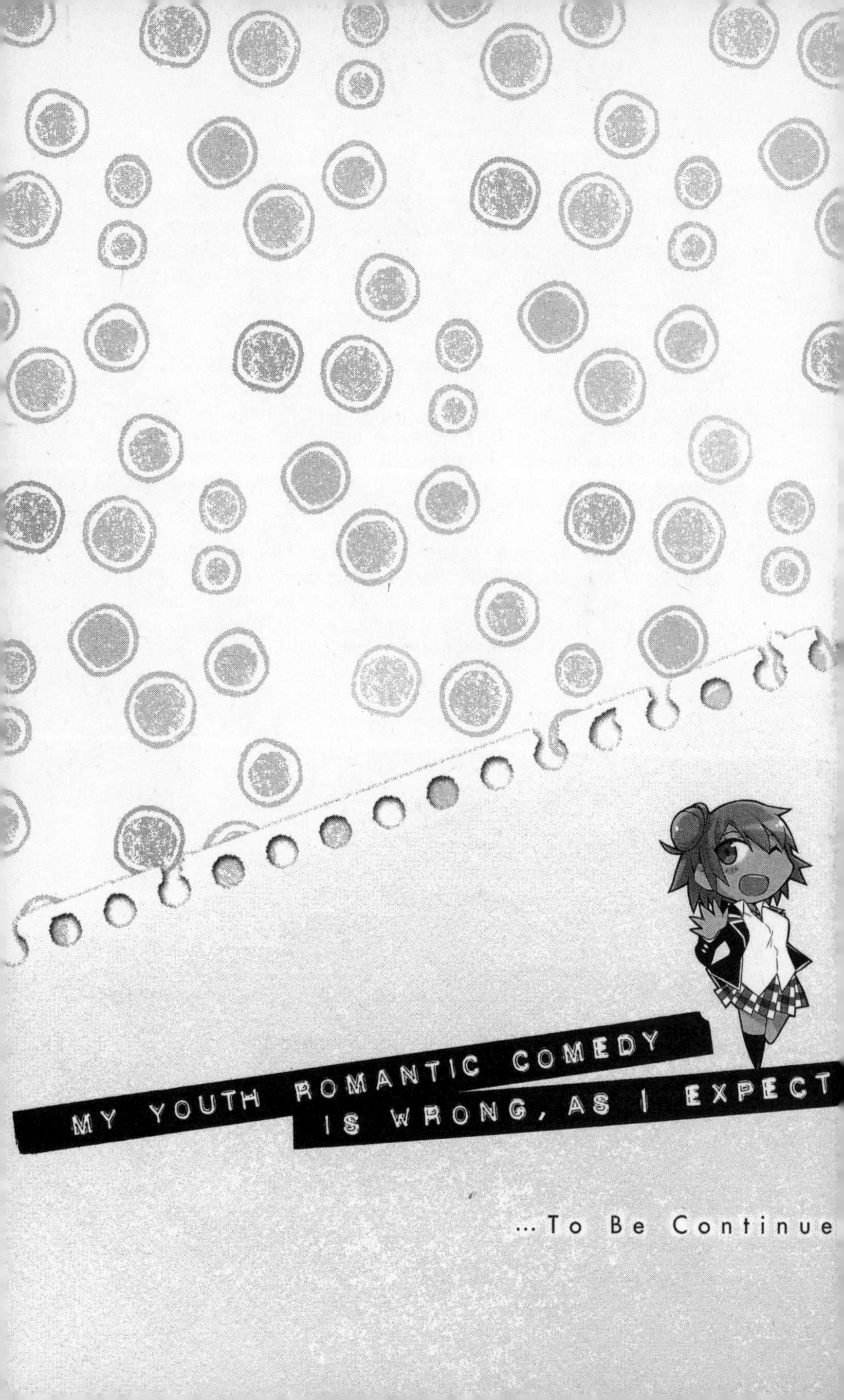
MY YOUTH ROMANTIC COMEDY IS WRONG, AS I EXPECT
...To Be Continue

AFTERWORD

THANK YOU VERY MUCH FOR BUYING THIS MANGA. THIS IS NAOMICHI IO.
I'M A NEWBIE HERE, AND IT'S NOTHING BUT FIRSTS FOR ME RIGHT NOW:
FIRST SERIALIZATION, FIRST PRINT VOLUME...
NOW THEN, THIS HAS BEEN MY YOUTH ROMANTIC COMEDY IS WRONG,
AS I EXPECTED: @COMIC, OTHERWISE KNOWN AS "COMIGAIRU" (NAMED
BY WATARU WATARI-SENSEI). WHAT DID YOU THINK? WHEN MY EDITOR
FIRST TALKED TO ME ABOUT ILLUSTRATING THIS BOOK, I THOUGHT,
"OH, HE ALWAYS TELLS SUCH FUNNY JOKES!"
...BUT HE WAS SERIOUS. HIS EYES WEREN'T SMILING.

ANYWAY, THE ORIGINAL NOVEL IS SUCH AN ELABORATELY
CONSTRUCTED WORK, SO AFTER READING IT MANY TIMES OVER AND
PILING UP DRAFT AFTER DRAFT, I TRIED MY BEST TO PUT IN ALL THE
PARTS THAT WOULD MAKE IT A REALLY FUN READ. BUT WHEN YOU'RE
MANGA-IZING SOMETHING, UNFORTUNATELY THERE ARE LOTS OF PARTS
YOU HAVE TO TAKE OUT. I'D LOVE IT IF YOU WERE TO READ THE ORIGINAL
NOVEL TO COMPLEMENT THIS MANGA.

FINALLY, I'D LIKE TO GIVE MY THANKS TO EVERYONE: FROM THE ORIGINAL
NOVEL, WATARU WATARI-SENSEI, PONKAN⑧-SAMA, ALL THE PEOPLE AT
THE EDITORIAL DEPARTMENT OF GAGAGA PUBLISHING,
MY EDITOR WHO GAVE ME THIS OPPORTUNITY, AND THE EDITORIAL
DEPARTMENT AT SUNDAY GX.

'☆' SCENE I HATED TO CUT

IT'S CROOKED.

SPECIAL THANKS:
YAMADA-KUN
SAKURAI-SAN
MATSUNAGA-KUN
KOUTAROU
TAKADA-
SENSEI
AKKII
MITSUKI

AND YOU,
THE READER

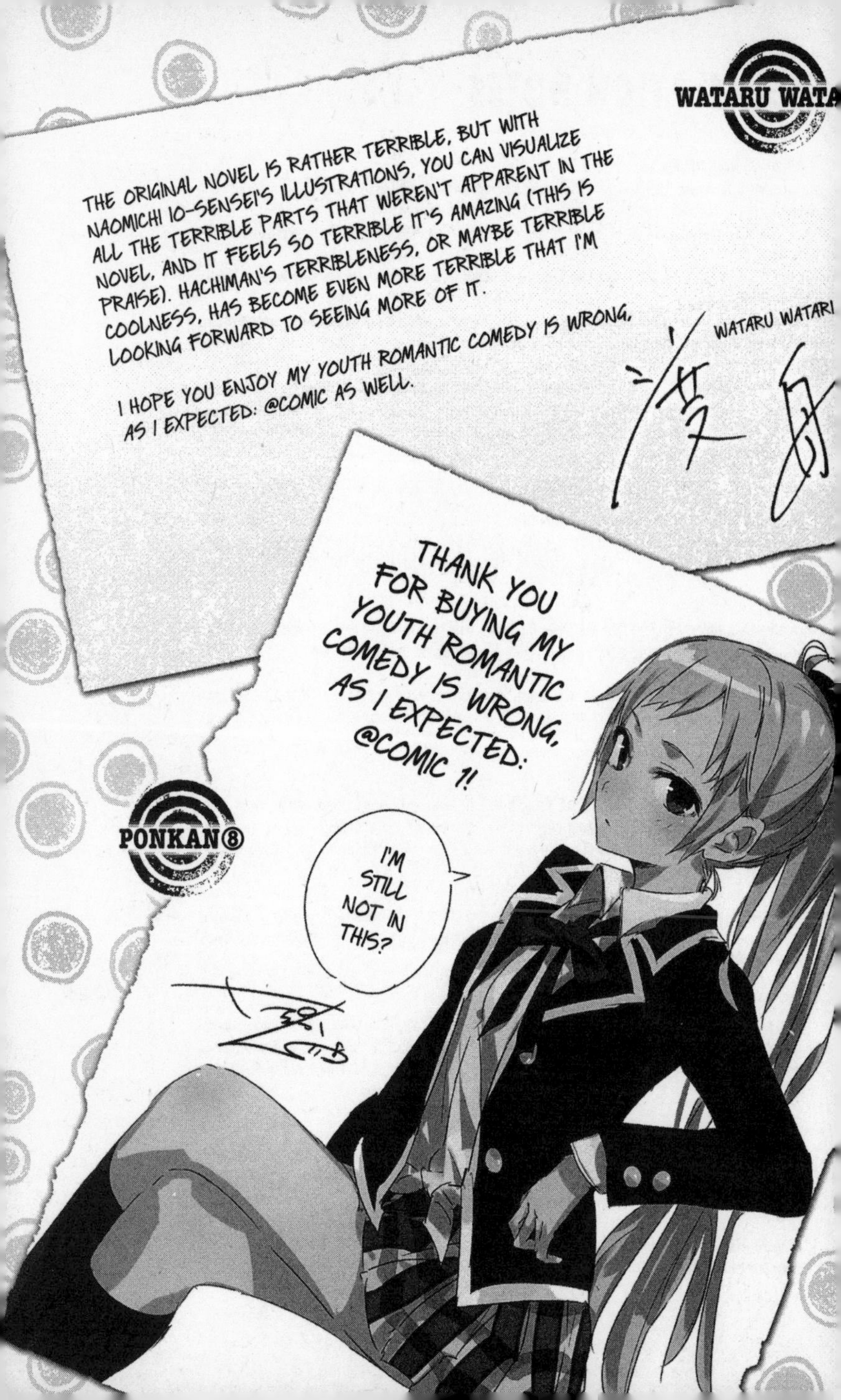
WATARU WATA
THE ORIGINAL NOVEL IS RATHER TERRIBLE, BUT WITH NAOMICHI IO-SENSEI'S ILLUSTRATIONS, YOU CAN VISUALIZE ALL THE TERRIBLE PARTS THAT WEREN'T APPARENT IN THE NOVEL, AND IT FEELS SO TERRIBLE IT'S AMAZING (THIS IS PRAISE). HACHIMAN'S TERRIBLENESS, OR MAYBE TERRIBLE COOLNESS, HAS BECOME EVEN MORE TERRIBLE THAT I'M LOOKING FORWARD TO SEEING MORE OF IT.
I HOPE YOU ENJOY MY YOUTH ROMANTIC COMEDY IS WRONG, AS I EXPECTED: @COMIC AS WELL.
WATARU WATARI
PONKAN⑧
THANK YOU FOR BUYING MY YOUTH ROMANTIC COMEDY IS WRONG, AS I EXPECTED: @COMIC 1!
I'M STILL NOT IN THIS?

TRANSLATION NOTES

COMMON HONORIFICS

no honorific: Indicates familiarity or closeness; if used without permission or reason, addressing someone in this manner would constitute an insult.

-san: The Japanese equivalent of Mr./Mrs./Miss. If a situation calls for politeness, this is the fail-safe honorific.

-sama: Conveys great respect; may also indicate that the social status of the speaker is lower than that of the addressee.

-kun: Used most often when referring to boys, this indicates affection or familiarity. Occasionally used by older men among their peers, but it may also be used by anyone referring to a person of lower standing.

-chan: An affectionate honorific indicating familiarity used mostly in reference to girls; also used in reference to cute persons or animals of either gender.

-sensei: A Japanese term of respect commonly used for teachers, but can also refer to doctors, writers, and artists.

PAGE 2

"Normies." The original Japanese term here is *riajuu*, a term nerds use to describe non-nerds. Literally, someone who feels fulfilled by real life. "Riajuu bakuhatsu shiro!" (Go blow up, normies!) is the name of a Hatsune Miku song about being mad at normal people for having fulfilling lives.

PAGE 12

Tsundere is a Japanese word that combines the terms *tsun-tsun* (prickly) and *dere-dere* (bashful). It refers to a character that is prickly and irritable on the outside but secretly sentimental.

"That's some long nosed sniper material. Are you one of the Straw Hat Pirates or what?" In Eiichiro Oda's *One Piece* manga, the long-nosed sniper Usopp is both a chronic liar and a member of the Straw Hat Pirates.

PAGE 18

"Think of it as the Hyperbolic Time Chamber." In Akira Toriyama's *Dragonball* manga, the Hyperbolic Time Chamber is a training room where time passes more slowly, allowing years of training to take place in mere days of real-world time. In Japanese it's known as the *Seishin to Toki no Heya* or the "Room of Spirit and Time."

"Or would it be easier to understand if I just called it *Revolutionary Girl Utena*?" *Revolutionary Girl Utena* is a 1997 anime directed by Kunihiko Ikuhara. It involves a sinister student council scheming to "crack the world's shell."

PAGE 21

"It's second-year head swell." Second-year head swell (kounibyou, literally "second year of high school disease") is a term Hiratsuka invents here to tease Hikigaya. However, it's based on an existing term, chuunibyou (literally "second year of middle school disease, translated in this book as "M-2 syndrome" — "M" for "middle school" and "2" for "second year").

PAGE 46

"Gundam Fight! Ready? Go!" In the *Mobile Fighter G Gundam* incarnation of the Gundam series, organized battle tournaments between various *mecha*, begins with this line. Like all of Hiratsuka's favorite anime, it's from the nineties.

"It would have been easier to understand if I'd said 'Robattle.'" "Robattle" refers to battles between robots in the Medabots anime series, which is much more obscure than Gundam.

PAGE 52

"No-waste ghost." The *mottainai obake*, or no-waste ghost, was the star of a number of public service announcement—style commercials in the early eighties. It would haunt children for wasting food while crying, "What a waste!" In this case, it's a waste that Yukinoshita is so beautiful.

PAGE 104

Gagaga Bunko published the *My Youth Romantic Comedy Is Wrong, As I Expected* light novel series in Japan.

PAGE 106

"She could kill me with a snort." The accompanying illustration is a visual reference to a boss battle with *Final Fantasy VI*'s Typhon, whose special attack is "Snort," which sends the character flying off the screen.

PAGE 107

"'Nationals?'" Both "Kunidachi City" and the word for "national" use the same kanji (characters that depict meaning) pronounced differently. In the original, Hikigaya makes fun of the idea that Hayama's team could never make it to the national championships by suggesting that he must mean he's going to Kunidachi City instead.

PAGE 134

"Bodhisattva Hachiman." Hachiman is a god of war in the Shinto tradition; with the arrival of Buddhism in Japan, he was integrated into that faith as a Bodhisattva, a human who has attained Buddhahood.

PAGE 136

"Muromachi period." In Japanese history, the Muromachi period refers to the time stretching from the mid-1300s to the mid-1500s, during which Japan was ruled by the Ashikaga shogunate. The period ended with the collapse of Japan into smaller factions. It is to this violent era, known as the "Sengoku" or "Warring States" period, that Zaimokuza is referring.

"The Seiwa Genji zealously worshipped him as a god of war." The Seiwa Genji were a powerful line of the Minamoto clan of Japanese nobility for hundreds of years, tracing their lineage back to Emperor Seiwa. The Kamakura and Ashikaga shogunates (as well as the and the Tokugawa shogunate) were both descended from the Seiwa Genji.

PAGE 147

"Character readings." In Japanese, small *hiragana* (phonetic characters) are often written above the kanji to explain how there are pronounced, and they are called "*ruby*." In manga and light novels, when someone has a special power move or attack, it is common to make up ruby using English words just to make a name that sounds cool but does not quite reflect the meaning of the kanji, often to the point of absurdity. In this case, the kanji say "Illusory Red Blade Flash" while the ruby above say "Bloody Nightmare Slasher" in English.

PAGE 152

"The important part is the illustrations." Light novels typically have an illustrated cover and full-art pages throughout the book in anime style, often drawn by popular artists, and a book's popularity can depend on the art just as much as the story.

MY YOUTH ROMANTIC COMEDY IS WRONG, AS I EXPECTED @COMIC 1

Original Story: **Wataru Watari**
Art: **Naomichi Io**
Character Design: **Ponkan⑧**
ORIGINAL COVER DESIGN/Hiroyuki KAWASOME (Graphio)

Translation: Jennifer Ward

Lettering: Bianca Pistillo

YAHARI ORE NO SEISHUN LOVE COME WA MACHIGATTEIRU. @COMIC Vol. 1 by Wataru WATARI, Naomichi IO, PONKAN⑧
© 2013 Wataru WATARI, Naomichi IO, PONKAN⑧
All rights reserved.
Original Japanese edition published by SHOGAKUKAN.
English translation rights arranged with SHOGAKUKAN through Tuttle-Mori Agency, Inc., Tokyo.

Yen Press
Hachette Book Group
1290 Avenue of the Americas
New York, NY 10104

www.hachettebookgroup.com
www.yenpress.com

Yen Press is an imprint of Hachette Book Group, Inc.
The Yen Press name and logo are trademarks of Hachette Book Group, Inc.

The publisher is not responsible for websites (or their content) that are not owned by the publisher.

Library of Congress Control Number: 2016931004

First Yen Press Edition: May 2016

ISBN: 978-0-316-31230-1

10 9 8 7 6 5 4 3 2 1

BVG

Printed in the United States of America